Islamic Law and Muslim Same-Sex Unions

Islamic Law and Muslim Same-Sex Unions

Junaid Jahangir and Hussein Abdullatif

LEXINGTON BOOKS
Lanham • Boulder • New York • London

Published by Lexington Books
An imprint of The Rowman & Littlefield Publishing Group, Inc.
4501 Forbes Boulevard, Suite 200, Lanham, Maryland 20706
www.rowman.com

Unit A, Whitacre Mews, 26-34 Stannary Street, London SE11 4AB

British Library Cataloguing in Publication Information Available

Library of Congress Control Number: 2016950765
ISBN: 978-0-7391-8937-5 (cloth : alk. paper)
eISBN: 978-0-7391-8938-2

∞™ The paper used in this publication meets the minimum requirements of American National Standard for Information Sciences—Permanence of Paper for Printed Library Materials, ANSI/NISO Z39.48-1992.

Printed in the United States of America

Contents

Foreword

Scott Siraj al-Haqq Kugle

It is an honor to be invited to write a foreword for this bold book. The two authors take up the challenge to articulate an authentically Islamic "middle way" toward the acceptance of gay and lesbian Muslims. They propose that Islamic norms of marriage can be adapted to same-sex couples. This can be done in such a way as to both help the couple regulate their relationship within Islamic ethics and urge the wider Muslim community to accept them as dignified and protected members of the community. This proposal requires a nuanced reassessment of Islamic scriptural authority and a deep critique of the Islamic legal tradition. This book offers a detailed foray into this delicate matter with scholarly rigor, abiding faith, and the aim to strengthening moderate Islamic practice that is compatible with democratic civil values.

The authors bring to this study their valuable skills and experience. They are deeply familiar with Islamic tradition. They adopt contemporary medical perspectives and advances in psychiatry. They believe that the Islamic legal tradition has always been framed by theories about human nature based on culture, medicine, and philosophy; as these frameworks change so also the Islamic legal tradition must change, so that it speaks authentically and meaningfully to humanity. Islam's universality is dependent on its adaptability and continuous reform, and Muslims' opinion about homosexuality is a vivid "litmus test" to show whether their Islam is adapting and healthy or is rather stagnant and deadly. After all, Islam is like water on which Muslims rely for nourishment and purification. Flowing water is clean, pure, and useful. Stagnant water becomes dirty, impure, and poisonous. Yet stagnant water is easily bounded and defined, while running water is complex, ever shifting its boundaries and flow over boundaries. Many Muslims prefer their religion to be like stagnant water, especially those scholars called *ulama* or the ones with authoritative knowledge, who gain power and prestige by asserting the proper bounds of religious practice. This book addresses the *ulama* and those who respect them, providing them tools and insights to make sure that their opinions about homosexuality are not based on stagnant stereotypes but rather on living principles.

This book builds upon previous studies that have been published over the last decade. It also makes importance advances in the growing literature about Islam and homosexuality, literature that is not just scholarly but also activistic in that it aims to change how Muslims live out their religion. This field of writing began in 2003, when the book *Progressive Muslims: On Gender, Justice and Pluralism* was published, in which I wrote a chapter on homosexuality and Islamic ethics; in it, I argued that Qur'anic verses are misinterpreted and hadith reports are wrongly validated such that the Islamic legal tradition unjustly penalizes homosexual Muslims. The ideas first presented in that chapter required deeper support, and so from 2004 to 2006 I wrote a full book on this subject, *Homosexuality in Islam: Critical Reflections on Gay, Lesbian and Transgender Muslims*, which was published in 2010. At the same time, Samar Habib was independently researching about Arabic and Islamic literature that addressed same-sex female relationships, which she completed as her PhD dissertation in 2007 and published as *Female Homosexuality in the Middle East: Histories and Representations* in 2009. She adopted a more cultural perspective, which sees Islam as an important component of Arab culture rather than as a universal religious tradition, which is the perspective that I adopt. Her book made a crucial intervention that focused attention on female sexuality and lesbian experience in Muslim communities, and she rightly argues that Islam was—and continues to be—shaped by Arab cultural norms and patriarchal prejudices. She continued to promote secular scholarship on homosexuality and Islam by editing a collection of essays by both Muslim and non-Muslim scholars, published in 2010 as *Islam and Homosexuality* in two volumes. The title she gave this collection reveals her agnostic stance over whether Islam can be reconciled with homosexuality and the essays include a variety of ideological positions on this question. Most notably, her collection included an essay by Junaid Jahangir on same-sex marriage in Islamic tradition, which is a precursor to the book he has coauthored here.

When I first began to publish about homosexuality and Islam, friends, both Muslim and non-Muslim, feared for my safety. There was an overwhelming feeling that Muslims were not only homophobic but also violent. Yet the outrageous violence of the September 11 attacks had the unintended consequence of strengthening moderate Islamic voices all over the world and spurring progressive Islamic voices in democratic nations. Muslim extremists had gone so far that there was nothing more to be feared from them. They had badly tarnished "conservative Islam" and revealed the irrational and inhumane side of conservative religious ideology. In this context, many Muslim activists and scholars adopted a newfound boldness to speak about what had been formerly considered unspeakable. They ignored stigma and censure to think out loud and in writing about issues that were formerly left unthought (to adopt the felicitous phrase from the late great Islamic philosopher Mohammed Arkoun—may he rest in God's mercy). The result of publications by Samar Habib, myself, and others is that there is now a space in discourse for informed discussion of homosexuality and Islam. This space is accepted, though it is contested. It exists in English, though this space of discourse is increasingly spilling over into other languages that Muslims use with their own cultural contexts.

Many up-and-coming scholars from the younger generation are now doing research on Islam's relation to issues of sexual orientation and gender identity (sometimes labeled SOGI for convenience). As undergraduate courses allow students to expand the scope of their thinking and master's degrees encourage Muslims to pursue PhDs, new theses and dissertations will turn into books and articles and blogs and reports. The gradual power of academic research, coupled with clinical medical practice and media publishing, has the effect of steadily moving water. It may not be dramatically visible but it slowly and gradually erodes boulders. Intractable prejudices are not as solid as they may appear at first.

The book in your hands represents the latest contribution to this field. It presents several important advances and deepens the existing discussion in many ways. It is written by believing Muslims for believing Muslims, and for this reason, it takes piety and rectitude very seriously. It is addressed to the *ulama* class, the traditional scholars and legal jurists who continue to shape Muslim public opinion on matters great and small. This class is not so easily definable as it used to be before colonialism dismantled or severely limited many traditional institutions of Islamic learning. Now media spokesmen through TV and internet are also increasingly considered to be *ulama.* Muslim professionals—who have training as doctors, lawyers, or engineers but also pursue Islamic learning—are increasingly functioning as leaders of Muslim communities who look to them as *ulama.* This book addresses this expanded contemporary *ulama* class and those who imitate them. The book uses their terminology and text sources, seeking to affirm the moderate and adaptive elements of the Islamic juristic tradition to come up with socially useful solutions to problems related to sexuality, sexual orientation, and gender identity. This book adopts the principles of the *ulama* while questioning the conservative rhetoric championed by many modern *ulama* spokesmen (and they are overwhelmingly male). This book is therefore a great challenge to conservative Muslims. It cannot be dismissed as secular, licentious, or heretical. It uses traditional principles that are essential elements to the

Islamic tradition to question conservatives who claim to uphold that tradition. It represents an argument for reform of tradition from within that tradition.

Readers who are already familiar with Islamic scripture and law will find much that is thought provoking here. Readers who are not familiar with this complex tradition and its terminology might have a hard time accessing this book's argument; such readers would benefit from first reading works such as Farid Esack's *Short Introduction to the Qur'an* or Mohammad Hashim Kamali's *Shari`ah Law: An Introduction*. It is hoped that the strength of this book—its intimate engagement with Islamic legal discourse—will not limit the scope of its readership.

One advance presented in this book is that it addresses upholders of the Islamic tradition in their own language. The book treats contemporary web-based authorities as ulama, so more populist Muslim audiences will find reference here to opinions of many famous internet Islamic authorities. They may be surprised to find how shallow are the opinions expressed as Islamic orthodoxy today, when compared to jurists with principles in the past. Another advance is that this book endeavors to integrate knowledge from previous scholarship in disparate fields. It brings together scholarship, both Islamic and secular, asserting that both are relevant and authoritative for Muslims living in globalizing contemporary societies. This book couples traditional and progressive Islamic scholarship, integrating into it insights from contemporary medical and sociological research. The book argues persuasively that Islamic theology and law must be based on the realities of scientific knowledge and technological society; Islam that compartmentalizes ritual and religion from the rough-and-tumble of social life does not live up to the example of Prophet Muhammad's teachings.

Another advance of this book is that it takes women's sexuality seriously. It addresses lesbian experience as an integral part of "homosexuality" rather than an afterthought. Though the coauthors are male, they make a conscientious effort to keep the focus on women's sexuality and not assume that male sexuality defines the field. It is difficult to do this, because the Islamic legal tradition was created by men (arguably for the benefit of men) and includes deeply patriarchal and misogynist assumptions. Yet the coauthors try their best to analyze how Qur'an interpreters and Islamic legal experts have discussed female homosexual interactions, and to forefront these experiences in their proposals for Islamic legal reform. My own work has been weak in this respect, which I readily admit and urged others to compensate for its lack, so it is heartening to see this book make necessary corrections.

Just as women are often marginalized in prior publications, so also Shii Muslims are too often ignored. In another significant advance, the coauthors of this book take Shiism seriously. Shii communities represent a minority group in the world's Muslim population (approximately 80 percent of the world's Muslim identify as Sunni in their sectarian allegiance, while 20 percent identify as some sort of Shii). Yet this book treats Shiism as an alternate religious discourse that is equal to Sunnism in its Islamic legitimacy and legal complexity. The book mainly addresses Sunni interpretations of Islam, but makes a serious effort to include Shii legal schools and hadith sources in its analysis. The coauthors address Ithna-`Ashari Shiism (the so-called Twelver Shii community) as representative of Shiism as a whole; this is justified in that the Twelver community is the largest Shii community worldwide and is the most vocal in engaging modern debates over the future direction of Islam. In addition, the ruling government of Iran, a regime based on a fundamentalist understanding of Twelver Shiism, is one of the only governments to actively execute homosexuals. Therefore, the focus on Twelver Shiism makes sense, though readers interested in other Shii communities—such as Ismailis or Zaidis or Alevis—might be disappointed to find their traditions neglected. Every book, after all, has its inherent limitations. It is hoped that this book's limited inclusion of Shii discourse will spur other scholars and activists to do deeper research on the diverse Shii communities, how they their treat homosexual members, and how they might approach reform internal to their own communities.

Yet another advance is that this book takes marriage seriously. It argues that Islamic marriage norms are applicable to same-sex couples, if those norms are reformed to eliminate patriarchal inequalities. In this argument, it takes very seriously the long-standing proposal by Muslim feminists to reform the customs of Islamic marriage to make the partners in a *nikah* more egalitarian, at least in their legal rights and responsibilities if not in their social roles. The same Islamic reforms that make heterosexual marriages more equitable will make homosexual marriages more possible.

The coauthors of this book make a strong argument that Muslim homosexuals can only prosper if they enter into same-sex partnerships that are analogous to *nikah* marriage, a contract designed to create a durable household and caring partnership that legalizes sexual pleasure for both participants. They mean that in this arrangement Muslim homosexuals can prosper as believers and persons who need sexual intimacy as an integral part of their living and flourishing; this would be a "middle path" between pious celibacy (an option often forced upon homosexual believers) and secular licentiousness (an option sometimes chosen when religious norms seem too steeped in stigma and stereotype). The coauthors also mean that in this arrangement, Muslim homosexuals prove that they are upstanding members of their religious community, equal to heterosexual married couples in piety and propriety, in rights and obligations. They imply that the more Muslim homosexuals opt for marriage (or arrangements that approximate contractual marriage), the more pressure there will be for mainstream Muslim communities to accept them with dignity. Conversely, the more that mainstream Muslim communities reform their norms of marriage to allow for same-sex partners, the more homosexual Muslims will be encouraged to embrace Islamic piety, hope for salvation along with other Muslim individuals, and contribute to their community's vibrancy rather than reject it or suffer in estrangement. The coauthors thus articulate a delicate circle of cause and effect. Progressive Islamic reform can expand the scope of diversity of individuals who can participate in Islam, and the participation of diverse persons in Islam can promote Islamic reform. This project affirms that authentic Islam is based on vital principles rather than reliant on boundary policing. It suggests that Islamic authorities should be finding ways to keep their principles living and flexible, rather than fixing orthodoxies that exclude many to empower a few.

While I was reading this book for the first time and contemplating about how to write this foreword, the US Supreme Court legalized same-sex marriage. While this was the result of decades of grass-roots activism and legal challenges to discriminatory laws in the United States, the Supreme Court's decision seemed sudden. What was largely unthinkable in many US contexts became a legal possibility in all US contexts. The federal law overturned a patchwork of state decisions, some of which banned same-sex marriage, some of which allowed it, and some of which compromised by allowing unions that were legally different from heterosexual marriage (and therefore inferior to it). Conservative religious groups that fueled bans on same-sex marriage in states and local communities were suddenly thrown on the defensive. It remains to be seen how religious institutions will react as their community members who are homosexual become more public about their identity and enter in same-sex marriages that are recognized in federal law and protected by constitutional guarantees to equal rights, privacy and privileges, and defense against discrimination. In the United States, there will emerge a new balance of the right to "pursue happiness" and freedom to "practice religion" without coercion by the state; religious communities will, out of necessity, adjust their practices as most of their members respect civic norms and extremists find themselves sidelined by gradual social change.

Yet in Muslim majority countries, this Supreme Court decision incited much condemnation. On the internet, violent homophobic rhetoric seemed normal in Islamic chat rooms even as a few Muslims dared to overlay their Facebook profiles with rainbow-colored filters in solidarity with homosexuals finally claiming an important legal right in one influential democracy. So this book will be published at a crucial time, as the debate about same-sex marriage reaches a crucial tipping point. At this point, I look back to what I wrote in 2006:

> Some Muslim readers will find the proposals above [Islamic reform to accommodate same-sex couples] to be utopian. But what begins as an unrealistic idea often gathers momentum until, after several generations, it is accepted as common sense. . . . Even if this proposal is not taken up by a broad consensus of Muslims in the West, a small minority of lesbian, gay, and transgender Muslims can adopt it to guide their own practice and strengthen their faith. . . . Indeed, we find individual Muslims acting upon reformist notions of the *shari'a* to guide their own conduct, even without the approval of their wider community. This is especially apparent when we turn to the issue of same-sex partnerships and marriage.[1]

This passage was published in 2010 in my book's chapter on same-sex marriage and partnership based on Islamic norms as a case example of how the *shari'a* might be reformed to better meet the requirements of justice and conscience. Even then, federally legalized same-sex marriage in the United States seemed remote. Now suddenly, due to the wisdom of a few judges, it is a reality. This throws an enormous challenge before the Muslim community in the United States. We will see whether its authorities can muster the wisdom and courage to face this challenge while living up to the Qur'anic dictum that "God commands that you act with justice and benevolence and generosity to those related to you, and God forbids transgression and injustice and oppression—God warns you that you might remember" (Qur'an 16:90). The book before you enables Muslims to see the issue of homosexuality and same-sex marriage in a new light, emphasizing justice and benevolence and a generous spirit that approaches the issue with an open mind and loving heart. If God wills, it will be part of their collective effort to live out the Qur'an's message in new and challenging times.

NOTE

1. Kugle, *Homosexuality in Islam*, conclusion of chapter 4; for examples of same-sex *nikah* in practice, see Kugle, Living Out Islam, 107–111.

Acknowledgments

We thank God first and foremost for enabling us to do this work and all the loved ones in our families, biological and adopted, for their support. We honor all the individuals who suffered from adversity that is unprovoked and unneeded. We hope that this book will help free vulnerable LGBT Muslims from the stranglehold of oppression in the name of religion that corrodes their body, mind, and soul.

Coauthor Junaid would like to thank his adopted family members, especially Rob Wells and Jay Smith and his friends at the Southminster-Steinhauer United Church and interfaith circles in Edmonton for standing by him through thick and thin.

We are extremely grateful to our dear brother and ally, Ayman Hossam Fadel, for his painstaking work with the transliteration. Not only did he help with editing but also caught some glaring errors, which escaped our eyes. We also acknowledge his help with the editing of our *Journal of Homosexuality* article "Investigating the Islamic Perspective on Homosexuality." Indeed, this book would not have been possible without his exceptional contributions.

Additionally, we thank Leigha Schuster for her swift and painstaking work on fixing the End Notes and bibliography to meet the proper format. We also thank our acquisition editors at Lexington, especially Eric Wrona, who approached us with the idea for the book, and Sarah Craig, who has helped us see this book through.

We are thankful to Ustad Scott Siraj al-Haqq Kugle for agreeing to write a foreword to our book, which has been years in the making. We also appreciate his pioneering contributions in this area and sincerely hope that our work will complement his body of work.

We are grateful for powerful scholars like Hashim Kamali, Kecia Ali, and Samar Habib, all of whom have advanced the study of Islamic scholarship, which we have drawn upon to complement our study of the primary texts. We are also thankful for the strong conversations we have had with our colleagues and critics at various Islamic forums, for it is their sustained interest that has helped hone our arguments.

All praise be to Allah, who creates whatever He wills, who has not created anyone in vain, and who has blessed his creations with a deep need for intimacy, affection, and companionship, and with the legitimate avenues to fulfill that need irrespective of gender, gender expression, or sexual orientation.

Introduction

The objective of this book is to address the plight of religiously observant gay and lesbian Muslims, who face immense duress from their biological as well as their larger faith-based family. Muslims who identify themselves as queer[1] or as gays and lesbians either live lonely celibate lives or have to accept living with sin because of great difficulty or inability to live without same-sex intimacy. In light of the Prophetic teaching on adopting the middle way, we argue for a way between the two polar extremes of sanctioning a free flow of desires or prescribing a lifelong foreign value of celibacy. Based on jurisprudential tools, we believe there might be enough scope for developing a case for Muslim same-sex unions.

The book is aimed at a readership that is acquainted with the fundamentals of the Islamic faith, as much of the arguments that are projected by online commenters and within Muslim spaces are eventually based on the Muslim texts and opinions of the past scholars. UK-based academic, Asifa Siraj points out in her study that amongst various variables like education, age, and gender, levels of religiosity is the most influential variable directly associated with intolerance and opposition to "homosexuality" and that having a higher level of education did not have an influence on such attitudes.[2] Moreover, there is a concerning trend amongst some of the more conservative members of the Muslim community and even intellectuals who at times equate any accommodation to gay and lesbian Muslims as not only sinful but even un-Islamic, therefore threatening a potential for excommunicating from Islam anyone who may want to open a path for accommodation of gay and lesbian Muslims within Islamic teachings and within the Muslim community.[3] In view of the finding that religiosity is the most influential variable behind homophobia and given the threats of excommunication by conservative Muslims scholars, the importance of this book cannot be further emphasized. While there are works by Scott Siraj al-Haqq Kugle, Samar Habib, and Hassan El Menyawi amongst others on issues pertaining to Muslim gays and lesbians, this book complements those efforts by deconstructing the arguments of conservative Muslim scholars. Hence, the Muslim tradition that is usually presented through the lens of conservative scholars is recast by deconstructing the reading of such scholars, who view the concerns of Muslim gays and lesbians with prejudice and contempt.

Much opposition to same-sex relationships in Muslim countries stems from cultural mores. The reality of same-sex relationships in the Muslim diaspora and increasingly within the young generation of queer Muslims living in Muslim countries is different from those who engage in exploitative sex with members of the same gender. Whereas same-sex relationships between constitutional queer people are marked by the presence of long-term commitments, companionship, and intimacy beyond sexual gratification, the sexual orientation of the involved partners is moot in the case of exploitative sex. As such, where the need for the recognition of a partnership of queer Muslim citizens of a country arises to access basic public benefits, no such recognition is warranted in the case of sexual encounters based on exploitation.

We also recognize that opposition to same-sex relationships arises because of the strong views held against the practice of heterosexual anal sex, and because of the fact that same-sex relationships have been predominately viewed in religious literature through their association with anal sex. However, it does not seem reasonable to reduce the needs of queer Muslims for companionship and intimacy to a specific sexual act, which in some sense may also serve to dehumanize queer Muslims. Furthermore, we find that even the supposed unanimity on the prohibition of heterosexual anal sex is contested based on the rulings of Shī'ī jurists and several Sunnī scholars. Thus, given that Muslim views on same-sex relationships have been informed by the phenomenon of exploitative sex and by the rulings on heterosexual anal sex, a renewed approach to addressing the plight of queer Muslims is warranted. This would entail revisiting the primary sources of Muslim knowledge—the Qur'an, Hadith, and jurisprudence—to indicate how strong opinions against same-sex relationships require further scrutiny.

To this end, we argue that the starting point would be to acknowledge that the Qur'anic verses on the people of Lūṭ (Lot) (usually used to support heterosexual norms) are addressing a different reality than that of queer Muslims. This is specifically so as the analogy between the people of Lūṭ, who, based on the linguistic and holistic contextual analysis of the relevant verses, are depicted to have exercised coercion and exploitation of vulnerable fellow human beings, and queer Muslims, who are denied their basic need for companionship and intimacy, is highly contestable. According to jurists, for an analogy to be operational, that is, in order to apply the ruling for one case to another, aside from the existence of a common element between the two cases, other elements should not stand in the way of the analogy. To the extent that coercive and exploitative sexual and nonsexual acts committed beyond basic human need by an oppressive majority are starkly divergent from the basic need for love, companionship, and intimacy by a vulnerable minority, there is sufficient reason to critique the analogy between the people of Lūṭ and queer Muslims. Furthermore, given that the practice of anal sex does not define same-sex relationships as this particular sexual act is absent in the context of lesbian and several gay relationships, the analogy between queer Muslims and the people of Lūṭ, who are at times depicted as engaging in the practice of homosexual anal sex in exegetical literature, is further weakened.

Having revisited the Qur'anic verses, we next analyze the Hadith (sayings attributed to the Prophet) based on the work of Muslim Hadith experts of previous ages. We find that there are about nine strands of Prophetic texts related to the people of Lūṭ and/or their actions and that there are three strands that are related to the *mukhannathūn* (effeminates) of Medina, which are also used at times to preach social ostracism of sexual minorities. Based on analyses of the transmission chains of all these 12 strands of texts, we find them to be suspect and weak in authenticity, which indicates that we do not have much confidence in their attribution to the Prophet. Furthermore, even taking these texts at face value, we conclude that given the marked difference between the people of Lūṭ and queer Muslims, the rulings on the former cannot be reasonably applied to the latter. In other words, while the primary sources of the Qur'an and the Hadith reference the conduct of the people of Lūṭ, they remain silent on the issue concerning queer Muslims.

Given this silence of the primary sources of Muslim knowledge, we state that the Prophet's Companions potentially understood the term *'amal qawm Lūṭ* (work of the people of Lūṭ) as a composite of apostasy and murder and perhaps coercive sexual conduct. The exegetical texts and others which are referenced in the History of Ṭabarī indicate a whole array of acts which have been associated with the people of Lūṭ. As such, when conservative Muslims claim that the chief sin of the people of Lūṭ was homosexual anal sex, they end up selecting one action amongst several including the cardinal sins of "associating partners with God" and "rejecting God's Messenger." Claims by conservative Muslims, who emphasize a specific sexual act, perhaps on the basis of personal disgust, do not find support with past jurists like Ibn Ḥazm (d. 1064), who clearly stated that the people of Lūṭ were destroyed for not believing in God.

While past jurists like Ibn Ḥazm delineate the immorality of anal sex between males based on the verses on the people of Lūṭ, by distinguishing between the exploitative and coercive acts of the people of Lūṭ and queer

Muslims, who are denied their basic need for sexual expression, we sustain the argument that rulings in the context of the people of Lūṭ cannot be reasonably applied to queer Muslims. We develop the argument that neither the Prophet's Companions nor their followers had a consensus on the understanding of later juristic terms of *liwāṭ* (sodomy) and *lūṭī* (sodomite). We also indicate weaknesses in the texts attributed to the Companions of the Prophet and argue that even accepting these narratives at face value, they raise more questions and do not provide a consistent directive on *liwāṭ*, let alone the issues concerning queer Muslims. Therefore, we argue that not only is there no express directive for queer Muslims in the principal sources of Muslim knowledge—the Qur'an and the Sunnah—but also there is no express directive to be found in either the conduct or the texts attributed to the *Salaf* (pious ancestors).

We next address the reasoning used by the past Muslim jurists in their condemnation of the specific act of *liwāṭ*, which contemporary conservative Muslims extend to prohibit same-sex relationships. We argue that the jurists have relied on extra scriptural sources to substantiate their arguments on the prohibition of *liwāṭ*. Essentially, given their sociocultural values, the jurists viewed *liwāṭ* as an act that puts the passive partner in a position of subordination and humiliation. Given their assumption that no man would willingly elect to be the passive partner, except for pecuniary reasons or disease, they had no reason to address the anachronistic issue of a same-sex legal contract.

Effectively, we reiterate that traditional opinions on the people of Lūṭ are limited in their scope to allow for their extension to issues concerning queer Muslims including that of same-sex unions. We argue that given the consensus amongst contemporary medical and psychiatry experts on the inner constitution of a minority of human beings toward the same sex, and given such an acknowledgment by several contemporary Muslim jurists, as noted by Dr. Hashim Kamali, a renewed approach to addressing the plight of queer Muslims, who are denied their basic need for sexual expression, is warranted. As such, we argue that given that Islam acknowledges sexual expression as a basic need, the prohibition of any sexual expression for queer Muslims does not sound reasonable, especially in view of textual arguments based on a weak analogy between the people of Lūṭ and queer Muslims. The fact that several contemporary conservative Muslims who issue religious rulings are relying more on test-based arguments than on textual arguments on the prohibition of same-sex unions suggests that the text-based prohibition of same-sex unions requires a closer inspection.

We also critique the opinions of contemporary conservative Muslims, who issue religious rulings, and indicate that their arguments are not necessarily reflective of the Muslim tradition. As such, we argue that instead of being motivated by the desire to retain the formulaic rulings, a renewed approach concerning queer Muslims should be motivated by higher Islamic values, based on Qur'anic and Prophetic teachings, that include the overriding juristic principles of alleviating hardship, adopting the middle way, in this case between celibacy and promiscuity, facilitating and easing the burden of coreligionists. Such principles would allow the move toward the institution of Muslim same-sex unions.

We point out that the Qur'anic verses 23:5–7 that condemn any person seeking sexual gratification outside the Muslim marriage contract/legal sanction as a transgressor keeps the door open for same-sex unions. Specifically, these verses seek to prohibit sexual activity outside of a legal contract/sanction and given that the question of same-sex unions has not been satisfactorily addressed within the Muslim tradition that did not recognize minority orientation toward the same sex given the limited knowledge of such issues during the Classical period when Muslim jurisprudence was being codified between the ninth and twelfth centuries, these verses do not stand in the way of a renewed approach toward addressing Muslim same-sex unions. Even if the position was taken to prohibit any form of sexual activity outside a legal contract/sanction between opposite gender spouses, these verses provide a general ruling, which are always open to exceptions as in the case of same-sex unions.

Basing the Muslim marriage contract on Qur'anic verses, 9:71 on mutual protectorship and 2:187 on spouses being garments to one another, provides an avenue to allow for the institution of Muslim same-sex unions. However, while we provide arguments for allowing for Muslim same-sex unions, we also acknowledge the limitations in some of the arguments that are advanced to this end. As such, it is the overriding of formulaic rulings by higher Islamic values of justice and human dignity and adopting a reasonable approach toward addressing the plight of gay Muslims that facilitates the case for Muslim same-sex unions.

This book is divided into seven chapters, the first of which sets the stage for addressing the issue by providing clarifications by distinguishing between gays and exploitative sex, distinguishing between gays and the *ma'buns* (receptive male partners in homosexual anal intercourse), between urges and sexual orientation, and by framing the issue as that of a legal contract for same-sex couples as opposed to the issue of permissibility of sexual acts.

The second chapter addresses the primary text of Muslim knowledge—the Qur'an. A linguistic and contextual analysis of the verses on the people of Lūṭ is provided along with an analysis of verses 23:5–7 that are quoted to forbid sexual activity outside the confines of marriage and *mulk yamīn* (ownership-based contract), to distinguish between Muslim gays and lesbians, whose issue is that of legitimate needs for intimacy and affections as opposed to the people of Lūṭ, who subjugated vulnerable travelers through coercion and inhospitality. The issue of Lūṭ's offer of his daughters is addressed as well as verses 4:15–16 that are being used by some contemporary scholars to prohibit same-sex unions but which were not used classically to address *liwāṭ* or *siḥāq* (both sexual activities viewed in the context of disease). Based on a renewed *qiyās* (analogical deduction), an alternate reading of the verses on the people of Lūṭ is provided and the criticisms to such a reading are deconstructed. It is argued that the primary text of Muslims is silent on the issue of a legal contract that would legitimize affection and intimacy for Muslim gays and lesbians.

The third chapter addresses the second source of Muslim knowledge—the Hadith texts that are attributed to the Prophet. These texts are divided into nine strands and they are all found to be extremely weak on the basis of both their transmission chain and the content that conflicts with other texts and verses of the Qur'an that clearly confine capital punishment for murder and *fisād fī al-arḍ* (anarchy on Earth). The three strands of Prophetic texts that address the *mukhannathūn* (effeminates of Medina), some of which are often quoted by conservative Muslims, are also shown to be weak on the basis of their transmission chain. The texts that indicate the conduct of the four Caliphs who succeeded the Prophet politically are also deconstructed along with the opinions of the *tābiʿūn* (the followers), which indicate that there was no consensus on the definition of terms like *liwāṭ*, *Lūṭī*, and *al-Lūṭīyya* before the time of the jurists. It is found that these terms possessed a wide array of meanings, and it seems that the specific understanding of sexual intercourse between men was projected onto these texts at a late stage. Thus, it is argued that the secondary texts are also silent on the issue of a legal contract that would legitimize affection and intimacy for Muslim gays and lesbians.

Since contemporary conservative Muslim scholars often reduce the concerns of Muslim gays and lesbians to anal sex, the fourth chapter addresses the texts pertaining to heterosexual anal intercourse in Sunnī jurisprudence and to a limited extent in the Shī'ī tradition, which indicates that the textual evidence against heterosexual anal intercourse is weak. Given the weakness of textual evidence, scholars use other arguments to prohibit the act, which include harm to the wife and the issue of noxiousness. We argue that even if the Hadith texts on heterosexual anal intercourse are construed as authentic enough to support the case of prohibition, given physiological differences between men and women due to the pleasure derived by males from the prostate, the prohibition from a heterosexual to a homosexual context is not readily transferable. Furthermore, given the difference of opinion through Shī'ī jurists, the argument of noxiousness does not carry much weight. Regardless, the supposed prohibition of anal sex in general does not influence the issue of Muslim same-sex unions that are not defined by a single sexual act of anal intercourse.

The fifth chapter addresses the opinions of the classical jurists on *liwāṭ*, which are divided into three categories. Essentially the jurists all upheld some punishment for *liwāṭ* and by analogy for *siḥāq*. The three categories of punishment include the death penalty for *liwāṭ* as a distinct crime, the same punishment as for *zinā* (fornication) by analogy and the *taʿzīr* (discretionary) punishment through the argument, proposed by the Ḥanafī jurists, that *qiyās* (analogical deduction) does not apply on the *Hudood* (five punishments prescribed in the Qur'an) and also on the basis of the silence of the primary and secondary texts on the issue. Ibn Ḥazm's deconstruction of the arguments of the jurists who upheld the death penalty in the case of *zinā* is delineated. However, Ibn Ḥazm's own deconstruction is applied on Ibn Ḥazm's upholding of *taʿzīr* through a text that is deemed weak. Based on such a deconstruction, the case for decriminalization of sexual activity between the same genders confined through a legal contract is presented and the same deconstruction methodology is further extended to question the reprehensibility of *liwāṭ* and by analogy *siḥāq*. Delineating the factors that define an activity as *qubḥ* (evil), it is found that same-sex relationships do not fall in that category, as they do not contain elements of oppression and falsehood. A limited view of Shīʿī jurisprudence is also provided. The point that the past jurists did not address the issue of a legal contract for same-sex couples, given the socioeconomic conditions and medical knowledge of their times, is sustained.

The sixth chapter addresses the arguments propounded by contemporary conservative Muslim scholars. It is shown that the arguments made by them, such as denying the existence of gays and lesbians or formulating *fiṭra*-based arguments, stand in contrast to the approach of the classical jurists, who based their opinions keeping in view the medical knowledge of their times, an approach that is rejected by contemporary conservative scholars when they eschew the consensus amongst medical and psychology professionals. The arguments based on treating the concerns of Muslim gays and lesbians as urges, caprice, and whims instead of the genuine human need for affection and intimacy are also deconstructed along with the *ijmāʿ* (consensus)-based arguments that are used to silence a meaningful discussion on the subject. The slippery slope arguments and those based on obedience and tests or trials are also deconstructed to indicate that such arguments do not have a reasonable and justified footing and that all such arguments violate the ethos of Islam, which rests on justice and human dignity. By carefully deconstructing the opinions of contemporary conservative Muslim scholars and invoking the silence of the Muslim texts and that of the classical jurists, the stage for Muslim same-sex unions is set.

In the seventh and final chapter, the case for Muslim same-sex unions is justified on the basis of the Islamic principle of alleviating *ʿusr* (undue hardship). By casting the issue as the need for a legal contract to allow for affection and intimacy for Muslim gays and lesbians, whose constitution is oriented toward the same gender, and on the basis of human dignity and justice to a people who are denied their humanity, the case for Muslim same-sex unions is substantiated. The marriage contract, which was also traditionally allowed by some jurists to the *khunthā mushkil* (intersex people), is shown to rest on the realization of *mawadda* (affection) and compassion, and it is argued that if such benefits are afforded to sterile couples and elderly women then there do not exist reasonable grounds to deny the same to same-sex couples. Given that marriage falls in the ambit of *muʿāmalāt* (social transactions) that are time and location specific and in light of changes such as the Tunisian family law reforms, the criticisms to same-sex unions on the basis of procedural issues are also deconstructed. Finally, Muslim academics and jurists are invited to help support efforts toward sanctioning same-sex unions that would protect our children, who identify as gays and lesbians, from the oppression of cloistered lives or that of lives lived in immense duress through false marriages of convenience to the opposite gender.

NOTES

1. While the word queer can represent any sexual or political minority, we will use it to refer to gays and lesbians.
2. Siraj, "The Construction of the Homosexual 'Other,'" 41–57.
3. Qadhi, "Dealing With Homosexual Urges."

Chapter 1

Some Clarifications

The subject of same-sex unions is usually addressed with strong opinions, at times based on intense moral disgust, which may be explained by a variety of factors, which include viewing queer Muslims through the lens of exploitative sex, depicting them as electing a deliberate morally wrong choice, equating them with the historical classification of individuals as *ma'buns*—men suffering from a disease of requiring receptive homosexual anal intercourse, and reducing the concerns of queer Muslims to the singular act of anal sex, which in general is deemed prohibited in Sunnī jurisprudence. These misconceptions need to be addressed and clarifications provided before undertaking any analysis of the Qur'an, Hadith, and jurisprudence in later chapters as the values one brings to the primary sources of Muslim knowledge influence their interpretation. Indeed, as will be shown in chapter 5, many instances of jurisprudential treatment of same-sex conduct have been influenced by the sociocultural milieu of the classical Muslim jurists.

In what follows, four clarifications are presented toward the case that queer Muslims cannot be defined as *ma'buns* and that their existence and concerns cannot be reduced to a single sexual act or manner of speech.

1.1 THE FIRST CLARIFICATION

The first clarification that deserves to be made is to separate queer Muslims from the phenomenon of exploitative sex between members of the same gender. Anecdotally, the many instances of same-sex conduct by straight males despite having recourse to their wives are not foreign to Muslim societies. This is an important point because usually men who engage in sexual activity with other men do not necessarily have a constitutional sexual orientation toward members of the same sex. Such people indulge in same-sex acts for a wide variety of reasons that could include making quick money[1] or perhaps procuring drugs. Furthermore, they might indulge in same-sex acts in the absence of access to women in prisons or in heavily gender-segregated cultures. Nadya Labi evokes this point through the experience of a Filipino expatriate in Saudi Arabia.

> Francis . . . reported that he's had sex with Saudi men whose wives were pregnant or menstruating; when those circumstances changed, most of the men stopped calling. "If they can't use their wives," Francis said, "they have this option with gays."[2]

Arno Schmidt also raises a similar point through his observations on subcultures of the Iranian society. His observation indicates how, like in Saudi subcultures, several males in the Iranian society pursue sexual encounters with males or youth with feminine features to be used as a surrogate for women.

> An Iranian "trick" . . . "will pick up Playboy, never Playgirl. He will turn to photos of women's rear ends. . . . He will point to the woman and point at you. He does not ask if you like her; he asks if you will be her."[3]

Observations on the conduct of some Saudi and Iranian males indicate that in many cases within Muslim societies, it is predominately straight males who pursue same-sex conduct outside the folds of a legal contract/sanction given the absence of the first best option of having intercourse with women. Such observations also indicate that the approach of other males or youth is a one-sided affair; for consent on part of the penetrated partner may not necessarily be assumed as such encounters occasionally include financial incentives for the passive partner or some kind of economic class-based or age-stratified exploitation of the weaker passive partner. Furthermore, the emphasis on penetrative sexual contact substantiates the point that by mimicking the sexual role in a heterosexual relationship, these straight males are using other males or youth as surrogates, especially so when intimacy, warmth, and companionship aspects of a relationship remain starkly absent in such encounters, which are principally based on the singular penetrative act performed to address frustration or satiate hypersexuality.

Naturally, viewed through this lens, many Muslims categorize same-sex conduct as a perversion which at times is inflicted on poor youth and madrassa students. It is through this sociocultural lens that many Muslims end up viewing the relationships that young queer Muslims hope to forge in the Muslim diaspora or within Muslim majority societies. However, the relationship between queer Muslims forged by bonds of love and the genuine need for intimacy and lifelong companionship cannot be reasonably compared to the sexual conduct of straight males who end up exploiting other males or youth with feminine features as surrogates for females.

It is in the context of such exploitative same-sex conduct between straight males and youth, as in the case of the Dancing Boys of Afghanistan,[4] or with the *mukhannathūn* (effeminates) that the past jurists issued their rulings to prohibit same-sex conduct. As such, it deserves to be reiterated that rulings within classical Muslim jurisprudence did not recognize sexual orientation and were simply based on outer actions. Indeed, given the absence of development in psychology, jurists as noted by the Shafi'i jurist al-Āmidī (d. 1233) based their opinions on the apparent, as hidden things were left to God,[5] which may include inner attributes like sexual orientation. However, Muslims also acknowledge the Prophet's teaching that actions are judged by their intentions,[6] which seems to suggest that a distinction needs to be made between superfluous sexual acts of straight males who one-sidedly pursue other males or youth to use as surrogates and the plight of queer Muslims, whose basic needs for intimacy and companionship have not been reasonably addressed within Muslim jurisprudence.

1.2 THE SECOND CLARIFICATION

The second clarification that needs to be made is that queer Muslims are not deliberately electing a morally wrong choice for same sex as their inner constitution does not allow them to marry opposite-sex spouses. Indeed, rulings within a classical Muslim jurisprudence distinguish between actions and leanings and are applicable only to the former. However, leanings, preferences, taste, or tilt as addressed within classical jurisprudence need to be distinguished from orientation or inner constitution of an individual as the former provide a sense of choice, fad, or changeable habit, whereas the latter indicate an integral or basic attribute of an individual, which, if unaddressed, would lead to immense duress on a person's life. Indeed, within classical jurisprudence, there have always been *rukhaṣ* (licenses) that alleviated and facilitated people under situations which placed undue duress on their lives.

There does not seem to be a belief in Muslim jurisprudence that all such licenses have been revealed or that there would not be further scope for licenses with changes in social conventions. As an instance, several contemporary Muslim scholars have issued the license to obtain interest-based mortgage for buying a house despite the fact that such an issue does not raise a life or death situation for a Muslim believer.[7] This is an important point to underscore as some Muslims who issue religious rulings are of the opinion that licenses are issued only under the life or death situation as in the case of the Qur'anic facility, based on verse 2:173, to consume pork under situations of extreme necessity. Indeed, in the context of same-sex unions for constitutional Muslim queers, living without any intimacy and companionship leads to a life of immense isolation and loneliness. This would go against the spirit of Islamic teachings and values that seek not to reduce but to enhance the welfare of human beings. To the extent that Islam recognizes the genuine needs of human beings and to the extent the Islamic law serves to enhance the welfare of believing Muslims, the past rulings on same-sex conduct based on tilt or leanings need to be replaced with a renewed approach that accounts for the sexual orientation of a minority of believing Muslims.

Support for viewing the issue concerning queer Muslims through the lens of orientation also comes from the observation that many contemporary Muslim psychiatrists and jurists have come to concede that orientation for the same sex is a constitutional part of a minority of human beings. Dr. Qazi Rahman, a lecturer at the University of London and coauthor of the book *Born Gay: the Psychobiology of Sex Orientation*,[8] has jointly stated:

> Ultimately, we believe this book will confirm what most of us have always intuitively felt: that our sexual preference is a fundamental and immutable component of our human nature.[9]

Likewise, Dr. Hashim Kamali from the International Institute of Advanced Islamic Studies in Malaysia has written that sexual orientation is increasingly considered inherent by not only science but also Islamic jurisprudence. He writes:

> Fiqh and science both confirm that sexual orientation is latent within each individual, emerging in complex interactions between one's biological make-up and early childhood. Current research is pushing slowly but steadily towards the conclusion that sexual orientation is largely inherent.[10]

1.3 THE THIRD CLARIFICATION

The third clarification that needs to be made is to distinguish between queer Muslims and the historical classification of individuals as *ma'buns*—men suffering from the disease of requiring receptive homosexual anal intercourse. Historically, according to Dr. Bassem Nathan, three medical opinions existed among medieval Arabs. While the first school considered same-sex conduct as deserving of punishment and the second simply focused on the mechanics of anal sex, the third school essentially provided a "congenital theory" for same-sex conduct. According to this school, *'ubna* (tilt toward receptive homosexual anal intercourse) results when the maternal sperm prevails over the paternal sperm.[11] It seems that the physician al-Rāzī (d. 925 CE) was a proponent of the third school. Based on the medical knowledge of his time, al-Rāzī stated that *'ubna* was the outcome of the contest between the female sperm and the male sperm.[12] According to Rosenthal, al-Rāzī considered *'ubna* to be genetic in that it was deemed incurable.[13] According to Ze'evi, based on al-Rāzī's writings, a homosexual male may have different physical traits than his heterosexual counterparts. Interestingly, Ze'evi indicates a chart, based on Arabic and Turkish texts of the sixteenth and seventeenth centuries, that illustrates how the shape of fingers can be associated with "homosexuals," drunks, and whores.[14]

According to Boswell, many Muslim scientific writers, besides al-Rāzī, believed that "homosexuality" was inherited. This corresponds with the third school indicated by Dr. Bassem Nathan. Apart from Muslim physicians, other scholars like the Nestorian Christian Ḥunayn ibn Ishāq (d. 873 CE)[15] and the Melkite Christian Qusṭā ibn Lūqā (d. 912 CE) also subscribed to the view that "homosexuality" was an inherent trait. In fact, Qusṭā ibn Lūqā provided a classification of men indicating some men are *yamīlu 'ilā* (disposed) toward women, some toward men, and some toward both.[16]

According to Sahar Amer, scholars also understood "lesbianism" as an inherent trait.[17] She quotes al-Kindī (d. 873 CE) stating, like Galen (d. 199/217 CE), that "lesbianism" was caused by heat generated in the labia which could only be reduced by orgasm with another woman. This viewpoint corresponds with the ideas of the second school mentioned by Bassem Nathan. Sahar Amer also mentions Yūḥannā ibn Māsawayh (d. 857 CE) as indicating that "lesbianism" was an outcome when a nursing woman eats celery, rocket, melilot leaves, and the flowers of a bitter orange tree. Likewise, the physician Al-Samaw'al ibn Yaḥyā (d. 1180) explained the physiological causes of lesbianism, specifically grinding, through rationales of coldness, shortness, deficiencies, or illnesses of wombs.[18] The viewpoints of al-Kindī, Ibn Māsawayh, and Ibn Yaḥyā indicate that "lesbianism" was explained on the basis of physical traits or childhood exposure to the effects of certain foods.

While it may be tempting to argue that past Muslim scholars, especially on the basis of the work by scholars like Boswell and Amer who have used "homosexuality" and "lesbianism," did have a theory of sexual orientation, yet it deserves to be underscored that they were trying to explain the "itch for receptive homosexual anal intercourse" and "itch for rubbing labias," which were viewed as a tilt toward bad habits, as opposed to sexual orientation, which alludes to an individual's inner constitution. Ze'evi's allusion to texts from the sixteenth and seventeenth centuries that associated "homosexuals" with drunks and whores suggests that past Muslim scholars were using a medical framework to explain habits like drinking and prostitution and as such equated same-sex conduct on a par with them, instead of viewing same-sex conduct on the basis of something more integral and constitutional like sexual orientation.

This distinction between the "tilt for receptive homosexual anal intercourse" and orientation toward a member of the same sex is usually missed when contemporary Muslims, who issue religious opinions based on their reading of the Muslim texts, equate queer Muslims with *ma'buns*. As an example, Hamza Yusuf refers to Muḥammad al-Dasūqī's (d. 1815) work to indicate that past Muslim scholars ruled on issues concerning queer Muslims. Yusuf quotes Muḥammad al-Dasūqī as having written that "it is discouraged [but not prohibited] for a eunuch (*khasi*) or homosexual (*maʾbūn*) to be a regular prayer leader" and that

> it is disliked [but still valid] for a maʾbūn to be an assigned leader of the obligatory prayers as well as for communal supererogatory prayers, but not tarawih, or travelers' prayers, or as someone who leads them on occasion. And the intended meaning of maʾbūn is a male who is effeminate in his speech, similar to a woman's speech, or someone who desires rectal intercourse but doesn't practice it, or someone who has practiced it but since repented yet, nonetheless, has set tongues wagging.[19]

This quote complements the information that is found under the section "Who is disliked to lead the prayer" in the Kuwaiti encyclopedia of *Fiqh*.[20] It is also clear from Muḥammad al-Dasūqī's comment that where *maʾbūn* refers to a man with a tilt toward receiving homosexual anal intercourse, Yusuf ends up conflating the individual classified on the basis of the tilt toward the singular act of receptive homosexual anal intercourse or on the basis of suffering from a disease or a bad habit with queer Muslims, whose inner constitution has been accepted as an integral part of his identity, which goes beyond the singular sexual act to encompass a life that includes the legitimate need for intimacy and companionship.

It is specifically this understanding of "homosexuality," including that of the past scholars of the third school as alluded to by Bassem Nathan, as the disease to engage in receptive homosexual anal intercourse, which has shaped the views of Muslim jurists. The contemporary conservative Muslim scholar al-Munajjid, for instance, writes that in Sharīʿa terminology, "homosexuality" refers to "inserting the tip of the penis into the anus of a male."[21] Likewise, "lesbianism" has been understood as referring to the action of "rubbing" as opposed to an orientation. Even in the sexual satirical literature of Niẓām al-Dīn ʿUbayd Zākānī (d. 1370), the debate is not between male and female genders but between anal and vaginal penetration.[22] Therefore, it is important to reiterate that while current Muslim scholars like Kamali and Rahman understand "homosexuality" through the lens of sexual orientation, past scholars and contemporary Muslims who lean on tradition conflate issues concerning the lives of queer Muslims with those of *ma'buns*, who have been classified as suffering from a supposed "congenital" disease to indulge in receptive homosexual anal intercourse.

1.4 THE FOURTH CLARIFICATION

This necessitates the fourth clarification, based on which the concerns of queer Muslims cannot be reduced to the issue of permissibility of sexual contact but rather involve holistic lives that include the need for intimacy and companionship. Indeed, just as the Muslim marriage contract places limits on the sexual expression of opposite-sex spouses, there may be similar restrictions placed on partners in Muslim same-sex unions formulated within an Islamic framework, which will have to be studied and discussed later. Indeed, not all queer Muslims indulge in the practice of homosexual anal intercourse, which further weakens the argument that conflates queer Muslims with *ma'buns* and substantiates the point that individuals cannot be defined by specific sexual practices.

As a matter of fact, some heterosexual Muslims indulge in anal sex. According to Shī'ī jurisprudence, anal sex is permissible with one's wife with her approval, albeit it is strongly disliked. Notwithstanding the rulings that prohibit heterosexual anal sex within Sunnī jurisprudence, several husbands insist on this act as evident from various online Islam Q&A websites. In fact, one sex columnist writes on the distinction between anal sex and being gay.

> Many gay men do not have anal sex. In fact, oral sex and mutual masturbation are more common than anal stimulation among gay men in long-term relationships. . . . Studies indicate that about 25 percent of heterosexual couples have had anal sex at least once, and 10 percent regularly have anal penetration.[23]

Given that many gay men do not indulge in homosexual anal sex and that the practice is moot in the case of lesbians, and given that many heterosexuals indulge in this act, the association between gay men and HIV infections is irrelevant where the risky activity of unprotected anal sex is absent. In fact, according to groups that work on HIV prevention, it is stigma and discrimination that drive sexual activity underground, thereby increasing the probability of HIV infections.[24] Furthermore, in the context of Sub-Saharan Africa, we would not erroneously associate AIDS with heterosexuals but rather with unprotected sexual intercourse. Thus, HIV and other diseases should be associated with unprotected sexual encounters rather than sexual orientation of individuals.

The four clarifications mentioned above indicate that queer Muslims should be viewed separately from the phenomena of exploitative sex, which is predominately observed within Muslim majority societies, and that queer Muslims have a constitutional orientation toward members of the same sex, which includes the legitimate need for intimacy and companionship so that they cannot be equated with the historical category of *ma'buns*, who have been portrayed as suffering from a congenital tilt, habit, or disease toward requiring receptive homosexual anal intercourse. Furthermore, based on the clarifications presented above, the concerns of queer Muslims cannot be reduced to the singular act of homosexual anal sex, which is irrelevant in the case of lesbians and several gay men.

These clarifications motivate a critical and detailed study of the fundamental sources of Muslim religious knowledge. While a detailed look into Shī'ī texts is beyond the scope of this work, the Qur'anic verses on the people of Lūṭ and the associated exegetical literature will be addressed in the next chapter, followed by a critical review of the Hadith canon in a chapter addressing the Sunnī texts and thereafter a critical look at the reasoning of the Sunnī jurists and, to a limited extent, some Shī'ī jurists in the successive chapters addressing texts on heterosexual anal intercourse and *liwāṭ*.

NOTES

1. Brad Hammer, "Gay for pay porn stars: Are they really gay?" *Huffington Post*, December 27, 2013, accessed August 2015.
2. Nadya Labi, "The Kingdom in the closet," *The Atlantic Magazine*, May 2007, accessed January 26, 2016, http://www.theatlantic.com/magazine/archive/2007/05/the-kingdom-in-the-closet/5774/.
3. Arno Schmitt and Jehoeda Sofer, *Sexuality and Eroticism among Males in Moslem Societies*, (New York: The Haworth Press, 1992), 66.
4. Frontline, *The Dancing Boys of Afghanistan*, PBS Documentary, 2010, accessed January 26, 2016, http://www.pbs.org/wgbh/pages/frontline/dancingboys/.
5. Christian Lange, *Justice, Punishment and the Medieval Muslim Imagination*, (Cambridge: Cambridge University Press, 2008), 193.
6. "An-Nawawi's 40 Hadith, Hadith No. 1," ahadith.co.uk, accessed January 25, 2016, http://ahadith.co.uk/hadithwithcommentary.php?id=441&cid=11.
7. European Council for Fatwa and Research's Resolution on "Permissibility of conventional mortgage under necessity," 1999, accessed January 26, 2016, http://www.globalwebpost.com/farooqm/study_res/i_econ_fin/ecfr-fatwa_mortgage.htm.

8. Glenn Wilson and Qazi Rahman, *Born Gay: The Psychobiology of Sex Orientation*, (London: Peter Owen, 2005).

9. " Wilson and Rahman," *Born Gay*, 11.

10. Mohammad Hashim Kamali, *Transgenders and Justice in Islam*, *New Straits Times*, November 24, 2011, accessed January 26, 2016, http://www.hashimkamali.com/index.php/publications/item/23-transgenders-and-justice-in-islam.

11. Bassem Nathan, "Medieval Arabic medical views on male homosexuality," *Journal of Homosexuality* 26 (1994): 37–9.

12. Dror Ze'evi, *Producing Desire: Changing Sexual Discourse in the Ottoman Middle East, 1500–1900*, (Berkeley: University of California Press, 2006), 38.

13. Franz Rosenthal, "Ar-Râzî on the hidden illness," *Bulletin of the History of Medicine* 52 (1978): 45–60, accessed January 27, 2016, http://williamapercy.com/wiki/images/Ar-Razi_on_the_Hidden_Illness.pdf.

14. Ze'evi, *Producing Desire*, 29.

15. Husain F. Nagamia, and Nasir Puyan, "Abū Zayd Ḥunayn ibn Isḥāq al-'Ibādī: a physician translator par excellence," *Journal of Islamic Medical Association of North America* 40 (2008): 9–14, accessed January 26, 2016, http://dx.doi.org/10.5915/40-1-5279.

16. John Boswell, "Revolutions, universals, and sexual categories," in *Hidden from History: Reclaiming the Gay and Lesbian Past*, ed. Duberman M., Vicinus M., Chauncey Jr, G, (New York: Meridian, 1989), accessed January 26, 2016, http://history.msu.edu/hst420/files/2013/03/Boswell__Revolutions__Universals__and_Se.pdf.

17. Sahar Amer, "Medieval Arab lesbians and lesbian-like women," *Journal of the History of Sexuality* 18 (2009): 215–36.

18. Samar Habib, *Arabo-Islamic Texts on Female Homosexuality, 850–1780 A.D*, (New York: Teneo Press, 2009).

19. Hamza Yusuf, "Tempest in a teapot: Islamophobia meets homophobia." Sandala, May 8, 2013, accessed January 27, 2016, https://www.sandala.org/blog/tempest-in-a-teapot-islamophobia-meets-homophobia.

20. Kuwaiti Encyclopedia of Fiqh, Entry: *khunthā mushkil*, 212 in الموسوعة الذهبية للحديث النبوي الشيف و علومه [*The Golden Encyclopedia of the Prophetic Golden Hadeeth and its Sciences*], 2nd edition, (London: Turath Publishing), CD-ROM.

21. "Why does Islam forbid lesbianism and homosexuality?" Islam QA, accessed January 25, 2016, http://islamqa.info/en/10050.

22. Afsaneh Najmabadi, "Types, Acts or What? Regulation of sexuality in nineteenth century Iran," in *Islamicate Sexualities*, eds. Kathryn Babayan and Afsaneh Najmabadi, (Cambridge: Harvard University Center for Middle Eastern Studies, 2008), 278.

23. "Not all gay men have anal sex," Alice! Health Promotion, Last modified June 13, 2008, http://goaskalice.columbia.edu/not-all-gay-men-have-anal-sex.

24. "HIV/AIDS At risk groups—other groups," Global Health Council, [n.d.], accessed January 26, 2016, http://web.archive.org/web/20110728031548/http://www.globalhealth.org/hiv_aids/risk_groups2/.

Chapter 2

Analysis of the Relevant Qur'anic Verses

There exists no Qur'anic verse that directly addresses same-sex relationships. The prohibition of same-sex relationships, however, is indirectly derived through *qiyās*—analogy from the verses on the people of Lūṭ. These verses are technically understood as pertaining to anal intercourse between males. According to the understanding of most exegetes and jurists, all these verses—(7:80–81; 26:160–166, 27:54–55, 29:28–29)—refer specifically to *liwāṭ*—anal intercourse between males, usually involving a youth, and this particular act is condemned as a major sin.[1] While some zealous conservative Muslims borrow from Western sodomy laws to define *liwāṭ* as involving private parts and the mouth, contemporary scholar Muhammad Salih al-Munajjid indicates how "homosexuality" has been defined in the Islamic tradition as follows.

> Homosexuality means having intercourse with males in the back passage. This was the action of the accursed people of the Prophet Lot. In Shariah terminology it refers to inserting the tip of the penis into the anus of a male.[2]

In contrast to past scholars like Ibn Ḥazm (d. 1064), conservative Muslims believe that the people of Lūṭ were destroyed primarily for same-sex conduct, which is conflated with *liwāṭ*. However, given the interpretation by substitution methodology of exegetes like Qurṭubī,[3] it seems that the understanding of the Qur'anic verses on the people of Lūṭ has been qualified by the later juristic term *liwāṭ,* which suggests that the culturally informed concept of *liwāṭ* was read back into the Qur'an.

When conservative Muslims claim that "homosexuality" is a major sin, they are basing their opinion on a derived rule as opposed to a clear-cut law found within the Qur'an, as in the case of intoxicants (5:90), pork (5:03), fornication (17:32), and incest (4:23). As a general rule, all major prohibitions of

Islam come mainly in the form of a direct and clear statement in the Qur'an. These statements generally use variants of the following words: "Do not," "Forbidden" or "penalty of Hell." Snippets of the following verses, depicting the prohibition of intoxicants, pork, fornication, incest, murder, slander, usury, gambling, disobedience to parents, and associating partners with God would substantiate this line of argument.

> . . . intoxicants and games of chance . . . are only an uncleanness, . . . shun it therefore . . . (5:90)
>
> Forbidden to you is that which dies of itself, and blood, and flesh of swine. (5:03)
>
> And go not nigh to fornication; surely it is an indecency and an evil way (17:32)
>
> Forbidden to you are your mothers and your daughters and your sisters. (4:23)
>
> Do not devour your property among yourselves falsely, . . . and do not kill your people. (4:29)
>
> Do not find fault with your own people nor call one another by nicknames. (49:11)
>
> Allah has . . . forbidden usury. . . and whoever returns (to it)—these are the inmates of the fire; they shall abide in it. (2:275)
>
> You shall not serve (any) but Him, and goodness to your parents. . . . say not to them (so much as) "Ugh" nor chide them. (17:23)

The above list indicates that in contrast to other sins, same-sex conduct, despite being branded as a major prohibition, surprisingly does not appear to be expressly and clearly prohibited in the Qur'an. Nonetheless, conservative Muslim scholars generally quote one of the three verses—7:81, 26:165–166, or 27:55—to substantiate their claim that same-sex unions stand prohibited in Islam. Apart from the use of the word *azwājikum* (wives) in verse 26:166, these verses more or less contain the same information.

> Most surely you come to males in lust besides females; nay you are an extravagant people (7:81)
>
> What! Do you come to the males from among the creatures? And leave what your Lord has created for you of your wives? Nay, you are a people exceeding limits (26:165–166)
>
> What! Do you indeed approach men lustfully rather than women? Nay, you are a people who act ignorantly (27:55)

Without paying attention to the context, some scholars extrapolate from such verses to apply them to all same-sex conduct. However, ignoring the context is contrary to the traditional methodology related to the applicability of *qiyās* (analogy), which applies only if the situations and circumstances of the two cases are similar and in the absence of other circumstances that render the analogy void. This suggests that the context of both situations, that of the people of Lūṭ on the one hand and Muslim gays and lesbians on the other, have to be meticulously studied to look at the parallels and differences in order to gauge the applicability of drawing a ruling from one case to another on the basis of *qiyās*.

As such, the verses indicate that the people of Lūṭ exceeded limits by approaching males as a collective nation, which suggests that the purport of the verses is different from addressing a minority of men and women whose constitutional orientation is toward members of the same sex. Moreover, where exceeding limits makes sense in the case of a collective community of married people, whose sexual and emotional human needs are met through their spouses, it is not clear how limits are exceeded in the case of a minority of gay men and women whom conservative Muslim leaders deny their genuine need for sexual expression by prescribing them to remain permanently celibate.

A better understanding of the people of Lūṭ story may help invoke a more suitable analogy from the story than what has been proffered by traditional exegetes that the people of Lūṭ were destroyed for *liwāṭ*. As such, it is also important to read verses 7:81, 26:165–166, and 27:55 holistically in the context of other verses that provide the background of the story of the people of Lūṭ in the Qur'an. Reading verse 7:81 in the context of the preceding verse 7:80 and verses 29:28 and 29:29, presented below, would indicate that it would be unreasonable to infer that these verses are alluding to contemporary same-sex relationships.

> And (We sent) Lūṭ when he said to his people: What! Do you commit an indecency which anyone in the world has not done before you? (7:80)
>
> And (We sent) Lūṭ when he said to his people: Most surely you are guilty of an indecency which none of the nations has ever done before you (29:28)
>
> What! Do you come to the males and commit robbery on the highway, and you commit evil deeds in your assemblies? (29:29)

Indeed, relationships based on commitment, reciprocity, equality, and love cannot be equated with conduct that included indulging in indecency, highway robbery, and actions perpetrated in public assemblies. Alternatively, how reasonable is it to assume that committing highway robbery, evil deeds in open assemblies, and being a responsible citizen in a committed same-sex relationship go hand in hand?

Exegeses from other verses on the people of Lūṭ also add to the understanding based on the aforementioned verses. Conservative Muslims usually quote verses that indicate Lūṭ's offering his daughters to deduce the point that heterosexual marriages are preferred to same-sex conduct. However, in traditional exegeses there has been much difference of opinion on whether Lūṭ really did offer his daughters, which casts doubt on the understanding that the verses are giving precedence to heterosexual marriages. Moreover, the fact that the people of Lūṭ were demanding that the male visitors be yielded to them and that Lūṭ was concerned about the protection of his guests indicates that the verses are not alluding to committed same-sex relationships but something else altogether. These verses, a detailed exposition of which will be undertaken later, are as follows.

> And when Our messengers came to Lūṭ, he was grieved for them, and he lacked strength to protect them. He said: O my people! These are my daughters, they are purer for you. . . . They said: Certainly you know that we have no claim on your daughters, and most surely you know what we desire. (11:77–79)
>
> They said: Have we not forbidden you from (other) people? He said: These are my daughters, if you will do (aught). . . (15:67–72)

However, apart from invoking the Qur'anic verses on the people of Lūṭ, conservative Muslims also quote verses that confine legitimate sexual relationships between a man and his wives or concubines to sustain the prohibition of same-sex relationships.

> And who guard their private parts, except before their mates or those whom their right hands possess, for they surely are not blamable, but whoever seeks to go beyond that, these are they that exceed the limits. (23:5–7)

These verses are referenced to indicate that the marriage contract—*nikāḥ*—only exists between men and women. The juristic rule *al-aṣl fī al-'abḍ*ā*ʿ al-taḥrīm*—the default status of sexual intercourse is prohibition, seems to have been derived on the basis of these verses and indicates that only *nikāḥ*—marriage contract—between men and women legitimizes sexual intercourse. However, this juristic rule is a point of *ijtihād*—independent reasoning and not based on the notion of *maʿlūm min al-dīn bi-l-ḍarūra*—religious doctrines known by necessity to be part of religious teachings.[4] As such, if the juristic rule of the prohibition of any sexual expression outside the folds of a marriage contract is based on independent reasoning, then it seems reasonable to raise two questions: first, whether the classical Muslim jurists actually addressed the marriage contract between two males or two females and second, whether same-sex sexual expressions are intrinsically *qubḥ*—evil and therefore prohibited or whether they are prohibited because of a lack of a legal relationship.

The argument that the past jurists did not address same-sex relationships within a legal contract can be based on the observation that the jurists viewed the marriage contract between an active or insertive partner and a passive or receptive partner. According to Kecia Ali, "Grammatical active and passive translate into socially and legally active and passive."[5] In the context of the verses on the people of Lūṭ, the Qur'an uses the words *dhakar* and *unthā* for men and women, which connote the meanings of nonreceptive and receptive entities, respectively. As such, linguistically in Arabic, consent in sex is implicitly assumed to exist between males and females and absent between same-sex couples. *Nakaḥa*—the transitive verb for the word *nikāḥ*—marital contract, which connotes both marriage and sexual intercourse, is used based on the assumption of female passivity, that is, a woman is not "married with" or had "sexual intercourse with" but rather "is married" or "done sexual intercourse to."[6] It may also be noted that just as the words *dhakar* and *unthā* respectively connote nonreceptive and receptive entities, Daniel Boyarin argues that the word *neqeba* for females in Talmudic Hebrew and Aramaic referred to orifice bearer and that gender was constructed on the basis of penetration and being penetrated.[7]

One can easily apply those same principles to a same-sex marriage contract with a little imagination to one partner assuming the more traditionally or predominantly masculine role and the other the more traditionally or predominantly feminine role. Such principles can apply even in the case if both partners wished to change roles, as one partner assuming the insertive role and the other the receptive role does not constitute an unequal relationship. Indeed, Islamic scholars have been able to come with lots of ingenious solutions to problems that are much more challenging than this one.

However, according to Sahar Amer, in medieval Arabic literature, as found in the stories of the Thousand and One Nights, two females Hayat al-Nufus and Budur are depicted as equal partners in their relationship, in that both were portrayed as active givers and passive recipients of same-sex intimacy.[8] Moreover, Frederic Lagrange indicates that implicitly based on the libel literature, the *fā'il* (active partner) can slide to becoming the *maf'ūl bihi* (passive partner) if he places "attraction for boys at the centre of his discourse."[9] Moreover, Rowson notes that apart from the category of *muajir* (receptive partner for money), there existed the *mubadil* (receptive partner in exchange for being the active partner).[10] However, even in the context of such literature, Kathryn Babayan indicates that women who engaged in sex with their female coequals in social and religious status were pathologized as *majnūn* (crazy),[11] just as the receptive male partners were pathologized as *ma'būns*. This indicates that same-sex legal contracts were simply not feasible as relationships were viewed on the basis of penetration and same-sex desire was viewed through the lens of pathology.

The viewpoint of male activity and female passivity within Islamic legal literature can also be substantiated based on Kecia Ali's observation that despite the fact that past jurists discussed the consequences of wildly improbable scenarios, there is a marked silence on the issue of females taking male concubines or females marrying people of the Book.[12] Texts do exist that allude to the issues of female taking male concubines such as the narrative that includes ʿUmar (d. 644) indicating that the interpretation that a woman gave to the Qur'anic verses 23:5–7 on taking male concubines was incorrect,[13] or a similar narrative involving two women, which indicates the friends of ʿUmar (d. 644) stating, "They disputed you on the book of God," thereby suggesting that they did not deem the understanding of the women as completely wrong.[14] However, it does not seem that the later jurists relied on these texts as they were deemed weak in their authenticity.

Kecia Ali references the jurist Shāfiʿī (d. 820) who provided the reason behind why a female could not take a male concubine. He reasoned that it was impermissible to make an analogy between different entities and alluded to the viewpoint that a man is the one who marries or takes a concubine and stands over a woman and a woman is the one who is married or taken as a concubine and does not stand over a man simply on the basis that she is different.[15]

In classical jurisprudence, legal sexual intercourse is made possible through *milk*—ownership or control, and as such Shāfiʿī and other jurists viewed *mahr* (dower) as the "vulva price," that is, payment made to have legal access to the wife's private parts.[16] In fact, within the Ḥanafī School of jurisprudence, in the absence of a legitimate reason to refuse sex, husbands could even forcibly have sex with their wives.[17] Given that legal sexual intercourse comprised of ownership of the female private part and a duty on the wife's part to submit to penetration in the absence of a legitimate excuse, and to the extent marriage was viewed as a form of slavery by scholars like al-Ghāzālī (d. 1111) wherein the husband could curtail the movement of his spouse, the question of a same-sex relationship between two equal entities would have been moot for the past jurists.

This also helps explain that for past jurists a consensual relationship between two free men would have been viewed as significantly worse than a coerced relationship between a free man and his male slave,[18] simply because another free man would not be subjected to ownership like a woman or a slave. As such, a marriage contract between two free men or two free women would not have been possible as the asymmetry in relationship between a male and a female would have been deemed to be absent between members of the same spouses based on the view that the husband was the active or insertive partner whereas the wife was the passive or receptive partner. In other words, the issue of another free man willingly submitting to the ownership of another male would have been considered absurd and viewed through the lens of *'ubna*—disease of the anus, as being receptive or passive was not a role deemed for nonafflicted males. Based on the jurist al-Āmidī's opinion that jurists decide on the basis of the apparent, not hidden, attributes, and given the absence of developments in human psychology, past jurists did not address the issue of same-sex relationships in a legal contract between gay men or lesbian women, but ruled on such relationships through the lens of external penetrative acts outside of a legal contract and rationalized through the lens of disease and considered such relationships as absurd.

While the past jurists did not rule on same-sex relationships in a legal contract between two free men or two free women, they did rule on same-sex conduct outside of a legal contract and within the context of slavery. They prohibited same-sex acts outside of a legal contract as stipulated by verses 23:5–7. The fact that some jurists took a permissive view on same-sex conduct within the context of a free man and his male slave[19] indicates that such jurists did not view same-sex acts as prohibited based on the rationale that such acts were inherently *qubḥ* (evil) but deemed them prohibited in the absence of a legal contract. Kecia Ali distinguishes intrinsically sinful acts as bestiality and necrophilia from acts outside the folds of a legal contract,[20] which include same-sex acts by analogy with fornication. Viewed in this light, the prohibition of same-sex relationships does not rest on the nature of the acts but on the absence of a legal contract between members of the same gender, which would have been considered absurd by the past jurists due to their sociocultural understanding that the husband was supposed to be the insertive partner who held his wife, the receptive partner, through an ownership contract.

That the prohibition of same-sex relationships rests on the absence of a legal contract, as opposed to the inherent nature of the acts, can also be discerned from the fact that sexual acts other than vaginal intercourse are not unanimously deemed prohibited within a legal contract. While contemporary Sunnī Muslim scholars hold strong opinions on heterosexual anal intercourse, deeming it prohibited, there is much difference of opinion on a whole array of other sexual expressions that include masturbation, oral sex, rimming, and use of sex toys. This indicates that the sexual expression between members of the same gender are not prohibited because of some intrinsic evil aspect of such acts but that these acts are prohibited in the absence of a legal contract that legitimizes such conduct.

2.1 THE RANGE OF SCHOLARLY OPINION ON ORAL SEX

Take for instance the sexual act of oral sex. The reasoning of those who deem it prohibited includes avoiding total nudity during sex, not reducing oneself to a "sub-animal level," indicating that the mouth is used for reading the Qur'an, mentioning that even lowly beasts do not indulge in such an act and noting that the mouth is not a receptacle for impurity for even the umbilical cord is not attached to the mouth of the fetus.[21] Other reasons that oral sex is prohibited are that the preseminal discharge is jurisprudentially considered impure, verse 2:222 directs Muslims to approach women in the manner God has commanded, which is construed as referring to vaginal intercourse, that oral sex is against modesty or deemed reprehensible according to past fatwās, and that conduct like masturbation, sex during menstruation, anal sex, and sodomy are accepted by the *kuffār*—infidels.[22] Furthermore, some contend that oral sex contravenes *adab*—proper Islamic behavior and goes against *fiṭra*—human nature.[23]

However, none of the reasons advanced for the prohibition of oral sex have a strong textual corroboration. The arguments that allude to proper Islamic behavior, immodesty, avoiding complete nudity during sexual intercourse, and reducing oneself to the level of animals or beneath them reflect personal taste and disgust. The argument that infidels accept sexual conduct like masturbation, sex during menstruation, and anal sex and so Muslims must reject such acts is a weak one to make. While sex during menstruation is forbidden by verse 2:222, masturbation is deemed permissible, as will be elaborated later, based on texts cited by Ibn Ḥazm and even based on verse 2:222. Heterosexual anal sex is not deemed forbidden in Shī'ī jurisprudence. While some Sunnī jurists use verse 2:222 to prohibit heterosexual anal intercourse, it is not generally used to forbid oral sex or sexual foreplay. The *fiṭra* argument seems to be stretched, for as noted before, it is generally understood in the context of man's disposition toward monotheism rather than specific sexual acts. Finally, the argument of having impurity in the mouth requires further scrutiny.

A difference of opinion exists within the four Sunnī schools of jurisprudence on the purity of secretions from the genitals. This difference of opinion seemingly stems from *qiyās*—analogical deduction—and the difference arises based on whether such secretions are compared to breast milk and spittle, which are deemed pure, or to feces and urine, which are considered impure. According to a conservative Muslim authority, Abu Ḥanīfa (d. 767) and Mālik ibn Anas (d. 795) consider semen as impure and whereas Shāfi'ī (d. 820) and Aḥmad ibn Ḥanbal (d. 855) deemed semen as pure, all deemed the preseminal liquid and its vaginal equivalent as impure.[24] However, another conservative scholar contends that jurists like Ibn 'Ābidīn (d. 1836) and Ibn Ḥazm (d. 1064) considered vaginal secretions as pure and the reasons that have been forwarded for such a position include the absence of texts deeming them impure, that things are pure unless a text deems them impure, the fact that vaginal secretions are not secreted from the urethra or anus, that such secretions are discharged even in the absence of sexual desire and that they do not necessitate *ghusl*—bathing to attain purity.[25]

Given the difference of opinion on genital secretions, which based on the reasoning of scholars seems to rest upon *qiyās*, it seems that there cannot be an absolute position on the impurity of genital secretions and thus the impermissibility of oral sex cannot be deemed absolute. It is perhaps for this reason that several scholars deem oral sex as permissible based on a wide array of reasons.

A group of Salafi scholars base permissibility of the act on the texts attributed to the Prophet that encourage foreplay between spouses. Shāfiʿī scholars also deem oral sex as permissible as one of the opinions of Shāfiʿī (d. 820) is presented as that falling short of heterosexual anal sex the whole body could be enjoyed.[26] Egyptian sexologist Heba Qutb's reasoning on permissibility is based on the fact that there exists no text that prohibits the act. This can be coupled with the fact that in Islamic jurisprudence, in the context of *muʿāmalāt* (social transactions) things are deemed permissible unless expressly prohibited. Dr. Ali Jumah's opinion is based on the reasoning that such an act between spouses keeps them away from illicit acts. Mālikī jurists claim there is no harm in the act. Some scholars believe that since genitalia are not dirty like the anus, therefore oral sex would be permissible. Contemporary scholar Sheikh al-Turayri's opinion on permissibility of oral sex is based on the arguments that, apart from heterosexual anal sex and sex during menstruation, all other acts are permissible between spouses, dislike of a practice does not render it impermissible, female genitals are not impure, and that the possibility of the existence of impurity does not render the act impermissible.[27]

It seems that the predominant reasoning behind the prohibition of oral sex hinges on the issue of impurity and hence harm, whereas permissibility is based on the argument of the absence of an express text that prohibits the act and the fact that acts are deemed pure and permissible otherwise. The impurity aspect is also contested as at least outer genitalia are deemed without impurity, which is reserved for urine and feces. That the aspect of impurity governs the permissibility of oral sex can also be noted from the opinion in Hanbali jurisprudence, based on which oral sex is permissible before penetration and is considered reprehensible after penetration and from the opinion that even though Shāfiʿī and Hanbali jurists consider sperm to be pure, they deem it unlawful to swallow.[28] However, to the extent impurity is absent and to the extent the harm of oral sex as studied in light of contemporary scientific knowledge is deemed next to negligible, the prohibition on oral sex cannot stand, especially given the stark absence of textual prohibition.

Textual arguments seem to take precedence over impurity arguments. This is why even though the anus is deemed impure because of the argument that noxiousness is always present in contrast to the vagina where noxiousness is present only during menstruation, given that usually the textual argument is made against heterosexual anal sex and sex during menstruation, any act related to the anus other than penetration is deemed permissible by those who uphold this line of reasoning. Thus, enjoyment of the anus without penetration is deemed permissible.[29] Notwithstanding the arguments of impurity and the concern of mimicking the actions of the people of Lūṭ, some contemporary scholars like Habeeb Alli deem not just touching but also rimming as permissible. While Habeeb Alli has asserted the prohibition of using anal toys, he allows for the use of vaginal toys.[30] Alli's opinion on the use of vaginal toys may have precedent in the opinion of Ḥasan Baṣrī (d. 728) who stated that there is no harm in a woman inserting an object in her vagina to protect herself from the desire to commit *zinā* (fornication).[31]

Thus, to the extent that acts like oral sex, rimming, and the use of sex toys are not considered prohibited, it may be concluded that in the context of same-sex relationships, the key issue at hand is not that the acts are intrinsically *qubḥ* (evil) but the absence of a legal contract that makes such acts permissible. As such, if sexual acts other than vaginal intercourse are not evil per se and that the jurists have not addressed the issue of a legal contract between members of the same sex or dismissed such a contract based on their notion of gender, as informed by the constructs of their times, then it stands to reason to revisit the opinion on same-sex relationships.

2.2 THE RANGE OF SCHOLARLY OPINION ON MASTURBATION

However, verses 23:5–7 have been subject to different interpretations. Several past scholars interpreted the verses to forbid any sexual activity including masturbation outside the folds of *nikāḥ*. They opine that since there is no text that permits masturbation, the *asl* (original proof) is prohibition[32] and as such one who masturbates would be transgressing limits.

According to online fatwa sites, Mālik (d. 795) opined that verses 23:5–7 defined the masturbator as one who exceeded limits,[33] whereas, Shāfiʿī (d. 820), using a similar argument, deemed masturbation to be prohibited and invoked verse 24:33 to counsel patience.[34]

> And let those who do not find the means to marry keep chaste until Allah makes them free from want out of His grace. (24:33)

Conservative Muslim scholars may allude to al-Ghāzālī (d. 1111) who advised that an unmarried person can fast, lower the gaze, or focus on an occupation that takes his mind away from carnal urges.[35] In line with verse 24:33, conservative Muslim scholars reference a Hadith, which indicates that the Prophet advised fasting to those who were unable to get married as fasting diminished sexual desire.

> We were with the Prophet while we were young and had no wealth whatever. So Allah's Messenger said, "O young people! Whoever among you can marry, should marry, because it helps him lower his gaze and guard his modesty (i.e. his private parts from committing illegal sexual intercourse etc.), and whoever is not able to marry, should fast, as fasting diminishes his sexual power."[36]

However, if verse 24:33 is viewed through the lens of the commentary of the exegete Ibn Kathīr (d. 1373), the picture that is delineated is not one of perpetual chastity as is advocated to gays and lesbians by contemporary Muslim scholars. Ibn Kathīr references texts from the Companions that indicate that the patience that is being suggested in this verse and even in the Prophetic directive is not one of a permanent situation but for a temporary time frame. He quotes texts from Ibn ʿAbbās (d. 687) and Ibn Masʿūd (d. 650) that indicate that Allah encouraged both free men and servants to get married and promised enrichment from his bounty if they were poor.[37] In the commentary on the verse, Ibn Kathīr also presents a text attributed to the Prophet that among the three upon whom there is a right upon Allah to help is the one who marries in order to remain chaste, and also mentions that the Prophet officiated the marriage of a man who was so poor that his *mahr* (dower payment) consisted of his teaching of the Qur'an to his spouse and that Allah provided that man whatever was sufficient for him and his spouse.[38] Thus, based on the commentary of the verse, the directive of patience cannot be construed to be for a permanent basis.

Habeeb Alli has expressed that the directive of fasting is not easily adoptable or for everyone given the contemporary culture and in fact during Ramadan, fasting can actually stimulate desire instead of inhibiting it.[39] Likewise, some state that "patience is a finite thing and one cannot expect people to be abstinent for years."[40]

Some reference an inauthentic Hadith attributed to Anas ibn Mālik (d. 712) that indicates that among the seven people who will be forever consigned to Hell are the "homosexuals" (giver and receiver) and those who indulge in masturbation.[41] Such strong opinions on masturbation are also upheld through other texts, such as the one mentioned by Ibn Jurayj (d. 767) that indicates that people who masturbate will be resurrected with their hands tied, and the one mentioned by Saʿīd ibn Jubayr (d. 714) that suggests that Allah punished an entire nation for playing with their genitals.[42]

Conservative Muslims invoke the tradition comprised of the jurists' opinions and the Hadith texts on masturbation, apart of course on *liwāṭ*, to prohibit any sexual activity outside marriage. It seems that they superimpose the understanding developed from this tradition onto verses 23:5–7 and those on the people of Lūṭ. It is interesting to note that based on the tradition as shaped by the above texts and opinions, both masturbation and *liwāṭ* are condemned in a parallel fashion. It is also interesting to note that extra-textual assumptions inform the rulings of the jurists on both masturbation and *liwāṭ*. Just as classical jurists viewed the receptive partners as suffering from *ʾubna*, conservatives like the Shīʿī scholar Muhammad Bāqir Qarashi opine, "Masturbators are afflicted by mental defects in addition to innate frailty and depression,"[43] whereas others allude to the health hazards of masturbation such as "weak sexuality, weak sperm, premature ejaculation, a curving of the penis (Peyronie's disease)."[44]

Likewise, just as the classical jurists associated humiliation with *ʾubna*, some past scholars associated shame with masturbation. For instance, Qurṭubī (d. 1273) asserted, "Masturbation is a shame on a low male, so what of a big man?"[45] Moreover, conservative Muslim leaders offer similar prescriptions to gay Muslims as they offer unmarried Muslims concerned about masturbation, which include fasting, eating and drinking in moderation, avoiding pornography, keeping good friends, admiring nature instead of the opposite gender, getting busy in worship and spiritual acts, and avoiding gatherings that bring men and women in close proximity.[46]

However, other jurists did not interpret verses 23:5–7 to forbid masturbation as an activity that exceeded limits. Ibn Ḥazm (d. 1064) shared Aḥmad ibn Ḥanbal's (d. 855) opinion, based on extra-textual analogy-based reasoning, that semen, being a bodily excretion, could be permissibly expelled as blood-letting. It is important to note that for Ibn Ḥanbal, the use of extra-textual reasoning on the issue of masturbation trumped any textual support against the act, on the basis of which other jurists deemed the act as exceeding limits. Thus, for Ibn Ḥanbal, it seems that based on extra-textual reasoning, the masturbation act did not exceed limits.

The jurists who followed Ibn Ḥanbal's school of jurisprudence added conditions to the permissibility of masturbation by indicating that it could only be allowed to avoid *zinā*—strictly defined as vaginal intercourse outside a marriage contract—and in the absence of having means to enter a marriage contract.[47] The reasoning of the Hanbali jurists suggests that notwithstanding the traditional understanding elicited from verses 23:5–7 and the Hadith that prescribed fasting in the absence of having means to enter a marriage contract, a sexual act, which otherwise is condemned severely and in a parallel fashion to *liwāṭ*, was deemed permissible. Their reasoning suggests that some juristic rule must have been invoked to address the texts.

Contemporary conservative Muslim scholar Shaikh Aḥmad Kutty actually compares the case of one who is concerned about committing *zinā* in the absence of a marriage contract with one who is allowed to eat pork upon starvation leading to imminent death.[48] In essence, the juristic framework of necessity and hardship, under which prohibitions are trumped, seems to be extended to a sexual act. Kutty's opinion also suggests that by viewing the case of an unmarried person in the necessity and hardship framework, masturbation is not treated as an act that exceeds limits. This raises the question that if a sexual function is viewed as a human need and masturbation, despite some texts that prohibit the act, is viewed as not exceeding limits, then on what basis is the human need of Muslim gays and lesbians for *mawadda* (affection) and companionship viewed as transgressing limits.

Some may allude to Ibn Taymiyya's (d. 1328) position that the necessity and hardship framework cannot be applied to sexual acts. Ibn Taymiyya stated that while the latter prohibition of blood, carrion, and pork was not absolute under dire situations, the prohibition of attributing partners to God, lewdness, and injustice is absolute in that it cannot be circumvented by the rationale of necessity or any other reason.[49]

However, other conservative Muslim scholars substantiate the use of the necessity and hardship framework to masturbation. Some categorize masturbation as a deviation, in a manner similar to the categorization of same-sex relationships, but invoke the juristic principle that "necessity is judged according to the circumstances that warrant it" and opine that to avoid fornication and any ensuing psychological disorders, the prohibition on masturbation would be relaxed.[50] It is important to note here that contemporary conservative Muslim scholars acknowledge psychological well-being apart from life or death situations in their use of the necessity and hardship framework.

Contemporary Muslim scholar Sheikh Salman al-Oadah, while acknowledging the difference amongst classical scholars on the permissibility of masturbation, states that even if the act were deemed unlawful, it can be expiated for by repentance and even suggests that people do not blame themselves for more serious sins as lying and backbiting as they do so for masturbation.[51] While al-Oadah states that a serious harm of masturbation is regret, al-Turayri states that guilt and distaste cannot be used as an evidence for the prohibition of an act.[52] Given that in some texts masturbation is viewed in conjunction with *liwāṭ* as a sin worthy of condemnation, it is interesting to note how scholars treat the two sexual conducts quite differently.

Based on Aḥmad Ibn Ḥanbal and Ibn Ḥazm's opinion, the act of masturbation is not viewed as intrinsically immoral and if this opinion is viewed in the context of the opinions of those who forbid masturbation, then it suggests that for those who prohibit masturbation, the issue is less about the inherent immorality of the act and more about the absence of a marriage contract within which masturbation between a husband and wife is allowed. In general, even if anal sex is deemed intrinsically immoral despite the weakness of the textual evidence, as will be noted in chapter 4, other forms of sexual conduct are deemed permissible and the issue at stake is not the permissibility of sexual acts, which do not exceed limits in vacuum, but only when committed with other individuals and as such the issue is the commission of sexual acts outside a legal contract.

Based on a linguistic analysis of these verses and alluding to the texts compiled by Ibn Ḥazm (d. 1064) that allow for masturbation, notwithstanding the criticisms leveled by some on these texts,[53] contemporary scholars like Ghamidi indicate that the verses are referring only to the prohibition of sexual activity committed with other individuals and as such there is no general principle or injunction that deems masturbation as prohibited or undesirable.[54]

Ghamidi distinguishes between sexual contact with other individuals or creatures, in which he includes adultery, bestiality, and homosexuality, from sexual gratification from objects. However, same-sex relationships cannot be lumped with adultery given that same-sex relationships cannot be viewed as exceeding limits unless a legal outlet were available and the lumping with bestiality seems problematic unless one were to deny the importance of mutual consent in sexual relationships.

Ghamidi goes against the classical grain to contest the prohibition of masturbation that has been upheld by the likes of Mālik (d. 795) and Shāfiʿī (d. 820). Ibn Ḥanbal and Ibn Ḥazm used extra-textual reasoning on the issue of masturbation. Kutty uses the framework of necessity and hardship; al-Oadah goes on to take a position similar to those past jurists who argued that nonpenetrative acts could be expiated by supererogatory works; and Alli states that fasting cannot be construed as a pragmatic approach in the contemporary context. Collectively, all of these positions suggest that if fasting cannot be viewed as a permanent solution, then based on extra-textual reasoning, that is, scientific information, consent, and how we understand gender, and given a framework of necessity and hardship, a juristic opinion can be formulated, which can go against the classical grain just as that of Ghamidi.

Notwithstanding the above analysis, as noted in the previous chapter, gay Muslims cannot be defined by a specific sexual act. As will be explored through the following analysis, there exists a strong case to distinguish between the people of Lūṭ and queer Muslims. Furthermore, the rule of marriage may perhaps be open to exceptional situations. In this regard, the accommodation of the marriage contract of the *khunthā mushkil*—intersex person with a male or female partner is noteworthy.[55] While the opinions of the jurists on the marriage of the *khunthā mushkil* will be addressed in a later chapter, a linguistic and contextual analysis of the verses of the people of Lūṭ follows next.

2.3 VERSES ON THE PEOPLE OF LŪṬ

The verses on the people of Lūṭ may be addressed through at least six different lines of arguments. First, Ibn Ḥazm's (d. 1064) passionate critique indicates that the people of Lūṭ were chiefly destroyed for their unbelief in God and rejection of His Messenger rather than *liwāṭ*, a point which is not contested by any traditional *Tafsīr*—commentary of the Qur'an.[56] This argument helps reject many weak Hadith and traditions that are used to prescribe horrific penalties for *liwāṭ*.

Second, the commentaries on verse 7:80 by Ibn Kathīr (d. 1373), Ṭabarī (d. 923), and Qurṭubī (d. 1273) can be examined more carefully. The history of Ṭabarī indicates:

> God's statement, "such as no one did before you in both worlds," refers to the fact that no male jumped upon a male before the people of Lot.[57]

Ibn Kathīr confirms that the people of *Lūṭ* invented deeds unfamiliar to men and other creatures that existed before them. In his work, he also references the opinion of Walīd ibn ʿAbd al-Malik (d. 715) that he would not have thought of *liwāṭ* had God not mentioned about the people of Lūṭ in the Qur'an.[58] Al-Bayḍāwī (d. 1286) also attributes the invention of the *fāḥisha*-abomination to the people of Lūṭ.[59]

> They did things that none of the children of Adam or any other creatures ever did before then. . . . This evil practice was not known among the Children of Adam before, nor did it even cross their minds, so they were unfamiliar with it before the people of Sodom invented it. (Commentary of Ibn Kathīr with variants in commentaries of Ṭabarī and Qurṭubī)[60]

Similar to the viewpoint of Ibn Kathīr, the Shīʿī Tafsīr compiled by Ayatollah Sayyid Kamal Faghih Imani and others suggests that the people of Lūṭ were the founders of the deed at least in the public meetings where sometimes they revealed their private parts.[61] In one of his responses, contemporary scholar Sheikh Mohamed el-Moctar el-Shinqiti substantiates this line of thought when he quotes Ibn al-Qayyim: "This (sin) was not known among Arabs during the lifetime of the Prophet."[62] Similarly, Khaled el-Rouayheb mentions that the Egyptian jurist Ibrāhīm al-Bājūrī (d. 1860) stated that the people of Lūṭ were the first to sodomize men and that Ibn Ḥajar al-Haytamī

(d. 1503) stated that no male animal is found to copulate with his like.[63] However, there is some evidence that suggests same-sex actions may have predated the time of the people of Lūṭ.

According to Biblical chronology, the destruction of Sodom and Gomorrah is dated around 1712 BCE, whereas according to archeological dating, the destruction of the cities of Bab edh-Dhra and Numeira, conjectured to be the sites of Sodom and Gomorrah, is dated about 2300 BCE.[64] Historical record traces same-sex conduct as far back as 10,000 years in the Melanesian region[65] and 40,000 years ago among aboriginal people of all racial lines.[66] The Mesolithic rock art in Sicily which shows male phallic figures has been interpreted to depict same-sex intercourse and falls between 10,000 and 5000 BCE.[67] In the context of the Mesopotamian society, Gordon Wenham states:

> From iconographic evidence dating from 3000 BC to the Christian era it is clear that homosexual practice was an accepted part of the Mesopotamian scene. This conclusion is confirmed by many literary and legal texts in which homosexual activity is mentioned.[68]

It is also interesting to note an Assyrian law code from the middle of the second millennium BCE that has a section on the penalty for rape of men[69] and the warning from a vizier in 2600 BCE Egypt against forcing sodomy upon youth.[70] This evidence suggests that concerns of subjugation of males through sex have been an issue since antiquity and may have been the issue in the context of the people of Lūṭ.

However, another exegete al-Rāzī (d. 1209), while conceding that the people of Lūṭ may have invented the abomination, claimed that the "homosexual" conduct in 7:80 may allude to the collective action of the people of Lūṭ rather than individual conduct, which also substantiates the need to study the verses more carefully, especially in light of better knowledge of sexuality, than has classically been done. Al-Rāzī's comment in the context of verse 7:80 is as follows.

> So, how can it be said: "No one of the people before beat you to it"? Even though the desire (sexual) asks us to do it always?
>
> The answer is in two possibilities:
>
> That we see many people finding this act as being dirty, therefore if the many found it dirty, then it is possible that many ages have passed without anyone doing it.
>
> Perhaps it is all of them that did that, and what was condemned was that the act was done by all rather than by individuals.[71]

Since the commentaries of al-Bayḍāwī, Zamakhsharī (d. 1143), and Jalālayn (d. 1459 and 1505) mainly stick to the linguistic background of the verses, it may be implied that they cover both arguments put forth by al-Rāzī.

The second reasoning by al-Rāzī invites the question as to why the people of Lūṭ engaged in *liwāṭ* at a collective level and necessitates a contextual analysis of the relevant verses. Moreover, according to our contemporary understanding, since gays and lesbians constitute a small minority of the population, verses 7:80, 29:28, and other allied verses are alluding to an entirely different phenomenon than that of same-sex relationships.

The third argument may revolve around the point of plucking verses out of their context. Conservative Muslims usually quote Qur'anic verses 7:81, 26:265–266, or 27:55 to assert the prohibition of homosexual conduct without necessarily alluding to the context such as that provided by verses 7:80 and 29:29.[72] The context is important for if the allied verses are ignored, then stand-alone verses could lead to inappropriate conclusions. For instance, it could potentially and wrongly be argued, based on verses 2:191 and 5:51, respectively,[73] that unbelievers are to be persecuted and the people of the Book not befriended.

In line with the third line of thought, the fourth argument may address the underlying purport of the Qur'anic verse as opposed to its superficial directive. An instance in this regard might be verses 26:128–129 on the people of ʿĀd who are being condemned for their vanity rather than for building tall monuments. Potentially, it may be argued that the people of Lūṭ are being condemned for their collective unbridled lust rather than anachronistic same-sex relationships. This line of thought is perhaps strengthened when one notes that the style of the two sets of verses 26:128–129 and 26:165–166 is quite similar.[74]

> Do you build on every height a monument? Vain is it that you do: And you make strong fortresses that perhaps you may abide. (26:128–129)
>
> Do you come to the males from among the creatures? And leave what your Lord has created for you of your wives? Nay, you are a people exceeding limits (26:165–166)

Continuing with this line of argument, where verse 29:29 refers to the people of Lūṭ ambushing travelers and committing highway robbery, Maududi's (d. 1979) commentary[75] on verse 7:90 depicts the people of Shuʿayb as ambushing trading caravans on the highway. This conduct of the people of Shuʿayb is addressed immediately after the verses on the people of Lūṭ in chapter 7 and seems to suggest that the conduct of the people of Lūṭ goes beyond sexual acts and rather motivated by aggression. However, since the sexual acts perpetrated by the people of Lūṭ are construed as exceeding limits in addition to their nonsexual aggressive acts, this necessitates a contextual analysis as to the nature of the sexual conduct of the people of Lūṭ on a collective scale.

2.4 A CONTEXTUAL ANALYSIS OF THE VERSES ON THE PEOPLE OF LŪṬ

The second, third, and fourth arguments are aimed at raising questions to motivate a revisiting of these verses. They form a prelude to both the contextual and linguistic analyses of the verses on the people of Lūṭ. A contextual analysis may form the fifth line of argument in developing a different understanding of the relevant verses from that of conservative Muslims. This argument can potentially build on verse 29:29. The "Qiṣaṣ al-Anbiyāʾ" texts, the traditions compiled in "Tārīkh Ṭabarī," and the "Tafsīr of Jalalayn" would bolster the argument based on verse 29:29. While some of the texts are from the *Isra'iliyyat* (narratives originating from Judeo-Christian sources), since they are sometimes used by those who condemn same-sex relationships, it is only reasonable to quote them to depict the whole picture of the conduct of the people of Lūṭ.

Essentially, the argument would be to emphasize the point of why the people of Lūṭ were destroyed as opposed to simplistically stating that they were destroyed for "homosexual" conduct. This contextual analysis would tend to bring in subtlety and nuance to an oversimplified understanding of the story of the people of Lūṭ. The crux of the argument is that verse 29:29 expressly states that the people of Lūṭ approached males and ambushed travelers and committed evil deeds in their assemblies. One of the Shīʻī commentaries on the Qur'an, the *Tafsīr nūr al-thaqalayn*, indicates that that the people of Lūṭ would perpetrate *liwāṭ* on youth to the extent that blood would pass from the anus[76] and demanded two of the three angels disguised as youths who had come to visit Lūṭ,[77] despite the fact that they were married.[78] Likewise, the commentaries of Qurṭubī (d. 1273), al-Bayḍāwī (d. 1260), Abu Ḥayyān (d. 1344), and some others also contain quotes from Ibn ʿAbbās (d. 687) that the people of Lūṭ were married and/or they had approached Lūṭ earlier for marrying his daughters.

> They [people of Lot] asked him before to marry his daughters but he refused since they are infidels and not good people. In their customs and traditions, if a man is refused by the father of a girl, then he shall never ask for her hand again.
>
> Their [people of Lot] custom was to marry only one woman, and they were all married, so providing his daughters for them was pointless for them. (Ibn ʿAbbās)[79]

The argument that the people of Lūṭ had wives can also be substantiated from the commentaries of al-Rāzī (d. 1209), Ṭabrasī (d. 1153), Samarqandī (d. 983), and Ṭabarī (d. 923) on verses 11:77–82, which provide explanations on Lūṭ's offer of his daughters. According to them, one possible explanation was that through the offer of daughters, Lūṭ was essentially telling the unruly mob to have sex with their own wives.

Like the Qiṣaṣ al-Anbiyā' by Rāwandī, the *Tafsīr nūr al-thaqalayn* also indicates that the root cause of their incurable disease and conduct was miserliness, which they perpetrated on travelers in order to drive them away.[80] They also threatened Lūṭ, who would secretly provide hospitality, that they would denigrate his guests.[81]

The conduct of the people of Lūṭ in open assemblies and on the highway is amply elaborated in the various *Qiṣaṣ*, Ṭabarī, and the Jalālayn texts. While some *Qiṣaṣ* texts indicate that the people of Lūṭ sodomized travelers during a period of famine, commentators like Jalāl al-Dīn al-Maḥallī (d. 1459) and Jalāl al-Dīn al-Suyūṭī (d. 1505) state that the people of Lūṭ sodomized travelers to drive them away from their prosperous land.[82] Regardless, a holistic view of these narratives and traditions paints a picture of coercive conduct of the people of Lūṭ. This then weakens any analogy between the people of Lūṭ and contemporary gays and lesbians. Excerpts of the Jalālayn and Qiṣaṣ narratives are provided below.

> They said: make it your tradition that if you take a stranger in your country, you penetrate him, and make him pay four Dirhams. People will not come to your place if you did that. (Tafsīr Jalālayn)[83]

> Greed and miserliness bid them follow its call, to the extent that if any strangers stopped to ask for their hospitality, they would rape them (faḍaḥahu) without sexual need, in order to dishonor them. They persisted in this behavior until they began to search out men and force themselves on them. (Qiṣaṣ al-Anbiyā' by al-Rāwandī)[84]

> The people went outside the city walls, searching for people whom they could debauch [yafjurūna bihi]. . . . It became a habitual custom for them with any stranger who wandered onto their lands. Corruption spread among them. (Qiṣaṣ al-Anbiyā' by al-Kisā'ī)[85]

> From far and beyond merchants came to Sodom with bags of gold, hoping to buy grain, but the Sodomites . . . forced the grain merchants to commit abominations with them in lieu of payment. (Qiṣaṣ al-Anbiyā' by al-Kisā'ī/Tha'labī)[86]

Likewise, the Shī'ī *Tafsīr* (commentary) compiled by Ayatollah Sayyid Kamal Faghih Imani and others indicates in the context of verses 7:80–81 that the miserly people of Lūṭ committed sodomy so that travelers would be afraid of being guests.[87] A similar viewpoint is found in an Ahmadi *Tafsīr* that indicates that the people of Lūṭ would not allow strangers enter their towns as they were in a state of war with their neighbors and so they would plunder wayfarers.[88]

The Tārīkh Ṭabarī texts[89] are diverse in nature in that they allude to a whole array of the crimes of the people of Lūṭ ranging from passing gas, lewdness, and intercourse to highway robbery, rape, and murder. Like other narratives, the authenticity of these narratives is questionable; however, they usually get sidelined when other weak texts are used to prescribe penalties for homosexual conduct. As such, these narratives deserve to be highlighted. The narratives that allude to lewdness and intercourse do not specify whether the conduct was consensual or forced. The narratives from Ibn Zayd and others are clear on the sexual aggression of the people of Lūṭ; however, the narrative from Mujāhid (d. 722) is open to interpretation. Likewise, without mentioning sexual aggression in the commentary for verses 26:165–166, Zamakhsharī (d. 1144) writes that the people of Lūṭ were condemned for exclusively penetrating males, while abandoning their wives. However, it is interesting to note that Zamakhsharī is only considering the active partner in the act of *liwāṭ*, which suggests that the act as defined by Zamakhsharī may not be consensual. Regardless, the less specific narratives may be qualified in light of the following narratives that allude to rape and murder.

- [Yūnūs → Ibn Wahb → Ibn Zayd]: Concerning God's statement, "And you commit abominations in your meetings," their meetings were the assemblies, and the abomination was their disgusting act which they would perform. They would accost a rider and seize him and mount him.
- [Yūnūs → Ibn Wahb → Ibn Zayd]: As for God's statement, "You cut the roads," the road is the way of the traveler. When the traveler, the son of the road, passed by them, they would block the road and perform with them that ugly deed.
- [Ibn Ḥumayd → Yaḥyā b. Wāḍiḥ → ʿUmar b. Abī Zāʾida → ʿIkrima]: Concerning his statement, "You commit abominations in your assemblies," it means they used to molest wayfarers, shortening those who passed by them. Footnote (on shortening): . . . form of torture, including a procrustean bed which was either too short or too long. The hapless wayfarer was made to fit the bed by force, which often resulted in his death.
- [Mūsā b. Hārūn → ʿAmr b. Ḥammād → Asbāṭ → al-Suddī → Abu Mālik and Abu Ṣāliḥ → Ibn ʿAbbās and Murra al-Hamdānī → Ibn Masʿūd and some Companions]: The quote, "And you commit abominations in your assemblies," means they would shorten everyone who passed by them, and that was the abomination.
- [Mūsā b. Hārūn → ʿAmr b. Ḥammād → Asbāṭ → al-Suddī → Abu Mālik and Abu Ṣāliḥ → Ibn ʿAbbās and Murra al-Hamdānī → Ibn Masʿūd and

some Companions]: (Lot's daughter) was afraid of what her people might do to them, so she went to her father and said, "Some young men want you at the gate of the city. . . . Let your people not seize them and violate them." His people had forbidden Lot to show hospitality to anyone; they had said to him, "Leave them to us. We will give hospitality to the men."

2.5 A LINGUISTIC ANALYSIS OF THE VERSES ON THE PEOPLE OF LŪṬ

Conservative Muslims contend that the phrases connoting "approaching males"—*A ta'tūna al-dhukrān* (26:165) or *lata'tūna al-rijāl* (7:81 and 27:55)—refer to *liwāṭ*, which is one among other crimes for which the people of Lūṭ were destroyed. It seems that by putting aside a holistic view of the relevant verses and simply focusing on these two phrases, conservative Muslims forbid homosexual conduct. Thus, the sixth line of argument comprises of a linguistic analysis of the Qur'anic Arabic text that specifically includes addressing these Arabic phrases. Conservative Muslims may translate the Arabic phrases as connoting "approaching males" in a manner similar to men approaching their wives in the context of verses 2:222–223 that use the verb *fa'tu-* approach of the same Arabic root as for the verb *atā* (approaching).

Given that *atā* has been used as a euphemism,[90] the phrases can be alternatively translated as connoting "aggressively pursuing nonreceptive males." Based on Edward Lane's Lexicon,[91] the verb *atā* denotes the meanings of "pursue," "hasten," and "the act of propelling or impelling—particularly of an arrow from a bow." Likewise, based on *Lisān al-'Arab*, the word *dhukran* used for males, in contrast to the word *unthā* for females, connotes a nonreceptive entity. When viewed through this lens, one may argue that forceful approaching of a nonreceptive entity constitutes rape.

However, one argument that is usually proffered in the context of the part "you approach men instead of women" used in verses 7:81 and 27:55 is that if we were to translate these verses to mean "raping men" instead of "approaching men," then that would imply erroneously that the verses are suggesting "raping women" instead of "approaching them." However, translating the phrase as "you rape men instead of women" would be incorrect as the word *ightiṣāb* (rape) has not been used directly in these verses. Instead, the translation "you approach men (nonreceptive entities) instead of women (receptive entities)" seems to be the appropriate translation and rape is inferred in the sense of approaching men, who are generally not receptive to the sexual advances of other men. Likewise, while women may not be receptive to the sexual advances of some men, based on the notion of gender as understood by the past jurists, women were assumed to be receptive to the sexual advances of men in general. This line of argument may be strengthened from a careful examination of the writings of the exegetes and jurists beyond the apparent verdicts of condemnation and prohibition of *liwāṭ* to investigate the assumptions and reasoning that led to their opinions.

Translating the phrases *A ta'tūna al-dhukrān* and *lata'tūna al-rijāl* to connote the pursuit of nonreceptive males may perhaps be more consistent with the classical understanding of the verses. As noted earlier, jurists and scholars like Abu Ḥanīfa (d. 767) and Ibn Taymiyya (d. 1328) believed, based on the sociocultural norms of their times, that no man in his right mind would allow another man to penetrate him unless for illness, money, or coercion.

Jurists referred to *'ubna*—illness described as requiring receptive homosexual anal intercourse in the context of *liwāṭ* when it was not inflicted on youth or male slaves. It is interesting to note that *liwāṭ* was associated with various segments of Muslim societies, including Muslim leaders, jurists, and *ḥuffāẓ*-memorizers of the Qur'an.[92] As noted by Rāghib Iṣfahānī (d. 1109), Muslim scholar Abdullah ibn Mubārak (d. 797) was alleged to have wanted tough men to alleviate his *'ubna*[93] and likewise jurists like Ibn ʿArabī (d. 1148) noted that the scholar al-Kisā'ī al-Kūfī (d. 804) openly confessed to engaging in same-sex conduct.[94] Likewise, al-Dhahabī (d. 1348) noted that while the Caliph Walīd ibn ʿAbd al-Malik (d. 715) was not a *kāfir* (disbeliever) or *zindīq* (heretic), he was rather an alcoholic and a *Lūṭī*, and he also noted that his brother Sulaymān ibn Yazīd (d. 717) alleged that he attempted to *rāwadanī ʿalā nafsī*—seduce him.[95]

Given that same-sex conduct was viewed in the context of illness or exploitation through money or coercion, and associated with vices that include alcoholism and incest, it is also possible that many narratives that involve allegations of *liwāṭ* or *'ubna* may have been manufactured, through which opponents were sought to be discredited. For instance, while Walīd has been alleged to have seduced his brother, in Tafsīr Ibn Kathīr, he is viewed as expressing contempt for *liwāṭ* and stating that if God had not mentioned about the people of Lūṭ, then people may not have indulged in such bad actions.[96] Likewise, al-Damīrī (d. 1405) noted that the Companion al-Ḥakam ibn Abi al-ʿĀṣ and Abu Jahl (d. 624) were *yurmā bi al-dā' al-ʿaḍḍāl*—allegedly known for having the tough disease, which refers to *'ubna.*[97] Abu Jahl has also been portrayed as suffering from *'ubna*, which he satisfied with stones instead of allowing himself to be penetrated.[98] However, such texts and those that involve the *mukhannathūn*—feminine males are inaccurately translated to construe the mentioned people as "homosexuals." For instance, the phrase *yu'tā fī duburih* in a text referred by al-ʿAynī (d. 855) has been translated to equate *mukhannathūn* with "homosexuals," whereas the appropriate translation of the phrase is, "a person taken from behind," that is, passive recipient of homosexual anal intercourse.[99]

The passive partner was predominantly a youth whose consent was not assumed in the act. Rowson references the term *ijāra*, which refers to the practice of a youth submitting to homosexual anal penetration for pecuniary reasons as opposed to any pleasure. He refers to the phrase by the jurist al-Jurjānī (d. 1089), "He takes from the basin and spends on the pitcher," which indicated the youth's interest in females, which he pursued by being a rent-boy.[100] He also refers to *dabīb* (creeping), the practice of initiating homosexual anal intercourse with a sleeping youth, which was not considered parallel to *ightiṣāb* (rape) as the youth was considered to not have suffered any permanent injury to his manliness.[101]

Both Abu Ḥanīfa and Ibn Taymiyya opine, as noted below, that the verses addressed the active partner instead of the passive partner, thereby substantiating the argument that the phrase *lata'tūna al-rijāl* in verses 7:81 and 27:55 is better understood as "pursuing nonreceptive males."

> In "liwāṭ," even though the active partner desires it, the passive partner does not by nature, and that is different from "Zinā," where the attraction happens on both sides. (Abu Ḥanīfa in Tafsīr al-Rāzī for 24:2)[102]

> The address was to the active partner because he was the one with the desire. . . . This is opposite to the passive partner for he has no sexual desire (for the act) to start with, except that it happens to him because of disease or money that he takes from the active partner or another aim. (Ibn Taymiyya in Tafsīr of chapter 24)[103]

Likewise, al-Rāzī (d. 1209), in his commentary of verse 7:81, states several reasons for why penetrating another male would be contemptible. These reasons include the view of such conduct as reversal of the male-female order and as such is unnatural. He further reasons that the passive partner suffers dishonor and humiliation. It is important to note that al-Rāzī defines *liwāṭ* by the act of homosexual anal intercourse in which the consent of the passive partner is not assumed since it would bring about severe dishonor and humiliation. Al-Rāzī's reasoning on the prohibition of *liwāṭ* can be paraphrased as follows.[104]

1. Sexual desire is mainly for procreation, despite the costs associated with rearing children.
2. The reversal of the active and passive roles of males and females in sexual conduct is unnatural.
3. Homosexual conduct is an end in itself rather than a means toward procreation.
4. The passive partner in "liwāṭ" suffers severe dishonor and humiliation.
5. "Liwāṭ" does not engender love and tenderness but animosity against the active partner and may lead the passive partner to kill the active partner.

6. Seminal fluid might lead to injury, diseases, and tumors in the anus as attested by the people of medicine.

It is clear that al-Rāzī's reasoning is extra-textual and informed by the models of sexuality of his time as is true for other jurists and exegetes. While al-Rāzī and other scholars can make the argument that procreative sex is needed for the maintenance of community and survival of the human species, they cannot extend that rule to every individual sexual act between any two people. The vast majority of scholars understood that sex has important legitimate functions other than procreation and they did not prohibit an older or infertile woman from marriage. Indeed, the example of the Prophet indicates that he married older women beyond the age of procreation.

It is also interesting to note from the sixth point that al-Rāzī is deferring to the medical profession on the issue of *liwāṭ*. The fact that medical opinions influenced the opinions of exegetes can be noted from the observations noted in the Shī'ī *Tafsīr* compiled by Ayatollah Sayyid Kamal Faghih Imani and others. The *Tafsīr* indicates that sodomy is a deviation that begins with cross-dressing among boys and girls, that it is like a psychic disease which intensifies with time, has destructive impacts on the limbs and the nervous system, and leads to reclusion and alienation from society.[105] This invites an interesting question of how much impact a change in medical opinion, given the contemporary medical and psychiatric opinion on the subject, would have on the Islamic jurisprudential treatment of *liwāṭ*.

Al-Rāzī's commentary includes texts from the Companions of the Prophet that substantiate the contextual analysis in Section 2.4 that the conduct of the people of Lūṭ was the subjugation of trespassers and later their own people. The following texts, referenced by al-Rāzī, are reflective of the common understanding of sexuality of his times.

> Al-Ḥasan said: They were penetrating men's anuses and they did not do it except to the strangers. 'Aṭā' reported from Ibn 'Abbās: This happened in them so much that they did it on each other.[106]

Given the statements referenced by al-Rāzī, some scholars explained that *liwāṭ* spread among the people of Lūṭ after they started to sodomize strangers, without having any sexual desire, to drive them away.[107] The commentary of al-Ṭabrasī (d. 1153) also references the following text from al-Ḥasan that the people of Lūṭ committed the abomination on strangers.[108] Likewise, the commentary of Jalālayn Maḥallī (d. 1459) and Suyūṭī (d. 1505) indicates that the people of Lūṭ sexually assaulted travelers, whereas other commentaries indicate explicitly that the people of Lūṭ only sodomized strangers.[109] Similarly, the scholar al-'Umari (d. 1788) mentioned that the people of Lūṭ sodomized youth and adult male strangers,[110] which indicates the power imbalance in their conduct.

The commentary of Ṭabrasī also substantiates the aggressive nature of their sexual conduct by associating the rape of travelers with the pelting of stones and elaborates on the words used in verse 29:29 *taqṭaʿūna al-sabīl* (cut off the highway) and *taʾtūna fī nadīkum al-munkar* (commit evil deeds in assembly), by alluding to various meanings of these words such as blocking procreation by not having sex with women, passing gas in assemblies, and highway piracy.[111] Ṭabarī (d. 923), in his commentary, seems to prefer the understanding of pelting stones at travelers and having sex with them as the main purport of verse 29:29.[112] Likewise, in the commentary of the phrase *taqṭaʿūna al-sabīl*, instead of construing it as cutting off progeny, Ayatollah Fadlallah (d. 2010) explains it as the people of Lūṭ cutting off the path of travelers, throwing rocks, and robbing them with a fine of 3 dirhams.[113]

The people of Lūṭ are depicted as indulging in a wide array of misconduct as captured by the word *fāḥisha* (abominations) used in verses 7:80 and 29:28. However, some might claim that the word *fāḥisha* refers specifically to the act of *liwāṭ* perhaps because of the particularizing article *al* (the) used before the word *fāḥisha* in verses 7:80 and 29:28. Some argue that the word *zinā* is mentioned without the definite article *al-*, whereas *liwāṭ* was mentioned with the definite article before the word *fāḥisha*.[114] Moreover, based on the understanding of most exegetes and jurists, all these verses—(7:80–81; 26:160–166, 27:54–55, 29:28–29)—refer specifically to *liwāṭ*.[115]

However, the word *fāḥisha* appears about 13 times in the Qur'an, three of which relate to actions of the people of Lūṭ through verses 7:80, 27:54, and 29:28, and whereas verse 17:32 uses the word to clearly point toward fornication, in all other instances the word is used to encapsulate a whole array of ugly acts that include, according to *Lisan al-ʿArab*, the meaning of "uttering bad words" as portrayed through the example of the Prophet admonishing ʿĀ'isha against such speech.[116] Moreover, a possible synonym for the word *fāḥisha*, *khabāʾith* (deeds of abomination), has been used in verse 21:74 on the people of Lūṭ, which like the word *fāḥisha* alludes to many evil acts as opposed to one specific act. It should also be noted that the definite article *Al* before the word *fāḥisha* suggests that all aspects of evil are encompassed,[117] thereby indicating that the word used in the context of the verses on the people of Lūṭ alludes to a whole array of evil activities as opposed to just one particular act.

Some even argue that since the word *fāḥisha* was used to refer to *zinā* in verse 4:15, the word *fāḥisha* used in verse 7:80 would refer to *liwāṭ* by analogy, which is not a strong argument, as according to some scholars, verse 4:15 alludes to prostitution.[118] Moreover, according to Ibn Ḥazm, the term *zinā* is not applied to *liwāṭ* whether in common usage or in the *Sunnah*.[119]

This further weakens deducing the meaning of *fāḥisha* as *liwāṭ* based on a supposed analogy with *zinā*.

Since the word *fāḥisha* has been used to denote indecency in verse 7:80, and the word *musrifūn*—"extravagance" or "transgressing bounds"—has been used in 7:81, the interconnectedness of the two words may be noted. Daryabadi (d. 1977) explains the word *fāḥisha* as follows:

> . . . in its general significance is "an excess; an enormity; anything exceeding the bounds of rectitude" but when particularized, signifies "adultery or fornication."[120]

This meaning of *fāḥisha* as exceeding the limits of ugliness is also substantiated through *Lisan al-ʿArab*. This suggests that both "abomination" and "extravagance" refer to a practice conducted in excess, especially given the alternative of lawful substitutes. This understanding also emerges from Ibn Ḥazm's (d. 1064) writings, when he states that nothing has been forbidden without the provision of an excellent substitute.[121]

Other assumptions behind the rulings of the jurists, whether explicit or implicit based on their understanding of sexuality, require a careful examination given our contemporary knowledge of sexuality. According to Ze'ev Maghen, the jurist al-Māwardī (d. 1058) assumed that pleasure was not generally derived from same-sex touching and the jurist al-Nawawī (d. 1278) assumed that a man is not normally the object of another man's desire.[122] Furthermore, Maghen states that the scholars of the Shāfiʿī and Ḥanbalī schools of jurisprudence indicate that even if a man derives pleasure from touching a boy, his ritual purity is not affected based on the premise that males are not generally attracted to males.[123] Thus, when the verses on the people of Lūṭ are viewed in light of these assumptions, it becomes apparent that the jurists understood that for the people of Lūṭ, pleasure was one-sided and also because of the fact the word *shahwa* (desire) was only used for the active participants.

Even if the people of Lūṭ are viewed as pederasts, because of al-Jurjānī's assumption, noted earlier, that the youth only submits to homosexual anal penetration for money that he uses to pursue females, no consent can be assumed on the part of the youths. Moreover, while several exegetes and jurists do not explicitly state the assumptions on *liwāṭ* in their work, for instance, the *fetva eminis* from the end of the sixteenth century addressed specific points of law and omitted legally irrelevant details,[124] information can be patched from the works of Abu Ḥanīfa, Ibn Taymiyya, and al-Rāzī to indicate that that they understood *liwāṭ* as a one-sided conduct that inflicted humiliation on the passive partner.

Zamakhsharī (d. 1144) defines the word *shahwatan* after the phrase *lataʾtūna al-rijāl* in verse 7:81[125] as pure desire, which does not generally include affection or gentleness. As such, the absence of a word that connotes affection or gentleness, which would qualify the use of the word *shahwatan,* implies that desire in the context of the people of Lūṭ occurred without affection or gentleness. In fact, Zamakhsharī indicates that their action is not motivated by any reason but desire and essentially describes them as being animalistic.[126] This understanding of the word *shahwatan* also connects appropriately with the meaning for the phrase *lata'tūna al-rijāl* as "a rush toward the unwilling/nonreceptive males." The understanding of "rushing toward males" also gets bolstered when one notes that the people of Lūṭ are described as rushing as depicted by the word *yuhrauna* in verse 11:78 or by the word *yastabshirūna*—"rejoicing"[127]—in verse 15:67, which according to the commentators depicted the fact that the people of Lūṭ were looking forward to sexually penetrating the guests. It is also interesting to note that the article *L* (the) is used to particularize men in the phrase *lata'tūna al-rijāl,* which may perhaps refer specifically to the traveling men visiting Sodom. This observation seems compatible with the narratives in Section 2.4 that indicate that the people of Lūṭ aggressively raped strangers.

Like Zamakhsharī, the Shīʻī Tafsīr compiled by Ayatollah Sayyid Kamal Faghih Imani and others indicates that the act of sodomy is bereft of affection, mercy, and intimacy.[128] Similarly, jurists like Ibn al-Qayyim (d. 1350), in the context of verse 7:81, depicted the people of Lūṭ with desire which did not contain love or compassion. In the following, apart from raising concerns on procreation, Ibn al-Qayyim clearly distinguishes between the acts of the people of Lūṭ and the relationships between men and women.

> The only thing that led them [people of Lūṭ] that way was only a desire, not the need for which the male is attracted to the female, and of meeting a need and pleasure to enjoy, and the appearance of love and compassion for which a woman forgets her parents, and remembers her husband.[129]

A contextual and linguistic analysis allows depicting the people of Lūṭ as highway robbers, murderers, and rapists. It may be argued linguistically that since the conjunction *wa* (and) has been used to separate three distinct crimes of the people of Lūṭ mentioned in verse 29:29, that is, *lata'tūna al-rijāl* (approaching males), *taqṭaʻūn al-sabīl* (cut off the highway), and *ta'tūna fī nadīkum al-munkar* (commit evil deeds in assembly), the crime of having sex with men, euphemistically referred to as "approaching males," should be separate from highway robbery and evil deeds committed in the assembly. However, the very fact that the conjunction "and" instead of "or" has been used indicates the compound nature of the acts of the people of Lūṭ. Furthermore, irrespective of whether the act of "approaching males" is deemed separately from other acts or not, verse 29:29 suggests that the misconduct of the people of Lūṭ was not limited to same-sex conduct but associated with other crimes.

Arno Schmitt states that in the old Arabic dictionaries, *'amal qawm Lūṭ* (act of the people of Lūṭ) is defined as an activity rather than as an inclination. He further adds that the Arabic synonyms on intercourse do not indicate reciprocity and that the Arabic language employs the construct *lāṭa bi* that indicates that sodomy is done on an object, usually a youth, instead of with an equal willing partner, which would require the use of the construct *lāṭa ma'a*.[130] He indicates that in most of the Hadith texts the dichotomy of the *'alā* (one on top) and *asfal* (one underneath) or the distinction between the *fā'il* (doer) and *maf'ūl bihi* (object) is found.

Schmitt's arguments can be qualified by the fact that the words *'alā* (one on top) and *asfal* (one underneath) are used to refer respectively to men and women and that desire on the part of females is implicitly assumed. However, the same cannot be assumed for the passive male partner for as noted earlier, Abu Ḥanīfa stated that in contrast to the active partner, the passive partner did not desire *liwāṭ*. Other jurists, who followed Abu Ḥanīfa's school of jurisprudence, like al-Kāsānī (d. 1191) and al-Marghinānī (d. 1197), have also echoed the view that *liwāṭ* is one-sided.[131]

Khaled el-Rouayheb's work indicates that the classical Qur'anic commentaries portrayed the people of Lūṭ as either pederasts or aggressive rapists and, in both cases, based on the juridical literature, they were assumed to be the penetrators.[132] He references many texts from 1500 to 1800 CE to delineate the understanding of scholars and jurists that being the passive partner in homosexual anal intercourse was associated with subordination and humiliation. Moreover, he clearly states that in many such contexts the act of penetration could not be termed sexual as it was not only dissociated from love and intimacy but also from desire and pleasure.[133]

Saleem Kidwai indicates that the passive partner on several occasions during the times of Muslim rulers in India were held responsible for killing the active partners for the humiliation caused to them.[134] As such, these texts and instances seem to substantiate the reasoning used by the jurists that the desire for *liwāṭ* was one-sided and that at times the passive partner would even kill the active partner for the humiliation caused. In fact, in one of the juristic manuals, the *Fatāwā-i-Khayriyya*, it is written that it would be permissible for a person to kill someone who intimidates him to sodomy.[135] This seems similar to the jurist Efendi (d. 1574) opining that it would be permissible for a woman to poison her husband who had divorced her, if she could not escape from him trying to have intercourse with her.[136] The idea that *liwāṭ* was one-sided is well entrenched to the extent that in pre-Islamic Arabia, Dhū Nuwās is reported to have been compelled to kill Dhu Shanātir to escape his advances. Even in the case of animals, Al-Jāḥiẓ (d. 868) is noted to have mentioned of the *'udār* animal that assaulted men anally, who would later die with a worm-infected anus, and of a horse,[137] castrated at an early age, who would pursue other horses, mules, and donkeys.[138]

While a contextual and linguistic analysis allows depicting the people of Lūṭ as rapists, Aleardo Zanghellini states that sociocultural norms like those of *muruwwa* (manliness), which associated being penetrated with humiliation and indignity, informed the opinions of the exegetes and jurists. Even a willing passive partner was viewed pathologically as homosexual anal intercourse was viewed as leading to "subordination, degradation, and emasculation." Zanghellini states that medieval jurists narrowly defined *liwāṭ* as homosexual anal intercourse and condemned the practice on the basis of the reversal of general norms, which according to them referred to the male being the active partner and the female being the passive partner.[139] This opinion is compatible with the linguistic analysis of the words *dhukrān* used for males to describe a nonreceptive entity and the word *unthā* for females that depicts a receptive entity. As such, based on a contextual analysis, while the people of Lūṭ can be viewed as aggressive rapists, based on a linguistic analysis, they can also be viewed as rapists in the sense that they were approaching males who were assumed to be nonwilling, nonreceptive entities even if the latter wanted to get penetrated.

In essence, difference of opinion on whether the conduct of the people of Lūṭ can be assumed as consensual or not is based on how the two Arabic phrases—*A ta'tūna al-dhukrān* (26:165) or *lata'tūna al-rijāl* (7:81 and 27:55)—are understood. Any other information extracted from the verses on the people of Lūṭ would be subsidiary to the understanding developed on the basis of these two Arabic phrases.

2.6 LŪṬ'S OFFER OF HIS DAUGHTERS

A similar difference of opinion on linguistics arises on the issue of Lūṭ's offer of his daughters mentioned in verses 11:78–79 and 15:67–72. Conservative Muslims may argue that the offer of daughters substantiates that heterosexual relationships are preferred to homosexual relationships. They question that if the crime of the people of Lūṭ was exclusively that of coercion and rape then why did Lūṭ offer his daughters up to the community to substitute for the male guests? Since a prophet of God cannot partake in injustice, conservative Muslims claim that the verse cannot allude to rape but rather consensual relations.

However, these verses pushed traditional exegetes to explain why a prophet of God might offer his own daughters to a crowd of transgressors. It is in the commentaries of the traditional exegetes and the meaning of key words from this verse and other allied verses that perhaps this issue can be effectively addressed. The various commentaries of al-Rāzī (d. 1209), Ṭabrasī (d. 1153), Samarqandī (d. 983), and Ṭabarī (d. 923) actually present two possibilities of understanding these verses. Either they qualify that Lūṭ offered his daughters for marriage, or perhaps more plausibly, Lūṭ is merely telling them to go back to their wives. According to the second opinion, at least it becomes apparent that despite being married, the people of Lūṭ persisted in debauching his male guests. The two possibilities from the four Qur'an commentaries are summarized below.

1. He offered his daughters for marriage.
2. He was really offering the women of his town, because a Prophet is the father of his people. . . . When he offered the women of the town, he was offering them to have sex with their own wives.[140]

The commentary of Qurṭubī (d. 1273) on verse 11:78 actually alludes toward two more potential understandings of the problematic part of Lūṭ offering his daughters. Qurṭubī raises the possibility that Lūṭ merely wished to prick the conscience of his people and therefore did not actually offer his daughters.

3. He was pointing to them that doing zinā with his daughters is ḥarām and doing it with his guests is worse. Here the example is one wanting to embezzle some money and the other would say: it is better to steal.
4. He was not offering anything but said that to make them go away.[141]

Based on the first and third opinion, conservative Muslims may argue that the commentators are perhaps advising of establishing opposite gender relationships against having same-sex relationships. This argument is sometimes bolstered by an allusion to the word *aṭhar* used in verse 11:78 to depict purity, and on the basis of this word, it is argued that since rape connotes aggression and oppression, it could not be the opposite of pure. Therefore, it is argued that the verse 11:78 is condemning same-sex unions by contrasting them to the pure alternative of heterosexual marriage. However, it is to be noted that the word *aṭhar* technically means purer or less dirty as opposed to its antonym *anjas* which means dirtier or less pure. Therefore, purer could simply be the less dirty of the two options and thus the opinion that Lūṭ was contrasting sexual misconduct with women, receptive entities, who would be more susceptible to the advances of males, with the rape of male guests, nonreceptive entities, who would not be susceptible to be encroached upon in that manner. This point gets bolstered by the third opinion which contrasts *zinā* with daughters to sexual conduct with guests.

According to another line of thought, the contrast between daughters and guests as a comparison between females and males is only part of the story. Another major comparison emphasizes the point that the daughters were Lūṭ's responsibility, and perhaps owing to the social norms of that age Lūṭ had the authority to offer them whereas he did not have authority to offer his guests. Lūṭ could offer his daughters, as the Shī'ī *Tafsīr* (commentary) compiled by Ayatollah Sayyid Kamal Faghih Imani and others indicates in the context of verse 15:71 that it could be possible that marriage with unbelievers was not legally prohibited at that time.[142] Therefore, the option of offering his daughters could be purer because he had the jurisdiction to do so whereas he did not have the authority to offer the guests, especially as he was obliged to protect them. Thus apart from the contrast between males and females, the dimension of jurisdictional authority makes deducing any ruling on same-sex conduct based on these verses more complex.

While the word *aṭhar* means purer, and therefore allows for the comparison between a dirty and dirtier option, the word *yataṭahharūn* used in verses 7:82 and 27:56, used for Lūṭ and his followers, connotes active purification, and therefore may be used to contrast people indulging in same-sex conduct with those who abstain from it. However, neither 7:82 nor 27:56 specifies that from a whole array of sins, rejecting God's Prophet, committing highway robbery, and other evil acts in assemblies, it was specifically the one act of homosexual anal penetration that distinguished Lūṭ's followers from the rest. This line of reasoning gets bolstered by al-Rāzī's commentary that the word *yataṭahharūn* (pure) could be understood in several different ways. It could refer to someone who abstained from sodomy, but it could also refer to someone who abstained from sin. Al-Rāzī further adds that perhaps this word was used by the people of Lūṭ to simply mock Lūṭ and his followers and as such did not carry a specific meaning. This would indicate that merely on the basis of the words *aṭhar* (purer) and *yataṭahharūn* (pure), one may not easily deduce that they are used specifically to condemn same-sex conduct.

It could further be argued that verse 11:78 is comparing sexual misconduct with women with the dirtier option of consensual sexual conduct with men; however, such a conclusion is not warranted from the text, which suggests that Lūṭ's guests simply were not susceptible to the advances of the people of Lūṭ. The verses paint a picture of the aggressive mob demanding access to the guests. On the offer of daughters, the people of Lūṭ state that they have no *ḥaqq* (right) on Lūṭ's daughters as opposed to *irba* (desire) (as used in verse 24:31) for them.[143] This indicates that the demand to access Lūṭ's guests was based on what they considered a "right" to access the trespassers of their city. It may be noted that one of the commentaries from the Ahmadiyyah community, even while prohibiting same-sex conduct on the basis of 7:81, actually points out that verses 11:78–79 are not dealing with sexual conduct but with the abuse of guests.[144]

According to the Ahmadi *Tafsīr*, while some commentaries suggest that the angels came to Lūṭ in the form of handsome boys or that upon hearing about them the people of Lūṭ rushed with sexual intent, the context does not warrant that, as based on 15:71, they did not exhibit pleasure but rather displeasure at Lūṭ's offering hospitality to strangers and that they had finally got the opportunity to settle old scores with Lūṭ.[145] The *Tafsīr* also indicates that Lūṭ's two daughters were already married in the town, that he offered them as hostages, and that there was no sexual intent involved in such an offer, but since the custom was to only have males as hostages, the people rejected that offer.[146]

The *Tafsīr* goes on to draw parallels between Lūṭ whose daughters were married to the townspeople and the Prophet, whose three daughters Ruqayya, Zaynab, and Umm Kulthum were married to the disbelievers, to suggest that God was comforting the Prophet by telling him that the disbelievers would be surely punished just as the people of Lūṭ, who at least did not persecute Lūṭ's daughters, were punished.[147] It indicates that just as Lūṭ's people prohibited him from entertaining outsiders, the Meccans prohibited the Prophet against strangers lest he should form alliances with them.[148] The *Tafsīr* also draws further parallels between the blinding of the people of Lūṭ and the strong gale that drove into the faces of the Meccans during the Battle of Badr blinding them and causing their defeat and just as the houses of Lūṭ's people were turned upside down, metaphorically the Meccan social order was overthrown as the poor Muslims rose to eminence and the mighty disbelievers slided down the social scale.[149] Thus, given such concordance between the story of Lūṭ and the life of the Prophet, the obsessive focus on same-sex unions seems unreasonably out of place.

The argument on the "right" to sexually subjugate travelers may also be supported from the Arabic word *nurīd*, which means "want" or "seek" but which in the context of verse 11:79 may connote "demand of an aggressive nature." It is interesting to note that a variant of *ḥāja*, *ḍarūra* or *ṭalab*, words that connote necessity or need, has not been used in place of *nurīd*. This contextual understanding of the word *nurīd* is supported by the observation that a variant word *rāwaduhu*, based on the same root, is used in verse 54:37, which according to al-Rāzī denotes a demand for action. A portion of verse 54:37 reads, "And they had demanded from him his guests, but we obliterated their eyes," which indicates that the people of Lūṭ demanded the guests for a particular action. Likewise, another variant of *nurīd*, based on the same root, appears in verse 12:30 as *turāwid*, which has been translated to connote seduction. The wife of Azeez did try to seduce Joseph and tore his shirt from behind in an attempt to force herself upon him. Thus, when the word *nurīd* is viewed in the context of verses 54:37 and 12:30, along with the next verse 11:80, which indicates the exasperation of Lūṭ when he says, "If only I had against you some power or could take refuge in a strong support," it seems to confirm the argument that verse 11:79 is alluding to sexual aggression.

The words used in verse 15:70 *A wa lam nanhaka ʿan-l-ʿālamīn*—Did we not forbid you from the world?—also suggest that the subject of these verses is the abuse of guests. The commentaries of Ibn Kathīr and Ṭabrasī, presented below, indicate that Lūṭ was banned from hosting and protecting guests so that they could use their custom to abuse and rape any wayfarers.

> He was banned from having guests (protecting anyone) at his house. This leaves strangers (unprotected) out for the people of the town to rape them. (Tafsīr Ṭabrasī for 15:70)[150]
>
> [Lūṭ] he was afraid that if he hosted them, then his people will find out and if he did not host them then his people will abuse them. (Tafsīr Ibn Kathīr for 29:33)[151]

Maududi's commentary on verse 15:67[152] mentions several incidents from the Talmud that depict the inhospitality of the people of Lūṭ. Poor travelers were robbed of their belongings, not given any food, and the dead were left stark naked without shrouds. Even one of the slaves of Abraham's wife, Sarah, was subjected to beating and sustained head injuries. Moreover, Lūṭ and his daughters were threatened that they would forfeit their right to live in Sodom if they offered kindness to poor travelers.

2.7 REVISITING 7:81, 26:165–166, AND 27: 55

Disregarding the contextual and heretofore linguistic analysis, verses 7:81, 26:165–166, or 27: 55 are often quoted to prohibit same-sex unions, and this necessitates a further linguistic analysis of these stand-alone verses. The following language and grammar-based approach to analyzing key words in these verses complements the previous contextual and linguistic analysis that already included the phrases *A taʾtūna al-dhukrān* (26:165) or *lataʾtūna al-rijāl* (7:81 and 27:55). Verse 7:81 reads:

> lataʾtūna al-rijāla shahwatan min dūni al-nisāʾ bal antum qawmun musrifūn (7:81)

The verb *atā,* usually translated as "approach," is understood to be mild in its essence, as an argument is made connecting this word with *f-aʾtū* in verse 2:223 wherein men are directed to approach their wives after they have cleansed themselves post menstruation.[153] Alternatively, according to Daayiee Abdullah, the use of the word *atā* also provides the meaning of "to rush like an uncontrolled stream of water, a flood of water without banks to guide it."[154] This alternate understanding of the verb *atā* makes sense given the context of the other violent crimes committed by the people of Lūṭ and also the fact that they were approaching men, who are generally nonreceptive to the sexual advances of other men. The use of the emphatic particle *la* before *ta'tūna* appears to strengthen this reasoning, which is perhaps why Zollner (2009) understands the verb as connoting aggression. However, another way to understand the verb *atā* is to recognize that it conveys the meaning of "approaching with intent," although either way the point of approaching nonreceptive males can be sustained.

Immediately after this verb, the definite article *al-* (the) is used to particularize men and the same is used later to particularize women, which may specifically refer to the traveling men visiting Sodom and the wives of the people of Lūṭ, respectively. The other key word in this verse is *shahwatan*, which, according to Edward Lane's lexicon, connotes excited or intense desire usually associated with food or carnal desires. It may be appreciated that the word *ḥubb* (love) or another variant that captures affection has not been used in this verse. Given the usage of *shahwatan* as opposed to *ḥubb* in verse 7:81 strengthens the point that the approach of the people of Lūṭ was sexual but bereft of mercy and affection. This understanding of the word *shahwatan*, as excited or intense carnal desire, also connects appropriately with the meaning for the previous words *lata'tūna al-rijāl* as "a rush toward the males."

However, this potential understanding of the verse raises the question, whether it would be fair to compare "rushing toward men" with "approaching women," since the words *min duni* (instead of) are used in the verse. This can be addressed by focusing on the understanding of *atā* as "approaching with intent," which is made more emphatic by the use of the particle *la* before *ta'tūna*. Moreover, it needs to be noted that the synonym of the word *rijāl* in verse 7:81 is *dhukrān*, as used in verse 26:165, and which according to Lisan al-'Arab means "male," "male genital," "hard/harsh," or "nonreceptive." Noting that the words *lata'tūna al-rijāl* in 7:81 and *A ta'tūna al-dhukrān* in 26:165 are synonymous and based on a holistic approach, it would be reasonable to elicit the understanding that approaching a nonreceptive entity with intent would mean that consent cannot be assumed on behalf of the nonreceptive entity. It may also be noted that in contrast to the word *dhukrān*, the word used for females is *unthā*, which has the connotation of receptivity. This linguistic analysis would then indicate that the classical Muslim framework operates with the notions of implied consent between opposite genders and therefore implied nonconsent between the same gender, specifically between two males. Thus, the question of comparing "rushing toward men" with "approaching women" becomes moot by recognizing the verb *atā* as "approaching with intent" and the word *rijāl* or *dhukrān* as referring to a nonreceptive entity, approaching which would provide a similar sense as that provided if the words *lata'tūna al-rijāl* were understood to reflect "rushing toward males."

It makes sense to understand *lata'tūna al-rijāl* as "rushing toward males" as opposed to mildly approaching them owing to the point on nonreceptivity. The understanding of "rushing toward males" also gets slightly bolstered when one notes that in verse 11:78, the people of Lūṭ are described as rushing, as depicted by the word *yuhrauna,* or in verse 15:67 as rejoicing, as indicated by the word *yastabshirūna*, which according to the exegetes depicted the fact that the people of Lūṭ were looking forward to sexually penetrating the guests. Indeed, the word *yastabshirun* connotes purely seeking sex, as opposed to affection or love, as it encapsulates the word *bashr,* which refers to skin.

It is argued that the verb *atā* that is captured in the words *A ta'tūna* when not followed by a preposition as *'alā* as in verse 7:81 does not lend itself to the meaning of force or coercion. As noted earlier, understanding *atā* in coercive terms would lead to a misogynistic translation of the phrase *lata'tūna al-rijāla shahwatan min dūni al-nisā'* as "you forcefully coerce men instead of women." Furthermore, it is argued that exegetical literature such as the Tafsīr Jalalayn, when translated to English, always shows that the word *atā* is translated as "to come."

However, while the absence of the preposition *'alā* might slightly alter the meaning, it is irrelevant to the discussion of verse 7:81 for this verse is not understood based on just one word but rather the context. The context reflects that two general groups of men and women are being compared in the verse and as such general rules indicate men reject the advances of other males for penetration whereas women generally are accepting of such an action. The verse does not mean that every female should accept every man who approaches her for penetration and nor does it assert that every male should reject a potential suitor. It simply compares the two groups in general and the language indicates that exceptions apply in terms of certain women rejecting certain men. Therefore, as noted earlier, approaching an entity for penetration is not automatically coercive but rather deemed coercive when someone not receptive to the activity is pursued and deemed passionate or desirable when someone receptive to the activity is approached. So far as translations of the exegetical literature are concerned, the English equivalents of the Arabic words do not necessarily reflect what the word actually means and the choice of the English equivalent merely reflects the choice of the translator and the understanding, or lack thereof, of the original Arabic text.

Sometimes it is insisted that had the purport of the verse been to expressly mention rape then the words connoting aggression such as *tukrihū*, as used in verse 24:33, or *ajbar* or *tadfaʿ**ūn*** should have been used in verses 7:81, 26:165–166, and 27: 55 instead of the word *lataʾtūna* (approach). However, such words have not seemingly been used in such a context in the Qur'an, which is perhaps why rape is addressed through *ḥirāba* (unlawful warfare) laws and not through some specific Qur'anic injunctions on rape. It is also to be noted that to some extent, owing to the seeming lack of distinction or the inability of the court to distinguish between rape and adultery, the Pakistan Hudood Laws have been a source of great persecution for Pakistani women living through such laws in the 1980s. Further light on the issue can also be shed when words like *al-ʿālamīn* (the worlds) and *wa-tadharūna* (and leave) as used in verses 26:165—166 are considered. It is also important to recall that the story of Lūṭ as mentioned in the Qur'an focuses on the active partner's action and not the passive partner. The Qur'an did not expressly delve into the disposition of the passive partner and as such their role in the action pursued by the active partner cannot be deemed as based on willingness given the textual evidence provided by jurists based on the natural fact that generally men do not submit to penetration. Nonetheless, verses 26:165–166 are reproduced below in Arabic.

> *A taʾtūna al-dhukrāna min al-ʿālamīn wa-tadharūna ma khalaqa lakum rabbukum min azwājikum bal antum qawmun ʿādūn* (26:165–166)

It is interesting to note that while the emphatic particle *la* is not used before the verb *atatoona* in verse 26:165, the word used in lieu of *al-rijāl* is *al-dhukrān* which carries with it the connotation of a nonreceptive entity, and which therefore retains the equivalence between the phrases *lataʾtūna al-rijāla* and *A taʾtūna al-dhukrāna*. The word *al-ʿālamīn* could possibly even help choose the first of the two traditions supplied by al-Rāzī in the context of verse 7:80 from Al-Ḥasan and Ibn ʿAbbās, where the former narrative emphasized the sexual conduct of the people of Lūṭ with strangers and the latter narrative emphasized the ensuing debauchery among their own people. Moreover, the word *wa-tadharūna* (and leave) substantiates Zamakshari's point in his commentary for 26:165–166, that the people of Lūṭ were condemned for exclusively penetrating males, while abandoning their wives. Thus, a purely linguistic analysis itself lends support to the thesis that the issue at stake was not the anachronistic same-sex unions issue but rather the extravagant approaching of nonreceptive travelers by men whose basic needs were being met with their spouses.

Another key word in verse 7:81 is *musrifūn*, which is used to describe the conduct of the people of Lūṭ. According to the Lisan al-ʿArab, the word comes from the root S-R-F, which gives the impression of water that is poured on earth but which does not nourish the plant or tree. The word *musrifūn* is used to describe people who spend beyond need or benefit or to describe people who exert effort in the wrong place. Traditional authorities would take this word to understand the verse as in the light of 2:223 that describes wives as tilth, thereby connecting the purpose of sexual relations with procreation. However, this understanding is open to exceptions as for infertile couples or the *khunthā mushkil* (ambiguous gender), who while being allowed to get married by classical authorities, do not have the ability to procreate. Likewise, al-Ghāzālī connotes that a woman may refuse to bear children to preserve her beauty.[155]

However, *musrifūn* alludes to people who go beyond genuine need, which in this context would refer to sexual need. In terms of exerting effort in the wrong place, this would mean pursuing generally nonreceptive males for extraneous sexual conduct over and above genuine sexual need. Also, by using the word *qawmun* (nation) before *musrifūn*, the Qur'an is making it clear that the whole nation of the people of Lūṭ is being condemned for their unbridled lust as opposed to any specific homosexual segment of the population. Likewise, the words *qawmun ʿādūn* (transgressing nation) and *qawmun tajhalūn* (ignorant nation) used in verses 26: 166 and 27:55 respectively always refer to the whole nation of the people of Lūṭ. Zamakshari, as mentioned earlier, is clear in his commentary on 26:166 that the transgression refers to the extravagant act of the people of Lūṭ of seeking sexual conduct beyond their spouses. Likewise, al-Rāzī highlights the words *tubṣirūn* and *tajhalūn* in his commentary on 27: 54–55. He addresses various possibilities of understanding both these words; however, if both these words are considered holistically, they seem to indicate that the people of Lūṭ were aware of both their erroneous conduct and its consequences and therefore far from being ignorant they acted ignorantly despite their knowledge. This clearly reflects that the conduct of the people of Lūṭ was that of open defiance despite having recourse to their spouses.

In conclusion, key words that denote demand—*nurīd*, *rāwaduhu* and *A taʾtūn*, in verses 11:79, 54:37 and 7:81 respectively, apart from the words that denote extravagance—*fāḥisha*, *musrifūn* and *ʿādūn* in verses 7:80, 7:81 and 26:166 respectively, and the concern on Lūṭ's guests expressed in verses 15:70 and 29:33, collectively suggest that the Qur'an is condemning inhospitality through subjugation of fellow human beings. The phrases "rushing toward males," "excited desire," particularized men and women and "excessiveness beyond need or benefit" in verse 7:81, and the phrases "the worlds," "and leave" and "spouses" in verses 26:265–166 holistically point to a picture that has limited scope to be applied to contemporary same-sex unions. Thus, based on a linguistic analysis that amplifies the contextual analysis on verses

7:80, 29:28–29, 11:78–79, and 15:67–72, it can be reasonably concluded that the condemnation of the people of Lūṭ is for their forceful and extravagant approaching of nonreceptive traveling males of different nations, even while their basic sexual needs were being fulfilled by their spouses, and this deportment in modern parlance is deemed nothing short of "rape." In short, based on either an analysis of the traditional commentaries or the holistic understanding of key Arabic words, the conventional analogous deduction of the condemnation of same-sex unions can be rejected.

On the basis of the heretofore analysis, it may be questioned that if the alternate thesis could be reasonably deduced based on the Qur'anic verses on the people of Lūṭ, then why has 1,400 years of Muslim scholarship never considered the possibility of the case for legal Muslim same-sex unions, since at least some Muslim jurists did consider rare scenarios such as the possibility of female-led prayers. However, concerns on female-led prayers or even in the case of females having sex with male slaves did arise respectively during the time of the Prophet (d. 632) and Caliph ʿUmar (d. 644). In contrast, the issue of constitutional gays and lesbians was not addressed by the classical jurists as the issue was viewed through the lens of superfluous desire as opposed to that of exclusive orientation toward members of the same gender and to rule over the latter would not have been possible in the absence of developments in the fields of psychology and psychiatry. As such, we do not have evidence that the question of a legal contract between two equal partners of the same gender was ever asked, for all the Hadith and juristic opinions are about sex between two males outside the scope of a legal contract.

To reiterate, when the verses on the people of Lūṭ are collected and analyzed contextually and linguistically, a strong case emerges to read these verses as alluding to acts of coercion and exploitation. Sex in this regard is devoid of love, tenderness, or even desire and pleasure, and is rather used as a weapon to subjugate vulnerable human beings.

2.8 VERSES 4:15–16

Given issues in conflating the case of gays and lesbians with the people of Lūṭ, some contemporary conservative scholars like Aḥmad Shafaat invoke verses 4:15–16 to draw rulings for same-sex conduct.[156] These verses read as follows:

> Those who commit unlawful sexual intercourse of your women—bring against them four [witnesses] from among you. And if they testify, confine the guilty women to houses until death takes them or Allah ordains for them [another] way. (4:15)

> And the two who commit it among you, dishonor them both. But if they repent and correct themselves, leave them alone. (4:16)

However, most scholars, both present and past, seem to refute this understanding. For instance, Rowson states:[157]

> Only one maverick commentator, the Mu'tazilite Abu Moslem Eṣfahāni (d. 934), understood two highly ambiguous verses (4:15–16) as referring to, respectively, female and male homosexual behaviour . . . while otherwise there was unanimous consent that the subject of both verses was heterosexual fornication.

This statement finds support in Maududi's commentary on the Qur'an as follows:

> Even less convincing is the opinion expressed by Abu Muslim al-Iṣfahānī that the first verse relates to lesbian relations between females, and the second to homosexual relations between males. It is strange that al-Iṣfahānī ignored the basic fact that the Qur'an seeks merely to chart a broad code of law and morality and hence deals only with fundamental questions.[158]

Likewise, Khaled el-Rouayheb writes:

> Not all scholars understood the verse (4:16) as applying to homosexual intercourse. In fact, even Ḥanafī commentators, whom one might expect to have exploited the verse in defence of their school's peculiar ruling on liwāṭ, interpreted the verse as applying to fornication between a man and a woman.[159]

Shafaat acknowledges that the majority of Muslim scholars reject the view that verses 4:15–16 provide penalty for same-sex conduct but also asserts that this view was recorded amongst other interpretations by the exegete Ibn Kathīr (d. 1373) and has been supported by recent scholars like Yusuf Ali (d. 1953) and both Thana Allah Panipati (d. 1810) and Muhammad Asad (d. 1992) who opined that these verses encapsulate both heterosexual and homosexual conduct. However, it deserves to be noted that the earliest Qur'anic Tafsīr *Asbab Nuzul* did not provide context for these verses and that the Tafsīr Ibn 'Abbās views 4:15–16 as depicting heterosexual adultery, a viewpoint supported by Ibn Kathīr, who, while narrating other opinions on 4:15–16, qualified them with the remark, "Allah knows best."[160]

Shafaat disagrees that verses 4:15–16 were abrogated by verse 24:2 in terms of the punishment for *zinā*, stating that there is no Hadith that provides such an understanding. He further argues that verses 4:15–28 form a united passage as they deal with various types of *fāḥisha* and that since verse 4:25, which mentions that slave women receive half the penalty for adultery for free women, was probably revealed after verse 24:2, which mentions the penalty of 100 lashes, therefore verses 4:15–16 would have been revealed after 24:2, thereby making the issue of 24:2 abrogating 4:15–16 moot. He further opines that since 4:15–16 do not abrogate verse 24:2, the Qur'an dealt with the common case of "natural sex" in verse 24:2 and less common case of "unnatural sex" in verses 4:15–16.

Based on a linguistic analysis of verses 4:15–16, Shafaat argues that the dual pronoun *alladhāni* (the two) is only used in verse 4:16 and asserts that the Qur'an uses the singular or plural pronoun elsewhere when it mentions *fāḥisha* as in verses 4:19, 4:25, 24:2, and 65:1. He further opines that if *alladhāni* were to refer to a male and a female, instead of two men, then this would imply that women are to be given punishment in addition to the punishment of indefinite punishment mentioned in verse 4:15. Moreover, he argues that the dual pronoun is not used in verse 4:15 just as it is used in verse 4:16 by asserting that homosexuality is more common among men rather than women.

Shafaat disagrees with the opinion that verse 4:15 refers to married women, whereas verse 4:16 refers to an unmarried man and woman, by arguing that this would leave out the punishment of married men. He argues that the phrase "the two who commit it" in verse 4:16 contains the pronoun "it," which can refer to the *fāḥisha* mentioned in verse 4:15 and as such this lends support to the view that both verses are to be interpreted in light of each other. He substantiates the point on interpreting the two verses together by claiming that whereas four witnesses are required to prove guilt in verse 4:15, no such requirement is set in verse 4:16, and this can be resolved by applying the rule of witnesses from 4:15 onto 4:16. Moreover, he rationalizes that since women are more adversely affected by accusations of sexual impropriety than men, the condition of four witnesses is explicitly stated for women and left implicit for men.

To counter the potential criticism of why the verses are not clear on the issue of same-sex conduct, Shafaat states that the meaning of these verses was clear at the time of revelation. Finally, he asserts that the focus of verses 4:15–16 is on rehabilitation rather than punishment and as such the Qur'an rejects the view that orientation toward the same sex is innate.

However, Shafaat's opinions can be critiqued on several counts. In Arabic grammar, while the dual pronoun *alladhāni* (the two) used in verse 4:16 represents the masculine, it is actually gender inclusive, which is perhaps why an overwhelming majority of classical jurists understood verse 4:16 to refer to *zinā* between men and women. However, even if verses 4:15–16 are to be used to refer to same-sex conduct, the point remains the sexual activity that is mentioned in these verses is one that takes place outside the legitimate folds of a legal contract, which is a separate issue than the one on determining a legal contract for same-sex couples.

Shafaat's argument that verses 4:15–28 form a united passage is based on the assumption that the main theme of the passage is *fāḥisha;* however, the passage also deals with the regulation of marriage and while there might be an overlap between the two issues, it is not enough to justify that verses 4:15–28 were all revealed at the same time. Furthermore, even if verses 4:15–28 were revealed at the same time, it cannot be concluded that they were revealed after verse 24:2. Shafaat focuses on the point that the punishment of 100 lashes mentioned in 24:2 can be halved for slave women mentioned in 4:25; however, that would lead to the absurd conclusion that the punishment of slave women for same-sex conduct should be half the quality of the punishment of confinement of free women.

Shafaat's point on the usage of dual pronoun in verse 4:16 and not in verse 4:15 based on the observation that male homosexuality is more common than female homosexuality belies the observation that a greater proportion of females are reported to be bisexual. Furthermore, while he tries to connect verses 4:15–16 with the common theme of homosexuality by arguing similar rules on witnesses, he fails to account for the understanding that the reason a plural pronoun is used in verse 4:15 to refer exclusively to women is that the import of the verse is prostitution, which is why Moiz Amjad argues that the punishment of confinement in verse 4:15 is severe as it prevents prostitution from spreading in society.[161]

Shafaat's argument that the verses are connected through the rule of using four witnesses to prove guilt belies jurisprudential precedent that in cases of nonpenetrative same-sex conduct, some schools allowed for two witnesses for proving guilt. Moreover, his point that the focus of the verses is rehabilitation seems to be a reading shaped by Catholicism-based arguments propounded by reparative therapy groups like NARTH, whose viewpoints on sexuality are at odds with those of the classical jurists, who while condemning *'amal qawm Lūṭ* never argued that same-sex desires were unnatural or could be changed.

Even within Shī'ī jurisprudence, verses 4:15–16 are not construed as having any bearing on same-sex sexual conduct. In contrast to Shafaat who claims that no Hadith supports the claim that verse 24:2 abrogated verses 4:15–16, Ṭabāṭabā'ī (d. 1920) opined that the Prophet stated that the phrase "until Allah ordains another way" refers to flogging mentioned in verse 24:2.[162] Furthermore, Ṭabāṭabā'ī asserted that nobody opined that the penalty of sexual conduct among females was abrogated, substantiating the argument that 4:15–16 do not refer to same-sex sexual conduct. He also referenced a text from al-Bāqir (d. 733), who upheld the opinion on the abrogation of 4:15 and mentioned that whenever a female committed indecency in the early days of Islam, she was socially ostracized, confined to a house, and provided food and drink. Ṭabāṭabā'ī substantiates this viewpoint by mentioning that similar opinions have been noted by Sunnīs through texts from Ibn 'Abbās (d. 687), Qatāda (d. 735), and Mujāhid (d. 722) amongst others.

The above analysis of the Qur'anic verses indicates that deducing the prohibition of same-sex relationships rests on the disputable *qiyās* (analogy) between the people of Lūṭ and gays and lesbians. The conduct of men chasing Lūṭ's guests is markedly different from that of committed same-sex couples raising a family together. As such, superimposing the framework of *liwāṭ*, which specifically refers to the singular act of homosexual anal intercourse in an age- and status-based asymmetrical context, on the lives of gays and lesbians does not seem reasonable.

2.9 SUPPORTING AN ALTERNATE READING OF THE VERSES ON THE PEOPLE OF LŪṬ

A legal maxim states that legal opinions should take into account changes of time and circumstances and as such, Kamali asserts that some jurisprudential rulings of earlier times may now be deemed unjust due to a different set of circumstances.[163] According to Kamali, the legal maxim that *ijtihād* (independent reasoning) is irrelevant in the presence of a *naṣṣ* (clear text) should be revised because of the possibility of fresh interpretation in a different context.[164] According to Ṭūfī, if the rules derived from the *naṣṣ* do not uphold the good, then the texts have to be reinterpreted.[165]

Given that the framework of *'ubna* and *ma'bun* is grossly outdated due to our increased understanding of human psychology and sexual orientation and given that the framework of *liwāṭ* that focuses on a single sexual act in the context of beardless boys and *ma'buns*, the application of both to the lives of gays and lesbians would be both unreasonable and unjust. This substantiates the critical analysis of the verses on the people of Lūṭ in this chapter and warrants a fresh reading as the classical jurists read those verses based on *qiyās* that equated the conduct of the people of Lūṭ with fornication.

A fresh reading of the verses is required also because textual reasoning that does not take into account human dignity and welfare has its limitations. Ibn al-Qayyim (d. 1350) asserted that the Sharīʿa is all justice, kindness, common good, and wisdom, and that any rule that departs from justice to injustice, from *maṣlaḥa* (public welfare) to *mafsada* (harm), is not part of Sharīʿa even if it is derived through literal interpretation.[166] Likewise, according to Turabi, if textual reasoning leads to *ḥaraj aẓīm* (extreme hardship), then the *maṣlaḥa* has to be given precedence and the purely hermeneutical interpretation is of no consequence.[167] Indeed, a majority of jurists have indicated that a mechanical reading of the text, which is devoid of wisdom and done only for conformity, should be avoided.[168]

Kecia Ali notes how past jurists bypassed even clear Qur'anic verses based on interpretive devices.[169] In the context of the verses on the people of Lūṭ, such devices may include *takhṣīṣ* (particularization) by bringing together two texts conjointly to bear on the legal problem at hand.[170] This suggests that instead of reading 7:81 on its own, it can be coupled with 29:29 to understand the phrase *lata'tūna al-rijāl* (approaching men) in its proper context of ambushing travelers. Another approach to verses 7:81, 26:65–66, and 27:55 that are often plucked out of context to prohibit same-sex unions is to note that the phrase "Allah does not like the extravagant" neither connotes a command nor a prohibition.[171] This is because the precise import of implicit injunctions in the form of praise or condemnation cannot be ascertained, that is, it is not clear whether they convey a ruling or mere warning or recommendation.[172] Thus, when verses 7:81, 26:65–66, and 27:55 describe the people of Lūṭ as extravagant, ignorant, or transgressing bounds, they are, strictly speaking, not prescribing a Sharīʿa law and the admonition is of the conduct of the people of Lūṭ, which is markedly different from the lives of believing gays and lesbians.

Another way to read these verses is to note that while jurists begin with the presumption to read the plain or literal meaning of the words, *qarīna* (extrinsic circumstances) may suggest reading the verses nonliterally.[173] Jurists may abandon the primary meaning in favor of another meaning based on context and circumstance.[174] This substantiates reading the words *rijāl* and *nisā'* not plainly as men and women but rather as nonreceptive and receptive entities respectively based on a linguistic analysis of the root words. Such a reading may be substantiated by noting that even for the seemingly clear word *banātī* (my daughters) in verse 4:23, jurists have debated whether the term includes illegitimate or adopted daughters.

A related relevant point is that according to the *arbāb al-khuṣūṣ* (partisans of specific reference), the rule for a general term does not apply to all members of the relevant class.[175] This suggests that the verses on the people of Lūṭ are open to exceptions in that *lata'tūna al-rijāl* would refer to predominately straight men pursuing other males as opposed to gay men, who are a minority like trans-men and intersex people.

An alternate reading of the verses on the people of Lūṭ also necessitates a renewed *qiyās*-based approach to deduce a reasonable understanding from these verses as opposed to simply superimposing them on the lives of Muslim gays and lesbians.

2.10 FORMULATING A BETTER *QIYĀS*—ANALOGICAL DEDUCTION

"Homosexuality" was viewed by past Muslim scholars on its own without any regard to the sexual orientation of the males involved and in the absence of a legal contract like *nikāḥ* (marriage) or concubinage, which was legally regulated in a world with slavery. In contrast, conservative Muslim leaders use the word "homosexuality" without a proper definition, although it seems that they use the word to refer to same-sex relationships whether sanctioned through a legal contract or otherwise. However, just as there are issues in conflating the people of Lūṭ with gays and lesbians through *qiyās*, there are issues in equating "homosexuality" with same-sex relationships bound by a legal contract. Some sympathetic conservative Muslim leaders may suggest that one may have a case-by-case look at the issue of constitutional gays and lesbians and tailor responses for them, perhaps suggesting celibacy for some, prescribing them to indulge in social work and adopting a slightly lenient approach toward others. However, Kamali notes that with change of time and place, a case-by-case approach may not be feasible.[176] This substantiates the importance of revisiting the *qiyās* (analogical deduction) approach of the past jurists.

The limitations in equating *liwāṭ* with same-sex relationships, and equating the people of Lūṭ with gays and lesbians, necessitate a renewed *qiyās* on the verses on the people of Lūṭ. Conservative Muslim leaders apparently feel that the predominant aspect of the analogy that equates the people of Lūṭ with gays and lesbians and *liwāṭ* with same-sex relationships is the act of homosexual anal intercourse. However, this leads to the problem in that the analogy does not fit as a specific act does not define the totality of same-sex relationships, which may not include the act of homosexual anal intercourse and which go beyond the sexual act to encompass the goods that are found in married life, such as pleasure, communication, emotional growth, personal stability, and long-term fulfillment,[177] as well as compassion and affection between the partners.

Qiyās requires that enough parallels have to exist between two situations or cases to extract a meaningful conclusion. More specifically, in order to extract an appropriate analogy, some critical shared elements have to be present and some critical negating elements have to be absent between two situations or cases. For instance, a drink cannot be considered prohibited if, while sharing its color with that of wine, it does not share the critical intoxicating property of wine. The *qiyās* is considered to be strong if the critical element or cause of prohibition is referenced from either the Qur'an or the Hadith as opposed to superficial observation. *Qiyās khafī* (hidden analogy), which is arrived through deeper reflection and analysis, is stronger than the usual *qiyās jalī* (obvious analogy) that is based on superficial similitudes, and is also more effective in repelling hardships, which is important as even a technically sound *qiyās* that goes against the overriding *maqāṣid* (objectives) of the Sharīʿa may be discarded.[178]

Just as verse 5:91 provides the *ʿilla* (effective cause) for the prohibition of intoxicants, which is that intoxicants keep one away from the remembrance of God, likewise verses 7:80, 11:77–79, 15:67–72, and 29:28–29 that form the context for verses 7:81, 26:165–166, or 27:55 that are usually quoted to prohibit "homosexuality" can be considered to determine the *ʿilla* that might enable one to make more appropriate conclusions on the verses on the people of Lūṭ. In doing so, one can avoid making superficial conclusions such as prohibiting a drink with the same color as wine or prohibiting same-sex relationships within the folds of a legal contract, both of which are not necessarily warranted by a reading of the relevant Qur'anic verses. Since the *qiyās* for which the *ʿilla* is extracted from the *naṣṣ* (text) is usually preferred to the *qiyās* based on superficial similitude, the often quoted verses 7:81, 26:165–166, or 27:55 on the people of Lūṭ will have to be complemented with verses 7:80 and 29:28–29 to obtain a more appropriate conclusion.

Verse 29:29 helps break the superficial analogy that is made by conservative Muslim leaders between the people of Lūṭ and gays and lesbians on the basis of the *ʿilla* of homosexual anal intercourse, which conservative Muslim leaders consider to be the defining feature of the people of Lūṭ. Relationships based on commitment, reciprocity, equality, compassion, and as mentioned in the Qur'anic verse 30:21—tranquility, mercy, and *mawadda* (affection)—cannot be equated with conduct that included indulging in indecency, highway robbery, and actions perpetrated in public assemblies. Alternatively, as noted earlier, how reasonable is it to assume that committing highway robbery, evil deeds in open assemblies, and being a responsible citizen in a committed same-sex relationship go hand in hand?

Likewise, as noted earlier, verses 7:80 and 29:28 also help break the superficial analogy between the people of Lūṭ and gays and lesbians. Generally, past exegetes, such as Ibn Kathīr (d. 1373), Ṭabarī (d. 923), and Qurṭubī (d. 1273), understood these verses as indicating that "homosexuality" started with the people of Lūṭ. The conclusion that same-sex conduct, whether forced or not, started from the people of Lūṭ does not stand the test of historical evidence. This further substantiates the argument that a renewed reading of the verses on the people of Lūṭ is warranted.

The exegete al-Rāzī (d. 1209), while conceding that the people of Lūṭ may have invented the abomination, also claims that the "homosexual" conduct in 7:80 may allude to the collective action of the people of Lūṭ rather than individual conduct, which only substantiates the argument that conduct of the people of Lūṭ was not one of gays and lesbians forging same-sex relationships through a legal contract but one perpetrated by the nation as a whole, all of whom could not have been constitutionally gays and lesbians unless one were to view the sexual orientation toward the same sex as a contagion.

Verses 7:80 and 29:28–29 seem to indicate that the collective action of the people of Lūṭ of pursuing other males, robbing them, and committing evil deeds in public assemblies indicate that the *ʿilla* (effective cause) behind the condemnation of the acts of the people of Lūṭ is not conduct of a minority that is based on compassion and affection, but one based on exploitation by the majority. This *ʿilla* behind the prohibition of the conduct of the people of Lūṭ based on texts would help formulate a stronger *qiyās* and hence more appropriate conclusions than one based on the superficial observation that the feature of homosexual anal sex equates the conduct of the people of Lūṭ with same-sex relationships.

Like verses 7:80 and 29:28–29, verses 11:77–79 and 15:67–72 also substantiate the argument that the *ʿilla* behind the condemnation of the acts of the people of Lūṭ is not conduct of a minority based on compassion and affection. Conservative Muslims usually quote verses 11:77–79 and 15:67–72, which indicate Lūṭ's offering his daughters to deduce the point that heterosexual marriages are preferred to same-sex conduct. However, in traditional exegetical works there has been much difference of opinion on whether Lūṭ really did offer his daughters, which casts doubt on the understanding that the verses are giving precedence to heterosexual marriages.

These verses indicate that the people of Lūṭ had forbidden him from providing hospitality and were demanding that the male visitors be yielded to them. The verses also indicate that Lūṭ was concerned about protecting his guests from the crowd that rebuffed the offer of his daughters by stating that they had no *ḥaqq*—right or claim on them and also expressed the *nurīd*—demand or want for the guests. Indeed, the language is not one of proposition and desire but one of coercion and demand, which indicates that the verses are not alluding to committed same-sex relationships but a conduct that is defined by coercion and exploitation.

The above textual analysis indicates that extracting the injunction of the prohibition of same-sex relationships in a legal contract does not follow from a *qiyās* based on the supposed common element of homosexual anal sex between the people of Lūṭ and gay men. The analogy does not hold in the case of lesbians and many gay couples whose sexual activity does not include the act of homosexual anal intercourse. Moreover, even if the act of homosexual anal intercourse formed part of the sexual conduct of some gay couples, the prohibition of the act is disputable as Shīʿī scholars contest the prohibition of heterosexual anal intercourse. The *qiyās* that equates the people of Lūṭ and gay people also falls short since, based on textual evidence, the collective action of the people of Lūṭ, as noted above, is textually defined by coercion and exploitation outside a legal contract. In short, equating gay people with the people of Lūṭ raises a lot of questions, which indicates that the analogy, and hence the prohibition of same-sex relationships, cannot be superficially based on a sexual act.

2.11 CRITICISM OF THE ALTERNATE READING

The approach of adopting an alternate reading of the verses to build a case for same-sex unions can be criticized as one breaking from the traditional scholarship of Islam. However, such criticisms can be contested based on the statements and reasoning of the past scholars, which depict how sociocultural norms and medical knowledge of the societies they lived in informed their viewpoints on the nature of same-sex relationships. The picture that emerges from medieval Islamic writings is one of widely practiced same-sex penetration of vulnerable populations that comprised mainly of male slaves and male youth. There may have been consensual sex between men but that was not the norm and as such would have been easily overlooked. If monogamous same-sex relationships existed, then they would have constituted a small minority and the scholars' responsibility was to protect the society and especially the vulnerable men from exploitation. Furthermore, even the consenting penetrated man was assumed to be afflicted by *ʾubna* and as such viewed as exploited by the many willing penetrating men of his locality.

Traditional scholars offered protection and dispensation to the vulnerable populations that comprised of male slaves, youth, and anyone who was coerced from any guilt or punishment. They, however, punished the person afflicted with *ʾubna* and even in such a case, some Shafiʿi scholars argued against capital punishment for the *maʾbūn* (male afflicted with *ʾubna*). Ibn al-Qayyim (d. 1350) seemed to apologetically explain that it is better for the receptive partner to die as punishment because he may die a martyr as opposed to remaining alive after the irreparable damage inflicted on him through penetration.

Viewed through this lens, homosexual acts in the society of the past scholars were closer to the practice of the people of Lūṭ than to the lives of loving same-sex couples in contemporary times, especially in the Western world. Thus, just as past scholars were informed by the reading of the texts and the actual practices of their populations, contemporary scholars have to inform their opinions by the same texts but by the very different practice of homosexuality in contemporary society rather than parrot opinions that are inapplicable to contemporary societies.

The Qur'anic verses are but one facet of consideration in the work of jurists, who also rely on the Prophetic Hadith literature as well as the narratives from the Companions and their followers, apart from the *qiyās*-based work of prominent founders of schools of Muslim jurisprudence. Therefore, chapter 3 would be aimed at analyzing the Hadith literature as well as the narratives from the Companions of the Prophet from both Sunnī and Shīʿī sources, whereas chapter 5 will present a critical reflection on the reasoning employed by both past and contemporary scholars on the prohibition of same-sex sexual conduct.

NOTES

Shakir's translation will be used for all of the Qur'anic verses in this chapter.

1. Everett K. Rowson, "Homosexuality In Islamic law," in *Encyclopaedia Iranica,* last modified March 23, 2012, accessed January 27, 2016, http://www.iranicaonline.org/articles/homosexuality-ii.

2. "Why does Islam forbid lesbianism and homosexuality?" Islam QA.

3. Scott Siraj al-Haqq Kugle, *Homosexuality in Islam: Islamic Reflection on Gay, Lesbian, and Transgender Muslims*, (Oxford: Oneworld Publications, 2010), 170.

4. We are grateful to Dr. Mohamed Fadel for this point.

5. Kecia Ali, *Marriage and Slavery in Early Islam*, (Cambridge: Harvard University Press, 2010), 179.

6. Ibid, 179.

7. Najmabadi, "'Types, Acts or What?" 292.

8. Sahar Amer, "Cross Dressing and Female Same-Sex Marriage in Medieval French and Arabic Literatures," in *Islamicate Sexualities*, eds. Kathryn Babayan and Afsaneh Najmabadi, (Cambridge: Harvard University Center for Middle Eastern Studies, 2008), 100.

9. Frederic Lagrange, "The Obscenity of the Vizier," in *Islamicate Sexualities*, eds. Kathryn Babayan and Afsaneh Najmabadi, (Cambridge: Harvard University Center for Middle Eastern Studies, 2008), 187.

10. Everett K. Rowson, "The Effeminates of Early Medina," *Journal of the American Oriental Society* 111, no. 4 (1991): 671–93.

11. Kathryn Babayan, "'In spirit we ate each other's sorrow': Female Companionship in seventeenth century Safavi Iran," in *Islamicate Sexualities*, eds. Kathryn Babayan and Afsaneh Najmabadi, (Cambridge: Harvard University Center for Middle Eastern Studies, 2008), 255.

12. Ali, *Marriage and Slavery in Early Islam*, 177.

13. Abū l-Fidā' Ismā'īl ibn 'Umar Ibn Kathīr, *Tafsīr Ibn Kathīr*. Commentary on verses 23:6, 29:33, الموسوعة الذهبية للحديث النبوي الشيف و علومه [*The Golden Encyclopedia of the Prophetic Golden Hadeeth and its Sciences*], 2nd edition, (London: Turath Publishing), CD-ROM.

14. Abu Bakr ibn Abi Shayba Abdullah ibn Muhammad ibn Ibrāhīm Ibn 'Uthmān, *Muṣannaf Ibn Abi Shayba*. Volume 5. In الموسوعة الذهبية للحديث النبوي الشيف و علومه [*The Golden Encyclopedia of the Prophetic Golden Hadeeth and its Sciences*], 2nd edition, (London: Turath Publishing), CD-ROM, 537.

15. Ali, *Marriage and Slavery in Early Islam*, 178–79.

16. Kecia Ali, *Sexual Ethics and Islam: Feminist Reflections on Quran Hadith.* (Oxford: Oneworld Publications, 2006), xxv, 4.

17. Ibid, 12.

18. Ibid, 96.

19. Ali, *Marriage and Slavery in Early Islam*, 182.

20. Ali, *Sexual Ethics and Islam*, 77.

21. Mufti Ebrahim Desai, "Fatwa on Oral Sex," Zawaj.com, accessed January 28, 2016, http://www.zawaj.com/articles/fatwa_oral_desai.html.

22. Muhammed Saeed, "Fatwa on Oral Sex," December 13, 2003, accessed January 28, 2016, https://8lan.wordpress.com/2011/01/24/fatwa-on-oral-sex/.

23. Hedaya Hartford, *Initiating and Upholding an Islamic Marriage*, (Damascus and Beirut: Dar al-Fikr, 2000), 156.

24. Sheikh Aḥmad Kutty, "Fatwa on Oral Sex," September 29, 2003, accessed January 28, 2016, https://8lan.wordpress.com/2011/01/24/fatwa-on-oral-sex/.

25. Ruqayyah bint Muḥammad Al-Muḥārib, "The Islamic Ruling on Female Secretion [Part Three]," The Message of Islam, accessed January 25, 2016, http://islamicstudies.islammessage.com/ResearchPaper.aspx?aid=303.

26. Gibril F. Haddad, "Oral Sex, Questions on Sexuality," Living Islam, accessed January 26, 2016, https://www.abc.se/~m9783/fiqhi/fiqha_e92.html.

27. Sheikh Abd al-Wahhab Al-Turayri, "Oral sex, Sexuality," *Islam Today,* accessed January 25, 2016, http://en.islamtoday.net/node/1514.

28. Musa Furber, "Is Oral sex permitted?" The Modern Religion, accessed January 26, 2016, http://www.themodernreligion.com/misc/sex/sex-oral.html.

29. Haddad, "Oral Sex."

30. Habeeb Alli, *Intimacy and the Sacred in Muslim Communities*, ed. Elizabeth Rahman (Bloomington: iUniverse Inc., 2011), 41–44.

31. Camilla Adang, "Ibn Ḥazm on Homosexuality. A Case-Study of Zahiri Legal Methodology," *Al-Qantara* 24, no. 1 (2003): 26.

32. Shaykh Muhammad Ibn Ameen, "The Islamic Ruling on masturbation," accessed January 26, 2016, http://www.ibnamin.com/masturbation_en.htm.

33. "Masturbation, Answer from Islam Online's Fatwa Bank at Islam-Online.net." Zawaj, December 14, 1999, accessed January 27, 2016, http://www.zawaj.com/articles/masturbation_islamonline.html.

34. "Ruling on masturbation and how to cure the problem," 329, Islam QA, accessed January 25, 2016, http://islamqa.info/en/329.

35. Mohammad Hashim Kamali, *Freedom of Expression in Islam*, (Cambridge: The Islamic Texts Society, 1997), 207.

36. Ṣaḥīḥ al-Bukhārī, Book 67, Hadith 3 and 4, in الموسوعة الذهبية للحديث النبوي الشيف و علومه [*The Golden Encyclopedia of the Prophetic Golden Hadeeth and its Sciences*], 2nd edition, (London: Turath Publishing), CD-ROM.

37. "The Command to Marry," Quran Tafsir Ibn Kathir, accessed January 26, 2016, http://www.qtafsir.com/.

38. Ibid.

39. Alli, *Intimacy and the Sacred in Muslim Communities*, 12.

40. Ronak Husni and Daniel L. Newman, *Muslim Women in Law and Society*, (London and New York: Routledge, 2007), 61.

41. Al-Hafith Abu Bakr Muhammad bin al-Hussain Al-Ajuree, *The Forbiddance of Homosexuality*, trans. Mustafa George Deberry, (Wilkes-Barre: Masjid At-Tawheed, 2010), 85

42. Ibid, 86.

43. Muhammad Bāqir Qarashi, "Combating Sexual Deviation," *Imam Reza Network*, accessed January 27, 2016, http://www.imamreza.net/eng/imamreza.php?id=3145.

44. Ibn Ameen, "The Islamic Ruling on Masturbation."

45. Ibid.

46. Sheikh `Atiyyah Saqr, "A Guide to Controlling One's Sexual Desire," Onislam, December 21, 2014, accessed January 28, 2016, http://onislam.orkiservers.com/english/ask-the-scholar/morals-and-manners/morals-and-values/174577-a-guide-to-controlling-ones-sexual-desire.html.

47. Zawaj, "Masturbation."

48. Shaikh Aḥmad Kutty, "Ask the Scholar," accessed January 26, 2016, http://www.asktheschoIar.com/question-details.aspx?qstID=1700.

49. Aḥmad ibn ʿAbd al-Ḥalīm Ibn Taymiyya, *Tafsīr Sūra Āl ʿImrān*, Tafsīr of do not make what is permitted prohibited; *Tafsīr Sūra Āl ʿImrān,* Tafsīr on the people of desire wish that you tilt, الموسوعة الذهبية للحديث النبوي الشيف و علومه [*The Golden Encyclopedia of the Prophetic Golden Hadeeth and its Sciences*], 2nd edition, (London: Turath Publishing), CD-ROM.

50. "'What is the fatwa on masturbation in Islam?' Islamic Ruling on Masturbation," Islam awareness, 2002, accessed January 26, 2016, http://www.islamawareness.net/Sex/fatwa_sex_003.html.

51. Sheikh Salman Al-Oadah, "Masturbation, Sexuality," IslamToday, accessed January 25, 2016, http://en.islamtoday.net/node/1513.

52. Al-Turayri, "Oral Sex."

53. Ibn Ameen, "The Islamic Ruling on Masturbation."

54. Javed Ghamidi, "Hifz al-Furuj (Guarding the Private Parts). Translated by Shehzad Saleem," Renaissance, accessed January 26, 2016, http://www.monthly-renaissance.com/issue/content.aspx?id=1242.

55. See the entry 'khuntha mushkil' in the Kuwaiti Encyclopedia of Fiqh.

56. Ibn Ḥazm, *Al-Muḥallā bi-l-Āthār: kitāb mā lā ḥadd fīh*: The question of the doing of the people of Lūṭ, in الموسوعة الذهبية للحديث النبوي الشيف و علومه [*The Golden Encyclopedia of the Prophetic Golden Hadeeth and its Sciences*], 2nd edition, (London: Turath Publishing), CD-ROM.

57. Abu Jaʿfar Muhammad ibn Jarīr Al-Ṭabarī, *The History of al-Ṭabarī: Prophets and Patriarchs*, trans. William Brinner, (Albany: State University of New York, 1986), 112–118.

58. Ibn Kathīr, *The History of Ibn Kathir—Bidaya and Nihaya*. Translated by Abul Fida Imad uddin Ibn Kathir Damishqi (Karachi: Nafees Academy Urdu Bazaar, 1988), Volume 9, 185.

59. Al-Bayḍāwī, *Anwār al-Tanzīl wa Asrār al-Taʾwīl.* Commentary on verses 7:80–82, in الموسوعة الذهبية للحديث النبوي الشيف و علومه [*The Golden Encyclopedia of the Prophetic Golden Hadeeth and its Sciences*], 2nd edition, (London: Turath Publishing), CD-ROM.

60. Ibn Kathīr, *Tafsīr Ibn Kathīr* for 7:81.

61. Ayatollah Sayyid Kamal Faghih Imani, et al. *An Enlightening Commentary into the Light of the Holy Qur'an, Parts 7 & 8*, trans. Sayyid ʿAbbās Sadr

Ameli, (Isfahan, Iran: Amir ul Mumineen Ali Library, 2005), Parts 7 & 8, 395–396, 487–488.

62. Mohamed El-Moctar El-Shinqiti, "Threats to Behead Homosexuals: Shari`ah or Politics?" Islamic Research Foundation International, accessed January 28, 2016, http://www.irfi.org/articles2/articles_2951_3000/Threats%20to%20Behead%20Homosexuals.HTM.

63. Khaled El-Rouayheb, *Before Homosexuality in the Arab-Islamic World, 1500–1800*, (Chicago: University of Chicago Press, 2005), 17, 115.

64. Rabbi Leibel Reznick, "Does archeological data support the Biblical story? Biblical Archeology: Sodom and Gomorrah, Science and Medicine," Aish.com, April 5, 2008, accessed January 27, 2016, http://www.aish.com/ci/sam/48931527.html.

65. James Neill, *The Origins and Role of Same-Sex Relations in Human Societies*, (Jefferson, NC: McFarland, 2011), 50.

66. Ibid, 72.

67. Margherita Mussi, *Earliest Italy: An Overview of the Italian Paleolithic and Mesolithic*, (New York: Kluwer Academic/ Plenum Publisher, 2001), 343–45.

68. Gordon Wenham, "The Old Testament attitude to Homosexuality," *Expository Times* 102 (1991): 259–363, accessed January 27, 2016, http://www.biblicalstudies.org.uk/article_attitude_wenham.html.

69. Neill, *The Origins and Role of Same-Sex Relations in Human Societies*, 83.

70. Ibid, 93.

71. Fakhr al-Dīn Abu Abdullah Muhammad ibn Umar ibn al-Ḥusayn at-Taymī al-Bakrī at-Ṭabaristānī Al-Rāzī, *Tafsīr al-Rāzī*. Commentary on verses 2:223, 7:80–81, 24:2, 24:31, in الموسوعة الذهبية للحديث النبوي الشيف و علومه [*The Golden Encyclopedia of the Prophetic Golden Hadeeth and its Sciences*], 2nd edition, (London: Turath Publishing), CD-ROM.

72. These verses condemn people of Lūṭ for approaching males as extravagant (7:81), exceeding limits (26:165–166) or ignorant (27:55). By ignoring the allied verses, traditional scholars uphold the prohibition of *liwat* and hence homosexual conduct.

73. And kill them wherever you find them, and drive them out from whence they drove you out. . . (2:191) O you who believe! do not take the Jews and the Christians for friends. . . (5:51)

74. The story of the people of Lūṭ may also be compared with that of the people of Saleh and the people of Thamood in the Qur'an. In all such cases, the emphasis is on the common theme of the rejection of God and His Messengers rather than a specific human conduct.

75. Syed Abul A'ala Maududi, *Towards Understanding the Qur'an*, trans. Zafar Ishaq Ansari, (Leicester: The Islamic Foundation, 2006), accessed January 26, 2016, http://www.tafheem.net/main800.html.

76. Ibn Jumuʿa, ʿAbd ʿAli, *Tafsīr Nūr al-Thaqalayn* (Qom: Intisharat Ismailiyan, 1415 AH/1994), 2: 375–407.

77. Ibid.

78. Ibid.

79. Al-Ṭabarī, *Tafsīr Ṭabarī*. Commentary on verse 11:78, in الموسوعة الذهبية للحديث النبوي الشيف و علومه [*The Golden Encyclopedia of the Prophetic Golden Hadeeth and its Sciences*], 2nd edition, (London: Turath Publishing), CD-ROM. Translation by Jamal Bakeer and the authors.

80. Ibn Jumuʿa, ʿAbd ʿAli. *Tafsīr Nūr al-Thaqalayn* (Qom: Intisharat Ismailiyan, 1415 AH/1994), 2: 375–407.

81. Ibid.

82. El-Rouayheb, *Before Homosexuality,* 126.

83. Jalāl al-Dīn Al-Suyūṭī, *Al-Durr al-Manthūr fī al-Tafsīr bi-l-Maʾthūr*, in الموسوعة الذهبية للحديث النبوي الشيف و علومه [*The Golden Encyclopedia of the Prophetic Golden Hadeeth and its Sciences*], 2nd edition, (London: Turath Publishing), CD-ROM.

84. Scott Siraj al-Haqq Kugle, "Sexuality, Diversity and Ethics in the Agenda of Progressive Muslims," in *Progressive Muslims*, ed. Omid Safi, (Oxford: Oneworld Publications, 2003), 214.

85. Ibid, 210.

86. Jan Knappert, *Islamic Legends: Histories of the Heroes, Saints, and Prophets of Islam*, (Leiden: E.J. Brill, 1985), 84. It is not clear whether the quote is from Thaʿlabī or Al-Kisāʾī.

87. Imani et al., *An Enlightening Commentary*, Parts 7 & 8, 395, 487.

88. Mirza Bashīruddin Maḥmūd Aḥmad, *The Holy Qur'an with English Translation and Commentary*, Volume 3, published under the auspices of Mirza Tahir Aḥmad, (U.K.: Islam International Publications Limited, 1988), accessed January 25, 2016, http://www.alislam.org/quran/tafseer/guide.htm?region=E1, 1103–1104.

89. Al-Ṭabarī, *The History of al-Ṭabarī,* 112–18.

90. We are grateful to Peter Gray for this point.

91. Edward William Lane, *Arabic-English Lexicon*, (Beirut: Librairie Du Liban, 1968), 14.

92. Ibn Kathīr, *The History of Ibn Kathir—Bidaya and Nihaya*, Volume 9, 185.

93. Al-Aṣbahānī, *Muḥaḍarāt al-Udabāʾ wa Muḥ*āwarāt al-Shuʿ*arāʾ wa-l-Bulaghāʾ*, Volume 1, 199.

94. Michael Muhammad Knight, "Queering the Qur'an," *Vice*, November 13, 2012, accessed January 26, 2016, http://www.vice.com/en_ca/read/queering-the-quran.

95. Al-Dhahabī, *Tārīkh al-Islām*, Volume 8, 294; *Siyar A'lām al-Nubalāʾ*, Volume 5, 373.

96. Ibn Kathīr, *The History of Ibn Kathir—Bidaya and Nihaya*, Volume 9, 185.

97. Al-Damīrī, *Hayāt al-Ḥaywān*, Volume 2, 247.

98. El-Rouayheb, *Before Homosexuality*, 45.

99. Al-ʿAynī, Badr al-Dīn. *ʿUmda al-Qārī Sharḥ Ṣaḥīḥ al-Bukhārī*, Volume 8, 403.

100. Everett K. Rowson, "The categorization of gender and sexual irregularity in medieval Arabic vice lists," in *Body Guards: The Cultural Politics of Gender Ambiguity,* eds. Julia Epstein and Kristina Straub, (New York: Routledge, 1991), 57.

101. Ibid, 67.

102. Translation by the authors.

103. Translation by the authors.

104. Al-Rāzī, *Tafsīr al-Rāzī* for 7:81. Translation by the authors.

105. Imani et al., *An Enlightening Commentary*, Parts 7 & 8, 490.

106. Al-Rāzī, *Tafsīr al-Rāzī* for 7:81. Translation by the authors.

107. El-Rouayheb, *Before Homosexuality,* 14–15.

108. Al-Ṭabrasī, *Majma' al-Bayān fī Tafsīr al-Qur'an*. Commentary on verses 7:80–82, in الموسوعة الذهبية للحديث النبوي الشيف و علومه [*The Golden Encyclopedia of the Prophetic Golden Hadeeth and its Sciences*], 2nd edition, (London: Turath Publishing), CD-ROM.

109. El-Rouayheb, *Before Homosexuality*, 126.

110. Ibid, 17.

111. Al-Ṭabrasī, *Majma' al-Bayān fī Tafsīr al-Qur'an*. Commentary on verse 29:28–30.

112. Abu Ali Fadhl ibn Ḥasan Al-Ṭabrasī, *Tafsīr Ṭabrasī*. Commentary on verse 15:70, in الموسوعة الذهبية للحديث النبوي الشيف و علومه [*The Golden Encyclopedia of the Prophetic Golden Hadeeth and its Sciences*], 2nd edition, (London: Turath Publishing), CD-ROM.

113. Email correspondence with Miqdaad Versi.

114. "He wants to repent from homosexuality and needs help," 27176, Islam QA, accessed January 25, 2016, http://islamqa.info/en/27176.

115. Rowson, "Homosexuality in Islamic Law."

116. From Hussein's monograph on verses 4:15–16.

117. "He Wants to Repent," Islam QA.

118. Moiz Amjad, "What is the Punishment for Adultery?" Renaissance Monthly Journal, Last modified May 1, 2002, http://www.javedahmadghamidi.com/renaissance/view/what-is-the-punishment-for-adultery.

119. Adang, "Ibn Ḥazm on Homosexuality," 24.

120. Abdul Majid Daryabadi, *Tafsīr-Ul-Qur'an Translation and Commentary of the Holy Qur'an*, Volume I, (Pakistan: Darul-Isha'at Urdu Bazar, 1991), 310.

121. Ibn Ḥazm, *Ṭawq al-Ḥamāma fī al-ulfa wa-l-Allāf* (Damascus: Maktaba 'Arafa. 1349 A.H./1929-30 C.E.), 139.

122. Ze'ev Maghen, *Virtues of the Flesh—Passion and Purity in Early Islamic Jurisprudence*, (Leiden: Brill, 2005), 261.

123. Ibid, 267.

124. Colin Imber, "Why you should poison your husband: A note on liability in Hanafi law in the Ottoman period," *Islamic Law and Society* 1, no. 2 (1994): 207.

125. Barbara Zollner, "Mithliyyun or Lutiyun? Neo-Orthodoxy and the debate on the unlawfulness of same-sex relations in Islam," in *Islam and Homosexuality*, ed. Samar Habib, (Santa Barbara: Praeger, 2010), 206–207.

126. Al-Zamakhshari, Commentary of 7:80, (Amman: Royal Aal al-Bayt Institute for Islamic Thought), accessed May 10, 2016, http://altafsir.com/.

127. "*Yastabshiruna*" can also be understood as seeking sex because the term "*bashar*" means skin.

128. Imani et al., *An Enlightening Commentary*, Parts 7 and 8, 395–96, 487–88.

129. Ibn al-Qayyim, *Al-Jawāb al-Kāfī li Man Sa'ala 'an al-Dawā' al-Shāfī* , 171. Translation by the authors.

130. Schmitt and Sofer, *Sexuality and Eroticism,* 14.
131. Ibid, 14.
132. El-Rouayheb, *Before Homosexuality,* 17.
133. Ibid, 14.
134. Saleem Kidwai and Ruth Vanita, *Same Sex love in India*, (New York: Palgrave McMillan, 2001), 113, 131–35.
135. Huseyn Hilmi Isik, "Uqubat—Penal Code," in *Seadet i Ebediyye - Endless Bliss*, 1st edition, Hakikat Kitabevi Publications No: 6, accessed January 26, 2016, http://imanveislam.com/kitaplar/english/read/endless6/013.htm.
136. Imber, "Why You Should Poison Your Husband," 214.
137. Pellat uses the word *ma'būn* for the castrated horse. It is not clear if Al-Jāḥiẓ used this word, and if so, whether he used it to mean passive recipient of anal intercourse or a castrated entity.
138. Charles Pellat, "*Liwāṭ*" The Encyclopedia of Islam, Volume 5, eds. C. E. Bosworth, E. Van Donzel, B. Lewis and Ch. Pellat, (Leiden: E.J. Brill, 1983), 776.
139. Aleardo Zanghellini, "Neither homophobic nor (hetero) sexually pure: contextualizing Islam's objections to same-sex sexuality," in *Islam and Homosexuality*, ed. Samar Habib, (Santa Barbara: Praeger, 2009), 206–207.
140. Translation by the authors.
141. Translation by the authors.
142. Imani et al., *An Enlightening Commentary*, Parts 7 and 8, 323.
143. We are grateful to Jamal Bakeer for this point.
144. Ahmad, *The Holy Qur'an*, Volume 3, 1105.
145. Ibid, 1104, 1301–1302.
146. Ibid, 1104–1105.
147. Ibid, 1303.
148. Ibid.
149. Ibid, 1304.
150. Al-Ṭabrasī, *Majma' al-Bayān fī Tafsīr al-Qur'an* for 15:70. Translation by the authors.
151. Ibn Kathīr, *Tafsīr Ibn Kathīr* for 29:33. Translation by the authors.
152. Maududi, "Towards Understanding the Qur'an."
153. We are grateful to an anonymous critic for this point.
154. Email correspondence with Daayiee Abdullah.
155. Tariq Ramadan, *Radical Reform: Islamic Ethics and Liberation*, (New York: Oxford University Press, 2008), 169.
156. Aḥmad Shafaat, "'Death Penalty For Homosexuality, Incest, And Bestiality.' Punishment for adultery in Islam: A detailed examination," March 6, 2005, accessed January 27, 2016, http://www.islamicperspectives.com/Stoning5.htm#Chapter5.
157. Rowson, "Homosexuality in Islamic law."
158. Maududi, "Towards Understanding the Qur'an."
159. El-Rouayheb, *Before homosexuality,* 122.
160. Ibn Abbas, Commentary of 4:15–16, (Amman: Royal Aal al-Bayt Institute for Islamic Thought), accessed May 10, 2016, http://altafsir.com/.
161. Amjad, "What is the Punishment for Adultery?"

162. Allama Muhammad Hussein Ṭabāṭabā'ī, *Tafsīr al-Mīzān*, ed. Husayn al-A'lamī, (Beirut: Manshurat Mu'assasat al-A'lamī li'l-Maṭbū'āt, 1394/1974), 2:211–225, 4:240–243.

163. Mohammad Hashim Kamali, "The Sharia, Law as the Way of God," in *Voices of Islam (5 vols.), Vol I: Voices of Tradition*, ed. Vincent J. Cornell, (Wesport, CT: Praeger Publishers, 2007), 169, 175.

164. Ibid, 158.

165. Anver Emon, *Islamic Natural Law Theories*, (Oxford: Oxford University Press, 2010), 162.

166. M. Hanif Lakdawala, "Muslim Intellectual Inertia and Ijtehad," *Islamic Voice* 13 no. 2 (February 1999): 146, accessed January 28, 2016, http://www.irfi.org/articles3/articles_4601_4700/muslim%20intellectual%20inertia%20and%20ijtehadhtml.htm.

167. Wael Hallaq, *A History of Islamic Legal Theories: An Introduction to Sunni Usul Al Fiqh*, (Cambridge: Cambridge University Press, 1999), 229.

168. Kamali, "The Sharia, Law as the Way of God," 168.

169. Ali, *Sexual Ethics and Islam,* xxi.

170. Hallaq, *A History of Islamic Legal Theories,* 74.

171. Ibid, 191.

172. Mohammad Hashim Kamali, *Principles of Islamic Jurisprudence*, 3rd edition, (Cambridge: The Islamic Texts Society, 2005), 198.

173. Mohammad Fadel, "Is Historicism a Viable Strategy for Islamic Law Reform? The Case of 'Never Shall a Folk Prosper Who Have Appointed a Woman to Rule Them," *Islamic Law & Society*, 2011, accessed January 26, 2016, http://papers.ssrn.com/sol3/papers.cfm?abstract_id=1712968.

174. Kamali, *Principles of Islamic Jurisprudence*, 118.

175. Fadel, "Is Historicism a Viable Strategy."

176. Kamali, *Principles of Islamic Jurisprudence*, 298.

177. John Corvino, "Homosexuality and the PIB Argument," *Ethics* 115 (April 2005), accessed January 26, 2016, http://johncorvino.com/academic/Corvino-PIB.pdf, 512.

178. Kamali, *Principles of Islamic Jurisprudence*, 333, 517.

Chapter 3

Analyzing the Hadith Tradition

The Prophet, Companions, and the Followers

Apart from the Qur'an, conservative scholars support their position by Hadith texts and opinions of the Muslim jurists. For the purposes of this chapter, the sayings of the Prophet, the Companions, and their followers—*tābiʿūn*—would all be categorized in the second source of Islamic knowledge—the Hadith. The narratives from the Prophet, his Companions, and their followers on same-sex conduct may be classified into five broad categories—first, Sunnī traditions that either condemn or call for the death penalty for homosexual conduct; second, Sunnī traditions that condemn adopting the behavior of the opposite gender; third, Sunnī traditions that report the rulings of the Companions on same-sex conduct; fourth, Sunnī traditions, mostly attributed to the followers, that are more of a descriptive nature; and fifth, Shī'ī traditions on same-sex conduct respectively between males and between females—*liwāṭ* and *siḥāq*. While the opinions of the past Sunnī jurists and to some extent Shī'ī authorities will be critically delineated in chapter 5, the texts that comprise the first four categories will be analyzed as follows along with Ibn Ḥazm's (d. 1064) critique of these texts.

3.1 CONDEMNATORY SUNNĪ TRADITIONS—SAME-SEX CONDUCT

There seem to be nine strands of Sunnī texts that are attributed to the Prophet. These texts, some of which are eschatological in nature, have the Prophet prescribe the death penalty for *liwāṭ*, define *liwāṭ* as adultery, or portentously express concern on Muslims engaging in *liwāṭ*. However, even contemporary conservative Muslim scholars like Sheikh Mohamed el-Moctar el-Shinqiti[1] have questioned the authenticity of these texts, specifically of those that have the Prophet prescribe the death penalty for *liwāṭ*. It is important to note that none of the nine strands of Prophetic texts are found in the more celebrated works of Bukhārī (d. 870) and Muslim (d. 875) because of the strong doubts that both these and other Hadith authorities have raised on these texts.

Apart from these nine strands of texts, there are other Hadith texts that are quoted on the net but which are not as strong enough as these already deemed weak nine strands of texts. One text that is often quoted reads, "When a man mounts another man, the throne of God shakes."[2] This text is found in the Shī'ī Tafsīr compiled by Ayatollah Sayyid Kamal Faghih Imani and others, and suggests that Allah's heaven trembles when *liwāṭ* is committed by the adolescent or when the act is committed on him.[3] The Tafsīr also presents the Hadith on the punishment by a rein of fire for kissing a boy lustfully.[4] Thus, even if the transmission chain of narrators is not investigated, it is clear that the text that indicates the shaking of God's throne mentions it in the context of exploiting adolescent youth.

Another text, which seems to be a composite of the texts presented in Sections 3.1.6 and 3.2.2, and supposedly referenced from Ṭabarānī (d. 970) and Bayhaqī (d. 1066), reads, "Four types of people get up in the morning while they are under the wrath of Allah and they sleep in the night while they are under the displeasure of Allah . . . those men who try to resemble women and those women who try to resemble men and those who commit sex with animals and those men who commit sex with men."[5] The same weaknesses that mar the texts in Sections 3.1.6 and 3.2.2 would also affect this composite text.

3.1.1 Hadith I[6]

A Prophetic narrative that is usually traced to Ibn ʿAbbās (d. 687), and deemed the most authentic in this category of Hadith, has been reported in different sources and is reproduced below in its variant forms.

> Whoever you find doing the deed of the people of Lūṭ, kill the one who does it and the one to whom it is done. (Sunan Abu Dawūd)
>
> The Prophet cursed the people that do the work of the people of Lūṭ. (Sunan al-Nasā'ī)
>
> Whoever you find doing the deed of the people of Lūṭ, kill the one who does it and the one to whom it is done. And whoever has sex with the animal then kill the man and the animal. (Musnad Ibn Ḥanbal)

So far as the authenticity of this strand of narratives is concerned, Bukhārī (d. 870) categorized the Hadith as *munkar* (implausible), especially given the issue of killing of the already violated animal. Likewise, other authorities like al-Nasāʾī (d. 915), Abu Dawūd (d. 889), Abu Ḥātim (d. 890), Yaḥyā ibn Maʿīn (d. 233 AH/852), Abu Zurʿa (d. 264 AH/883), and Darāquṭnī (d. 995), who terms this Hadith as *matrūk* (abandoned), all impugn the authenticity of this narrative.[7] Moreover, the fact that this Hadith has been related only from ʿIkrima (d. 723–24), only one of the six principal students of Ibn ʿAbbās, and given the reservations of authorities like Ibn ʿUmar (d. 693), Saʿīd ibn al-Musayyib (d. 715), and Mālik ibn Anas (d. 795) against ʿIkrima as untrustworthy only casts further doubt on the authenticity of this narrative.[8] Moreover, it is surprising to note that while this Hadith is deemed the most authentic in this category of narratives, it suffers from weakness in each of the narrators in the transmission chain apart from the fact that ʿIkrima has been branded as a liar by some Hadith authorities.

3.1.2 Hadith II

The second Prophetic narrative, traced back to Abu Hurayra (d. 681), is reproduced below.

> Stone the upper and the lower, stone them both. (Ibn Māja)

The authenticity of this narrative has been impugned, essentially by the branding of one of the narrators in the transmission chain, ʿĀṣim ibn ʿUmar, as weak by authorities like Yaḥyā Ibn Maʿīn (d. 233 AH/852), Abu Ḥātim (d. 890), Ibrāhīm al-Juzjānī (d. 872), and Hārūn ibn Mūsā al-Farwi (d. 867), apart from the celebrated Bukhārī, as well as al-Nasāʾī, who in fact termed the Hadith as *matrūk* (abandoned).[9] In fact, according to Sheikh Mohamed el-Moctar el-Shinqiti, except for Ibn Ḥibbān (d. 965) among the early scholars and al-Albani (d. 1999) from amongst the contemporary ones, no other scholar seems to have deemed the narratives in 3.1.1 and 3.1.2 as authentic. El-Shinqti goes to state that Hadith experts deem Ibn Ḥibbān's opinions as unreliable if they are not substantiated by other Hadith experts and likewise al-Albani's opinions pale in comparison with the doubts raised on these narratives by celebrated authorities like Bukhārī, Ibn Maʿīn, and Ibn Ḥajar (d. 1449) amongst others.[10]

3.1.3 Hadith III[11]

The third Prophetic narrative, traced back to Jābir ibn Abdullah (d. 697), is reproduced below in its variant forms.

> Whoever does the work of the people of Lūṭ, kill him.
>
> I fear most for my people is the work of the people of Lūṭ.

The authenticity of this narrative has been impugned by authorities like Yaḥyā ibn Saʿīd al-Qaṭṭān (d. 198 AH/817) apart from the celebrated Mālik (d. 795) and Aḥmad ibn Ḥanbal (d. 855) in relation to one of the narrators in the chain Abdullah ibn Muhammad ibn ʿAqīl (d. 686).[12]

3.1.4 Hadith IV

The fourth Prophetic narrative equates sexual conduct between males with adultery and it seems that it is perhaps from this narrative some jurists equated same-sex sexual conduct with *zinā* and therefore prescribed the same penalty for same-sex sexual conduct as that prescribed for *zinā*.

> If a man comes to a man (for sex) then they committed adultery.

The authenticity of this narrative has been impugned by authorities like Abu al-Fatih, Muhammad ibn Wāsiʿ al-Azdī (d. 127AH/744), Ṭabarānī (d. 970), and Abu Ḥātim (d. 890) who declared one of the narrators in the transmission chain, Muhammad ibn ʿAbd al-Raḥmān al-Qushayrī, as a liar.

3.1.5 Hadith V

The fifth Prophetic narrative, traced back to both Abu Hurayra (d. 681) and Ibn ʿAbbās (d. 687), is eschatological in its essence and refers to a speech he gave in Medina.

> . . . and whoever penetrates a woman or a child or a man in their anuses then he comes on the day of judgment smelling worse than the dead animal until he goes to hell. (Musnad al-Ḥārith)

The authenticity of this narrative has been impugned by authorities like Abu Zurʿa (d. 264 AH/883), Abu Ḥātim (d. 890), and Darāquṭnī (d. 995), apart from the celebrated Bukhārī and Aḥmad ibn Ḥanbal, who held reservations against one of the narrators, Dawūd ibn al-Maḥbar (d. 206 AH/821–22), in the chain of transmission.[13]

3.1.6 Hadith VI[14]

The sixth Prophetic narrative, traced back to Abu Hurayra, is also condemnatory in nature, albeit it mentions same-sex sexual conduct with a whole array of other behaviors. Sometimes, in order to draw out the gravity of *liwāṭ*, it is mentioned that the Prophet never cursed anyone thrice except for *liwāṭ*.[15]

> Cursed, cursed, cursed, who does the work of the people of Lūṭ. Cursed who marries a woman and her daughter. Cursed who cursed something of his parents. Cursed who had sex with animals. Cursed who changed the boundaries of the earth. Cursed who slaughters for other than Allah. And cursed who takes allies other than his allies.

The authenticity of this narrative has been impugned by authorities like Abu Ḥātim (d. 890), Ibn Ḥibbān (d. 965), al-Nasāʾī (d. 915), Darāquṭnī (d. 995), and the celebrated Bukhārī (d. 870), all of whom cast doubt on the trustworthiness of one of the narrators, Hārūn al-Taymī, in the transmission chain.[16]

3.1.7 Hadith VII[17]

The seventh narrative, traced back to Al-Nuʿmān ibn Bashīr al-Anṣārī (d. 684), is actually presented as depicting the words of the angel Gabriel as opposed to those of the Prophet.

> O Muhammad, a blessed people your nation, except that they have remnants of the works of the people of Lūṭ.

The authenticity of this narrative has been impugned by authorities including Bukhārī and Aḥmad Ibn Ḥanbal, both of whom cast doubt on the trustworthiness of one of the narrators, Mujālid ibn Saʿīd (d. 761–2), in the transmission chain.[18]

3.1.8 Hadith VIII[19]

The eighth Prophetic narrative, similar to the third narrative and likewise traced back to Jābir ibn Abdullah (d. 697) but eschatological in essence, is reproduced below.

> The most I fear for my people after me is the work of the people of Lūṭ, so my nation will have to wait for anguish if the women are (sexually) happy with women and the men with men.

The authenticity of this narrative has been impugned by authorities who questioned the trustworthiness of the narrators in the transmission chain. Essentially, ʿAbd al-Raḥmān ibn Thābit ibn Thawbān has been deemed weak, whereas the other narrators in the chain, al-Ḥasan ibn Jarīr and ʿUthmān ibn Saʿīd, have been categorized as unknown.[20]

3.1.9 Hadith IX[21]

The ninth and final Prophetic narrative in the category of condemnatory Hadith, traced back to Jābir ibn Abdullah, is reproduced below.

> If adultery became widespread, then taking female slaves will become widespread and if Lūṭism (having sex with males in the anus) increased, then God will raise his hand from creation and will not care in which valley they meet their end. (also in Mu'jam Kabīr of Ṭabarānī)

The authenticity of this narrative has been impugned by authorities who have essentially cast doubt on the trustworthiness of 'Abd al-Khāliq ibn Zayd ibn Wāqid, one of the narrators in the transmission chain, accusing him of fabrication.[22]

The strongest amongst these nine strands of texts, classified as Hadith I, appears in Sunan of Abu Dawūd (d. 889), which, as noted earlier, has been impugned not only by authorities like Mālik (d. 795) and Bukhārī but also by Abu Dawūd himself. Likewise, several authorities including Bukhārī, Mālik, Yaḥyā al-Qaṭṭān (d. 198 AH/817), Yaḥyā ibn Ma'īn (d. 233 AH/852), Ibrāhīm al-Juzjānī (d. 872), Abu Zur'a (d. 264 AH/883), Abu Ḥātim (d. 890), al-Nasā'ī (d. 915), Ṭabarānī (d. 970), Darāquṭnī (d. 995), and even Ibn Ḥanbal (d. 855), who is known to have accepted weak hadith over *qiyās* (analogy), had cast doubts on the authenticity of these Prophetic texts by recourse to a whole array of opinions, including treating the texts as *munkar* (implausible) or *matrūk* (abandoned), by branding the narrators in the transmission chain as liars or fabricators, by deeming the narrators as untrustworthy, unknown, or weak, or by emphasizing the weakness of the entire transmission chain.[23]

The absence of any authentic narrative traced back to the Prophet may also be bolstered by Ibn al-Qayyim's (d. 1349/1350) statement that the danger of pederasty was absent during the Prophet's time.[24] Likewise, the Syrian belletrist Aḥmad al-Barbīr (d. 1817), based on the absence of love poetry for boys, and the Egyptian scholar Mar'ī ibn Yūsuf al-Karmī (d. 1624) both opined that Arabs in pre-Islamic and Islamic times were not inclined toward pederasty,[25] which also substantiates the absence of any authentic narrative traced back to the Prophet on *liwāṭ*. In contrast, one researcher has indicated that the Quraysh tribe of the Prophet contained many passive homosexuals,[26] which seems to be reflected when Abu Jahl is depicted as suffering from *'ubna*, which he satisfied with stones instead of allowing himself to be penetrated.[27] Likewise, Kugle notes that Salah al-Din Munajjid (d. 2010) documented the existence of same-sex practices among both men and women in pre-Islamic Arabia.[28] However, given the text that depicts that the first person to have been suspected of *liwāṭ* was in 'Umar's time[29] casts doubt on the thesis that the Quraysh contained many *ma'buns*-passive homosexuals.

3.2 CONDEMNATORY SUNNĪ TRADITIONS—GENDER EXPRESSION

Apart from these texts, there exist three strands of texts, classified as follows, that seem to condemn the *mukhannath*-feminine male/masculine female, which are sometimes used by conservative scholars to condemn gays and lesbians. However, it is important to note that the *mukhannathūn* of Medina cannot be classified as "homosexual"[30] as the *'ubna* disease was rarely associated with the *mukhannathūn.*[31] While jurists like Ḥaṣkafī (d. 1677) defined the *mukhannath* as the one penetrated like a woman,[32] many jurists have been clear that effeminacy is not evidence of *liwāṭ*.

The texts in this section depict the Prophet as banishing the *mukhannathūn*. However, Hadith experts have also deemed all three strands of texts as weak based on their analysis of the transmission chains. Notwithstanding the fact that one of these texts appears in the canon of Bukhārī, authorities like Qatāda (d. 735), Ibn Ḥajar al-ʿAsqalānī (d. 1448), Mālik, Yaḥyā ibn Maʿīn, Abu Zurʿa, and Abu Ḥātim among others had cast doubts on the authenticity of these Prophetic texts by branding the narrators in the transmission chain as liars or fabricators, by deeming the narrators as questionable or unknown or by expressing concern in the transmission chain not connecting back to the Prophet.[33] Even if one disregards the weakness in the transmission chain, based on *matn* (content) analysis, it cannot be reasonably concluded that the *mukhannathūn* in the texts were exiled for their innate characteristics.

3.2.1 Hadith I

The strongest Prophetic narrative that is traced back to Umm Salama (d. 680) and ʿĀ'isha (d. 678) actually has the Prophet prohibiting a *mukhannath* from entering their quarters. This narrative is reproduced below in its two variant forms.

> The mukhannath said to the brother of Umm Salama: If God opened Ṭa'if to you tomorrow, then I will lead you to daughter of Ghīlān, for she comes forward with four and backwards with eight. The Prophet said: "This man does not enter on you after this."
>
> ʿĀ'isha said to a mukhannath in Medina: "Would you tell us about a woman to get her engaged to Abdullah ibn Abu Bakr?" Upon hearing the mukhannath's description, the Prophet responded: "Get out of Medina to Ḥamrā' al-Asad and in it will be your house."

The authenticity of this Hadith has been questioned by the fact that the tracing of the narrative is not unique, that is, either it leads to ʿĀ'isha or

Umm Salama. The other issue is that one of the narrators, Hishām ibn ʿUrwa (d. 772), has been deemed weak by Hadith experts, specifically because of the observation that the transmission chain is not appropriately connected to the Prophet. However, despite these limitations, this narrative still appears to be stronger than any of the narratives in Section 3.1, which necessitates a *matn* (content)-based analysis of this narrative.

Ibn Ḥajar al-ʿAsqalānī (d. 1448)[34] writes that the *mukhannath* in question was allowed in female quarters owing to his innate disposition, that is, absence of sexual attraction toward women. However, it is also important to note that, according to Rowson,[35] the presence of attraction toward males cannot be assumed in the context of the *mukhannath* of Medina. Regardless of the innate disposition of the *mukhannath* mentioned in this narrative, Ibn Ḥajar mentions that he was exiled either because of his exposing private matters of women or because he exhibited sexual desires for females. In either case, one may reasonably conclude, as does Kugle,[36] that the *mukhannath* was exiled because of his untoward behavior and not because of his innate characteristics. It may also be interesting to note that according to some sources, two other *mukhannath* were exiled to Ḥamrā' al-Asad or Dhī al-Ḥalīfa, depending on the narrative, to join the *mukhannath* mentioned in this Hadith.[37] Thus, even if one disregards the weakness inherent in this strand of narratives, based on *matn* (content)-based analysis, it cannot be reasonably concluded that people could be exiled based on their innate characteristics, whether their inner constitution is that of a *mukhannath* or by any analogy a gay or lesbian in the contemporary context. It may also be noted that Kugle[38] also concludes that the *mukhannath* was exiled for spreading lewdness and not because of innate characteristics.

3.2.2 Hadith II

The second strand of Prophetic narratives, traced back to Ibn ʿAbbās, Abu Hurayra, and Ibn ʿUmar, is reproduced below in its variant forms.

> The Prophet distanced the men that try to look like women and the women who try to look like men and He said: "Get them out of your houses and ʿUmar exiled so and so." (Ibn ʿAbbās)[39]
>
> The Prophet said take the mukhannathūn out of your houses and the Prophet made one leave and ʿUmar did too. (Ibn ʿAbbās)[40]
>
> The Prophet cursed or exiled the men that try to resemble women and the women that try to resemble men and the ones that ride the wilderness alone. (Abu Hurayra)[41]
>
> The Prophet cursed or exiled the men that try to resemble women and the women that try to resemble men. (Ibn ʿUmar)[42]

The strongest amongst these narratives is the first one as it appears in the relatively more authentic Ṣaḥīḥ Bukhārī text. However, given that it has come from ʿIkrima, who, as noted earlier, has been branded as a liar by authorities like Ibn ʿUmar, Saʿīd ibn al-Musayyib (d. 715), and Muhammad ibn Sīrīn (d. 728), apart from the reservations held by Mālik ibn Anas and Qatāda (d. 735), it severely weakens the strength of this narrative.[43] The fact that the next narrator, Yaḥyā ibn Abi Kathīr (d. 749), in the transmission chain, has also been accused of fabrication only adds to this weakness.[44] These criticisms suggest that this Hadith is not on par with the other Hadiths of Bukhārī and may even be considered weak by some scholars. The authenticity of the second narrative, also recorded in a relatively authentic work Muṣannaf ʿAbd al-Razzāq (d. 744), has also been questioned, as, like the first, it has been traced back to Ibn ʿAbbās through ʿIkrima and Yaḥyā ibn Abi Kathīr.

The third and fourth narratives appear in Musnad Ibn Ḥanbal, a compilation that includes Hadith as long as a liar does not narrate them. However, such Hadith may suffer from other weaknesses. The latter two narratives fall short of the authenticity test, as one of the narrators, Tayyib ibn Muhammad, in the Abu Hurayra narrative has been deemed as an unknown person,[45] whereas Thuwair, one of the narrators in the Ibn ʿUmar narrative, has been deemed as a liar by Sufyān al-Thawrī (d. 778), and he has also been deemed questionable by several authorities like Yaḥyā ibn Maʿīn, Ibrāhīm al-Juzjānī, Abu Zurʿa, and Abu Ḥātim.[46]

Like the narratives in 3.2.1, these narratives also mention the exile of the *mukhannathūn* from Muslim households; however, these narratives appear to be much weaker based on the investigation of the transmission chains. One key difference between the narratives in 3.2.1 and this section is that these also allude to ʿUmar following in the footsteps of the Prophet. Ignoring the weaknesses in the transmission chains, one may note that Ibn Ḥajar al-ʿAsqalānī mentions in his work *Fatḥ al-Bārī* that ʿUmar acknowledging the beauty of a good-looking man decided to exile him to Basra to join his previously exiled friend Naṣr ibn Ḥajjāj. It is interesting to note that the man was exiled to the then cosmopolitan town of Basra to join his friend as opposed to a barren desert. No matter how tempting it may be to conclude that perhaps ʿUmar's decision to exile the man, to a cosmopolitan town as opposed to letting him stay in the more rigid environment of the desert Arabs, may have been the starting point for the rights of differently oriented persons, it would be best to avoid any unnecessary speculation. Furthermore, while Ibn Ḥajar records that Abu Dhuayb requested ʿUmar to exile him to Basra where Naṣr ibn Ḥajjāj had already been exiled, other texts indicate that Naṣr ibn Ḥajjāj was previously exiled as the Medinese women were tempted by his good looks,[47] which does not allow for making any conclusions about the sexual orientation of the exiled people.

Ibn Ḥajar also mentions that on the basis of these narratives which merely mention exiling the *mukhannathūn*, the Hadith that mention killing of the active and passive partner in homosexual intercourse, as seen in Sections 3.1.1 and 3.1.2, might be classified as weak; however, such a conclusion would be weakened by the fact that not one *mukhannath* was proved or accused of being a passive partner in sex with another male. Not discounting Ibn Ḥajar's point, the severe weaknesses in the narratives mentioned in 3.1.1 and 3.1.2 have already been noted and as such they may not require further proof, if any, to discredit them. Nevertheless, ignoring the weaknesses in the transmission chains, these narratives can be potentially abused by some to preach a strong social ostracism of gay and lesbians on the basis of a derived analogy with the *mukhannath*.

3.2.3 Hadith III

The third and final strand of Prophetic narratives traced back to Abu Hurayra and Abu Saʿīd al-Khudrī (d. 682–4, 693), is respectively reproduced below.

> A mukhannath was brought to the Prophet with Henna on his hands and feet. It was said to the Prophet: "He is imitating women." So, the Prophet ordered that he be exiled to al-Naqīʿ. They said: "O Prophet of Allah: Should we not kill him?" He replied: "I was forbidden from killing the ones that pray." (Abu Hurayra)[48]

> A mukhannath was brought to the Prophet with Henna on his hands and feet, so the friends of the Prophet started to hit him with their shoes. The Prophet said: "Be careful of this one and his friends for your women." The friends said should we not kill him. The Prophet replied: "I was forbidden from killing the ones that pray." (Abu Saʿīd al-Khudrī)[49]

It may be noted that the transmission chains are quite weak for both narratives, even though the first narrative appears in the more noted work of Sunan Abu Dawūd. It has been noted by experts that one of the narrators in the first narrative, Abu Yasār al-Qurashī,[50] is an unknown and that another narrator, Al-Khaṣīb ibn Jaḥdar,[51] in the second narrative was deemed as a liar by the authority Yaḥyā ibn Maʿīn. Disregarding the weakness in the transmission chain, if the content of the Hadith is analyzed, it may be noted that the penalty of exile was not mentioned in one of the versions and only caution was suggested by the Prophet in the specific context of access by the *mukhannath* to female quarters. Therefore, as in the context of the narratives in 3.2.1, the issue at stake is one of any lewdness that could impact women rather than that of the innate characteristics of the *mukhannath* and certainly not same-sex sexual conduct.

3.3 CONDEMNATORY SUNNĪ TRADITIONS: THE COMPANIONS

Apart from the texts attributed to the Prophet, there exist other texts that mention the conduct of the Companions and the opinions of their followers—the *tābiʿūn*. In what follows, narratives from senior Companions Abu Bakr (d. 634), ʿUmar (d. 644), and ʿAli (d. 661) apart from other notable authorities like Ibn ʿAbbās (d. 687) and Ibn Zubayr (d. 692) are delineated.

3.3.1 Abu Bakr—The First Caliph

The most notable incident mentions the first Caliph burning a man at the behest of ʿAli. While this incident does not appear in the relatively strong works of Bukhārī and Muslim, it does appear in both the works of Bayhaqī (d. 1066) and Ṭabarī (d. 923). The narrative traced back to Ṣafwān ibn Salīm is reproduced below.

> Khālid ibn al-Walīd wrote to Abu Bakr during his reign that he found a man in some of the Arab areas who was penetrated like women. Abu Bakr gathered a group of friends of the Prophet for counsel. The one with the most severe opinion was ʿAli who said: "This is a sin that only a single nation committed before us and God punished them in the way you know. I suggest that we burn him in the fire," and so they agreed that he be burnt. Abu Bakr wrote to Khālid that he be burnt.[52]

The authenticity of this narrative is brought into question by noting that one of the narrators ʿAbd al-ʿAzīz ibn Abi Ḥāzim (d. 800/184 AH) has been referencing the works of the fabricator Sulaymān ibn Bilāl, although this critique is tempered by the fact that ʿAbd al-ʿAzīz ibn Abi Ḥāzim quoted this narrative from his father as opposed to referencing Sulaymān ibn Bilāl.[53] Moreover, while the work of Bayhaqī itself contains the observation that this narrative is not connected all the way back to Abu Bakr himself, it does indicate that three variant narratives as traced back to ʿAli through Jaʿfar ibn Muhammad (d. 765) and Abu Layla also exist. One of these alternate narratives indicates that ʿAli had someone stoned and burnt, whereas another narrative indicates that ʿAli had a married man stoned for committing the actions of the people of Lūṭ.[54] A text supposedly attributed to Ibn ʿAbbās indicates that ʿAli had two people burnt and Abu Bakr had a wall toppled over them.[55] The variant narratives may refer to different incidents, which further casts doubt on the authenticity of the Abu Bakr narrative.

However, the presence of these alternate narratives makes it unlikely to easily dismiss the narrative on burning or stoning those who commit the acts of the people of Lūṭ on the basis of critiquing the transmission chain. Since this narrative does not appear to be as weak as those found in Section 3.1, this would entail conducting a *matn* (content)-based analysis. One critique that has been leveled on the basis of content is that there exist stronger Hadith-based proofs that prohibit Muslims from executing capital punishment with fire as only God has the prerogative to do so and this puts the authenticity of these narratives into question, unless Abu Bakr or 'Ali was not aware of those Hadith. Two instances of narratives that forbid killing with fire are reproduced below. The first is traced back to the Prophet through Abu Hurayra and the second is actually traced to Ibn ʿAbbās who references the Prophet in his statement.

> The Prophet said: "I ordered you earlier to burn so and so, but no one should punish with fire except Allah, so do not burn the two of them but instead kill them." (Abu Hurayra)[56]

> Some zanādiqa (atheists) were brought to 'Ali and he burnt them. The news of this event, reached Ibn ʿAbbās who said: "If I had been in his place, I would not have burnt them, as Allah's Apostle forbade it," saying, "Do not punish anybody with Allah's punishment (fire)." I would have killed them according to the statement of Allah's Apostle, "Whoever changed his (Islamic) religion, then kill him."[57]

Based on the Ibn ʿAbbās narrative, it becomes clear that instances that depict 'Ali having someone burnt actually are possibly linked with the issue of apostasy. Notwithstanding authenticity issues, just as in the case of the Abu Bakr narrative, it may be deduced simply based on the content that '*amal qawm Lūṭ* was understood as a compound crime that involved rejecting God's message after having been convinced of its veracity. Likewise, given that verse 5:32 makes the exception for capital punishment only for murder and spreading mischief further casts doubt into reading capital punishment for same-sex sexual conduct on the basis of these narratives.

Kugle indicates that Abu Bakr had the alleged person burnt for compound actions that included apostasy and highway robbery, as Kugle critiques that it would seem implausible for a person nicknamed as *Fujā'a* (Lion) to have been passively penetrated. Given the desert Arab norms, it would have been likelier that he would have been the active penetrator, and thus, Kugle mentions that perhaps the note on the apostate getting penetrated was a later fabrication.[58] The fact that the words *liwāṭ* and *Lūṭī* were defined later by the jurists adds to the Qur'anic analysis in chapter 2 that the people of Lūṭ were condemned for the compound action of rejecting God's Prophet and *fisād fī al-arḍ* (corruption on earth), as mentioned in verse 5:32, through highway robbery. This line of reasoning is substantiated from another source that mentions that the person in the narrative, Iyas ibn Abdullah ibn Yalail, not only left Islam along with his tribe Bani Amer but also killed the followers of the Prophet in their tribe.[59] Moreover, Ibn ʿAbd al-Barr (d. 1071) mentions in his book *Istidhkār* that the perpetrator in question was actually a chief of his tribe who not only left Islam but also killed Muslims in large numbers. Thus, a contextual analysis thoroughly discredits the much popular Abu Bakr burning narrative, which then implies that any deduction from this narrative for loving same-sex unions would be extremely far-fetched.

3.3.2 ʿUmar—The Second Caliph

A relatively authentic narrative, that casts doubt upon the Abu Bakr narrative as it indicates that the first indicant of any homosexual behavior was noted at the time of the second Caliph, has been traced back to ʿĀ'isha via Shihāb Zuhrī (d. 741/2), and reported in the Muṣannaf ʿAbd al-Razzāq as follows.

> The first to be suspected of the ugly deed (the work of the people of Lūṭ) was at the time of ʿUmar, who ordered some of the young men from Quraysh not to sit with him.[60]

So far as the authenticity of this narrative is concerned, all the narrators in the transmission chain appear trustworthy, and based on the words used, "the ugly deed," it becomes apparent that one specific action has been mentioned as opposed to the more general description *ʿamal qawm Lūṭ* (actions of the people of Lūṭ). Any critique of this narrative, which is not found in relatively more authentic texts of Bukhārī or Muslim, would then require a *matn* (content)-based analysis. While the ugly deed in question has not been defined in the narrative, the possibility of anal penetration may not be excluded from the text. It is interesting to note that the person in the narrative was neither punished nor exiled, as the *mukhannath* allegedly were, and likewise only some young men, as opposed to all, were prohibited to associate with him, perhaps because the man was not found guilty but only suspected of the deed. Moreover, since the men who perform "the act of the people of Lūṭ" generally meant men who like to have sex with young men or adolescent boys who have not yet shown their beards, ʿUmar may have only ordered the vulnerable from sitting next to the man. However, not much can be concluded on the basis of this narrative, neither that the purport of ʿUmar's decision was social ostracism as he did not forbid everyone to sit with the man and nor that the Caliph was prescribing a tolerant approach toward alleged homosexual conduct, specifically if one were to note that the good-looking man allegedly exiled by ʿUmar was sent to a metropolis Basra rather than a barren desert, for both would amount to mere speculation in the absence of additional proof. It is also important to note that later jurists including Ibn Ḥazm, whose approach is deemed as being the most soft amongst the five Sunnī schools of jurisprudence, did not rely on this narrative to prescribe any ruling on homosexual conduct.

3.3.3 'Ali—The Fourth Caliph

While there do not appear to be narratives indicating that the third Caliph ʿUthmān (d. 656) dealt with the issue of homosexual conduct, three variants of a narrative traced back to Al-Qāsim ibn al-Walīd exist in the work of Bayhaqī. One of these narratives is reproduced below.

'Ali stoned a Lūṭī

So far as the authenticity in terms of the transmission chain of this narrative is concerned, while both Ibn Maʿīn and Al-ʿIjlī deem Qāsim ibn al-Walīd as trustworthy, another expert Ibn Saʿīd, in contrast, indicated that he did make mistakes.[61] This weakness in the transmission chain may then indicate either that similar narratives on 'Ali traced back to Jaʿfar ibn Muhammad and Abu Layla, as noted in Section 3.3.1, are also weak as they too are found in the works of Bayhaqī, or that three weak narratives put together could provide some proof on 'Ali stoning someone for homosexual conduct, specifically anal penetration. However, according to contemporary scholar Sheikh Mohamed el-Moctar el-Shinqiti, the scholars of Hadith mention that the traditions indicating that 'Ali adopted the opinion of stoning the sodomite are even weaker than the Hadith mentioned in 3.1.1 and 3.1.2, which were already deemed to be extremely weak.[62]

Narratives which use the word *Lūṭī* may be critiqued on the basis of *matn* (content)-based analysis as it seems the word *Lūṭī* or *liwāṭ* did not appear to have a concrete meaning during the time of the Companions and as such was a product of later juristic work, which would then cast further doubt on the authenticity of the narrative based on the *matn* (content) of the text. While Section 3.4 will build the case for the fact that the words *Lūṭī* and *liwāṭ* did not have concrete meanings during the times of the Companions, it may be worth noting that some Shī'ī jurisprudential scholars may use these narratives to prescribe capital punishment for homosexual conduct, while tolerating anal intercourse with wives and perhaps male slaves.[63] In contemporary times, Ayatollahs Ṭabāṭabā'ī, Sistānī and Lankarānī have all deemed anal intercourse with one's wife permissible, but undesirable, given the consent of the wife. It may also be argued that if such narratives were indeed authentic, then the later jurists would not have disagreed on addressing homosexual conduct and in fact would have relied specifically on these narratives for guidance.

3.3.4 Ibn ʿAbbās—Paternal cousin of the Prophet

Apart from the narratives supposedly describing the conduct of the Caliphs, there also exist texts that indicate that some prominent Companions enforced capital punishment for homosexual conduct. One such narrative attributed to Ibn ʿAbbās and traced back through ʿIkrima is reproduced below.

> If a virgin male is found on 'al-Lūṭīyya' then he is to be stoned.[64]

There appear to be four variants of these narratives, some of which are deemed quite weak as they are traced back through ʿIkrima, who has been accused of lying, as noted before, whereas other variants do not include ʿIkrima but do include another narrator later in the chain, Ibn Khathīm, who was impugned as a soft Hadith person in the same source, the *Sunan Kubrā*, that delineated these narratives. So far as content-based analysis is concerned, just as in the case of the narrative on 'Ali, it may be noted that the word *al-Lūṭīyya* would need to be defined as it did not have a concrete meaning during the time of the Companions. While some may argue that the particularizing *al-* has been used in the construction of the world *al-Lūṭīyya* and as such the word would refer to a particular action, specifically anal intercourse between males predominately in the context of pederasty, disease, and slavery, it may also be noted that *al-* has other meanings beyond its role of particularizing a word. Moreover, as in the case of the Abu Bakr narratives, a heavy penalty as stoning could only have been enforced on a more serious or compound crime. It may also be appreciated that the words in the narrative are not Ibn ʿAbbās's words but paraphrased by the later followers, which further substantiates the claim that these words were not in vogue during the time of the Companions. Moreover, given the fact that one of the narrators in the transmission chain, Mujāhid (d. 722), believed that anal intercourse between males was to be prescribed the same penalty as that for *zinā*, according to which unmarried adulterers are flogged as opposed to stoned, lends further reason to doubt the authenticity of this text. Thus, both through critiquing the content of the text and the weakness in the transmission chain, these narratives by Ibn ʿAbbās cannot be used as a proof to condemn homosexual conduct, let alone loving same-sex unions.

3.3.5 Ibn Zubayr—Abu Bakr's Grandson and ʿĀ'isha's Nephew

The narrative attributed to Ibn Zubayr is strong enough at least by the standards of Aḥmad ibn Ḥanbal on the basis of the transmission chain,[65] although the texts on homosexual conduct from Ibn Zubayr are deemed as untrustworthy by Ibn Ḥazm as he notes that some of the narrators are unknown.

This narrative traced back to ʿAtā' ibn Abi Rabāḥ (d. 734/735) is reproduced below.

> I witnessed Ibn Zubayr bring seven who were in liwāṭa. Four of them married and three unmarried. So, he had the four married ones stoned and the three unmarried flogged according to the Ḥadd (of Zinā), while Ibn ʿUmar and Ibn ʿAbbās were in the mosque.[66]

Notwithstanding Ibn Ḥazm's reservations on the transmission chain, on the basis of content-based analysis, a similar critique can be leveled on this text, as was employed in the case of the 'Ali and Ibn ʿAbbās narratives, in that the usage of the word *liwāṭa* would need to be defined as it did not have a concrete meaning during the time of the Companions. While this critique would weaken the strength of this narrative, the fact that the text distinguishes between married and unmarried perpetrators would indicate that anal penetration could indeed be the purport of this text. However, given the fact that later jurists did not use these narratives to specify the penalty of homosexual conduct would cast doubt on the authenticity of this narrative. It is also important to note that given the fact that Ibn ʿAbbās is mentioned in the narrative and is not reported to have contested the punishment would cast further doubt on the Ibn ʿAbbās narrative in Section 3.3.3, for in that narrative the unmarried perpetrator was condemned to death. Alternatively, it could mean that Ibn ʿAbbās considered this punishment acceptable, although he himself preferred otherwise.

In summary, chief amongst the Companion narratives is the incident of Abu Bakr (d. 634), which has not only been deemed weak but it also leads to the alternate viewpoint that since the so-called "homosexual" was executed as he had killed many Muslims during the Ridda Wars,[67] it may reflect that the Companions understood the phrase *'amal qawm Lūṭ* as a composite of apostasy, murder, and perhaps penetration of other males. This supports the viewpoint that the understanding of the words *Lūṭī* and *liwāṭ* as exclusively connoting homosexual anal intercourse was a product of later juristic work. It is, therefore, interesting to note that when some conservative Muslims make the argument that no jurist refers to a highway robber as a *Lūṭī* and that the word is exclusively used to refer to the one involved in homosexual anal intercourse, they have to take into account that such words did not have a precise meaning during the time of the Companions or the *tābiʿūn*.

3.4 DEFINITION-BASED SUNNĪ TEXTS—THE *TĀBIʿŪN*

While the Hadith narratives in Sections 3.1 and 3.2 could be simply critiqued on the basis of the severe weaknesses in their transmission chains, the narratives in

Section 3.3, despite being absent in relatively more authentic and notable works, did require a content-based analysis, specifically on the usage of the terms like *Lūṭī* and *liwāṭ*, to investigate their authenticity. It was contested that there did not exist concrete meanings for these words during the time of the Companions. The usage of these terms motivates the need for this section, which would focus on showing that there did not exist a concrete and unanimous understanding of the terms like *Lūṭī* and *liwāṭ* during the time of the Companions, let alone during the time of the Prophet. Texts, mostly attributed to the *tābiʿūn* (followers), exploring the definition of such terms are analyzed as follows.

The argument that the words *Lūṭī* and *liwāṭ* and other terms coined for homosexual conduct are later juristic creations can be supported by noting that there was no consensus amongst the *tābiʿūn* on these terms. Apart from the nine strands of Prophetic texts on *liwāṭ* and three strands of texts on the *mukhannathūn*, and aside from the texts associated with the Companions, there exist four strands of texts on the usage of the words coined from *Lūṭ*, several of which are attributed to the *tābiʿūn*.

3.4.1 Penalty for the Possible Slander—*Lūṭī*

Notwithstanding authenticity issues of these narratives, the first strand of the *tābiʿūn* texts explores the penalty or lack thereof of slander through the usage of words derived from *Lūṭ*. There exist three variants of a text that is traced back all the way to the Prophet through ʿIkrima via Ibn ʿAbbās that appear in the *Sunan Ibn Māja*, *Tirmidhī*, and the *Mustadrak*. However, only the version that appears in the *Sunan Ibn Māja*, which is reproduced below, contains both the terms *Lūṭī* and *mukhannath*.

> If a man called the other "you mukhannath" flog him twenty times and if a man called the other "you Lūṭī" flog him twenty times.[68]

So far as the authenticity of this strand of narratives is concerned, it may be noted that the Tirmidhī text was deemed unknown by Tirmidhī (d. 892) himself whereas the Mustadrak narrative was deemed incorrect by Thahabi. In the context of the above Ibn Māja (d. 887) version of the text, one of the narrators in the transmission chain, Dawūd ibn al-Hussein, was impugned by Abu Ḥātim by noting from others that whatever he narrated from ʿIkrima was weird.[69] The accusation against ʿIkrima as a liar only further weakens the narrative. Thus, it may be concluded that the text attributed to the Prophet stands extremely weak and even if this weakness were ignored, not much can be concluded on the definition of the term *Lūṭī*.

A second text, reproduced below, is traced back to Shihāb Zuhrī and Qatāda, and is found in the Muṣannaf ʿAbd al-Razzāq, which is a relatively authentic source of *athar* texts, that is, narratives attributed to the Companions and the *tābiʿūn* as opposed to *athat* texts attributed to the Prophet.

> (For) a man who calls another 'O Lūṭī'; they responded: No 'Ḥadd' (prescribed punishment)[70]

It may be noted that this text contradicts the first text, where 20 lashes have been prescribed for slandering a person with the word *Lūṭī*. Given that the first text is relatively weaker, precedence would have to be given to the second text on this issue, based on which, it could be plausibly reasoned that if the word *Lūṭī* really referred to some male involved in anal intercourse with another, then such slander would be expected to carry a punishment, specifically if one were to accept that anal penetration carried the penalty equivalent to that for *zinā* or perhaps worse than that. Therefore, the absence of any punishment for slander would imply that the word *Lūṭī* perhaps did not have the later concrete juristic meaning of one involved in anal penetration with another male. This conclusion then casts further doubt on some of the narratives in Section 3.3 related to the Companions of the Prophet, many of which contained terms like *Lūṭī*, *liwāṭ*, or *Lūṭism*, and which either prescribed punishment for anal penetration between males as that for *zinā* or as for a worse crime.

The third text, found in the *Muṣannaf* of Ibn Abi Shayba (d. 849), distinguishes between *Lūṭī* and *'amal qawm Lūṭ* by stating that slander by the second but not the first term leads to a *ḥadd* penalty. The narrative traced back to Farqad al-Subkī (d. 729/30) is as follows:

> A man called another "you Lūṭī." . . . Al-Ḥasan and Muhammad both said: "No Ḥadd punishment on him," whereas al-Ḥasan qualified "except if he says: you do the work of the people of Lūṭ."[71]

Like the second text, this one indicates that the meaning of the word *Lūṭī* did not have a concrete meaning prior to the time it was given a specific meaning by the jurists. It is interesting to note that there was a distinction between the terms *Lūṭī* and *'amal qawm Lūṭ* where the latter connoted contemptible conduct. However, *'amal qawm Lūṭ* does not necessarily carry the specific meaning of anal intercourse between males but carries within it a whole array of compound crimes ranging from disbelief in God, highway robbery, to evil deeds in open assemblies. This point is substantiated not only from the Qur'anic text 29:29 but also from the analysis on the Abu Bakr narrative. Thus, based on the third text as well, it may be concluded that the absence of any specific meaning for the term *Lūṭī* further weakens some of the narratives attributed to the Companions in Section 3.3.

Moreover, in light of the Abu Bakr narrative, it would perhaps be reasonable to state that the Companions understood the story of the people of Lūṭ as that of coercion and exploitation, whereas later jurists understood it as exclusively referring to homosexual anal intercourse. In fact, based on the opinions of jurists and scholars, as noted in chapter 2, even later jurists understood *liwāṭ* as sexual exploitation and that only in the last 100–200 years has the word taken the meaning of "homosexuality" as we understand it today.

3.4.2 Positive Reference—*Lūṭī*

While the texts in 3.4.1 indicated that the word *Lūṭī* with potential negative connotations did not have a concrete meaning prior to jurisprudential work, the next narrative, traced back to the Prophet, but not expressly attributed to him, through Sinān ibn Salama (d. 714), indicates that the word *Lūṭī* in fact carried a positive connotation, perhaps referring to the few steadfast followers of the Prophet Lūṭ. Based on verses 26:168–172, the Shī'ī *Tafsīr* compiled by Ayatollah Sayyid Kamal Faghih Imani and others indicates that a group of believers supported Lūṭ by their intense protest, although others dismissed them.[72] Likewise, an Ahmadi *Tafsīr* indicates that a party of believers was saved along with Lūṭ and not just his daughters.[73] Given this context, the Ibn Salama text reads:

> A man called another "O Lūṭī"; this was taken to Sinān ibn Salama who responded, "What a good man you are, if you were of the people/followers of Lūṭ."[74]

Notwithstanding authenticity issues, this text does indicate that the term *Lūṭī*, which later obtained the concrete meaning as one involved in homosexual anal intercourse, clearly did not have a specific meaning during the time of the Prophet, for it could plausibly have meant the steadfast followers of Lūṭ. This text, like those in Section 3.4.1, would then cast doubt on the authenticity of the narratives in Section 3.3 attributed to the Companions of the Prophet. It could be speculated that perhaps these words were later interjected in those narratives, thereby weakening their validity.

It is also interesting to note that Arno Schmitt has stated that in some contexts the Arabic word *Lūṭī* referred not only to masculine hooligans, wrestlers, and ruffians but also to merrymakers, fools, showmen, dancers, singers, and musicians.[75] This connotation of the word *Lūṭī* may be contrasted with the later juristic works as that of Qāḍīkhān (d. 1196), who stated in his work that the invective *Lūṭī* necessitates a *ta'zīr*-discretionary punishment,[76] or the jurists, who prescribed 80 lashes for slander of unlawful intercourse with a boy by the word *Lūṭī*.[77]

3.4.3 Reference to Anal Intercourse between Males—*al-Lūṭīyya*

The third strand of the tābiʿūn texts provides a sexual connotation to the terms *al-Lūṭīyya* (feminine version of *Lūṭī*) and *liwāṭ* by referring to anal intercourse with wives as the minor *liwāṭ* or by referring to enema as "the edge of the works of the people of Lūṭ." Notwithstanding authenticity issues, the third strand of the *tābiʿūn* texts contrasts with the first strand of the *tābiʿūn* texts that specifically rule out any penalty for slander through the word *Lūṭī*. There are two texts, reproduced below, one traced back to Qatāda and another to Mujāhid, the first of which carries the possibility that the term *al-Lūṭīyya* could specifically have been understood as anal intercourse between males.

> Abdullah ibn ʿUmar said that it (anal intercourse with wife) is the little 'al-Lūṭīyya' (Qatāda)[78]

> It is an edge of the works of the people of Lūṭ . . . the enema (Mujāhid)[79]

There does not appear to be a direct definition of the terms *al-Lūṭīyya* or *al-Lūṭīyya Kubrā* and as such any meaning for these terms is only potentially derived from these texts, which raises the question whether the strength of just these indirect narratives, in contrast to the several others in Section 3.4, is sufficient enough for the later meticulous jurists to specify their opinions on *liwāṭ* or *al-Lūṭīyya*. A variant of the text referring to Ibn ʿUmar has been recorded by both Ibn Ḥanbal and al-Nasāʾī, although the latter deemed it weak.[80] This variant text has come through different transmission chains, which are deemed weak. Notwithstanding authenticity issues, the text version narrated from ʿAmr ibn Shuʿayb and recorded by Ibn Ḥanbal is paraphrased below.

> He was asked about the man who comes to a woman in her anus. He said: this is the little "Liwāṭ."[81]

It seems rather strange that the texts that would expressly define a specific conduct, which would form the base for other conduct, would be absent whereas some texts would exist that would indirectly allude to the base conduct by particularizing the derived conduct with the definite particle *Al*. This would seem to cast doubt on the authenticity of these narratives, as two other narratives traced back to Qatāda exist that indicate that the meaning of *Lūṭī* was not concretely defined. One of these two Qatāda narratives was noted as the second text in 3.4.1, whereas the other Qatāda text found in Muṣannaf Ibn Abi Shayba is reproduced below.

> A man said to Abi al-Aswad "You Lūṭī," so he responded "May Allah have mercy on Lūṭ" and he did not take any offense.[82]

Had the term *Lūṭī* meant one involved in homosexual anal penetration, the situation would have been grave and treated as a case for slander, specifically given the norms among seventh- and eighth-century Muslims on *muruwwa*-manliness; yet the text mentions that Abi al-Aswad did not take any offense to being called a *Lūṭī*. Thus, contradictory texts, traced back to Qatāda, shed doubts on the texts that seem to indirectly define *al-Lūṭīyya*. Notwithstanding authenticity issues, it may be noted that even on the basis of accepting the Mujāhid text at face value, one cannot simply deduce that if enema were the edge of the work of the people of Lūṭ, then homosexual anal sex necessarily was the work of the people of Lūṭ, as the phrase *'amal qawm Lūṭ*, as noted in Section 3.4.1, carries within its scope a whole array of compound crimes ranging from disbelief in God and highway robbery to evil deeds in open assemblies. Thus, the two principal texts in this section, when viewed in the holistic context of other texts, get weak enough to deduce any potential definitions, specifically, for the terms *Lūṭī* and *al-Lūṭīyya*.

3.4.4 Absence of a Concrete Meaning—*Lūṭī*

It appears that there existed no consensus amongst the *tābi'ūn* on the usage of words coined from *Lūṭ*. The fourth strand of the *tābi'ūn* texts makes this point clear. One such text attributed to one of Abu Ḥanīfa's teachers—Ibrāhīm al-Nakha'ī (d. 713), found in the *Muṣannaf 'Abd al-Razzāq*—indicates the term *Lūṭī* was not completely or universally understood as referring to homosexual anal intercourse.

> About a man who called another man "*Lūṭī*," Ibrāhīm said: His intent, he is to be asked what he meant?[83]

According to this text, the term *Lūṭī* required explanation as it did not have the precise meaning of a person involved in homosexual anal intercourse. Given the life span of 'Abd al-Razzāq as-Ṣan'ānī (d. 833), the author of *Muṣannaf 'Abd al-Razzāq*, it may be concluded that even around 772 CE, 150 years after the Prophet's migration, there was no consensus on the meaning of words, which were defined by the later jurists.

This text therefore casts further doubt on some of the narratives attributed to the Companions in Section 3.3 that they prescribed a penalty for homosexual anal intercourse either equivalent to that for *zinā* or for a worse crime. Moreover, even if the narratives of the Companions in Section 3.3 are accepted at face value, the analysis in Section 3.4 makes it clear that terms like *Lūṭī* did not have a specific meaning prior to the time of the later jurists. Moreover, the reports indicating the conduct of the Companions are not binding Hadith and the obligation to follow these reports depends on the existence of consensus around them. The point on following the precedent of a Companion will be further explored in the section on *ijmāʿ* (consensus) in chapter 6.

Overall, based on a holistic appraisal of the texts in Section 3.4, it may be concluded that while *ʿamal qawm Lūṭ* (works of the people of Lūṭ) was condemned, it was neither clearly defined by the Prophet or His Companions and as per the Abu Bakr narrative and the Qur'anic text 29:29 it could mean a compound array of crimes ranging from rejecting God's Prophet, highway robbery to committing evil acts in open assemblies. Thus, the Companions did not have concrete meanings for terms like *Lūṭī*, *al-Lūṭīyya* or *liwāṭ* and as such the texts in Section 3.4 cast doubts on the narratives in both Sections 3.1 and 3.3, specifically those that contain these later juristic terms. In fact, it deserves to be noted that one cannot find the accepted contemporary meaning of these terms in the old Arab dictionaries because there is no record of their use before the works of the jurists. For instance, one may deduce from the following Lisān Al-ʿArab dictionary note that the term(s) depicting those involved in homosexual anal intercourse were coined at least after the time of the Prophet.

> Layth said: Lūṭ was a Prophet who Allah sent to his people, who rejected him and continued with what they did, so people derived from his name a term for an act for those who do what his people did.[84]

It may also be noted that the narratives in Section 3.4 that specifically delineate opinions of the *tābiʿūn* are strong only when there exists a consensus in their opinions, for difference of opinion would require one to elect the relatively more correct opinion amongst them. Thus, given that there was no consensus amongst the *tābiʿūn* on the meaning of the words, which were later used by the jurists to define homosexual anal intercourse, further doubt may be cast on the narratives in Section 3.3 that specifically employed these terms. Finally, based on the overall Sections 3.1–3.4, one may conclude that it would be intellectually dishonest to extract rulings for same-sex sexual conduct, let alone loving same-sex unions on the basis of a whole array of traditions that are deemed weak based on both the transmission chain and the content-based authenticity checks. It is perhaps due to this reason that none of these narratives appear in the relatively more authentic works of Bukhārī, Muslim, or Mālik's *Muwaṭṭaʾ*.

3.5 THE SIX RULINGS THAT PRESCRIBE THE DEATH PENALTY: THE REFUTATION OF IBN ḤAZM[85]

It was noted from the aforementioned sections that Prophetic Hadith on homosexual conduct are weak enough to preclude deducing any legal rulings from them, a point that has been conceded by several scholars. Likewise, it was noted that no authentic text from either the Companions or their followers exists to deduce any ruling either. In fact it was noted that there was sufficient difference of opinion amongst the followers as to the very meaning of the terms *Lūṭī* and *al-Lūṭīyya*, whose meaning was made concrete only during the time of the jurists, an observation that casts further doubt on those narratives that specifically used these terms. This section is aimed at continuing with this line of refutation, by delineating Ibn Ḥazm's critique of these narratives.

According to Camilla Adang, Ibn Ḥazm presents seven types of rulings on homosexual conduct as defined specifically by homosexual anal intercourse, of which he refutes six types of rulings, all of which prescribe capital punishment for such conduct. Whereas Sections 3.1–3.4 were classified according to whether the narratives were traced back to the Prophet, the Companions, or their followers, Ibn Ḥazm actually lumps narratives from the Companions and the followers together on the basis of the defined penalty.

Of the six types of rulings that prescribe capital punishment, the first indicates that both the active as well as the passive partner, regardless of their marital status, are to be burnt alive. These texts allude to the Abu Bakr narrative in Section 3.3.1, although they are traced back to either Ibn Wahb, who indicates that the perpetrator was burnt after execution by the sword as per the Prophetic directive that only God had the prerogative to do so, or to Ibn Samaan, who indicated that the perpetrator was burnt alive. Ibn Zubayr, in contradiction to the narrative reported in Section 3.3.4, Hishām ibn ʿAbd al-Malik (d. 743), and Amir al-Qasri are also reported to have ordered the burning of men alive during their times. However, Ibn Ḥazm impugns the authenticity of these texts by confirming that the Abu Bakr and 'Ali texts that depict burning of the perpetrators have a broken transmission chain, that Ibn Samaan was attested as a liar by Mālik ibn Anas, that the clear Prophetic directive forbade killing by fire, and that the narratives alluding to Ibn Zubayr contain weak links.

The second ruling that is traced back to Ibn ʿAbbās through Qāḍī Aḥmad ibn Ismāʿīl ibn Dulaym prescribes that both the perpetrators be thrown from a high mountain and subsequently pelted with stones. The third ruling, based on the narratives corresponding to Sections 3.3.3 and 3.3.4, traced back to both 'Ali, through Muhammad ibn Saʿīd ibn Nabāt (d. 1037/8), and Ibn ʿAbbās respectively, indicates that both the perpetrators are to be stoned regardless of their marital status. For the third ruling, apart from these narratives, texts from the subsequent generation of scholars like Shihāb Zuhrī, who the jurist Mālik ibn Anas greatly relied on, and Ibrāhīm al-Nakha'ī, who was one of the teachers of the jurist Abu Ḥanīfa, are also included. The narratives of both Shihāb Zuhrī, which were also accepted by Shāfiʿī, and that of Ibrāhīm al-Nakha'ī, are reproduced below.

If anyone deserves to be stoned twice, it is the Lūṭī (Ibrāhīm al-Nakha'ī)

A Lūṭī should be stoned, whether he is muḥṣan or not (Shihāb Zuhrī)

Ja'far Ṣādiq (d. 765) is also noted as having asserted that one who commits the act of *liwāṭ* deserves to be stoned twice.[86] Regardless, it is worth noting that while the current Ibrāhīm al-Nakha'ī narrative prescribes stoning the *Lūṭī* twice, the narrative in Section 3.4.4 attributed to Ibrāhīm al-Nakha'ī mentioned that the meaning of the term *Lūṭī* was unclear. Thus, if the meaning of the term *Lūṭī* is not clear, then any ruling, specifically, that prescribes the death penalty, cannot be deduced from the current text. Moreover, the authenticity of the current text is also brought into question. Likewise, given that Shihāb Zuhrī died around 741–742 CE and that the Ibrāhīm al-Nakha'ī text, in Section 3.4.4, mentioned clearly that even around 702–772 CE, the term *Lūṭī* was not completely or universally understood as referring to homosexual anal intercourse, bring into doubt the authenticity of the current Shihāb Zuhrī text as well. Likewise, the Shihāb Zuhrī narrative, presented as the second text in 3.4.1, which indicated that there was no penalty for a person who called another *Lūṭī*, only casts further doubt on the current Shihāb Zuhrī text.

The fourth ruling, traced back to Ibn ʿAbbās, indicates that both the active and passive partners are to be executed by the sword. There then appear to be three contradictory rulings based on the texts traced to Ibn ʿAbbās, which raise doubts as to the authenticity of these texts and therefore the second, third, and fourth rulings. In fact, Ibn Ḥazm contends that texts from Ibn ʿAbbās, Ibn Zubayr, and Ibn ʿUmar are traced through unknowns in the transmission chain of narrators, and therefore he further states that it would be inappropriate to accept any opinion supposedly attributed to the Companions on this subject.

The fifth and sixth rulings actually differentiate between the perpetrators on the basis of their position in the act and their marital status, and henceforth their legal status, respectively. The fifth ruling is not traced back to the Companions or their followers but to the opinion of a later Shafi'i jurist Abu Ja'far Muhammad ibn 'Ali ibn Yūsuf, according to whom the passive partner is stoned regardless of his marital status. According to the fifth ruling, the active partner is punished as a fornicator, that is, he is stoned if married but flogged if unmarried. While the opinions of the jurists will be considered in chapter 5, for now it suffices to note that Ibn Ḥazm expresses his disagreement with this viewpoint based on his analysis of the Qur'an.

The sixth ruling, in contrast to the fifth ruling, is independent of the position of the perpetrators in homosexual anal intercourse but prescribes the penalty for fornication to both partners, that is, they are stoned if married but flogged if unmarried. This ruling is based on the Ibn Zubayr narrative, as in

Section 3.3.5, that indicated the tacit approval of Ibn ʿAbbās and Ibn ʿUmar. However, Ibn Ḥazm contends that the narratives, attributed to both Ibn Zubayr and Ibn ʿUmar, as noted earlier, contain weak links in the transmission chain and therefore stand refuted. Likewise, he refutes the opinions of Ḥasan al-Baṣrī (d. 728) and some others who maintain the same ruling or add exile for a year to the penalty for the active partner. In fact, Ibn Ḥazm generally refutes these rulings by reiterating that the term *zinā* is never equated with *liwāṭ* either in common usage or in the Prophet's authentic directives, which would also cast doubt on the narratives in Section 3.3 that used words like *Lūṭī* and *al-Lūṭīyya* as well, and by taking recourse to the principal source of Muslim knowledge—the Qur'an.

As part of his general refutation of these six rulings, Ibn Ḥazm falls back to verse 25:68 and the Prophet's directive that prohibited taking life except for three cases—that is, fornication after marriage, apostasy, and murder. He further contests that if it is forbidden to spill the blood of a person, Muslim or otherwise, with the exception of the three cases, then capital punishment could not be enforced on any person, whether iniquitous or contrite, based on flawed texts that are supposedly used to substantiate the six rulings that prescribe capital punishment for homosexual anal intercourse.

Based on his reading of the relevant Qur'anic verses, Ibn Ḥazm further contests that given the people of Lūṭ were destroyed on the basis of both their abominable conduct and their rejection of God's Prophet, and given that Lūṭ's wife was not involved in the works of the people of Lūṭ, but merely abetted them, and given the observation that Lūṭ's people were also blinded, would all weaken the case of those who propose capital punishment for homosexual anal intercourse on the basis of the Lūṭ narrative in the Qur'an. This is because the proponents of capital punishment would be inconsistent in their methodology if they would prescribe death for one involved in the act of homosexual anal intercourse but who did not disbelieve in God's Prophet, and likewise they would be inconsistent in their methodology by not prescribing the same penalty for abetters of the act or for that matter by not blinding those who accosted others for perpetrating the act.

Finally, Ibn Ḥazm states that going by the reasoning of the proponents of the death penalty, people who tamper with weights and measures should be burned, and people who wound another person's she-camel should be executed because the people of Shuʿayb and Ṣāliḥ were destroyed respectively for those reasons mentioned in the Qur'an. Thus, by drawing out their contradictions and by indicating that they would be acting against the verses they quote by being inconsistent in their approach, Ibn Ḥazm effectively refutes the proponents of the first six rulings.

In conclusion, the first ruling that prescribes death by burning, and the next three rulings that prescribe death by stoning or by sword of both the active and passive partners, irrespective of their marital status, are all deemed weak. Likewise, the fifth and sixth rulings that seem to have been based on analogy with *zinā* (fornication) are deemed weak because either they are a product of *qiyās* (analogy)-based methodology, an approach rejected by the Ẓāhirī school of Ibn Ḥazm, or that they rest on weak narratives that allude to Ibn ʿAbbās, Ibn Zubayr, and Ibn ʿUmar, and which contradict other weak narratives, as noted in Sections 3.3.4 and 3.3.5, attributed to the same Companions. In short, Ibn Ḥazm argues that it would be inappropriate to accept any opinion supposedly attributed to the Companions on this subject.

3.6 INDIRECT CONDEMNATION OF SAME-SEX RELATIONSHIPS—THE *ʿAWRA* TEXTS

Given the aforementioned weaknesses in the above texts, sometimes contemporary conservative Muslim authorities use an indirect condemnation of same-sex relationships. The argument goes that if Muslims are not allowed to look at the *ʿawra* (prescribed covered body parts) of the same gender, then the issue of same-sex relationships becomes moot. Such an argument fails to account for the point that prior to marriage Muslims are forbidden to look at the *ʿawra* of the opposite gender as well and as such superimposing the *ʿawra* texts on the issue of a legal contract for same-sex couples itself is irrelevant and inappropriate.

The Hadith recorded in *Ṣaḥīḥ Muslim* and also narrated by Ibn Ḥanbal, Abu Dawūd, and Tirmidhī, and which is traced back to Abu Saʿīd al-Khudrī (d. 682/693) indicates that the Prophet stated:

> A man should not look at the *ʿawra* of another man nor should a woman look at the *ʿawra* of another woman. A man should not be in one garment with another man nor should a woman be in one garment with another woman.

There are conflicting reports on the authenticity of this Hadith.[87] While one of the transmitters, Al-Ḍaḥḥāk ibn ʿUthmān, was deemed as trustworthy by Ibn Ḥanbal, Yaḥyā ibn Maʿīn, and Abu Zurʿa mentioned that he was not strong and Abu Ḥātim, while confirming his trustworthiness concluded that his Hadith is not used as a proof. Likewise, while Ibn Ḥibbān deemed him trustworthy, Bukhārī did not include his Hadith in his work.

In his explanation of this Hadith,[88] al-Nawawī (d. 1277) asserts that according to this text, men and women are also forbidden to look at the *ʿawra* of the same gender, just as they are forbidden to look at the *ʿawra* of the opposite gender by consensus. Al-Nawawī compares looking at the *ʿawra* of the same gender with that of the opposite gender, which suggests the acknowledgment of the existence of sexual attraction between same genders. However, contextually it also seems that the issue is one of modesty as in another text the Prophet is reported to have prohibited a woman touching another wearing only one garment as she might describe her to her husband and it would be as if he sees her.[89] Thus, while modesty is enjoined upon all Muslims, construing the prohibition of same-sex unions from this text would not be reasonable as that would mean one could easily deduce the prohibition of heterosexual marriage.

Since looking at the *ʿawra* of the opposite gender is prohibited except under the exception of necessity or marriage, this suggests the existence of exception to the general rule of not looking. As such, one may conclude that a legal contract between same-sex couples may provide an exception to the rule of not looking. Since this Hadith cannot be taken as providing an absolute rule without exceptions, the issue of not looking at the *ʿawra* is irrelevant to the issue of a same-sex legal contract. Likewise, in the context of Hadith texts that call for separating the beds or blankets of children over the age of 10 regardless of gender, the issue at hand is not the prohibition of same-sex unions but of curbing sex outside a legal contract. In short, same-sex unions cannot be deemed prohibited based on such Hadith texts but would require other proofs for prohibition.

NOTES

Translation of all texts in this chapter is by the authors.

1. Mohamed El-Moctar El-Shinqiti, "Should beheading be the penalty for homosexuals," The Brunei Times, June 13, 2008, accessed January 26, 2016, http://www.bt.com.bn/friday_special/2008/06/13/should_beheading_be_the_penalty_for_homosexuals.
2. "Islam and Homosexuality," Mission Islam, accessed January 26, 2016, http://www.missionislam.com/knowledge/homosexuality.htm.
3. Imani et al., *An Enlightening Commentary,* Parts 7 and 8, 286.
4. Ibid, 306.
5. Al-Ṭabarānī. *Muʿjam Awsaṭ*, Hadith No. 4976, Shuab Eman book, in الموسوعة الذهبية للحديث النبوي الشيف و علومه [*The Golden Encyclopedia of the Prophetic Golden Hadeeth and its Sciences*], 2nd edition, (London: Turath Publishing), CD-ROM.
6. Muhammad Shams al-Ḥaqq al-ʿAẓīm Ābādī, *ʿAwn al-Maʿbūd fī Sharḥ Sunan Abu Dawūd,* Volume 6, in الموسوعة الذهبية للحديث النبوي الشيف و علومه [*The Golden Encyclopedia of the Prophetic Golden Hadeeth and its Sciences*], 2nd edition, (London: Turath Publishing), CD-ROM, 100–101.
7. Yūsuf ibn ʿAbd al-Raḥmān Al-Mizzī, *Tahdhīb al-Kamāl*, Volume 2, 4, 8, 11, 13, 14, 16, 20, 22, 27, 30, 31, in الموسوعة الذهبية للحديث النبوي الشيف و علومه [*The Golden Encyclopedia of the Prophetic Golden Hadeeth and its Sciences*], 2nd edition, (London:

Turath Publishing), CD-ROM, Volume 2, 43, 186; Volume 22, 169; Volume 14, 158–160.

8. Ibid., Volume 20, 278–82.
9. Ibid., Volume 13, 517–19.
10. El-Shinqiti, "Should Beheading Be the Penalty for Homosexuals."
11. Ibn ʿAbd al-Barr, *Al-Istidhkār fī Sharḥ Madhāhib ʿUlamāʾ al-Amṣār*, Volume 7, in الموسوعة الذهبية للحديث النبوي الشيف و علومه [*The Golden Encyclopedia of the Prophetic Golden Hadeeth and its Sciences*], 2nd edition, (London: Turath Publishing), CD-ROM, 495.
12. Al-Mizzī, *Tahdhīb al-Kamāl*, Volume 16, 79–85.
13. Ibid., Volume 8, 445–48.
14. al-Ḥākim Al-Naysabūrī, *Mustadrak*, Volume 4, in الموسوعة الذهبية للحديث النبوي الشيف و علومه [*The Golden Encyclopedia of the Prophetic Golden Hadeeth and its Sciences*], 2nd edition, (London: Turath Publishing), CD-ROM, 396.
15. Mohd Elfie Nieshaem Juferi, "The Consensus on Homosexuality and The Illiteracy of Christian Polemicists," *Bismika Allahuma*, September 18, 2007, accessed January 26, 2016, http://www.bismikaallahuma.org/archives/2007/the-consensus-on-homosexuality-and-the-illiteracy-of-christian-polemicists/.
16. Al-Mizzī, *Tahdhīb al-Kamāl*, Volume 30, 121.
17. Abu Muhammad al-Ḥārith ibn Muhammad ibn Dāhir Al-Tamīmī, *Musnad al-Ḥārith*, Volume 2, in الموسوعة الذهبية للحديث النبوي الشيف و علومه [*The Golden Encyclopedia of the Prophetic Golden Hadeeth and its Sciences*], 2nd edition, (London: Turath Publishing), CD-ROM, 565.
18. Al-Mizzī, *Tahdhīb al-Kamāl*, Volume 27, 221.
19. Sulaymān ibn Aḥmad ibn Ayyūb al-Lakhmī Al-Shāmī, *Musnad al-Shāmiyyīn*, Volume 1, 2, in الموسوعة الذهبية للحديث النبوي الشيف و علومه [*The Golden Encyclopedia of the Prophetic Golden Hadeeth and its Sciences*], 2nd edition, (London: Turath Publishing), CD-ROM, 104.
20. Aḥmad ibn ʻAli. Mukhtaṣar al-Kāmil fī al-Ḍuʿafāʾ Al-Maqrīzī, Volume 4, in الموسوعة الذهبية للحديث النبوي الشيف و علومه [*The Golden Encyclopedia of the Prophetic Golden Hadeeth and its Sciences*], 2nd edition, (London: Turath Publishing), CD-ROM, 281.
21. Al-Shāmī, *Musnad Al-Shāmiyyīn*, Volume 2, 205.
22. Muhammad Ibn Ḥibbān, *Al-Majrūḥīn*, Volume 2, in الموسوعة الذهبية للحديث النبوي الشيف و علومه [*The Golden Encyclopedia of the Prophetic Golden Hadeeth and its Sciences*], 2nd edition, (London: Turath Publishing), CD-ROM, 149.
23. For details see: Al-Mizzī, *Tahdhīb al-Kamāl*, Volume 2, 43, 186; Volume 8, 445–48; Volume 13, 517–19; Volume 14, 158–60; Volume 16, 79–85; Volume 20, 278–82; Volume 22, 169; Volume 27, 221; Volume 30, 121; Al-Maqrīzī, *Mukhtaṣar al-Kāmil fī al-Ḍuʿafāʾ*, Volume 4, 281; Ibn Ḥibbān, *Al-Majrūḥīn*, Volume 2, 149.
24. Joseph Norment Bell, *Love Theory in Later Hanbalite Islam*, (Albany: State University of New York Press, 1979), 129.
25. El-Rouayheb, *Before Homosexuality*, 77–78.
26. Marc Daniel, "Arab Civilization and Male Love," trans. Winston Leyland, in *Reclaiming Sodom*, ed. Jonathan Goldberg, (New York: Routledge, 1994), 60.
27. El-Rouayheb, *Before Homosexuality*, 45.
28. Kugle, "Sexuality, Diversity, and Ethics," 222.

29. ʻAbd ar-Razzāq Al-Ṣanʻānī, *Muṣannaf ʻAbd al-Razzāq*, Volume 7, 11, in الموسوعة الذهبية للحديث النبوي الشيف و علومه [*The Golden Encyclopedia of the Prophetic Golden Hadeeth and its Sciences*], 2nd edition, (London: Turath Publishing), CD-ROM, 243.
30. Rowson, "The Effeminates of Early Medina."
31. Rowson, "The Categorization of Gender," 71.
32. El-Rouayheb, *Before Homosexuality,* 22.
33. For details see: Ibn Ḥajar al-ʻAsqalānī, *Fatḥ al-Bārī*, Volume 12, 160; Al-Mizzī, *Tahdhīb al-Kamāl*, Volume 4, 430; Volume 20, 278–82; Volume 31, 508–10; Al-Rāzī, *Al-Jarḥ wa-l-Taʻdīl*, Volume 3, 396; Volume 4, 498; Ābādī, *ʻAwn al-Maʻbūd fī Sharḥ Sunan Abu Dawūd.*
34. Ibn Ḥajar al-ʻAsqalānī, *Fatḥ al-Bārī*, Volume 12, 160; also see Ibn ʻAbd al-Barr, *Al-Tamhīd li Mā fī al-Muwaṭṭaʼ min al-Maʻānī wa-l-Asānīd*, Volume 22, 272–73.
35. Rowson, "The Effeminates of Early Medina."
36. Kugle, *Homosexuality in Islam,* 92–96.
37. Abu Bakr Aḥmad ibn Ḥusayn ibn ʻAli ibn Mūsā al-Khusrawjirdī Al-Bayhaqī, *Sunan al-Bayhaqī al-Kubrā*, Volume 4, 8, in الموسوعة الذهبية للحديث النبوي الشيف و علومه [*The Golden Encyclopedia of the Prophetic Golden Hadeeth and its Sciences*], 2nd edition, (London: Turath Publishing), CD-ROM, 224.
38. Kugle, *Homosexuality in Islam,* 90–97.
39. Ṣaḥīḥ al-Bukhārī, Nikah chapter: the forbidding of entering on the women of effeminate men, in الموسوعة الذهبية للحديث النبوي الشيف و علومه [*The Golden Encyclopedia of the Prophetic Golden Hadeeth and its Sciences*], 2nd edition, (London: Turath Publishing), CD-ROM.
40. Al-San'ani, *Muṣannaf Abdul Razzāq*, Volume 11, 242.
41. Ibn Ḥanbal, *Musnad Aḥmad*, in الموسوعة الذهبية للحديث النبوي الشيف و علومه [*The Golden Encyclopedia of the Prophetic Golden Hadeeth and its Sciences*], 2nd edition, (London: Turath Publishing). CD-ROM, "Musnad Abu Huraira."
42. Ibn Ḥanbal, *Musnad Ahmad*. "Musnad Abdullah Ibn ʻUmar."
43. Al-Mizzī, *Tahdhīb al-Kamāl*, Volume 20, 278–282.
44. Ibid., Volume 31, 508–510.
45. Muhammad ibn Idris ibn al-Mundhir al-Hanẓali Al-Rāzī, *Al-Jarḥ wa-l-Taʻdīl*, Volume 2–4, 9, in الموسوعة الذهبية للحديث النبوي الشيف و علومه [*The Golden Encyclopedia of the Prophetic Golden Hadeeth and its Sciences*], 2nd edition, (London: Turath Publishing), CD-ROM, 498.
46. Al-Mizzī, *Tahdhīb al-Kamāl*, Volume 4, 430.
47. "The story of ʻUmar's exiling of Naṣr ibn Hajjaaj from Madinah,'" 201633, Islam QA, accessed January 25, 2016, http://islamqa.info/en/201633.
48. Abu Dāwūd Sulaymān ibn al-Ashʻath al-Azdī Al-Sijistānī, *Sunan Abu Dawūd*, Chapter: rule of the *mukhannathūn*, in الموسوعة الذهبية للحديث النبوي الشيف و علومه [*The Golden Encyclopedia of the Prophetic Golden Hadeeth and its Sciences*], 2nd edition, (London: Turath Publishing), CD-ROM.
49. Al-Ṭabarānī. *Muʻjam Awsaṭ*, Volume 5, in الموسوعة الذهبية للحديث النبوي الشيف و علومه [*The Golden Encyclopedia of the Prophetic Golden Hadeeth and its Sciences*], 2nd edition, (London: Turath Publishing), CD-ROM,194.
50. Ābādī, *ʻAwn al-Maʻbūd fī Sharḥ Sunan Abu Dawūd.*

51. Al-Rāzī, *Al-Jarḥ wa-l-Ta'dīl*, Volume 3, 396.
52. Al-Bayhaqī, *Sunan al-Bayhaqī al-Kubrā,* Volume 8, 232.
53. Abu Ja'far Muhammad ibn 'Amr Ibn Mūsā al-'Aqīlī, *Kitāb al-Ḍu'afā' al-Kabīr*, Volume 3, in الموسوعة الذهبية للحديث النبوي الشيف و علومه [*The Golden Encyclopedia of the Prophetic Golden Hadeeth and its Sciences*], 2nd edition, (London: Turath Publishing), CD-ROM, 10.
54. Al-Bayhaqī, *Sunan al-Bayhaqī al-Kubrā,* Volume 8, 232.
55. Ibid.
56. Ṣaḥīḥ al-Bukhārī, Volume 3, 1098.
57. Ṣaḥīḥ al-Bukhārī, Volume 9, Book 84, Number 57.
58. Kugle, *Homosexuality in Islam,* 137–140.
59. Ibn 'Abd al-Barr, *Al-Tamhīd li Mā fī al-Muwaṭṭa' min al-Ma'*ā*nī wa-l-Asānīd*, Volume 5, 22, in الموسوعة الذهبية للحديث النبوي الشيف و علومه [*The Golden Encyclopedia of the Prophetic Golden Hadeeth and its Sciences*], 2nd edition, (London: Turath Publishing), CD-ROM, 316.
60. Al-San'ani, *Muṣannaf Abdul Razzāq*, Volume 11, 243.
61. Ibn Ḥajar al-'Asqalānī, *Tahdhīb al-Tahdhīb*, Volume 8, in الموسوعة الذهبية للحديث النبوي الشيف و علومه [*The Golden Encyclopedia of the Prophetic Golden Hadeeth and its Sciences*], 2nd edition, (London: Turath Publishing), CD-ROM, 305.
62. El-Shinqiti, "Threats to Behead Homosexuals."
63. Ābādī, *'Awn al-Ma'būd fī Sharḥ Sunan Abu Dawūd*, Volume 6, 141.
64. Al-Bayhaqī, *Sunan al-Bayhaqī al-Kubrā,* Volume 4, 322.
65. Al-Rāzī, *Al-Jarḥ wa-l-Ta'dīl*, Volume 9, 295.
66. Al-Bayhaqī, *Sunan al-Bayhaqī al-Kubrā,* Volume 8, 233.
67. Ibn 'Abd al-Barr, *Al-Tamhīd li Mā fī al-Muwaṭṭa' min al-Ma'ānī wa-l-Asānīd*, Volume 5, 316.
68. Abū Abdullah Muḥammad ibn Yazīd ibn Mājah al-Rab'ī Al-Qazwīnī, *Sunan Ibn Mājah*, Volume 2, in الموسوعة الذهبية للحديث النبوي الشيف و علومه [*The Golden Encyclopedia of the Prophetic Golden Hadeeth and its Sciences*], 2nd edition, (London: Turath Publishing), CD-ROM, 857.
69. Sulaymān ibn Khalaf Al-Bājī, *Al-Ta'dīl wa-l-Tajrīḥ li Man Kharraja 'anhu al-Bukhārī fī al-Jāmi' al-Ṣaḥīḥ*, Volume 2, in الموسوعة الذهبية للحديث النبوي الشيف و علومه [*The Golden Encyclopedia of the Prophetic Golden Hadeeth and its Sciences*], 2nd edition, (London: Turath Publishing), CD-ROM, 565.
70. Al-San'ani, *Muṣannaf Abul Razzāq*, Volume 7, 429.
71. Ibn 'Uthmān, *Muṣannaf Ibn Abi Shayba*, Volume 5, 498.
72. Imani et al., *An Enlightening Commentary*, Parts 7 & 8, 308.
73. Ahmad, *The Holy Qur'an*, 1297, 1299.
74. Al-San'ani, *Muṣannaf Abul Razzāq*, Volume 7, 429.
75. Schmitt and Sofer, *Sexuality and eroticism,* 12.
76. Lange, *Justice, Punishment and the Medieval Muslim Imagination,* 220.
77. El-Rouayheb, *Before Homosexuality,* 137.
78. Al-San'ani, *Muṣannaf Abul Razzāq*, Volume 7, 429.
79. Ibn 'Uthmān, *Muṣannaf Ibn Abi Shayba*, Volume 5, 34.

80. Ibn Ḥajar al-ʿAsqalānī, *Talkhīṣ al-Ḥabīr*, Volume 3, Book of Nikāḥ, Chapter that addresses anal intercourse, in الموسوعة الذهبية للحديث النبوي الشيف و علومه [*The Golden Encyclopedia of the Prophetic Golden Hadeeth and its Sciences*], 2nd edition, (London: Turath Publishing), CD-ROM, 179–186.
81. Ibid.
82. Ibn ʿUthmān, *Muṣannaf Ibn Abi Shayba*, Volume 5, 498.
83. Al-San'ani, *Muṣannaf Abul Razzāq*, Volume 7, 426.
84. Ibn Manẓūr, *Lisān al-ʿArab*, Volume 7, in الموسوعة الذهبية للحديث النبوي الشيف و علومه [*The Golden Encyclopedia of the Prophetic Golden Hadeeth and its Sciences*], 2nd edition, (London: Turath Publishing), CD-ROM, 396.
85. This section owes much to Adang, "Ibn Ḥazm on Homosexuality."
86. Imani et al., *An Enlightening Commentary*, Parts 7 and 8, 286.
87. Al-Mizzī, *Tahdhīb al-Kamāl*, Volume 13, 273–274.
88. *Ṣaḥīḥ Muslim*. Volume 4, in الموسوعة الذهبية للحديث النبوي الشيف و علومه [*The Golden Encyclopedia of the Prophetic Golden Hadeeth and its Sciences*], 2nd edition, (London: Turath Publishing), CD-ROM, 30.
89. Adang, "Ibn Ḥazm on Homosexuality," 28.

Chapter 4

Sunnī Narratives on Heterosexual Anal Intercourse

Ityān bi-l-dubur

As noted in chapter 1, one particular sexual act does not define the lives of queer Muslims and as such does not stall the move toward Muslim same-sex unions. Nonetheless, the objective of this chapter is to investigate how Islamic textual sources address the specific issue of heterosexual anal intercourse and what bearing, if any, would that have on the issue of male same-sex conduct let alone same-sex unions.

A critical review of both the Sunnī and Shī'ī texts on heterosexual anal intercourse is presented to indicate the weakness of the textual evidence against the act. Despite the fact that conservative Muslims who issue religious opinions derive the ruling of the prohibition of heterosexual anal intercourse from the Sunnī texts of jurisprudence, the ruling on this sexual act does not seem to be clear within Sunnī jurisprudence. It is due to the weakness in the textual evidence that some Sunnī authorities have taken a neutral position on the issue, whereas many Shī'ī authorities have deemed the act to be permissible with the wife's permission, although they deem the act to be detestable.

The texts, which are presented below, are classified into three categories based on whether they stand neutral, forbid, or allow for anal intercourse between married heterosexual couples.

4.1 TEXTS ON PROHIBITION: THE ABU HURAYRA, IBN ʿABBĀS, KHUZAYMA IBN THĀBIT REPORTS, THE TIRMIDHĪ, AND IBN MĀJA TEXTS

Four texts, paraphrased below, are traced back to Abu Hurayra (d. 678), and out of which three indicate that the person who indulges in heterosexual anal intercourse either rejects the message of the Prophet, becomes accursed, or an apostate. The fourth text actually is eschatological in essence and seemingly depicts that such a person would perhaps be bereft of God's mercy on Judgment Day. The first text has been narrated by al-Nasāʾī (d. 915), Bukhārī (d. 870), Abu Dawūd (d. 888), Aḥmad ibn Ḥanbal (d. 855), and Bayhaqī (d. 1066) as follows:

> The Prophet said: Cursed is the one who enters a woman in her anus.

One of the narrators of this text Suhayl ibn Abi Ṣāliḥ has been deemed as unreliable or weak by Hadith experts like Abu Ḥātim (d. 890) who suggested that Suhayl's Hadith may be quoted but may not be used as evidence of the actual saying of the Prophet and likewise, Hadith experts like Ibn Ma'in (d. 233 AH/852) stated that Hadith scholars stay away from Suhayl's narratives.[1]

While the second text was compiled by Abu Dawūd, Aḥmad ibn Ḥanbal, al-Nasāʾī, and Ibn Māja (d. 887), it has been deemed weak by al-Bazzār who indicated that one of the narrators in the transmission chain, Ḥārith ibn Mukhlid, is not well known. Likewise, Yaḥyā ibn Saʿīd al-Qaṭṭān (d. 198 AH/817) raised his doubts on the interconnectivity of Ḥārith ibn Mukhlid with Suhayl ibn Abi Ṣāliḥ, the next narrator in the chain, who was also deemed to be unreliable or weak by Hadith experts. This text is paraphrased below.

> God does not look, on the Day of Judgment, at a man who approached a woman from her anus.

This text also appears to be compiled by Tirmidhī (d. 892)[2] in whose chain of narrators, Sulaymān ibn Ḥayyān, has been critiqued by Hadith experts for his poor memory and for having committed lots of errors. Ibn Ma'in (d. 233 AH/852) stated that while Ibn Ḥayyān is a truthful person, his narratives may not be used as evidence of the actual saying of the Prophet. Likewise, another narrator in the transmission chain, al-Ḍaḥḥāk ibn ʿUthmān ʿAbd Allah ibn Khālid, has been critiqued by Hadith experts like Abu Zurʿa (d. 264 AH/883), who stated that al-Ḍaḥḥāk was unreliable, by Ibn ʿAbd al-Barr who stated that al-Ḍaḥḥāk was prone to mistakes, and by both Ibn ʿAbd al-Barr and Abu Zurʿa (d. 264 AH/883), who stated that his narratives may not be used as evidence of the actual saying of the Prophet.

The third text compiled by Abu Dawūd, Aḥmad ibn Ḥanbal, and Tirmidhī has been evaluated strangely by Tirmidhī himself as according to him this report was received only from one individual, Ḥakīm al-Athram. Likewise, Bukhārī expressed his concerns by stating that it is not known if the narrator Abu Tamimah heard the report from Abu Hurayra. Abu Bakr al-Bazzār actually goes further than Tirmidhī and Bukhārī, in questioning the authenticity of the text, by forcefully not only labeling the report as weird but also outrightly stating that any transmission from Ḥakīm al-Athram is deemed of no consequence. This text is paraphrased below.

> Whoever comes to a menstruating woman or to a woman in her anus, or, whoever came to a soothsayer and believed in what he said, then he rejected what was revealed to Muhammad.

Another variant of the Abu Hurayra text compiled by al-Nasāʾī through Shihāb Zuhrī (d. 741/2) was deemed weird by al-Nasāʾī himself as Shihāb Zuhrī merely held the opinion that anal intercourse with women should not be committed but did not base his opinion on a Hadith text. Al-Nasāʾī also states that one of the narrators in the chain, ʿAbd al-Malik ibn Muhammad al-Ṣanʿānī, who was evaluated negatively by experts like Dahīm and Abu Ḥātim, was perhaps confused.

The fourth Abu Hurayra text, paraphrased below, was compiled by al-Nasāʾī, who traced it back to Abu Hurayra through Mujāhid (d. 722), has also been deemed weak as two of the narrators in the transmission chain, Abu Bakr ibn Khamīs and Layth, have been evaluated as weak.

> Whoever approaches men or women in the anus becomes a kāfir.

A variant of this text has been traced back to Ibn ʿAbbās (d. 687),[3] and has been recorded by luminaries like Tirmidhī, al-Nasāʾī, Ibn Ḥibbān, al-Bazzār, and Aḥmad ibn Ḥanbal. There are several chains for this text, some of which are deemed "*mawqūf* (interrupted)" in that they do not reach back to Ibn ʿAbbās. Al-Bazzār has recorded the relatively stronger chain; however, even in this transmission chain, one of the narrators, Abu Khālid al-Ahmar, was evaluated as either having a bad memory or that he was prone to error and in fact the expert Ibn Ma'in (d. 233 AH/852) did not deem his narrative as an evident proof.[4] Another chain, which is considered strong in the transmission chain, is reported by al-Nasāʾī through Mu'ammar. Notwithstanding authenticity critiques, the narrative is paraphrased below.

> A man asked Ibn ʿAbbās about coming to a woman from her anus. He responded: You ask me about Kufr.

There are two other narratives recorded by Tirmidhī.[5] The first one simply has the Prophet forbid the practice of anal intercourse with women through the following words.

> Do not enter your women in their anus.

In one transmission chain of this narrative, one of the narrators, Abu Mu'āwiya, has been critiqued by Hadith experts like Ibn Kharrāsh and jurists like Aḥmad ibn Ḥanbal who have both stated that Abu Mu'āwiya is not reliable when he reports from anyone other than al-A'mash, which is not the case for this narrative. Likewise, another narrator in the same transmission chain, 'Āsim al-Aḥwal, has been critiqued by Hadith experts as being an unknown, having poor memory, or as having a poor character. In another transmission chain of this narrative, Hadith experts have stated that narratives reported by one of the narrators in the transmission chain, ʿAbd al-Malik ibn Muslim, are not reliable enough to be imputed to the Prophet.

The second narrative recorded by Tirmidhī imputes the following statement to the Prophet, which has been critiqued by Hadith experts as two narrators in the transmission chain, Yaʿqūb ibn Abdallah al-Ash'arī and Sa'īd ibn Jubayr (d. 714), were deemed as being unreliable.

> [You may enter your women in any style] from front or behind, but keep away from the anus and the menstrual periods.

Another textual report paraphrased below, which seems similar in content to the Tirmidhī texts, is traced back to Khuzayma ibn Thābit (d. 657), and was referenced by Shāfiʿī (d. 820).

> A man asked the Prophet about entering women from behind. The Prophet asked him to specify if the question was about approaching from the back to enter the front or the anus. He continued: Allah does not shy away from the truth. Do not enter women from their anuses.

So far as the authenticity of this report is concerned, al-Nasāʾī and other experts deemed one of the narrators in the transmission chain, ʿAmr ibn Uḥayḥa, as weak and unknown. A variant of this text that simply mentions the latter *God does not shy from the truth. Do not come to the women from their anuses* part of the text has been narrated from 'Ali ibn Ṭalaq and has been recorded by luminaries like Tirmidhī, al-Nasāʾī and Ibn Ḥibbān.[6] However, the authenticity of all such texts is questionable as they all come from weaker sources as stated by Shāfiʿī (d. 820).[7]

Ibn Māja (d. 887) also compiled a variant of this narrative as follows,[8] wherein one of the narrators in the transmission chain, Ḥajjāj ibn Arṭā, was deemed unreliable and characterized as erroneously ascribing narratives to people by Hadith experts like Ibn Maʿīn (d. 233 AH/852). Likewise, other Hadith experts directed to ignore the narratives of Ḥajjāj ibn Arṭā, or stated that his narratives are not reliable enough to be imputed to the Prophet.

> God is not ashamed of the truth [the Prophet said it three times]. Do not enter women in their anuses.

Another narrator in the transmission chain of the above narrative, ʿAmr ibn Shuʿayb, was critiqued by Hadith experts like Abu Dawūd, who stated that his narratives did not constitute even half an evidence to be imputed to the Prophet, and Yaḥyā al-Qaṭṭān, who classified his narratives as being insignificant. Likewise, another narrator in the transmission chain of the above narrative, Abdallah ibn Haramī, was critiqued as he had only reported a single Hadith from Khuzayma ibn Thābit, which contained lots of weaknesses in its transmission chain.

There appear to be severe weaknesses in all the aforementioned Abu Hurayra and Ibn ʿAbbās texts as well as the Tirmidhī and Ibn Māja texts on heterosexual anal intercourse on the basis of the transmission chain authenticity checks. Even if the weakness in the transmission chain were to be sidelined, the content of these texts, specifically that which is eschatological in nature or that which deems perpetrators of heterosexual anal intercourse as apostates or as transgressors against God's revelation, seems incompatible with the overall spirit of Islamic teachings. Indeed, many Ḥanafī jurists stated that claiming anal intercourse with a wife or female slave as permitted did not necessitate *kufr* (unbelief).[9] For instance, Masʿūd ibn ʿUmar at-Taftāzānī (d. 1389) asserted, "To declare liwāṭa (sodomy) on one's wife as allowed is no heresy."[10] In contrast, in contemporary polemical discourse, sometimes discussions on the right of queer Muslims to same-sex unions are marred by epithets of *kāfir* (apostate) and charges of *kufr* (apostasy).

4.2 TEXTS ON NEUTRALITY

While a majority of the texts seem to indicate the prohibition of heterosexual anal intercourse, there exist other texts that seem to refute the understanding that a consensus opinion against heterosexual anal intercourse could be reached based on textual evidence.[11] A variant text of the Khuzayma ibn Thābit report, mentioned in the previous section, draws out the point of nonprohibition if not outright neutrality. This second variant of the narrative, paraphrased below, has a weakness in the transmission chain as one of the narrators, Haramī ibn Abdullah, was deemed as an unknown by the Hadith experts. The text indicates Abdullah ibn 'Ali ibn Al-Sāʾib responding to the man's question as opposed to the Prophet.

> A man asked Muhammad ibn Ka'b about (anal intercourse) who referred the question to Abdullah ibn 'Ali ibn al-Sāʾib who responded "this is filthy even if permitted."

Notwithstanding authenticity issues, it appears from the *matn* (content)-based analysis of the Khuzayma ibn Thābit variant texts that the issue of legality of the act did not seem to be settled. In fact, the following comment from al-Bazzār, a well-known Hadith compiler, effectively summarizes the status of the texts on the subject.

> I do not know in this field a (single) Hadith that is "Ṣaḥīḥ-correct," neither in permission nor in prohibition, and everything narrated from Khuzayma is not Ṣaḥīḥ, period.

In fact, a similar conclusion is reached by the jurist Shāfi'ī (d. 820), who mentioned, that there does not exist strong evidence for or against the act of heterosexual anal intercourse and that logic would suggest that the activity were permissible.[12] Shāfi'ī has also been referenced as arguing with Muhammad ibn al-Ḥasan on the implication for the legality of heterosexual anal intercourse based on the fact that intercourse was allowed in belly folds and thighs, which are not considered tilths, apart from the vagina, which is usually deemed as the tilth based on verse 2:223.[13]

In contrast, some contemporary Muslims who issue religious opinions have argued that Shāfi'ī deemed the act to be prohibited by quoting him as saying, "I do not give any permission to that; in fact, I deem it prohibited." They also argue that Shāfi'ī considered a Hadith which had the wordings "do not enter women from their rears" to be *ṣaḥīḥ* (authentic).[14] However, it deserves to be noted that quoted Hadith has wordings of the Tirmidhī, Khuzaymah ibn Thābit, and Ibn Māja texts, which were deemed to be inauthentic by several Hadith experts as noted in Section 4.1. Moreover, it is noted in jurisprudence that given conflicting statements of a jurist, as in the case of Shāfi'ī who issued conflicting opinions in his lifetime, one opinion may be preferred over the other specifically in the absence of strong textual proofs.

Notwithstanding the opinion of contemporary Muslims on the prohibition of heterosexual anal intercourse, the opinions of al-Bazzār and Shāfi'ī indicate that there do not exist authentic narratives on the legality of heterosexual anal intercourse, which seems to suggest, at least on the basis of Abdullah ibn 'Ali ibn al-Sā'ib's opinion, that prohibition of the act is based more on personal disgust than on the basis of any textual evidence. Prohibition of the act may also be based on *qiyās* (analogical reasoning) as in the case of al-Ghāzālī (d. 1111) who argued that since the reason behind the prohibition of sexual intercourse during menstruation was noxiousness and since noxiousness was always present in the anus, therefore the prohibition of anal intercourse would be stricter than the prohibition of vaginal intercourse during menstruation.[15]

While contemporary writer Ruqaiyyah Waris Maqsood opines on the prohibition of the act by alluding to the Tirmidhī and Ibn Māja Hadith, as noted in Section 2.2.1, she also refers to the trauma a woman experiences on being subjected to such an act.[16] According to Ibn al-Qayyim (d. 1350), anal intercourse fails to satisfy a woman's sexual desire, deprives her of her right, and as such construed the act as filthy and unnatural.[17] Likewise, contemporary scholar Moiz Amjad, acknowledging the weakness of textual evidence, upholds the prohibition of anal intercourse in general on the basis of *fiṭra* (nature)-based arguments rather than alluding to any text.[18] He also argues that narratives on the prohibition of heterosexual anal intercourse, as seen in Section 4.1, do not appear in the three most accepted collections of Hadith, that is, the Ṣaḥīḥ Bukhārī, the Ṣaḥīḥ Muslim, and the Muwaṭṭa' of Mālik, which casts further doubt on the authenticity of such narratives.

Prohibitions based on *qiyās* are contestable as rulings based on *qiyās* in Islamic jurisprudence are open to challenge and are rarely considered final. Indeed, where the Shī'ī school of jurisprudence rejects *qiyās*, the Ẓāhirī school of Ibn Ḥazm (d. 1064) was built on the principle of rejection of *qiyās*. In a similar spirit, Ibn Taymiyya (d. 1328) quotes Aḥmad ibn Ḥanbal (d. 855) that jurists made the most mistakes in the fields of *ta'wīl* (allegorical interpretation) and *qiyās*.[19] Just as the weakness in analogy-based rulings has been acknowledged, most theologians do not accept arguments based on "natural prohibitions" and that perhaps such arguments were first developed to counter arguments which could not be rationally refuted.

It is also interesting to note how some conservative Muslims who issue religious rulings end up conflating the issue with the destruction of the people of Lūṭ who are characterized as being accustomed to the evil habit of homosexual anal intercourse, which perhaps explains the taboo that is associated with the subject,[20] and which also reinforces the preclusion of any meaningful discussion on the plight of queer Muslims.

4.3 TEXTS ON PERMISSIBILITY—THE IBN 'UMAR TEXTS

While there appear to exist texts that seem to prohibit heterosexual anal intercourse, enjoyment of the anus without penetration was deemed licit in Muslim jurisprudence as in the work of al-Nawawī (d. 1278).[21] Likewise, al-Zabīdī (d. 1790) opined on the issue as follows.

> To enjoy the backside without entering the rectum is permissible, because with that exception, all parts of a woman's body may be enjoyed by the husband.[22]

Notwithstanding authenticity issues, there also exist competing texts that actually allow for the act of heterosexual anal intercourse. Three variants of a text, paraphrased below,[23] that is traced back to Ibn 'Umar (d. 693) through Nāfiʿ (d. 735), actually indicate that verse 2:223 actually allows for heterosexual anal intercourse on the basis of Ibn ʿUmar's understanding of the Qur'anic text. One of these texts has been mentioned by Bukhārī (d. 870) in his commentary of chapter 2 of the Quran, and the other by Mālik (d. 795), though not in his Muwaṭṭa', which is why some Mālikī jurists like Abu Muhammad Abdullah ibn Ibrāhīm al-Aṣīlī[24] have allowed for the act[25] whereas others hold it prohibited.

> Ibn ʿUmar asked: Do you know Nāfiʿ, why this verse (2:223) was revealed to us? . . . When people did not like the fact that one of the men of Medina had anal intercourse with his wife, God revealed this verse (Your women are your tilth). Nāfiʿ asked: Coming to her from the back in the vagina? Ibn ʿUmar replied: No, in her anus. (Mālik ibn Anas variant)

> Once Ibn ʿUmar read chapter 2 until he came to the verse and asked Nāfiʿ: Do you know for what was it revealed? Nāfiʿ responded in the negative. Ibn ʿUmar replied it was revealed for that (anus) and then he continued. (Bukhārī variant)

> Ibn ʿUmar mentioned about the verse (2:223): He comes to her ________ (anus) (Bukhārī variant)

However, some contemporary Muslims who issue religious opinions at the Islamweb site have argued that Ibn al-Qayyim (d. 1350) had refuted the misconception that the Ibn ʿUmar texts allowed for heterosexual anal intercourse and equated Ibn ʿUmar's narratives with those of Ibn ʿAbbās (d. 687).[26] However, they do not quote Ibn al-Qayyim's refutation, and the Ibn ʿAbbās text they reference, as follows, does not provide any indication of the prohibition of heterosexual anal intercourse.[27]

> Ibn ʿAbbās said regarding verse 2:223: "Your wives are as a tilth unto you; so approach your tilth when or how you will; but do some good act for your souls beforehand and fear Allah, and know that ye are to meet him (in the Hereafter), and give (these) good tidings to those who believe."

While the Islamweb site does not indicate how the prohibition of heterosexual anal intercourse can be construed from the statement of Ibn ʿAbbās, the online Tafsīr of Ibn Kathīr (d. 1373) indicates that in the context of verse 2:223, Ibn ʿAbbās commented that the "tilth" referred to the place of pregnancy and that intercourse can be had however one liked as long as it took place in the *farj* (genital).[28] In another text, recorded by Abu Dawūd (d. 888), Ibn ʿAbbās is reported to have said that Ibn ʿUmar erred in his interpretation of the verse of tilth.[29] Likewise, a text referring to the opinion of Ibn ʿAbbās on heterosexual anal intercourse has been traced to Saʿīd ibn Jubayr (d. 714) through Ibn Jarīr and Ibn Abi al-Ḥātim as follows:

> Ibn ʿAbbās responded to man's query: Is there any tilth in the posterior? If what you say were correct then the verse of menstruation would be abrogated, because if that place was not open (because of blood) you would go into this (other) place! But his verse means "whenever you like" in the night or day![30]

The opinion that intercourse takes place in one valve was echoed by Ibn Jurayj (d. 767) through a Hadith, whose transmission chain is not provided in Ibn Kathīr's commentary, and also Aḥmad ibn Ḥanbal (d. 855), who referenced a Hadith, classified as *ḥasan* (good) but not *ṣaḥīḥ* (authentic) by Tirmidhī, which indicates that intercourse takes place only in one valve.[31] A Hadith text that is traced to Jābir ibn Abdullah (d. 697) through Ibn ʿAsākir (d. 1175) also indicates that intercourse takes place in the same valve.[32]

Both the Islamweb site and the online Tafsīr of Ibn Kathīr reference a narrative by Nāfiʿ, as follows, that seems to suggest that people were slandering Nāfiʿ by stating that he allowed for the permissibility of heterosexual anal intercourse.

> Imam al-Nasāʾī (d. 915) reported via Kaʿb ibn ʿAlqama that Abu al-Nadhar asked Nāfiʿ (d. 735): It is being reported from you that you related a statement from Ibn ʿUmar, which suggests that he allowed having sex in anus. He replied: They lie about me.[33]

The narrative continues with Nāfiʿ clarifying the reason behind the misunderstanding that he allowed for the act of heterosexual anal intercourse. The Islamweb version ends the narrative with Ibn ʿUmar's explanation that verse 2:223 referred to the context of vaginal intercourse. While the version in the Tafsīr of Ibn Kathīr does not contain Ibn ʿUmar's allusion to vaginal intercourse, it indicates that the transmission chain narrators are authentic.

Likewise, with the indication that the transmission chain narrators are authentic, Tafsīr Ibn Kathīr also contains a narrative reported by Abu Muhammad Abdullah ibn ʿAbd al-Raḥmān Dārimī (d. 868) in his *'Musnad'*-compilation that indicates Ibn ʿUmar's questioning whether a Muslim would commit the act of heterosexual anal intercourse.

> Saʿīd ibn Yasār Abu al-Ḥubāb asked Ibn ʿUmar, "What is your position on having sex with women in the rear?" . . . and clarified that he meant "anal intercourse." Ibn ʿUmar questioned . . . "Does a Muslim do that?"[34]

It is clear that Ibn Kathīr in his *Tafsīr* (commentary) argues for the prohibition of heterosexual anal intercourse by alluding to texts related to Ibn ʿAbbās, Ibn Jurayj, Nāfiʿ, and Ibn ʿUmar, whose transmission chains he considers authentic. He marshals all the evidence that would seemingly oppose the Ibn ʿUmar texts that allow for heterosexual anal intercourse, one of which was recorded by Bukhārī. However, it is interesting to note that Ibn Kathīr neither critiqued the transmission chain of the Bukhārī text nor explained why it was incorrect.

The Islamweb site indicates that no report from Bukhārī allows for anal intercourse with one's wife.[35] However, instead of recording any text on the prohibition of heterosexual anal intercourse, Bukhārī recorded a variant of the Ibn ʿUmar narrative on the permissibility of heterosexual anal intercourse.

Neither the Islamweb site nor the online Tafsīr of Ibn Kathīr critique the Bukhārī text that seemingly allows for the act of anal intercourse and rather marshal texts that indicate the prohibition of the act. However, the marshaled evidence, none of which is strong enough to stand against the Bukhārī text, has to be viewed with skepticism.

Another reason why the Ibn ʿAbbās, Ibn Jurayj, Nāfiʿ, and Ibn ʿUmar texts reported in the Tafsīr of Ibn Kathīr have to be viewed with skepticism is because the Tafsīr also contains other texts, marshaled as evidence for the prohibition of heterosexual anal intercourse, which, as noted in Section 4.1, have already been deemed weak by past Hadith expert authorities.

The Tafsīr of Ibn Kathīr reports the Khuzayma ibn Thābit narrative along with the 'Ali ibn Ṭalaq variant, classified as *ḥasan* (good) by Tirmidhī. However, as noted in Section 4.1, the Khuzayma ibn Thābit narrative was critiqued by Hadith authorities. The Tafsīr of Ibn Kathīr also reports a variant of the second Abu Hurayra text noted in Section 4.1, which is attributed to Ibn ʿAbbās and has been reported by Tirmidhī, al-Nasāʾī, Ibn Ḥibbān (d. 965), and Ibn Ḥazm. However, as noted earlier, several Hadith experts have critiqued the authenticity of the narrative of this text.

The marshaling of inauthentic or weak textual evidence seemingly against the Ibn ʿUmar texts is not limited to the Tafsīr of Ibn Kathīr. The Islamweb site has seemingly also presented the first and second Abu Hurayra texts, as noted in Section 4.1, without indicating how the past Hadith authorities have severely critiqued such texts.

Finally, while Tafsīr of Ibn Kathīr and the Islamweb site have marshaled texts, which indicate Nāfiʿ stating that people lied about him on the subject and Ibn ʿUmar questioning whether a Muslim indulged in the act, several past authorities referenced the Ibn ʿUmar texts in a fashion that seemed to confirm the permissibility of the act.

While Ṭabarī (d. 923) recorded Ibn ʿUmar's commentary on verse 2:223 on the permissibility of heterosexual anal intercourse, Ibn ʿAbd al-Barr (d. 1071) stated that traditions wherein Ibn ʿUmar accepts the permissibility of heterosexual anal intercourse are *ṣaḥīḥ*—authentic and well known.[36] Likewise, Ṭabarānī (d. 970), Ḥasan ibn Sufyān along with al-Ḥākim al-Naysābūrī and Abu Naʿīm have all recorded an Ibn ʿUmar narrative whose transmission chain was deemed *ḥasan* (good) as follows.

Ibn ʿUmar stated: "This verse [2:223] was revealed to the Prophet with respect to the permissibility of anal intercourse."[37]

Likewise, a text traced to Abu Saʿīd al-Khudrī (d. 682/693) through good transmission chains from Ibn Rahwayh, Abu Ya'la, Ibn Jarīr, Al-Ṭaḥāwī (d. 935), and Ibn Marduwayh (d. 1019) indicates that the verse of tilth was revealed after people thought ill of a person who had heterosexual anal intercourse.[38]

In light of the weak and selective evidence marshaled by conservative Muslims through the Islamweb site and the online Tafsīr of Ibn Kathīr, as noted above, a clear prohibition of heterosexual anal intercourse cannot be sustained.

4.4 THE POSITION OF THE JURIST MĀLIK IBN ANAS (D. 795) AND THE *SALAF* (PIOUS ELDERS)

As noted earlier, apart from Bukhārī, the jurist Mālik ibn Anas, founder of the Mālikī school of jurisprudence, also reported the Ibn ʿUmar narrative, though not in his Muwaṭṭaʾ. Just as there is a report on Ibn Abi Mulayka's using oil for anal intercourse with a slave girl, there also exist texts recorded by Suyūṭī (d. 1505) and al-Alūsī (d. 1854) that seem to indicate that Mālik himself indulged in the act of heterosexual anal intercourse.[39]

However, as in the Nāfiʿ and Ibn ʿUmar context, the online Tafsīr of Ibn Kathīr and the Islamweb site reference a text from Abu Bakr ibn Ziyād Naysābūrī, as follows, which indicates that Mālik expressed that people fabricated lies against him on the subject.

Ismāʿīl ibn Rūḥ asked Mālik ibn Anas, "What is your position on having sex with women in the anus?" Mālik replied, "You are not an Arab! Does sex occur but in the place of tilth (pregnancy)? Do it only in the farj (vagina)." Ismāʿīl responded, "People claim that you allow that practice." He said, "They fabricate lies against me, they fabricate lies."[40]

However, both the online Tafsīr of Ibn Kathīr and the Islamweb site fail to address the weakness in the narratives that allege that Mālik himself indulged in the act of heterosexual anal intercourse. Moreover, they seem to ignore other narratives that present Mālik's opinion on the permissibility of heterosexual anal intercourse, which were referenced by al-Jaṣṣāṣ (d. 981), Ibn Qudāma (d. 1223), and Shawkānī (d. 1834) as follows:

al-Jaṣṣāṣ recorded that Abu Bakr said: "It is well known that Mālik allowed it [anal intercourse] but his companions deny it because it was a nasty statement. In fact, it is well known and cannot be rejected by their denial."[41]

> Ibn Qudāma recorded that Mālik said: "I have never met someone that I deem a religious role model who doubts that it [anal intercourse] is permissible."[42]

Likewise, Shawkānī recorded a narrative through Ṭaḥāwī, whose transmission chain include Aṣbagh ibn al-Faraj and ʿAbd al-Raḥmān Ibn al-Qāsim, which reports Mālik's statement similar to but more extensive than the Ibn Qudāma version.

> Mālik said: "I have never met someone that I deem a religious role model who doubts that entering a woman in the anus is permissible." After reciting portion of 2:223, he continued "What could be clearer than this?"[43]

While ignoring these texts, the Islamweb site and the online Tafsīr of Ibn Kathīr state that the *Salaf* (pious elders), which includes the Companions and two generations that followed them, condemned the practice of heterosexual anal intercourse or deemed it tantamount to *kufr* (disbelief). The array of *Salaf* that both sources refer to includes Saʿīd ibn Musayyib (d. 715), Abu Salama, ʿIkrima, Ṭāwūs, ʿAṭāʾ, Saʿīd ibn Jubayr (d. 714), ʿUrwah ibn al-Zubayr (d. 713), Mujāhid ibn Jabr (d. 722), and al-Ḥasan. The Islamweb site also indicates that similar strong opinions, apart from Mālik ibn Anas, were held by the other three founding fathers of the extant four Sunnī schools of jurisprudence.[44]

However, alternate sources indicate that a large group among the Salaf that included Muhammad ibn Kaʿb al-Quraẓī (d. 735) and ʿAbd al-Malik ibn al-Mājishūn apart from Nāfiʿ, Ibn ʿUmar, Mālik ibn Anas, and Saʿīd ibn Musayyib (d. 715) deemed heterosexual anal intercourse to be permissible.[45] Similar to Thanaullah Panipati (d. 1810) and Ibn Kathīr, al-Shawkānī (d. 1834) recorded in his book *Nayl al-Awṭār* that "anal intercourse with women is the statement of the jurists of Medina."[46]

Ibn Shaʿbān and Muhammad ibn Saḥnūn (d. 256 AH) also narrated the permissibility of heterosexual anal intercourse from a large number of *Tābiʿūn*—followers. Indeed, the Tafsīr of Qurṭubī records the following statement.

> Ibn al-ʿArabī mentioned that Ibn Shaʿbān attributed the statement [on anal intercourse] to a large group of Ṣaḥāba—Companions and Tābiʿūn—followers.[47]

It becomes clear from the above analysis that the issue of heterosexual anal intercourse in Sunnī jurisprudence is not as clear as is usually considered, and that there exists conflicting evidence for both the permissibility and prohibition of the act. As such, a clear prohibition of heterosexual anal intercourse cannot be sustained.

4.5 THE COMMENTARY OF AL-RĀZĪ (D. 1209)

The argument for permissibility of heterosexual anal intercourse revolves around Ibn ʿUmar's understanding of the verse of tilth (2:223). This verse, part of which is reproduced below, has been interpreted differently by scholars on the basis of the key words used in the text, namely, "*Ḥarth*-tilth" and "*faʾtū ḥarthakum annā shiʾtum*—so go to your tilth as you will."

> Your women are a tilth for you so go to your tilth as you will . . . . (2:223)

According to the commentary of al-Rāzī (d. 1209),[48] traditional scholars have differed on the interpretation of *ḥarth* (tilth), that is, whether the tilth mainly refers to bearing children or whether it refers to something beyond that, which could include mutual spiritual and emotional fulfillment of the couple involved. In fact, traditional scholars have advanced arguments for both interpretations. Likewise, there was a difference of opinion on the phrase "so go to your tilth as you will," in that whether it included non-sexual approaching of the spouse or just focused on the sexual aspect of the approach. Furthermore, the word *annā* can easily accommodate meanings of both "when you will" and "where you will" and it is in the second sense that the verse has been traditionally used for the permissibility of anal sex with the wife.[49]

In conjunction with verse 2:222, which mentions the phrase "*min ḥaythu amarakum Allah*—from where God has ordered you," traditional scholars have voiced another difference of opinion on whether the verses allow for only vaginal intercourse or also allow for heterosexual anal intercourse as left to the discretion of the couple involved. However, support for the latter has come from a minority of Sunnī scholars, including some Mālikī scholars who, according to secondary sources,[50] have even allowed for anal intercourse with male slaves, based probably on analogy with female concubinage, and Shī'ī scholars who substantiate their opinions based on their narratives as traced back to Ja'far al-Bāqir (d. 733), some of whom actually, like their Mālikī counterparts, have allowed for anal intercourse with male slaves.[51]

In conclusion, given the absence of clear or authentic textual evidence for or against heterosexual anal intercourse, difference of opinion on the issue is based on the interpretation of verses 2:222–223. The absence of strong textual evidences possibly explains why past authorities like al-Bazzār and Shāfiʿī, as noted in Section 4.2, adopted a more neutral position on the subject. Moreover, to the extent that the Ibn ʿUmar texts are deemed authentic enough, a case may even be made for the permissibility of heterosexual anal intercourse. The Qur'anic Path group online, which sidelines the Hadith texts, already allows for the permissibility of the act based on the argument that just as the primary function of the mouth for talking and eating does not influence the permissibility of oral sex, likewise, even if the primary purpose of the anus was not for penetration, that still does not make the act prohibited.[52]

The above analysis also seems to suggest that, given the absence of clear textual evidence on the basis of traditional scholarship, the issue of heterosexual anal intercourse does not warrant as much a taboo as exists within conservative Muslim circles, since there existed difference of opinion on the issue. Furthermore, it also appears that the prohibition of the act, to the extent that al-Ghāzālī's arguments are reflective of those of other Muslim scholars, is based on disgust and analogy, which essentially hinders the discussion on same-sex unions within conservative Muslim circles.

In conclusion, the discussion about the permissibility of anal intercourse with wives or female slaves does not pose hindrance to the wider question of whether there is space for same-sex unions Islamically. Suppose one concludes that the Hadith clearly and unequivocally prohibit anal intercourse with wives or concubines, so on that basis *qiyās awlā* (better fitting analogy) may be used to argue as follows. Since anal intercourse with wives and concubines is prohibited, it would be more fitting for it to be prohibited between two males, and therefore the case for same-sex union is moot. However, this argument can be rejected for at least two reasons.

First, anal intercourse with women is not the same as between men for while there is no physiological reason for women to enjoy the act, there is a clear physiological reason for some men, indeed a minority, to enjoy the process of prostatic massage. Second, even if one concludes that anal intercourse is prohibited irrespective of gender, it still does not hinder accepting same-sex unions as they are not defined by a single supposedly prohibited sexual act, for there is more to intimacy than mere anal intercourse.

4.6 HETEROSEXUAL ANAL INTERCOURSE IN SHĪ'Ī JURISPRUDENCE

Muslim authorities in Sunnī jurisprudence categorically forbid heterosexual anal intercourse. However, acknowledging the differing viewpoints on the verse of tilth and conflicting textual evidence in the tradition, many authorities in Shī'ī jurisprudence adopt a different view. Zayn al-Dīn al-'Āmilī (d. 1558) noted the Shī'ī position to deem the act of heterosexual anal intercourse as *karāha mughallaẓa*—nearly prohibited but not actually prohibited based on the textual evidence and interpretation of the verse of tilth.[53]

While some past and a few contemporary Shī'ī authorities forbid the act, many including past authorities like Shaykh al-Mufīd (d. 1022), Shaykh Ṭūsī (d. 1067), Sharīf al-Murtaḍā (d. 1044), and Ibn al-Muṭahhar al-Ḥillī

(d. 726 AH) deem the act *makruh*—detestable but not sinful.[54] Based on the widely held Shī'ī opinion, Shī'ī authorities in contemporary times like Ayatollah Lankarānī (d. 2007) ruled that while the act is undesirable, abominable, and beneath human dignity, it would be permissible with the wife's consent and provided no harm is caused to either partner.[55] Likewise, contemporary authority Ayatollah Sistānī has ruled that while the act is strongly undesirable, it is permissible based on the wife's agreement.[56]

As in the Sunnī tradition, the Shī'ī tradition contains conflicting textual evidence on heterosexual anal intercourse. A Hadith quoted by Ja'far al-Ṣādiq (d. 765) indicates that the Prophet stated that the anus of women is forbidden. However, al-Ḥillī (d. 1325) and al-'Āmilī (d. 1558) critiqued the transmission chain of this Hadith.[57] In contrast, a text from Abdullah ibn Abi Ya'fūr, whose transmission chain has been deemed authentic, indicates that Ja'far al-Ṣādiq opined that there is no problem with anal intercourse if the wife agrees,[58] and recited the verse of tilth (2:223) to substantiate his position.[59] However, both 'Ali Reza (d. 818), who expressed personal dislike for the act, and Ja'far al-Ṣādiq have also cautioned that since a woman is a means of pleasure, she should not be harmed.[60] Thus, as in the Sunnī tradition where the 'Ali ibn al-Sā'ib's text alluded to personal disgust, it seems that the Shī'ī position is also informed by personal dislike in the absence of strong textual evidence against heterosexual anal intercourse.

Muhammad Ḥusayn Ṭabāṭabā'ī (d. 1981) indicated in his Tafsīr al-mīzān that notwithstanding the detestability of the act, the permissibility of heterosexual anal intercourse does not depend on the verse of tilth but rather on verse 15:71, which depicts Lūṭ offering his daughters to the mob knowing well that they were not seeking vaginal intercourse.[61] The Shī'ī texts that allude to verse 15:71 for the permissibility of heterosexual anal intercourse include the text traced back to 'Ali Reza (d. 818) through Shaykh Ṭūsī (d. 1067) and the text traced back to Ḥasan ibn 'Ali (d. 670).[62]

Ṭabāṭabā'ī also opined that deriving the prohibition of heterosexual anal sex on the basis of the words "as Allah ordered you" in the verse of tilth 2:223 would be difficult and considers it to be the weakest argument. He reasoned that the verse is merely granting permission to establish sexual relations after menstruation and as such is not prescribing an obligation.[63] Ṭabāṭabā'ī's opinion on verse 2:223 only confirms the observation in Tafsīr of al-Rāzī, according to which traditional scholars have differed on the interpretation of verse 2:223.

In conclusion, the Shī'ī position can be projected as one of permissibility of heterosexual anal intercourse with the proviso that the wife's consent needs to be sought along and the qualifier that the act is deemed to be *makruh* (detestable). If the wife disagrees, then the Shī'ī position is that as a precaution, it would be *wajib* (obligatory) to abstain from the act.[64] In some sense, the Shī'ī position is not too different from the opinions upheld by Sunnī authorities like al-Bazzār and Shāfi'ī, as noted in Section 4.2, who took a neutral position on the issue citing the absence of strong textual evidence against the act. Shāfi'ī acknowledged that there is not a single *ṣaḥīḥ* (authentic) Hadith for or against the act and asserted his opinion on prohibition on the basis of poor taste.

To reiterate, there exist contradicting Hadith and reports on the act of heterosexual anal intercourse, where some texts prohibit the act and others from Ibn 'Umar allow for it. The Hadith in Bukhārī does not explicitly mention the *dubur* (anus) but leaves a blank, which leads to the impression that the text allowed for the act and therefore Bukhārī shied away from mentioning it expressly. At most, the better designations of the narrators in the transmission chains are "accepted" and "truthful good in Hadith" both of which are not accepted as strong designations.

It is also important to underscore that in the absence of strong textual evidence against the act, Sunnī and Shī'ī authorities provided their opinions on the basis of considerations of noxiousness, personal disgust, and avoiding harm. The case of the prohibition of anal sex on women appears in the context of women generally not desiring or wanting such an act. Given the absence of the prostate, pleasure in this case is derived by the penetrating men and not the receptive women. Thus, even if the Hadith texts are construed as authentic enough to support the case of prohibition, given physiological differences between men and women due to the pleasure derived by males from the prostate, the prohibition from a heterosexual to a homosexual context is not readily transferable. In short, the detestability or prohibition of heterosexual anal intercourse is based on these extra-scriptural considerations, which regardless do not influence the issue of Muslim same-sex unions that are not defined by a single sexual act of anal intercourse. Regardless, the next chapter delves into the reasoning of the classical jurists on *liwāṭ*—homosexual intercourse between males in the context of disease and subordination.

Acknowledgment: This section draws heavily on Ibn Ḥajar al-'Asqalānī, *Talkhīṣ al-Ḥabīr*, Book of Nikāḥ, chapter that addresses anal intercourse.

NOTES

Unless the reference is from an online source, translation of the texts is by the authors.

1. Amjad, "Narratives on the Prohibition of Anal Sex."
2. This paragraph draws from Ibn Ḥajar al-'Asqalānī, *Tahdhīb al-Tahdhīb*, referenced in Moiz Amjad, "Narratives on the Prohibition of Anal Sex."

3. The Ibn ʿAbbās text and its variants based on varying narrators in the transmission chain can be found in Ibn Ḥajar al-ʿAsqalānī, *Talkhīṣ al-Ḥabīr*, Volume 3, 179–186.

4. Al-Mizzī, *Tahdhīb al-Kamāl*, Volume 11, 397.

5. Amjad, "Narratives on the Prohibition of Anal Sex."

6. Ibn Ḥajar al-ʿAsqalānī, *Talkhīṣ al-Ḥabīr*, Volume 3, 179–86.

7. Ibn Ḥajar al-ʿAsqalānī, *Talkhīṣ al-Ḥabīr*, Volume 3, 181; Al-Suyūṭī, *Al-Durr al-Manthūr fī al-Tafsīr bi-l-Maʾthūr,* Volume 1, 266, see the comment by BOY-NICE, "Shiasm revealed."

8. Amjad, "Narratives on the Prohibition of Anal Sex."

9. El-Rouayheb, (2005), *Before Homosexuality,* 124.

10. Schmitt and Sofer, *Sexuality and Eroticism,* 14.

11. Ibn Ḥajar al-ʿAsqalānī, *Talkhīṣ al-Ḥabīr*, Volume 3, 179–86.

12. Ibn Ḥajar al-ʿAsqalānī, *Talkhīṣ al-Ḥabīr*, Volume 3, 181; Al-Suyūṭī, *Al-Durr al-Manthūr fī al-Tafsīr bi-l-Maʾthūr,* Volume 1, 266, see the comment by BOY-NICE, "Shiasm revealed."

13. Ṭabāṭabāʾī, *Tafsīr al-Mīzān.*

14. 'Is anal sex permitted in the Shafi'i school?' IslamQA, April 10, 2012, accessed January 26, 2016, http://islamqa.org/shafii/shafiifiqh/30067.

15. Haddad, "Oral Sex."

16. Ruqayyah Waris Maqsood, *The Muslim Marriage Guide*, (New Delhi: Goodword Books, 2005), 144–45.

17. Ibid.

18. Amjad, "Narratives on the Prohibition of Anal Sex."

19. Aḥmad ibn ʿAbd al-Ḥalīm Ibn Taymiyya, *Majmūʿ Fatāwā*, in الموسوعة الذهبية للحديث النبوي الشيف و علومه [*The Golden Encyclopedia of the Prophetic Golden Hadeeth and its Sciences*], 2nd edition, (London: Turath Publishing), CD-ROM.

20. IslamOnline Fatwa Committee, "Islamic Ruling on Anal Sex. Reprinted from IslamOnline's Fatwa Bank," accessed January 26, 2016, http://www.zawaj.com/articles/ruling_anl_sx.html.

21. Haddad, "Oral Sex."

22. Ruqayyah Waris Maqsood, *The Muslim Marriage Guide*, (New Delhi: Goodword Books, 2005), 144–45.

23. Ibn Ḥajar al-ʿAsqalānī, *Talkhīṣ al-Ḥabīr*, Volume 3, 179–86.

24. Al-ʿAynī, Badr al-Dīn. ʿ*Umda al-Qārī Sharḥ Ṣaḥīḥ al-Bukhārī*, Volume 8, 403. Reference from Chapter Fourteen: Nasibi propaganda relating to sexual ethics, Shia Pen, accessed January 25, 2016, http://www.shiapen.com/comprehensive/mutah/nasibi-propaganda-of-sexual-ethics.html.

25. Ali, *Marriage and Slavery in Early Islam*, 182.

26. "Fatwa #: 86457, Anal Sex Strictly Forbidden," Islamweb, accessed January 26, 2016, http://www.islamweb.net/emainpage/index.php?page=showfatwa&Option=FatwaId&Id=86457.

27. Ibid.

28. Ibn Kathīr, "The Reason behind revealing Allah's Statement: 'Your Wives are a Tilth for You.'"

29. Ṭabāṭabā'ī, *Tafsīr al-Mīzān*, verse 2:222–223.
30. Ibid.
31. Ibn Kathīr, "The Reason behind revealing Allah's Statement: 'Your Wives are a Tilth for You.'"
32. Ṭabāṭabā'ī, *Tafsīr al-Mīzān*, verse 2:222–223.
33. Ibn Kathīr, "The Reason behind revealing Allah's Statement: 'Your Wives are a Tilth for You.'"
34. Ibid.
35. "Anal Sex Strictly Forbidden," Islam web.
36. "Chapter Fourteen: Nasibi propaganda relating to sexual ethics," Shia Pen.
37. Ibid.
38. Ṭabāṭabā'ī, *Tafsīr al-Mīzān*, verse 2:222–223.
39. "Chapter Fourteen: Nasibi propaganda relating to sexual ethics," Shia Pen.
40. Ibn Kathīr, "The Reason behind revealing Allah's Statement: 'Your Wives are a Tilth for You.'"
41. Al-Jaṣṣāṣ, *Aḥkām al-Qur'an*, Volume 2, 40, reference from Shia Pen, "Chapter Fourteen: Nasibi propaganda relating to sexual ethics."
42. Al-Maqdisī, *Al-Mughnī*, Volume 8, 132, reference from Shia Pen, "Chapter Fourteen: Nasibi propaganda relating to sexual ethics."
43. Al-Shawkānī, *Tafsīr Fatḥ al-Qadīr*, Volume 1, 354, reference from Shia Pen, "Chapter Fourteen: Nasibi propaganda relating to sexual ethics."
44. "Anal sex strictly forbidden," Islam web.
45. Al-Qurṭubī, *Tafsīr al-Qurṭubī*. Commentary of 2:223, (Amman: Royal Aal al-Bayt Institute for Islamic Thought), accessed May 10, 2016, http://altafsir.com/.
46. "Chapter Fourteen: Nasibi propaganda relating to sexual ethics," Shia Pen.
47. Ibid.
48. See Al-Rāzī, *Tafsīr al-Rāzī* on verse 2:223.
49. Amr Shalakany, "Comparative Law as Archeology: On Sodomy, Islamic Law and the Human Rights Activist," Draft: October 9, 2006, accessed January 27, 2016, http://www.utexas.edu/law/centers/humanrights/events/speaker-series-papers/Shalakany.pdf, 26.
50. Adang, "Ibn Ḥazm on Homosexuality," 9.
51. Ābādī, *'Awn al-Ma'būd fī Sharḥ Sunan Abu Dawūd*, Volume 12, 99.
52. "Does the Qur'an prohibit anal sex between husband and wife?" Quranic Path, accessed January 27, 2016, http://www.quranicpath.com/misconceptions/anal_sex.html.
53. "Chapter Fourteen: Nasibi Propaganda Relating to Sexual Ethics," Shia Pen.
54. Ibid.
55. "Anal Intercourse," The Official website of Grand Ayatollah Muhammad Fazel Lankarani, accessed January 27, 2016, http://www.lankarani.com/eng/faq/a.php.
56. Ahlul Bayt Foundation, Rulings of Grand Ayatollah Sistani, Marriage.
57. Sayyid Muhammad Rizvi, *Marriage and Morals in Islam*, (Ahlul Bayt Digital Islamic Library Project, Ontario, Canada), accessed January 27, 2016, http://www.al-islam.org/marriage-and-morals-islam-sayyid-muhammad-rizvi/chapter-three-islamic-sexual-morality-2-its#c-marriage.

58. Ibid.
59. "Chapter Fourteen: Nasibi Propaganda Relating to Sexual Ethics," Shia Pen.
60. Rizvi, "Chapter 3, The Islamic Sexual Morality."
61. Ṭabāṭabā'ī, *Tafsīr al-Mīzān*, verse 2:222–223.
62. Al-Kashani, *Tafsir Kashani*. Commentary of 11:78, (Amman: Royal Aal al-Bayt Institute for Islamic Thought), accessed May 10, 2016, http://altafsir.com/.
63. Ṭabāṭabā'ī, *Tafsīr al-Mīzān*, verse 2:222–223.
64. Rizvi, "Chapter 3, The Islamic Sexual Morality."

Chapter 5

Revisiting Muslim Jurisprudence

The eponymous founders of the four extant Sunnī schools of jurisprudence—Abu Ḥanīfa (d. 765), Mālik (d. 795), Shāfiʿī, (d. 820) and Ibn Ḥanbal (d. 855)—and their followers can be classified into three groups based on their position on *liwāṭ*. Essentially, all classified *liwāṭ* as a sin, which is understandable given their understanding that *liwāṭ* inflicts subordination and humiliation on the passive partner, which in many cases was a beardless youth who submitted for pecuniary reasons as opposed to pleasure. In contrast to the observation in Arabic literature that the onset of beards meant decline in attractiveness, Lagrange shows that one of the libels indicates how someone went crazy over another's budding beard.[1] However, even in the case of adult males, the jurists assumed that since *liwāṭ* inflicts humiliation on the passive partner, the only way someone could submit to homosexual anal penetration was due to disease related to the anus-*ʾubna*.

Despite the fact that *liwāṭ* inflicted humiliation on the receptive partner, jurists decided to punish the *ma'buns* (receptive partners suffering from *ʾubna*) as well, as it could be that the jurists were dismayed by the apparent availability of such men to others in their location through prostitution or in the general context of *ʾubna*. Sexual practice with free men in the context of *ʾubna* was not monogamous, which may have been deemed as a danger to society and to the social order because in such cases sex is not regulated. In contrast to such sexual practice with free men that was not tolerated, some scholars and indeed the society at large may have tolerated sex between the master and his male slave, as it was regulated.

Moreover, jurists assumed that the active partner's attraction toward youth was not a sole desire toward them but the same that was directed toward women and therefore could be sated with lawful female partners.[2] Khaled el-Rouayheb has also noted that in the medieval Arabic texts, a man was generally depicted as being drawn toward the feminine features of the boy rather than his masculine features and as such men were assumed to be attracted to women.[3] Moreover, al-Nawawī (d. 1278) is also quoted as having stated that the male youth is like a woman as his beauty is similar to a woman's beauty and that he is desired as she is desired.[4] Furthermore, in the disputation theme in poetry, where love of women was contrasted with the love of boys, there was never a theme of men being attracted toward other men with masculine features.[5] As such, the exegetes and jurists viewed sexual activity between males as based on an age- and status-stratified asymmetrical relationship between unequal partners, which stands in contrast to contemporary gay relationships between equal partners.[6]

Ibn Sīnā (d. 1037) portrayed the passive partner as spiteful, ill-tempered, and effeminate and that any treatment was futile.[7] He denied a genetic cause for the disease, which he blamed on imagination and prescribed hunger, vigils, detention, and beating to break the desire.[8] However, al-Rāzī (d. 925) considered *ʾubna* to be genetic in that it was a result of the maternal sperm overpowering the paternal sperm at conception. While he prescribed enemas and sensual massages of the private parts, based on the Galenic model of humoral effect,[9] by good-looking maids and slaves, he also stated that the disease if prolonged would be incurable.[10] In his medical work, Dāwūd al-Anṭākī (d. 1599) explained *ʾubna* through the presence of a boric substance in the veins of the rectum that caused an itch in the anus, which prompted the person to seek penetration.[11] Al-Anṭākī opined that *ʾubna*, which, outside the medical literature, was explained in terms of a worm-infected anus, was either inherited or acquired through penetration by the effect of pungent semen, and he suggested the remedies of rubbing the anus with ash from the burnt hair of a hyena's right thigh or by using potions of lapis lazuli, agaric, aloe, mastic, or clove with yogurt.[12]

Likewise, the physician al-Kindī (d. 873), seemingly based on Galen (d. 200), deemed that *siḥāq* was explained by an itch in the labia and Yūḥannā ibn Māsawayh (d. 857) indicated that *siḥāq* was a consequence of a nursing woman eating celery, rocket, melilot leaves, and flowers of a bitter orange tree.[13] Islamicate medical tracts also indicate that the human body would have a feminine or masculine, active or passive, and penetrating or penetrated type of sexuality.[14] Medical texts also indicated that abstinence was associated with the accumulation of seminal fluids in testicles or ovaries leading to pain, weakening of eyesight, and tumors in testicles or ureters and as such regular intercourse or masturbation was prescribed to avoid such illnesses.[15] Sex with male youths was not advisable as only a healthy young woman's womb, in contrast to old, ugly or weak women, provided scope to properly absorb semen.[16]

According to Khaled el-Rouayheb, medical paradigms were assimilated into the Islamic religious discourse in previous centuries,[17] and as such the jurists addressed *'ubna* based on the medical knowledge of their times. Based on the knowledge of their times, some jurists also prescribed cures; for instance, Ja'far al-Ṣādiq (d. 765) is reported to have suggested that a person suffering from *'ubna* sit on a chopped off hump of a camel.[18] Likewise, as will be noted in Section 5.5, jurists like Ramlī (d. 1550) seemingly issued juristic opinions on allowing for a kiss to avoid the lover's death based on such medical theories. As such, it may be reasonable to revisit the extra-scriptural assumptions used by the past jurists in deriving their rulings.

It is also interesting to note that *liwāṭ* was associated with various segments of Muslim societies including Muslim leaders, jurists, and *ḥuffāẓ*—memorizers of the Qur'an.[19] Where Shaykh Ḥasan al-'Aṭṭār (d. 1835) of Al-Azhar University was known for sodomy, the rural Shaykh Sulaymān of Nāḥiyat al-'Asal was noted for having around "one hundred and sixty" youth.[20] The scholar Sinān al-Dīn al-Amasī (d. 1578) had written on the practices of certain Sufi sects of the sixteenth century that learned scholars and court leaders would take pride in keeping and buying male youths, whereas others would not marry women but rather keep male youths as *zawjāt al-safar* (travel wives), *ghulām al-firāsh* (bed boy), or *khāsikiyya* (favorite).[21] This seems to suggest that *liwāṭ* was generally perpetrated in the context of power imbalance between a leader, jurist, or adult on the one hand and a youth or male slave on the other. In the context of soldiers away from women, it was noted that they used subservient males of other localities and treated them as women.[22]

Male slaves were sexually used by their masters[23] and at times this was sanctioned by some Mālikī jurists and some Shī'ī scholars[24] on the basis of *mulk yamīn*—ownership of the right hand—rationale that allowed sexual relationship with female concubines.[25] While a majority of jurists did consider such use of male slaves prohibited, a *Ḥadd* penalty was not implemented in violation of the prohibition on the basis of semblance of the conduct with lawful conduct with female concubines.[26] According to Ibn al-Humām (d. 1456), based on *ijmā'* (consensus), there was no *Ḥadd* penalty on a man who had *liwāṭ* with his male slave.[27] In fact, according to Arno Schmitt, only the Ḥanbalī jurists were unambiguous in their condemnation of sodomizing male slaves.[28] While male slaves did not have much legal recourse in cases of *liwāṭ*, jurists like Ibn al-Qayyim (d. 1350) ruled that the male slave was justified in running away from his master to avoid *liwāṭ*.[29] The Ḥanafī al-Kawākibī (d. 1685) clearly stated that based on the phrase "what their right hand possesses" verses 23:6 and 70:30, which generally alluded to female concubines, there were those who deemed *liwāṭ* with male slaves permissible.[30]

It becomes apparent that the jurists were articulating opinions based on their assumptions on human sexuality and the sociocultural values of their times. Wael Hallaq mentions that the Muslim scholar Muhammad Shahrur (b. 1938) indicated that the jurists were simply articulating the Weltanschauung of their times and as such cannot be blamed for the positions they adopted and that therefore, doctrines of the traditional schools of jurisprudence as well as the traditional interpretations of the Qur'an are not binding on modern Muslims as these interpretations and doctrines were based on assumptions based on the knowledge base of their times.[31]

Notwithstanding Shahrur's opinion, since many contemporary Muslims believe that the rulings postulated by the founding fathers of the four extant schools of Sunnī jurisprudence cannot be taken lightly, it is imperative to investigate the reasoning behind their rulings. Given their underlying assumptions and based on their sociocultural values, the jurists categorized *liwāṭ* as a sin; however, they greatly differed on the punishment. Their opinions and justifications, which are classified into three groups on the basis of the punishment for *liwāṭ*, that is, capital punishment, the *zinā* punishment, and the *taʿzīr* punishment, are presented below followed by the case for decriminalization of same-sex acts based on Islamic law in Section 5.4 and finally revisiting the reasoning behind the moral reprehensibility of *liwāṭ* in Section 5.5.

5.1 THE CAPITAL PUNISHMENT

Mālik (d. 795), on the basis of a question he asked an elder of Medina—Shihāb Zuhrī (d. 741/2), opined that both the active and passive partners in *liwāṭ* should be killed irrespective of their marital status.[32] This opinion is not based on a Prophetic text but rather based on Mālik's deference to the scholars of Medina, specifically Shihāb Zuhrī. Furthermore, Shihāb Zuhrī has another opinion, according to which the punishment for *liwāṭ* is similar to that of *zinā* (fornication) in that married perpetrators of *liwāṭ* are lapidated whereas unmarried perpetrators are flogged.[33] There is also a narrative traced back to Shihāb Zuhrī according to which there is no prescribed punishment for the one who slanders another with the invective "you *Lūṭī*."[34] This is important to note since slander is one of the five principal crimes that include theft, highway robbery, fornication, and murder for which the Qur'an stipulates a punishment.[35]

Ibn Ḥazm (d. 1064) critiqued scholars for referring to Shihāb Zuhrī's opinions without providing arguments rooted in the Qur'an and the Hadith texts. He indicated that such scholars would accept Shihāb Zuhrī's opinions, whenever his opinions correspond with their own.[36] Furthermore, on the basis of a Prophetic text and the Qur'anic verse 25:68, he argues that the capital punishment cannot be inflicted except for apostasy, fornication, and homicide.[37] As such, the case of the scholars who propose the capital penalty for *liwāṭ* without equating it to *zinā* is extremely weak. In fact, some scholars, like Javed Ghamidi,[38] based on verse 5:32, even argue that the death penalty is reserved only for murder or for disorder through terror or persecution.[39]

Like Shihāb Zuhrī, Shāfi'ī (d. 820) and Ibn Ḥanbal (d. 855) also supported this punishment through one of their opinions. Unlike Mālik, who relied on Shihāb Zuhrī's opinion, they substantiated their argument through a Prophetic text, noted in Section 3.1.1, or by referring to the narratives that depict the opinions and conduct of the Companions Abu Bakr (d. 634), 'Uthmān (d. 656), 'Ali (d. 661), and Ibn 'Abbās (d. 687).[40] However, the Prophetic text they referenced is part of the nine strands of Prophetic texts, alluded to in Section 3.1, whose authenticity has been questioned by Hadith experts like Bukhārī (d. 870) and Muslim (d. 875). Furthermore, even Mālik who could have substantiated his opinion with this text does not report it in his collection of Hadith—Al-Muwaṭṭa'.

Ibn Ḥazm impugned the authenticity of the texts that depict the conduct of the Companions by confirming that the Abu Bakr and Ali texts that depict burning of the perpetrators have a broken transmission chain, that one of the narrators in the transmission chain, was attested as a liar by Mālik and that the clear Prophetic directive forbade killing by fire.[41] Likewise, he stated that the reports that are traced back to Ibn 'Abbās have been transmitted by "all kinds of unknown people" and therefore cannot be relied upon.[42] It is important to reiterate that Mālik did not base his ruling on the texts that depict the conduct of the Companions, since he deemed them weak by doubting the trustworthiness of one of the narrators, and instead resorted to one of the opinions of Shihāb Zuhrī, an elder from Medina.

Some writers mention that texts that depict the opinions of the Companions 'Umar (d. 644) and 'Uthmān (d. 656) indicate that both suggested the capital punishment for the perpetrators of *liwāṭ*.[43] 'Uthmān (d. 656) is also credited with acting upon the advice of 'Ali (d. 661) who prescribed the punishment of 100 lashes; however, these traditions were not recorded in the authoritative collections such as those of Bukhārī and Muslim.[44] Furthermore, apart from Ibn Ḥazm's general refutation of the opinions on capital punishment, there exists another opinion attributed to 'Umar, according to which 'Umar simply asked some young men to not sit with a person suspected of *liwāṭ*.[45] While this text also is not found in the relatively more authentic Hadith compilations of Bukhārī and Muslim, it is interesting to note that 'Umar did not ask all men to dissociate themselves from this particular individual but only some of the young men. It deserves to be noted that 'Umar's specification of young men only substantiates the assumptions made by the jurists that *liwāṭ* was generally perpetrated on youth.

As noted earlier in chapter 3, the texts that depict the conduct of Abu Bakr do so in the context of apostasy and murder, which, apart from transmission chain weakness issues, further weakens the case to extend the capital punishment from the context of apostasy and murder to exclusive cases of *liwāṭ*. Ibn Ḥazm also disputed the case of those scholars, including Mālik,[46] who deduce a penalty for *liwāṭ* based on the context of the people of Lūṭ. He contested that since the people of Lūṭ were destroyed for their abominable conduct and rejection of God's Prophet, scholars who deduce the capital penalty for *liwāṭ* 'would be inconsistent in their methodology if they prescribed capital punishment for perpetrators of *liwāṭ* who did not disbelieve in God's Prophet. Furthermore, he argued that people who tamper with weights and measures should be burned, and people who wound another person's she-camel should be executed because, like the people of Lūṭ, the people of Shuʿayb and Ṣāliḥ were destroyed respectively for those reasons as mentioned in the Quran.[47] Thus, by drawing out the contradictions and inconsistencies in their approach, Ibn Ḥazm effectively refuted the proponents of capital punishment for *liwāṭ*.[48]

Finally, the texts that depict the opinion of Ibn ʿAbbās that the perpetrators of *liwāṭ* must be killed were not considered authentic enough to allow his students like Mujāhid Ibn Jabr (d. 722) to prescribe the same punishment.[49] The opinions of *tābiʿūn* like Mujāhid indicate that either the texts that depict the opinions and conduct of the Companions are not trustworthy or alternatively the *tābiʿūn* felt that the opinions of the Companions on *liwāṭ* were not binding. In the context of finding proofs for rulings, jurists like al-Shawkānī (d. 1834) have stated that Muslims are required to follow the Qur'an and the Sunnah and as such the opinion of a single Companion cannot constitute proof.[50] Even Abu Ḥanīfa is reported to have said that in the absence of guidance from the Qur'an and Sunnah, he may resort to an opinion of a Companion and may either follow or abandon it.[51]

Given that the opinion of the capital punishment for *liwāṭ* without any qualifications cannot be reasonably defended from the primary sources, the Qur'an and the Sunnah, and given that the texts that depict the opinions and conduct of the Companions are not trustworthy, and given that many jurists did not reference Shihāb Zuhrī's opinions, with Ibn Ḥazm going so far as to refute his position, and given that even contemporary scholars like Sheikh Mohamed el-Moctar el-Shinqiti have critiqued the capital punishment for *liwāṭ*, it may be concluded that scholars who still uphold capital punishment may not have carefully engaged with the tradition. Moreover, given that the Qur'an directly and explicitly addresses prohibitions such as those on intoxicants and gambling (5:90), pork (5:03), fornication (17:32), incest (4:23), usurpation and murder (4:29), slander (49:11), usury (2:275), disobedience to parents and associating partners with God (17:23) through the variants of the words, "do not," "forbidden," or "penalty of Hell," and given that the

Qur'an has not addressed *liwāṭ* in as direct a manner as leads one to question whether the capital punishment can be substantiated on the basis of the vague treatment of the issue in the Qur'an.

In other words, the typical prohibitions in the Qur'an appear in the form of negative commands that start with *lā taf'al* (do not), through the usage "God forbids," through *nafy al-ḥall* (denial of permissibility) or through a command that requires avoiding something and that implicit injunctions that praise or condemn a conduct do not precisely indicate whether the objective is command and prohibition or warning and recommendation.[52] As such, the case for capital punishment for *liwāṭ* cannot be reasonably substantiated on the basis of the people of Lūṭ verses, as has also been indicated by Ibn Ḥazm. As such, since scholars are informed by their sociocultural values, and given that some may not have carefully engaged with the tradition, allows us to carefully revisit the opinions of the next group of jurists who opined that the punishment of *liwāṭ* should be the same as that for *zinā*.

5.2 PUNISHMENT OF *ZINĀ*

While one opinion from Shāfi'ī (d. 820) and Ibn Ḥanbal (d. 855) supports the punishment by killing, it is Mālik (d. 795) who seems to have been the predominant proponent of the capital punishment for *liwāṭ*. Shāfi'ī and Ibn Ḥanbal and many of the followers of their schools are better known to have prescribed the punishment for *zinā* for *liwāṭ*. The jurists who support this punishment substantiate their case by texts that indicate that the Companion Ibn Zubayr (d. 692) meted out the punishment for *zinā* to perpetrators of *liwāṭ*.[53] However, Ibn Ḥazm contends that texts from not only Ibn Zubayr but also other Companions are traced through unknowns in the transmission chain of narrators and therefore he suggests that it would be inappropriate to accept any opinion supposedly attributed to the Companions on *liwāṭ*.[54]

Ibn Ḥazm also emphasized that the term *zinā* is never equated with *liwāṭ* either in common usage or in the Prophet's authentic directives.[55] Given Ibn Ḥazm's doubts on the authenticity of the texts on *liwāṭ* attributed to the Companions further bolsters the case made in Section 3.4 that narratives attributed to the Companions that use words like *Lūṭī* and *al-Lūṭīyya* were a product of later development. It is also interesting to note that the Hadith, which were deemed weak in chapter 3, and the texts depicting the Companions' opinions and conduct with respect to *liwāṭ*, were only compiled in a series of monographs starting from al-Haytham b. Khalaf al-Dūrī (d. 919) and that these compilations were being produced as late as the seventeenth century.[56] This would suggest that a strong position against *liwāṭ* only began to emerge between the tenth and the seventeeth centuries, whereas there may have been relatively more ambiguity on the issue prior to that time period.

The equation of the *liwāṭ* punishment with that of *zinā* is also supported by other jurists as Ibrāhīm al-Nakha'ī (d. 715), supposedly one of the teachers of Abu Ḥanīfa (d. 765). However, like Shihāb Zuhrī (d. 741/2) whose opinion on *liwāṭ* informed Mālik's (d. 795) ruling, Ibrāhīm al-Nakha'ī is attributed with more than one opinion on the punishment of *liwāṭ*. Specifically, the opinions attributed to him support all three rulings on the punishment of *liwāṭ*, that is, capital punishment, punishment of *zinā*, and discretionary punishment.[57] This ambiguity in opinions further weakens the case of those who propose the punishment of *zinā* for *liwāṭ*.

Apart from the Ibn Zubayr texts, several jurists also substantiated the penalty of *zinā* for *liwāṭ* through a Prophetic text that defines the perpetrators of *liwāṭ* as perpetrators of *zinā*. However, this Prophetic text is considered weak by several Hadith experts as one of the narrators in the transmission chain is deemed a liar, whereas another is categorized as unknown.[58] Another reason why the punishment of *zinā* is not deduced from this Prophetic text is that another Prophetic text also equates *siḥāq* (tribadism) between women to *zinā*. However, Ibn Ḥazm refutes this report as one of the narrators is deemed as a weak transmitter and unconnected with other narrators in the transmission chain.[59] Thus, both Prophetic reports that equate *liwāṭ* and *siḥāq* with *zinā* are considered weak based on the critique of the transmission chain. It is also important to note that aside from transmission chain issues, several jurists opined that these texts are figuratively associating *liwāṭ* and *siḥāq* with *zinā*, to indicate that *liwāṭ* and *siḥāq* are sinful acts.[60] As such, they argued against punishment of *zinā* for *liwāṭ*.

Several Shāfi'ī and Ḥanbalī jurists, however, as well as a minority of Ḥanafī jurists used *qiyās* (analogical deduction) to equate *liwāṭ* with *zinā* and as such applied the punishment of *zinā* to *liwāṭ*. They analogized *liwāṭ* with *zinā* by reasoning that since both acts involved penetration and that the objective in both acts was the pursuit of sexual desire.[61] Despite the differences between *liwāṭ* and *zinā*, many jurists applied *qiyās khafī* (hidden analogy) to apply the *ḥadd* penalty of *zinā* to *liwāṭ*. However, *qiyās* involves juristic speculation and a ruling based on *qiyās* is considered weak and rarely final. The methodology of *qiyās* to determine the causes and objectives of divine injunctions has been critiqued by Mutazilah, Ẓāhirī, Shī'ī, and some Ḥanbalī scholars.[62] Furthermore, Ḥanafī jurists reject the use of *qiyās* in divinely ordained punishments, including *zinā*, and attribute a legal maxim in this regard to Abu Ḥanīfa.[63] Likewise, the Mālikī jurists have rejected the use of *qiyās* of *liwāṭ* to *zinā*.[64] Given the disagreements on analogizing *liwāṭ* to *zinā* by jurists from many schools, the Ḥanafī jurist Ibn al-Humām (d. 1457) stated that everybody disagreed on the analogy.[65]

In order to apply the ruling of *zinā* to *liwāṭ* through *qiyās* there must not only be important common elements between the two acts but also no significant factors that might impede the analogy. As noted earlier, jurists who applied the punishment of *zinā* to *liwāṭ* reasoned that the elements of intercourse and desire were common between *zinā* and *liwāṭ*. However, jurists who disagreed with this analogy fell back to the definition of *zinā* and indicated sufficient differences between the two acts. Ḥanafī jurists like Abu Yūsuf (d. 767) and Shaybānī (d. 805) defined *zinā* as the penetration of a *farj* (genital) by another *farj* in a legally prohibited manner to satisfy carnal desire in a desired object.[66] Based on this definition and other factors, several differences between *zinā* and *liwāṭ* break the analogy between the two acts.

Past scholars including Abu Ḥanīfa did not consider the anus to be *farj*[67] and this violates the condition of the penetration of a *farj*. Ḥanafī jurists like Samarqandī (d. 1144) and Kāsānī (d. 1191) clearly defined *zinā* as the insertion of the penis into the vagina.[68] A minority of Shāfi'ī and Ḥanbalī jurists prescribed 100 lashes to the passive partner in *liwāṭ* on the basis of the understanding that the *Ḥadd* of *zinā* applied to cases where the vagina was penetrated.[69] Likewise, differentiating between *zinā* and *liwāṭ*, Shāfi'ī, in one of his opinions, also argued that the passive partner should not be killed irrespective of his marital status.[70] Distinguishing between the two acts, some scholars also opined that *mahr* (dower payment) did not become incumbent on anal penetration as the anus was not acquired through a marriage contract.[71] Likewise, by alluding to a report, which indicates the Prophet defining *zinā* as a man illicitly obtaining from a woman that which he can lawfully obtain from his wife, Ibn Ḥazm also defines *zinā* as involving a penis and vagina. While some scholars may argue that linguistically the term *zinā* applies to all acts outside marriage or *mulk yamīn*, Ibn Ḥazm indicates that another Prophetic report, which indicates the genitals disproving or confirming the act of *zinā* committed by limbs, alludes to the subsequent pregnancy and therefore confirms that *zinā* involves a penis and vagina.[72]

Several scholars also distinguished between the two acts by arguing that a person's oath on not committing *zinā* remained intact if he instead committed *liwāṭ*. Furthermore, and notwithstanding authenticity issues of the texts, they argued that had the Companions equated *liwāṭ* with *zinā*, they would not have differed in their opinions on *liwāṭ*.[73] Scholars also emphasized that, in contrast to *liwāṭ*, *zinā* included the danger of procreation for a child born outside a legally sanctioned relationship, and whose pedigree would be eternally disputed, may grow up without a father.[74] Furthermore, they argued that *liwāṭ* was half as less widespread than *zinā* as there was only one solicitor in the act in that they assumed that males generally do not desire to be penetrated and therefore, deterrence through punishment was not merited to the same extent as that for *zinā*.[75] This last point is also substantiated by the assumptions made explicit by al-Rāzī, Abu Ḥanīfa, and Ibn Taymiyya, as noted in Section 2.5, that given the humiliation and subordination associated with the act, the passive partner in *liwāṭ* generally does not desire to be penetrated unless it were for pecuniary or other reasons.

Given that the *zinā* punishment cannot be reasonably supported on the basis of texts, which are deemed weak, and even on the basis of analogy, which was rejected by many jurists, it may be concluded that scholars who still uphold the *zinā* punishment for *liwāṭ* may not have carefully engaged with the tradition. It is also important to note that the past jurists who prescribed the *zinā* punishment essentially rejected deducing any ruling from the verses on the people of Lūṭ for *liwāṭ*, especially given the fact that contemporary conservative Muslims try to situate gays and lesbians in the context of the people of Lūṭ. Moreover, given that many past jurists did not prescribe the punishment for *liwāṭ* based on the verses on the people of Lūṭ, it seems that *liwāṭ*, *Lūṭī*, and other allied terms were technical in nature and did not entirely correspond to the definition of the acts of the people of Lūṭ. As such, given that many past jurists critiqued the *zinā* punishment for *liwāṭ* allows us to carefully revisit the opinions of the next group of jurists who opined that instead of either capital or *zinā* punishment, a discretionary punishment is warranted for *liwāṭ*.

5.3 THE *TA'ZĪR*—DISCRETIONARY PUNISHMENT

Amongst the past jurists, while the Mālikīs supported capital punishment and the Shāfi'ī, Ḥanbalī as well as a minority of Hanafis predominately supported *zinā* punishment for *liwāṭ*, the majority of Hanafis supported discretionary punishment.[76] It seems that this approach toward *liwāṭ* emerged from one of the three opinions of Ibrāhīm al-Nakha'ī, as noted in Section 5.2, and continued through Abu Ḥanīfa[77] to Dāwūd al-Ẓāhirī (d. 883), founder of the Ẓāhirī school, and hence to the Ẓāhirī jurist Ibn Ḥazm. Jurists like Sarakhsī (d. 1096) and Kāsānī (d. 1191) stated that *liwāṭ* did not have a legally prescribed punishment, whereas according to Ibn al-Humām (d. 1456), there is no legally prescribed injunction against *liwāṭ* based on the Qur'an, Hadith, or any *ijmā'* (consensus) on the issue.[78] In fact, Kāsānī passed over the Hadith on *liwāṭ* as he deemed their evidence not even worthy of refutation.[79] Given the absence of any legally prescribed punishment, some Ḥanafī jurists stated that any whipping should not exceed 39 lashes, that is, one less than the lowest *Ḥadd* punishment that constitutes 40 lashes.[80] Ibn Ḥazm went so far as to state that based on a Prophetic text that no man should be beaten with more than 10 lashes except for in the case of divinely sanctioned punishments.[81]

As noted in Section 5.2, Ibn Ḥazm rejected opinions based on the weakness of the texts that equated either *liwāṭ* or *siḥāq* (tribadism) with *zinā*. He also refuted Shihāb Zuhrī's position, who prescribed hundred lashes for *siḥāq*, a penalty deduced from the equivalence of *liwāṭ* and *siḥāq* with the gravest and least severe forms of *zinā*, respectively.[82] As such, he prescribes the same penalty for *liwāṭ* and *siḥāq* based on the following Prophetic text.

> If it is true that there is no Ḥadd punishment for this person because neither God nor His Prophet prescribed a penalty, then the rule is that the person did something "munkar-wrong." Therefore, the "munkar-wrong" needs to be corrected by employing the "ta'zīr-discretionary" penalty, which is below the Ḥadd punishment, by hitting the person not any more than the Prophet's order, and by removing his harm away from the people.[83]

Ibn Sīnā's (d. 1037) medical opinion on curing *'ubna*, as noted in Section 5, seems quite similar to the prescription of detention and beatings mentioned in this text. Likewise, while, Ibn Ḥazm does not appear to be clear on the imprisonment for women,[84] he proposes imprisonment for an unspecified duration of time for men, and substantiates this opinion on the basis of part of the Qur'anic verse 5:2 that reads, "And cooperate in righteousness and consciousness, and do not cooperate in sin and aggression," as well as, on the basis of a narrative from Ibn 'Abbās, which forms one of the three strands of texts noted in Section 3.2, which indicates that the Prophet distanced *mukhannathūn* (effeminate men) and the *mutarajjilāt* (masculine looking women).[85] However, this text has been deemed weak as two of the narrators have been deemed as liars or fabricators in the transmission chain, and because of the reservations expressed by authorities like Mālik and Qatāda.[86] Moreover, the application of the report is further weakened, as noted in Section 3.2, on the basis of the incorrect equivalence between effeminate men and those involved in *liwāṭ*. It also deserves to be noted that while refuting weak Hadith, Ibn Ḥazm himself relied on weak Hadith to substantiate his opinions as in the case of his accepting the second Abu Hurayra text on heterosexual anal intercourse as noted in Section 4.1.

Ibn Ḥazm also argues that not warding off the harm of the active and passive partners involved in the act of the people of Lūṭ from the public would be akin to abetting transgression.[87] As such, while he is clearly against the *Ḥadd* punishment, he emphasizes the *ta'zīr* penalty of beatings and detention. His opinion is based on the view that *fi'l qawm Lūṭ* (act of the people of Lūṭ), which by his time specifically meant *liwāṭ*, was a major sin like the consumption of pork or wine and like *zinā*, and that anyone deeming any of them permissible would be a *kāfir* (unbeliever) or *mushrik* (associationist) who may be executed.[88] To the extent that scholars are quick to point that a particular act is forbidden because of a particular verse, hadith, or *ijmā*ʿ, the lack of any such reference in Ibn Ḥazm's statement is noteworthy. Regardless, in contrast, Ibn ʿĀbidīn (d. 1836) stated that claiming the permissibility of *liwāṭ* with male slaves did not necessitate *kufr* (unbelief).[89] As such, when anal sex is ignored and on noting that frottage or rubbing is permissible between legal spouses, the prohibition and subsequent punishment of same-sex acts rests not so much on the *qubḥ* (intrinsically evil) aspect of same-sex acts, as is the case with bestiality and necrophilia, but rather on the absence of a legal relationship between members of the same sex.[90]

According to ʿAbd al-Jabbar's (d. 1025) work, *qabīḥ* (evil) is characterized by *ẓulm*, which includes the elements of injustice, unfairness, oppression, and tyranny.[91] ʿAbd al-Jabbar actually lists various *wujūh* (grounds) to define evil, which include *ẓulm* (wrongdoing), *ʿabath* (uselessness), *kadhb* (lying), *kufru niʿma* (ingratitude for a favor), *jahl* (ignorance), *irādatul qabīḥ* (willing evil), *amrul qabīḥ* (commanding evil), and *taklīfu mā lā yuṭāq* (imposing unattainable obligations).[92] In contrast, according to ʿAbd al-Jabbar, good is characterized by *ʿadl* (justice), *naf*ʿ (benefit), *ṣalāḥ* (advantage), *ṣidq* (truthfulness), and *irādatul ḥasan* (willing good).[93] Similarly, based on the works of Abu al-Ḥusayn al-Baṣrī (d. 1044), an act is deemed detestable if it contains the elements of oppression, falsehood, and purposelessness, in the absence of which the act is deemed permissible.[94] Likewise, based on the works of Sharīf al-Murtaḍā (d. 1044), an act is not reprehensible if it does not contain the elements of oppression, desirability of the detestable, or burdening with the impossible.[95] Given the definition of *qubḥ* as including the elements of injustice, unfairness, oppression, tyranny, falsehood, and purposelessness, it becomes difficult to define sexual acts between same-sex couples bound within a legal contract as *qubḥ*.

It seems that for Ibn Ḥazm, marital status and the position of the partners in the sexual act are irrelevant when prescribing the penalty for any illegal sexual conduct outside the folds of *nikāḥ* as according to him both *liwāṭ* and *siḥāq* are but cases of illegal *farj* (genital) contact. This point is substantiated by the fact that Ibn Ḥazm refers to the Prophetic texts on shielding one's *ʿawra* (prescribed covered body parts) from the same gender person, and on not joining the same gender person under one cover.[96] Ibn Ḥazm's referring to illegal *farj* (genital) contact also seems to substantiate the view that sex between members of the same gender is problematic because of its occurring outside the fold of a legal relationship, in contrast to being deemed as *qubḥ* (intrinsically evil), and therefore it is perhaps for this reason that *liwāṭ* is viewed as a major sin or gravely immoral.

Ibn Ḥazm, while rejecting any *Ḥadd* punishment on the basis of the verses on the people of Lūṭ, nonetheless uses those verses to specifically view *liwāṭ* as gravely immoral. Ibn Ḥazm opined that the act of the people of Lūṭ is hideous and despicable.[97]

> The act of the people of Lūṭ is one of the major sins and forbidden abominations, like consuming pig meat, or carrion, or blood, or wine; [like] adultery, and the remaining acts of disobedience. He who permits it—or any of those things which we have mentioned—is an unbeliever; an associationist (mushrik) whose life and wealth are free for the taking.[98]

Ibn Ḥazm lumps *liwāṭ* with the consumption of pork, carrion, and blood, which were separated by Ibn Taymiyya from shirk, lewdness, and injustice in his commentary on Surah Nūr. Ibn Taymiyya argued that while the prohibition on the latter is absolute, the prohibition of the former is contingent on the situation. Moreover, Ibn Ḥazm's opinion on the excommunication of the one who allows for the permissibility of *liwāṭ* is countered by that of Ibn ʿĀbidīn. Moreover, Ibn Ḥazm's view may be revisited by noting that, notwithstanding the aggressive nature of the acts of the people of Lūṭ as noted in Section 2.4, such acts occurred outside the folds of a legal relationship. The possibility of a legal relationship between members of the same sex would have been an anachronistic absurdity for Ibn Ḥazm and other jurists, for whom, as noted by Kecia Ali, same-sex relationships would have been a categorical impossibility.[99]

While Ibn Ḥazm prescribes detention and beatings that do not exceed 10 lashes for correction, deterrence, and removing harm from the public, and notwithstanding Shāfiʿī's opinions on the *zinā* punishment for *liwāṭ*, Shāfiʿī, after mentioning the texts that depict the conduct of 'Ali and the opinion of Ibn ʿAbbās, which Ibn Ḥazm and others have deemed weak, also presents an alternate opinion on *liwāṭ* from a past scholar who, while equating *liwāṭ* with *zinā*, prescribed no *Ḥadd* punishment for *liwāṭ*.

> Shāfiʿī mentioned that their companion said: There is no Ḥadd punishment and his "Iḥrām" remains intact if he performs the act while in "Iḥrām" unless he ejaculates. However, some of his friends disagreed with him. He added: The "Lūṭī" is like the person who commits zinā—but not worse. Shāfiʿī mentioned: Allah allowed sex with women in two ways, marriage and "mulk yamīn," while the other [liwāṭ] is prohibited from all angles.[100]

It is not clear whether the past scholar in Shāfiʿī's narrative prescribed any *taʿzīr* punishment that includes beatings or detention. At the very least, however, this narrative supports the third group of jurists who opined that there was no *Ḥadd* punishment for *liwāṭ* and emphasizes the prohibition of *liwāṭ* by alluding to the absence of a legal relationship as opposed to the *qabīḥ* (inherently evil) nature of *liwāṭ*. To the extent that Shāfiʿī defined *ijmāʿ* (consensus) as based on the entire Muslim community,[101] this only substantiates the view that there is no *ijmā*ʿ on the punishment for *liwāṭ*. Furthermore, the opinion that there is no *Ḥadd* punishment for *liwāṭ* and that it does not violate the perpetrator's *Iḥrām* seems to cast *liwāṭ* as a minor prohibition as opposed to a major one like *zinā*, which invokes the *Ḥadd* penalty and violates the person's *Iḥrām*.

While jurists in this group rejected both capital and *zinā* punishment in the absence of a legally prescribed injunction, and prescribed a less severe *ta*ʿ*zīr* punishment, they viewed *liwāṭ* as morally reprehensible. Ḥanafī jurists like Ibn al-Humām stated that moral reprehensibility did not necessitate a legally prescribed punishment and as such drinking urine is not punished like drinking wine.[102] Some argued that while all major sins were deemed abominable, not all had divinely sanctioned punishments and as such based on verse 6:151, the sins without legal punishments were simply to be avoided[103] and that the punishment would take place in the Hereafter and not in this world.[104] Likewise, according to two Ḥanafī jurists of the sixteenth and seventeenth centuries CE, the punishment for *liwāṭ* would be worse in the Hereafter given the absence of both *Ḥadd* punishment and the expiation of sins.[105] In contrast, Ibn Ḥazm indicated that major sins could be nullified through repentance and countered by good actions, each of which is worth ten times as a major sin.[106]

On the other hand, while prescribing the *ta*ʿ*zīr* penalty for *liwāṭ* that comprised of beatings and imprisonment, the Ḥanafī jurists ruled that repeat offenders warranted capital punishment.[107] In contrast, the Shafiʻi jurists, based on the *zinā* punishment, prescribed repetitive 100 lashes for repeat unmarried male offenders.[108] Likewise, as noted in Section 5.2, while Shāfiʿī, in one of his opinions, was lenient to the passive partner in that he argued that the passive partner should not be given capital punishment irrespective of his marital status, the Ottoman codes based on Ḥanafī jurisprudence prescribed a fine for the active partner and both beatings and fine for the passive partner.[109] This difference of opinions even in the *ta*ʿ*zīr* penalty indicates that the jurists were simply a product of their legal training and sociocultural values of their times.[110]

While Abu Ḥanīfa deemed *liwāṭ* as a nonmutual act, the Ottoman penal codes distinguish between rape and sex acts between males in that rape rupturing the anus was punishable by death, abduction of boys was punishable by castration or a heavy fine, whereas abduction of *mukhannath* led to the punishment of *zinā* or fine on both the abductor and the *mukhannath*, and sexual acts between dancing boys was punishable by fine based on their low economic status.[111] The Ottoman penal codes seem to suggest that cases of *liwāṭ* were perpetrated in the context of aggressive conduct of coercion, or exploitation of boys and the *mukhannathūn* through the perpetration of a humiliating and subordinating act, which seems to substantiate the linguistic analysis in Section 2.5.

The above review indicates that while Ibn Ḥazm classified *liwāṭ* as a major sin based on his reading of the verses on the people of Lūṭ, he prescribed a *taʿzīr* penalty for both *liwāṭ* and *siḥāq*. This viewpoint would be supported by a majority of Ḥanafī jurists and it also seems to have been supported by at least one early scholar as referenced by Shāfiʿī. There existed variations in the *taʿzīr* punishment for cases of same-sex conduct, based on the degree and extent of the offense such that the scope of *taʿzīr* punishments ranged from there being no penalty in lieu of supererogatory works, nominal fines, 10 lashes and/or detention to possible castration, 100 lashes, and even death for rapists and repeat offenders.

5.3.1 The 'Taʿzīr-Discretionary' Punishment—Nonpenetrative Acts

While, *liwāṭ* was deemed a major sin, which merited a *taʿzīr* punishment according to the third group of jurists, nonpenetrative acts were not considered *liwāṭ* but rather minor sins, which either merited a *taʿzīr* penalty or supererogatory works for expiation. The *ʿuqūbāt* (penal code) under the Ottomans also mentions that masturbation if done out of pleasure would merit a *taʿzīr* penalty, which may perhaps put nonpenetrative sexual acts at the same level as that of masturbation committed for pleasure.[112] This may be bolstered by Bouhdiba's assertion that *siḥāq* incurred the same penalty as that for autoeroticism, although he also includes bestiality and necrophilia as well in that list which tempers such equations.[113]

Acts like kissing, caressing, and *mufākhadha* (intercrural intercourse) between males, while deemed reprehensible, were not categorized as constituting *liwāṭ*.[114] Such acts, and to which one may add *siḥāq* for equivalence, were deemed as minor sins by jurists like al-Bujayrimī (d. 1806) who opined that they became major sins if committed repeatedly and by jurists like Ibn Ḥajar al-Haytamī (d. 1503) who opined that they became major sins if committed in conjunction with another minor sin like abusing a neighbor's trust.[115] Some assert that the gravity of such sins increases if they are justified.[116] Others opine that acts like touching, kissing, embracing, and informal interaction are all major sins based on verse 17:32 and that the majority, like al-Bujayrimī, agree that persistence of minor sins amounts to a major sin.[117]

Some scholars believed that the word *lamam* (venial faults) used in verse 53:32, which alludes to forgiveness to those who commit venial faults but shun major sins, referred specifically to nonpenetrative sexual acts.[118] Others opine that *lamam* refers to minor or major sins committed inadvertently based on verse 3:135, even though this verse does not contain that word, but they also temper this understanding on the basis of their understanding of verse 4:31 that *lamam* refers to minor sins, which may be forgiven through acts of worship and good deeds.[119] According to al-Jāḥiẓ (d. 869), some

Companions of the Prophet interpreted the word *lamam* in verse 53:32 to include kissing, touching, or even other nonpenetrative sexual acts.[120] While jurists like al-Shirbīnī (d. 1570) opined that acts falling short of intercourse merited the *taʿzīr* penalty, others like the Mālikī jurist al-Zurqānī (d. 1688) assumed that such minor sins, even if committed *ma'a al-iṣrār* (repeatedly and willfully) would be expiated by supererogatory works, even if the perpetrator did not repent as based on the understanding of the verse 11:14 that indicates that good deeds remove evil deeds.[121] In short, the concern of the two Ḥanafī jurists, who opined that the punishment for *liwāṭ* would be worse in the Hereafter, may be tempered by the opinions of other jurists, especially on nonpenetrative sexual acts.

To the extent that acts falling short of penetration are deemed minor sins, and acknowledging the difference of opinion amongst jurists concerning such acts, it may be opined that no punishment may be warranted and that there is scope for expiation of such sins even if they are done repeatedly.

5.3.2 Female Sexual Act—*Siḥāq*

As in the case of sexual acts between males, where *liwāṭ* is singled out and predominately dealt with in jurisprudence, the same is true in the case of sexual acts between females, where *siḥāq* (rubbing) is singled out in jurisprudence. Unlike *liwāṭ* however, where penetration is involved, *siḥāq* is described as grinding or rubbing and as such those who ascribe the capital punishment for *liwāṭ* do not apply the same for *siḥāq*. Nonetheless, a similar contempt is exhibited for *siḥāq* as it is viewed as an act outside the folds of a legal contract. Sometimes this contempt is rationalized by reference to texts that juxtapose acts between females with those of the people of Lūṭ or the people of Rass as mentioned in the Qur'an.

According to a text reported by al-Muttaqī al-Hindī (d. 1567), the 10 reasons for the destruction of the people of Lūṭ include women having sex with each, people playing with pigeons, beating drums, cutting beards, whistling, and wearing silk.[122] The list of some trivial vices in the list only raises the question on the authenticity of such texts and substantiates the point that personal distaste and contempt may have driven the construction and subsequent circulation of these texts. Regardless, just as the conduct of the people of Lūṭ included exploitative conduct, likewise, according to al-Nuwayrī (d. 1333), based on one text, the people of Rass were involved in idol worship, and began the practice of swapping and sodomizing their wives, which led women to grind with one another.[123] However, while the people of Rass are discussed in verses 25:38–39 and 50:12–14, the Qur'an does not connect them with lesbianism and neither do Zamakhsharī (d. 1143),[124] Ibn Kathīr (d. 1373), or Ṭabarī (d. 923) in their exegetical commentaries. Thus, the connection between the people of Rass and *siḥāq* does not seem to be justified.

Ibn Qudāma (d. 1223) is noted as having supported the position that two women involved in *siḥāq* are fornicators and a similar point is presented through a Hadith text by Al-Ṭabarānī.[125] However, such opinions are not justified under classical jurisprudence, especially given the fact that the definition of fornication for the purpose of Islamic law is specific to vaginal penetration by penis and as such *zinā* does not include *liwāṭ* or *siḥāq*.[126] The opinion that a lesbian's testimony is not acceptable on the basis of her being an evildoer is also presented[127]; however, according to Kamali, while a mufti bases his *fatwā* on religious considerations, a judge must only look at objective evidence and as such a pious individual in a court case is not treated differently from an impious person or one without a religion.[128] Moreover, the issue of testimony is irrelevant to the issue of a legal contract for a same-sex couple.

Scholars like al-ʿIzz ibn ʿAbd al-Salām (d. 1263) opined that a Muslim woman is not permitted to uncover in front of a woman who engaged in *siḥāq*, because she is an evildoer who can describe intimate parts to others.[129] Likewise, in the context of the Hadith on prohibiting women from sleeping under one blanket, the narrative that comes from Ibn Masʿūd (d. 650) also indicates the reason of the possibility of a woman describing another to her husband, thereby enabling him to virtually see the other woman.[130] However, as in the case of the *mukhannath* who was banished from the Prophet's household, this describes the concern on modesty and appropriate behavior. Furthermore, the issue of not looking at the *ʿawra* is irrelevant to the issue of a same-sex legal contract wherein the issue of not looking at the *ʿawra* becomes irrelevant.

The above analysis indicates how applying the framework of *siḥāq*, as addressed by the classical jurists, to the concerns of lesbians would be neither appropriate nor reasonably justified.

5.4 DECRIMINALIZATION OF SAME-SEX ACTS

As noted in Section 5.3, given that the question of same-sex legal relationships would have been absurd to the past jurists and that same-sex acts were viewed outside the scope of a legal relationship may substantiate the view that as opposed to any *qubḥ* property of same-sex acts, it is the absence of a legal relationship that seems to have been the main reason behind the reprehensibility, prohibition, and punishment for *liwāṭ* and nonpenetrative sexual acts that may include *siḥāq*. However, while the moral reprehensibility of nonpenetrative sexual acts including *siḥāq* may be explained by the absence of a legal relationship, jurists have provided further rationales behind the moral reprehensibility of *liwāṭ* which will be explored in Section 5.5.

To the extent that nonpenetrative sexual acts outside a legal relationship are considered minor sins, which, according to some jurists, even if repeatedly committed could be expiated through supererogatory works, according to other jurists, such sinful acts could be punished through some *taʿzīr* penalty. However, it seems that a case for decriminalization, that is, waiving of any punishment, at least for such acts, could be substantiated by revisiting Muslim jurisprudence on the rationale behind punishment. As such, al-Qarāfī (d. 1285) argued that sins whose secular harms were inconsequential enough to not merit any legal punishment as a severe penalty would be disproportionate relative to the harm of the sin whereas a proportional penalty would be insufficient to deter the commission of such sins.[131]

In the context of *liwāṭ*, a similar tension in the prescription of a punishment is also noticed in Ibn al-Qayyim's (d. 1350) statement when he indicates that it might be better to inflict capital punishment on the passive partner as being penetrated was akin to being damaged beyond repair as he was "given a death after which no life is wished," which he tempers by stating that the passive partner would become a martyr if he were killed as capital punishment would be a transgression against such a person.[132] As such, Ibn al-Qayyim, despite being a Ḥanbalī scholar, whose jurisprudence school either upheld capital or *zinā* punishment for *liwāṭ*, seemingly suggests that the punishment for the passive partner is disproportionate to the committed sin. However, he also notes, based on the sociocultural values of his time, that being penetrated was akin to being vanquished perhaps through the dishonor associated with the act. This dishonor associated with the act has even been noted in the dream literature; for instance, al-Nābulsī (d. 1731) mentioned that to dream of penetrating a rival indicates that one will get the better of him in real life, whereas being penetrated by him would indicate the reverse.[133] However, nonpenetrative acts including *siḥāq* are not usually associated with such dishonor or subordination associated with *liwāṭ*, which, as noted before, would be explored in greater detail in Section 5.5.

According to Ibn Ḥazm, the *taʿzīr* penalty that includes detention and beatings is based on the premise of correction or rehabilitation and removing the harm of the crime from the public. However, as noted in Section 5, physicians like al-Rāzī (d. 925) not only indicated a genetic cause but also notwithstanding cures, conceded the incurability of *ʾubna*. To the extent that one accepts the genetic cause for *ʾubna* or *siḥāq* would suggest that any punishment based on the premise of correction or rehabilitation would not meet its objective. Jurists like the Ḥanafite Kāsānī (d. 1191) indicated that given the rationale of punishment as deterrence, if the offender persists with the crime even after the *ḥadd* punishment, then no further punishments may be warranted.[134] Given Kāsānī's view that *liwāṭ* did not have a legal punishment, and to the extent the limited scope of correction or rehabilitation, even based on medieval Galenic models used by physicians like al-Rāzī, is accepted, the case for decriminalization of same-sex conduct may be supported.

According to the Universalist school traced back to Abu Ḥanīfa, who stated that all human beings, irrespective of their innate, inherited, or gained attributes, are inviolable based on their humanity, law is required to punish crimes that violate people's rights or disrupt social order, whereas sins that do not harm others or disrupt the social order are not required to be punished.[135] To the extent that nonpenetrative acts including *siḥāq* do not disrupt the social order or violate the rights of others, the case for decriminalization of same-sex conduct may be supported. The argument for decriminalization, that is absence of any punishment for at least nonpenetrative same-sex conduct in the household of a same-sex couple, does not automatically translate to the acceptance of same-sex unions, but it does constitute the necessary starting point for the case for such unions.

So far, the decriminalization of same-sex acts was addressed outside the confines of a legal relationship. The rationales of rehabilitation and deterrence were addressed and to the extent that nonpenetrative sexual acts including *siḥāq* were not deemed to be *qubḥ* (intrinsically evil) and, according to some jurists, deemed as minor sins which could be washed through supererogatory works even if repeatedly committed, the case for decriminalization of same-sex acts was substantiated. Even the issue of anal sex between gay couples is different from that of *liwāṭ* in that the latter was viewed in the context of age- and power-stratified asymmetrical relationships and in the context of a possibly incurable disease—*'ubna*. To the extent anal sex between gay couples is markedly different from *liwāṭ*, the issue of all sexual acts between couples has to be viewed from a lens different than that of *liwāṭ*. Nonetheless, based on verses 23:5–7, sexual acts outside a legal relationship remain morally reprehensible even if decriminalized.

Given Kecia Ali's observation, as noted in Section 5.3, that the question of same-sex legal relationships has not been countenanced by past jurists, and for whom the question would have been anachronistically absurd, and given the above analysis, especially in Section 5, that the past jurists based their opinions in the overwhelming context of pederasty and power-imbalanced relationships with male slaves and foreign males treated as women, and based on the medical knowledge of their times and in the absence of developments in psychology, the issue of same-sex relationships warrants a renewed approach.

While the case for same-sex unions will be considered later in this paper, to the extent that same-sex legal relationships have not been addressed by past jurists, who addressed acts outside the scope of legal relationships and notwithstanding verses 23:5–7, and given that the primary sources, the Qur'an and Sunnah, have not explicitly ruled on same-sex unions, same-sex acts within a civil legal relationship may be viewed through the notion of *'afw* (waiver). A Prophetic text mentions that halal is permitted, ḥarām is prohibited, and matters on which the lawgiver is silent are *'afw*, which indicates that the Sharī'a does not cover every issue.[136] Alternatively, matters on which there is revelational silence are *'afw* (not obligatory, which literally means ignorable).[137] According to Shāṭibī (d. 1388), the category of *'afw* falls between *ḥalāl* (lawful) and *ḥarām* (forbidden) and is also subject to further interpretation.[138] Given the dichotomy between matters which are *ta'abbudī* (not rationally understood) that include ritual cleanliness and worship, and matters which are *'ādī* (rationally understood) that include marriage, Shāṭibī argues that the term *bid'a* (innovation) applies to the former and not the latter,[139] which provides scope to reasonably address the issue of same-sex legal relationships, especially when old customs no longer provide for legitimate human needs given new developments in society.[140]

The silence of the primary sources and the absence of verdicts from the jurists, who could not possibly have addressed the issue of same-sex unions given the absence of contemporary developments in psychology and social changes that have led to equal rights, does not automatically lead toward the permissibility of same-sex legal relationships. However, such silence does indicate that the traditional prohibition of same-sex acts outside a legal relationship cannot be extended to gay and lesbian Muslims within the confines of a legal relationship. While the traditional rationales behind the proscription of *liwāṭ* will be addressed in Section 5.5, based on the above analysis, the case for decriminalization of at least nonpenetrative sexual acts including *siḥāq*, especially within the confines of a legal relationship, may be warranted.

5.5 THE REPREHENSIBILITY OF LIWĀṬ

Jurists predominately addressed same-sex relationships through extramarital *liwāṭ*, which was viewed as an act over and above the legitimate sexual need of a male that was to be fulfilled through a legal contract with a spouse or concubines. *Liwāṭ* is distinguished from homosexual anal intercourse in that it was viewed through the lens of disease or exploitation that involved the active partner with a beardless youth, strangers, or *mukhannathūn* suffering from *'ubna*. On the other hand, anal intercourse between consenting partners does not contain the elements of exploitation or disease, and this weakens the case for superimposing the framework of *liwāṭ* on to the intimate life of gay couples.

While the analogy between *liwāṭ* and homosexual anal intercourse is contestable, it is also reasonable to delve into the reasoning employed by the jurists, especially of those who opined that *liwāṭ* was more abominable than *zinā*. It is important to underscore that, like contemporary Muslim scholars, past jurists were influenced by their own sense of right and wrong, natural and unnatural,[141] and as such it is important to consider the assumptions behind their rulings. As such, some argued that the texts that condemn *liwāṭ* are more severe in tone than those that condemn *zinā* and that God destroyed a nation for the inviolability of the anus but did not destroy any nation for the inviolability of the vagina.[142] However, this line of argument has been accounted for by Ibn Ḥazm and other jurists, as noted in Sections 5.1 and 5.2, in that they viewed these texts as weak and did not base their opinions on the analogy of the perpetrators of *liwāṭ* with the people of Lūṭ, thereby substantiating the point that the people of Lūṭ were not specifically destroyed for *liwāṭ*.

Other jurists appealed to nature and argued that in contrast to *zinā*, *liwāṭ* was repulsive to people of sound character and that the act was so abominable that it had not occurred to humans prior to the people of Lūṭ.[143] Furthermore, some argued that *liwāṭ* was perpetrated due to animalistic desire, which meant sexual drive without affection, on the part of the active partner and *ʾubna* or effeminacy on the part of the passive partner.[144] However, apart from the fact that morality is not based on disgust, this line of argument is countered by al-Rāzī and by the historical record to the extent of its accuracy, as noted in Section 2.3, where both indicate "homosexual" practices prior to the people of Lūṭ. Likewise, it was noted in Section 2.3 that jurists like Ibn Ḥajar al-Haytamī (d. 1503) stated that male animals do not engage in same-sex copulation and as such this creates a tension between claims that the active partner's desires were animalistic and the argument that the acts of same-sex penetration did not exist within the animal kingdom. Finally, effeminacy is not necessarily associated with *liwāṭ* as in Section 3.2 it was noted that the *mukhannathūn* of early Medina are not associated with "homosexuality" let alone *liwāṭ*. So far as *ʾubna* is concerned, it is clear the jurists based their opinions on the current medical knowledge of their times, based on which, and in contrast, other jurists like the Shāfiʿi al-Ramlī (d. 1550) opined that kissing the object of one's affection, which included a youth, was a duty if in line with the then medical theory that such frustration would contribute to the lover's death.[145] A similar opinion is attributed to a certain Walī al-Dīn al-ʿIrāqī in the context of Ḥanbalī scholars.[146] Even Ibn al-Qayyim (d. 1349/1350) has mentioned that glances and kisses should be tolerated as a lesser evil given the likely alternative of the greater evil of the lover's death.[147]

The moral reprehensibility and subsequent prohibition of *liwāṭ* was also rationalized through other arguments chief amongst which was the concern for procreation, which was also evoked through an appeal to a Shī'ī text that depicts Ali (d. 661) opining that permission of *ityān al-ghulām* (penetration of youth) would lead to men dispensing with women and disrupting procreation.[148] On the rationale behind the prohibition of sodomy, the Shī'ī *Tafsīr* compiled by Ayatollah Sayyid Kamal Faghih Imani and others provides the viewpoint of both Ja'far al-Ṣādiq (d. 765) and 'Ali al-Riḍā's (d. 818) that if men and women pursue sodomy, procreation would be ceased.[149] The Shī'ī commentary of the Qur'an, the *Tafsīr nūr al-thaqalayn*, also presents a text attributed to the Prophet that states that God instills feminine desires in a person who allows himself to be sexually used. Likewise, the commentary presents Ja'far al-Ṣādiq's opinion that some males have inverted wombs in their anus and experience feminine desires and that a male will be unable to rid himself of desiring male youths if he persists in such conduct till he turns 40.[150]

The authenticity of the Shī'ī texts is not clear especially when apart from any transmission chain issues, it is noted that these texts vacillate between describing *liwāṭ* as penetrating male youth and having feminine desires to get penetrated. Furthermore, the same tension is observed in the narratives that depict Iyas ibn Abdullah ibn Yalail as a passive partner in *liwāṭ*, who was allegedly executed by Abu Bakr, as noted in Section 3, as given his role in the Ridda wars of killing Muslims and given his nickname of *Fujā'a* (Lion), he is depicted as an aggressive person. This also raises concerns that since the words *liwāṭ*, *Lūṭī*, and other allied terms did not have a precise meaning even during the time of the *tābi'ūn*, as noted in Section 3.1, any texts attributed to the Prophet and the Companions which contained such terms may more likely have been later imputations. Moreover, it may be instructive to emphasize that Abu Ḥanīfa, as noted in Section 5.1, had stated that in the absence of guidance from the Qur'an and Sunnah, he may follow or abandon the opinion of a Companion. This is especially so if the opinion was relatively obscure and it was not clear that other Companions had heard of it to properly critique it. As such, if there was no consensus among the Companions, then a sole opinion does not necessarily count as formulating the basis of a religious ruling.

So far as procreation is concerned, in the verse that alludes to Adam and Eve, the scope of the verse is *mu'ayyan* (specific) as opposed to *'āmm* (general),[151] which means that the purport of the verse is not universal. Furthermore, even if the universality of the verse is argued, general rules are always open to exceptions in jurisprudence. It is also important to emphasize that no Qur'anic verse or Hadith indicates that procreation is the teleology of marriage[152] and that the purpose of marriage, based on verse 30:21, is rather tranquility, compassion, and *mawadda* (affection) between spouses.[153] Al-Ghāzālī (d. 1111) had stated that a woman may resort to contraception even where the motive was the preservation of her beauty, and as such the purpose of sexual act was beyond procreation toward the fulfillment of a need involving the man and woman's right to pleasure.[154] Kecia Ali has also noted that in authoritative premodern texts, the wife's main duty was not child-rearing or home-making but rather sexual availability,[155] and that many jurists defined the purpose of marriage not through procreation but through sexual enjoyment.[156] Infertility in itself is not a stigma as a woman is not obliged either by the Qur'an or Sunnah to bear children.[157] Furthermore, the Prophet himself did not have children with each of his wives as he also married older women, including his first wife Khadija (d. 619), several of whom were elderly or sterile.[158]

While the reasons mentioned so far do not seem to be sufficiently strong to deem *liwāṭ* as morally reprehensible, another rationale behind the prohibition and reprehensibility of *liwāṭ* was the noxiousness associated with penetrating the anus.[159] Given that the Qur'anic verses do not specify the act of the people of Lūṭ, exegetes like Qurṭubī and Ṭabarī had to interpret the verse through substitution and analogy, and Muslim jurists defined *fi'l qawm Lūṭ* (acts of the people of Lūṭ) as anal intercourse to the extent that *liwāṭ*,[160] and especially its allied terms like *al-Lūṭīyya*, have been used for anal intercourse between a man and woman.

However, there seem to be three strands of Hadith texts on *ityān bi-l-dubur* (penetrating the anus), presented in chapter 4, that depict prohibition, permission, or maintain a neutral stand on the act.[161] The texts that seem to prohibit the act, depict the perpetrator of heterosexual anal sex as accursed, rejecting the message of the Prophet, committing *kufr* (apostasy) or in an eschatological manner indicate that such a person would be bereft of God's mercy on Judgment Day. These texts have been deemed weak on the basis of the transmission chains by authorities like Yaḥyā ibn Ma'īn (d. 233 AH/852), Abu Ḥātim (d. 890), Bukhārī (d. 870), Tirmidhī (d. 892), and al-Nasā'ī (d. 915), among others, by deeming the narrators as unknown, having a bad memory, prone to error or generally evaluated negatively, by deeming the texts as strange, weird, without consequence, or by deeming the texts as *mawqūf* (interrupted).[162] Apart from transmission chain issues with these texts,[163] they are countered by other texts that either allow or maintain a neutral stand on the act. Furthermore, while the text, also weak on the basis of the transmission chain, which takes a neutral stand by indicating that heterosexual anal intercourse is filthy even if permitted,[164] refers to noxiousness, the texts that prohibit the act do not mention noxiousness as a reason behind the reprehensibility or prohibition of the act.

There have also been jurists, especially in the Shī'ī schools, who deemed *liwāṭ* as not impermissible between a man and wife based on their interpretation of verses 2:222–223[165] and who suggest avoiding the act as an obligatory precaution without the wife's consent[166] to avoid any harm to her. Likewise, amongst some Sunni jurists, the word *anna* in verse 2:223 encompassed the meanings of both "when you will" and "where you will" and has been understood to legitimate heterosexual anal sex in the latter sense.[167] Amongst some Muslims, verse 2:223 is not used to prohibit anal sex between opposite-gender spouses according to their reasoning that the primary purpose of a body part does not have to be penetration for it to be enjoyed sexually.[168] This reasoning echoes that of Shāfi'ī in one of his narratives where he reasons that intercourse between thighs or belly folds was not prohibited despite the fact that both were not qualified as tilth.[169] Many Ḥanafī jurists stated that claiming anal intercourse with a wife or female slave as permitted did not necessitate *kufr* (unbelief).[170] For instance, Mas'ūd Ibn 'Umar at-Taftāzānī (d. 1389) asserted, "to declare liwāṭa (sodomy) on one's wife as allowed is no heresy."[171] Likewise, jurists like Ibn 'Ābidīn (d. 1836), as noted in Section 5.3, even stated that claiming the permissibility of *liwāṭ* with male slaves also did not necessitate *kufr* (unbelief),[172] which may be viewed in light of the observation, noted in Section 5, that several jurists upheld such permissibility.

Given that noxiousness does not reasonably account for the reprehensibility or prohibition of *liwāṭ*, another rationale provided against that act was the waste of semen, a point also substantiated by alluding to the word *musrifūn* (transgressors) used to describe the people of Lūṭ in verse 7:81.[173] However, Ibn Ḥazm mentions the opinions of several Companions and *tābi'ūn* that not only indicated no issues with spilling semen but also advised youth to practice masturbation in order to avoid fornication.[174] According to the Lisān al-'Arab, the word *musrifūn* comes from the root S-R-F, which gives the impression of water that is poured on earth without nourishing the plant or tree. The word is used to describe people who spend beyond need or benefit or to describe people who exert effort in the wrong place. As such, the word alludes to people who go beyond their need, including legitimate sexual need. Moreover, in terms of exerting effort in the wrong place, in the context of verse 7:81 this may mean, as also noted in Section 2.5, pursuing nonreceptive males for superfluous sexual conduct over and above genuine sexual need. Also, by using the word *qawmun* (nation) before *musrifūn*, the Qur'an is indicating that the whole nation of Lūṭ is being condemned for their actions as opposed to any specific "homosexual" segment of the population.

While several jurists deemed *liwāṭ* as more morally reprehensible than *zinā*, for instance, Abu Ya'ala al-Farra (d. 1066) opined that *liwāṭ* is worse than *zinā* as the vulva can become lawful through a legal contract,[175] there were others who argued otherwise. Ibn Ḥazm referenced a Hadith that lists *zinā* with one's neighbor's wife as one of the worst crimes and since *liwāṭ* is not mentioned, he invalidated the Mālikī position that *liwāṭ* is worse than *zinā*.[176] Several jurists opined that *zinā* was more morally reprehensible in that it led to confusion of lineages, and that since people are more zealously protective of females, in contrast to males, they may venture out to kill the one who commits fornication with them.[177] As noted in Section 5.3, according to a past scholar alluded to by Shāfiʿī, *liwāṭ* was deemed no worse than *zinā*. Likewise, as noted in Section 5.2, jurists raised concerns of children growing up without fathers in the context of *zinā*. As such, based on such consequences, *zinā* was deemed more morally reprehensible than *liwāṭ*, and also, as noted in Section 5.2, because of the observation that *liwāṭ* cases were fewer in number than those of *zinā*. Likewise, while al-Nawawī (d. 1278) is quoted as having stated that male youths are more worthy of prohibition as access to vice in their case is easier,[178] especially when Zaylaʿī (d. 1342–43) is also noted as indicating that *liwāṭ* occurs as or more frequently than *zinā*,[179] Marghīnānī's (d. 1197) 'Hidaya' indicates that Islam allowing marriage to women and substantiating marriage through prohibiting *zinā* constitute deterrence against *zinā* and as such a crime with more deterrents in place is deemed more vicious.[180] Similarly, amongst contemporary thinkers, referring to the gravity of *zinā*, Moiz Amjad asserts that *zinā* is not a crime against an individual but the society as it destabilizes the foundations upon which a stable society is built.[181]

Many postclassical Ḥanafī jurists supported the position of the Shafiʿi jurist al-Qazwīnī (d. 1095) that "homosexuality," as defined by the desire to penetrate the anus, was an *ʿāha* (flaw) or *qabīḥ* (inherently evil) because the anus was not a place for intercourse.[182] However, on the basis of the Mutazilite jurist al-Baṣrī (d. 1085), it is not clear how an act can be deemed detestable if the elements of oppression, falsehood, or purposelessness are absent from the act[183] and on the basis of the scholar al-Murtaḍā (d. 1044), an act cannot be deemed reprehensible if it does not contain falsehood, oppression, and in the absence of information from God or any obligation that is impossible to meet.[184] As such, the Ḥanafī jurist Ibn al-Walīd (d. 1119) argued that *liwāṭ*, like wine, would be permissible in Paradise as the evil consequences of the disruption of procreation and noxiousness will be absent in Paradise. Likewise, scholars like Zīrikzāde (d. 1601) argued for the allowance of *liwāṭ* in Paradise based on verses 76:19 and 41:31 that allude to the beardless youth of Paradise.[185] Given this difference of opinion, al-Ḥafnī (d. 1767), the rector of al-Azhar, stated that *liwāṭ* in Paradise was held as permissible by some on the basis of the absence of reproduction and excrement in Paradise.[186]

Scholars like al-Alūsī (d. 1854) who argued against Ibn al-Walīd's position essentially referred to *liwāṭ* as being against natural disposition by alluding to the pathology of being penetrated,[187] that is, *'ubna*, as the issue was understood given the medical knowledge and sociocultural values of al-Alūsī's times. Likewise, while jurists like al-Nābulsī (d. 1731) stated that the desire for male youth was unnatural as looking at women was more likely to give rise to lust and hence *ṭabīʿī* (natural),[188] others like Zaylaʿī (d. 1342–43) and Sarakhsī (d. 1096) stated respectively that people of sound reason coveted both the vagina and anus and that in the absence of divine law, one could not differentiate between the two.[189] Regardless, it seems that the *qubḥ* (inherently evil) aspect of *liwāṭ*, as upheld by some jurists, in contrast to noxiousness and reproduction, which have been addressed above, depends more so on *ʾubna* as the contributing factor in explaining the flaw in the disposition toward *liwāṭ*.

To the extent that none of the reasons presented so far—severe tone of forbidding texts, repulsion, disruption of procreation, noxiousness, and the waste of semen—serve as reasonable explanations indicates that *ʾubna* seems to have been a significant factor in accounting for the reprehensibility of *liwāṭ*. It is perhaps *ʾubna* that formed the underlying assumption when jurists opined that the reprehensibility of *liwāṭ* is based on the notion of the male and female respectively being the active and passive partners in sex[190] or that the male or the anus was not created for the purpose of sexual penetration.[191] Ibn Qudāma (d. 1223) echoes this notion when he states that the male is not a place of intercourse for another male even if he were owned as a slave.[192] Likewise, the Ottoman Grand Mufti Efendi's (d. 1574) specified that the people of Lūṭ had intercourse with *rijāl* (males) instead of *ghilmān* (youths),[193] especially since sexual intercourse between adult males was viewed as an anomaly connected to violence/rape or more so to the *ʾubna* disease.[194] The characterization of *ʾubna* as a disease, based solely on medical theories of the time, found its way into theology and juristic rulings. Such a characterization may have led jurists to look at the penetrator as someone taking advantage of a diseased individual and may have also led them to ignore the sexual desire and need of the receiver/passive partner as illegitimate since such desires were viewed to have originated due to disease.

As noted in Section 2.5, on the basis of Khaled el-Rouayheb's work, it becomes clear that the context of *liwāṭ* generally involved violence apart from *ʾubna* and pederasty, in that *liwāṭ* was perpetrated without not only love and intimacy but also desire and pleasure. The scholar al-Alūsī (d. 1854) noted that some people in his time used *akhdhan li-l-thaʾr* (sodomy to seek revenge).[195] As such, a Druze chieftain in 1701, noted as a notorious womanizer, was gang-raped and left naked by around 20 Turcoman soldiers.[196] Likewise, poetry contained themes of penetration not out of desire but to subordinate and humiliate the other; for instance, a deputy judge at a Damascus court Ibrāhīm al-Ghāzālī (d. 1678) lampooned a contemporary by versifying that he would sodomize the contemporary, if not with a penis, due to disgust, then with a piece of wood.[197]

Even discounting violence, the above seems to suggest that the jurists worked with the notions of implicit consent and nonconsent in sexual intercourse. The religious scholar al-Rāghib (d. 1108–09) described a woman sodomizing an effeminate man with a dildo as an ultimate sexual irregularity,[198] which suggests that it is the penetration of a male whether with a penis or a dildo that is a concern, especially given the medical model where a male is deemed the penetrator and the female the penetrated, and that switching these roles was deemed to seemingly reverse such "natural" roles, which authorities unanimously prohibited.[199] Likewise, according to al-Rāghib, *siḥāq* (tribadism) was explained through the aversion to phallic objects and penetration,[200] which seems to suggest that when jurists state that *siḥāq* went against the natural order, they are essentially alluding to a medical model based on the nonreceptive male and the receptive female. This view may also be substantiated through the words *dhakar* and *unthā* used to refer to males and females in the Qur'an, as noted in Section 2.5, which contain meanings of nonreceptive and receptive entities respectively, and as such, given the notion that only a male suffering from the *'ubna* disease would submit to dishonor associated with penetration may explain why sexual intercourse between males was considered reprehensible.

It is clear from the above that the jurists addressed same-sex encounters either in the context of pederasty or between male adults within the scope of violence or disease and dishonor associated with the act of getting penetrated, which they deemed reprehensible, and as such the question of same-sex legal relationships was irrelevant. As noted in Section 5, they operated with the medical model of the penetrator and the penetrated in the context of sexuality where implicit consent was assumed to be absent on the part of the passive partner who was either coerced or who submitted for pecuniary or disease-related reasons. Even in the context of *mubādala* (taking turns), a consensual relationship cannot be assumed as, according to al-Rāghib, pecuniary reasons underscored the decision of the partners to allow penetration in lieu of penetration.[201]

Jurists opined in the context of the medical model that relied on categories of the penetrated and penetratee, which suggests that their understanding of consent in sexual activity was heavily based on that model. As such, one Mālikī text in the *Mawāhib al-Jalīl* that prescribes ritual cleanliness after consensual or coerced sexual activity, and which is present in variant forms,[202] reads as follows:

> The Sunnah has prescribed ghusl as obligatory when two circumcised parts meet, that being when the glans is wholly inserted even when both do not ejaculate, if they are both adult Muslims, in the vagina or the anus, while sleeping, awake, consensual or coerced, two men or just one man.

However, in contrast to the words *riḍā* (consent) or *ikhtiyār* (choice),[203] the word used in such texts is *ṭaw'an*, which is properly translated as "not coerced" and therefore it is inappropriate translation that leads one to misconstrue "consent" on the part of the passive partner in *liwāṭ*. While the word *ikrāh* (coerced) is used to depict that the passive partner was forced into an act, the word *ṭaw'an* (not coerced) does not suggest that the passive partner consented as we understand "consent," but rather acted out of reasons that included financial considerations or *'ubna*, thereby violating the norms based on the penetrator-penetratee medical model.

Just as the jurists' understanding of "consent" is different from the contemporary understanding, so too is their understanding of what constituted exploitation. As such, strictly speaking, even the victim of rape could be regarded as a fornicator or sodomite whose punishment was removed due to *shubha* (resemblance) caused by duress involved in the act.[204] Notwithstanding the opinion that duress does not render fornication permissible but simply removes legal liability,[205] according to one juristic manual, the act of getting penetrated becomes permissible, but better not done, under duress.[206] However, getting penetrated due to *'ubna* was treated as morally and religiously reprehensible,[207] and that the person who committed *liwāṭ* for pecuniary reasons was a *Lūṭī* just as the one who committed *liwāṭ* for pleasure,[208] despite the fact that, according to some jurists, prostitution with women constituted *shubha*—resemblance to mitigate punishment,[209] and as such according to a Mālikī manual, the passive partner in *liwāṭ* was to be given the capital punishment if he "consented," that is, if not coerced.[210]

The fact that jurists did not mitigate punishment on the basis of *'ubna* or exploitation related to financial considerations should not be surprising given their understanding of exploitation and any associated liability.[211] As an example, it may be noted that Marghīnānī (d. 1197) presented the opinions of Ḥanafī jurists like Zufar (d. 775), who indicated that the person who kills under duress is liable for the murder, as opposed to the one who compelled the person, and Abu Yūsuf (d. 798), who opined that neither was liable, and Shaybānī (d. 811), who stated that necessity did not render the permissibility of murder.[212] Likewise, based on the incident where the Prophet did not hold a Jewish woman liable for gifting a poisoned sheep, the jurist Sarakhsī opined that the person who deceives another to drink poison is not liable for murder as the person who drank had exercised choice and therefore committed suicide.[213] Moreover, according to Ḥanafī jurists, while *ikrāh* (duress) nullifies consent, it does not negate choice[214] and as such the punishment was not mitigated for the receptive partner in *liwāṭ*. Thus, disregarding the distinction between *zinā* and *liwāṭ*, despite the fact that the Meccan jurist Ibn Ḥajar al-Haytamī (d. 1566) noted that fornication was associated with dishonor of the passive receptive party, whether the woman or the *al-malūṭ bihi* (sodomized),[215] and that several Ḥanafī jurists noted that *liwāṭ* was one-sided in that consent would be implicitly absent on the part of the passive partner, several jurists did not mitigate punishment for the passive partners.

However, while several jurists prescribed punishment based on their understanding of "consent," "exploitation," and "liability," other jurists mitigated punishment based on their understanding of *zinā* and *mulk yamīn* (ownership of the right hand). Thus, minority Mālikī jurists allowed sexual relationship with male slaves, as noted in Section 5, whereas minority Shafi'i and Ḥanbalī jurists mitigated the death punishment for the passive partner based on the understanding that the *zinā* penalty did not apply to an orifice other than the vagina.[216] Likewise, as noted in Section 5.3, a majority of Ḥanafī jurists and Ẓāhirī jurists like Ibn Ḥazm opined that there was no legally prescribed punishment but *ta'zīr* punishment, which varied drastically, on the basis of the methodology used by the jurists, from there being no punishment to lashes and/or detention to capital punishment for repeat offenders.

Based on the above analysis, the severe tone of forbidding texts, repulsion, the disruption of procreation, noxiousness, and the waste of semen do not serve as reasonable explanations for the reprehensibility of *liwāṭ*, which predominately occurred in the context of pederasty or violence. It seems that *liwāṭ* was deemed reprehensible based on the medical model that relied on the penetrator-penetratee categories and as such deviations from those categories, including women using dildos on men, were viewed as sexual irregularities. It is perhaps this reason that jurists held the penetration of men as a greater perversion than the penetration of male youth, who were desired for their predominantly feminine attributes. Given the absence of development in psychology, jurists as noted by the Shafi'i jurist al-Āmidī (d. 1233) based their opinions on the apparent, as hidden things were left to God,[217] which may include inner attributes like sexual orientation. Moreover, jurists may have looked at *'ubna* as an irregularity that does not occur often and therefore could be ignored. This is similar to declaring a minority opinion even from the early generations of Muslims as *shādhdh*—irregular and not worthy of consideration and study.

While several jurists generally understood the desire to penetrate the vagina or anus as natural, and opined that the desire toward male youth was excessive or superfluous in addition to the basic desire to penetrate women, they accepted the then prevalent medical theory that the passive male partner was afflicted with *'ubna*. Thus, while, addressing *liwāṭ*, jurists have not addressed the issue of same-sex relationships, which would have been anachronistically absurd for them, for gays and lesbians, who they could not acknowledge given that they based their rulings on the apparent instead of hidden or inner attributes. As such, it does not seem reasonable to extend the reprehensibility of *liwāṭ* to possible same-sex legal relationships.

5.6 SAME-SEX ACTS IN SHĪ'Ī JURISPRUDENCE

Shī'ī texts are sidelined by the Sunnī tradition in part due to difference in methodology. However, it may be helpful to investigate how the Shī'ī texts address same-sex conduct in order to obtain a comparative view on the issue and to determine any extra-scriptural considerations that informed the rulings of the Shī'ī authorities. A detailed analysis of the transmission chains of the Shī'ī texts is beyond the scope of this work and as such only a critical review of the content of these texts on male same-sex conduct is presented below followed by the same for female same-sex conduct in a separate section.

Shī'ī narratives on same-sex conduct extensively address anal intercourse between males as well as nonpenetrative sexual conduct. A narrative traced back to Ja'far al-Ṣādiq indicates that the Prophet stated that God invests a person with female lust if he allows himself to be sexually molested.[218] A variant text indicates that the opinion belonged to 'Ali instead of the Prophet. The content seems to suggest that the sexual act in question does not contain the element of reciprocity but is inflicted on another individual.

Texts attributed to 'Ali (d. 661) indicate that the punishment of the *Lūṭī*—perpetrator of homosexual anal intercourse—is that of fornication, that is, he is stoned if he were *muḥṣan*—married and/or had access to female concubines, and given 100 lashes otherwise.[219] However, this opinion of 'Ali contrasts with his other opinions in which he is alleged to have ordered the punishment of burning. Another text attributed to 'Ali indicates that the *Lūṭī* is punished even in the absence of penetration when he mounts another man and that if he penetrates the anus of another man, then he commits disbelief by doing so.[220] In the context of a text attributed to 'Ali, the commentator 'Ali Akbar Ghefari opined that the act is equivalent to *kufr* (disbelief) in terms of its punishment in the Hereafter, and is deemed equivalent to blood shedding.[221]

Contemporary Muslim leader Miqdaad Versi[222] references a text attributed to 'Ali (d. 661) that indicates his verdict, based on a Prophetic directive, on a man who confesses four times to committing *liwāṭ* that he had a choice between stroke on neck by sword, hanging by a mountain with hands and legs tied, and being burnt by fire. This text, which is found in the works of al-'Āmilī (d. 1693), is deemed *ṣaḥīḥ* (authoritative) in Shī'ī jurisprudence. However, as noted in Sections 3.3.1 and 3.3.3, and according to contemporary Sunnī scholar Sheikh Mohamed el-Moctar el-Shinqiti,[223] the texts attributed to 'Ali on the punishment of *Lūṭī*s are deemed extremely weak. The punishments attributed to 'Ali, especially those on burning, contradict other Prophetic texts that forbid punishment with fire. Moreover, some scholars are of the opinion that even if 'Ali burnt the *zanādiqa* (criminal dissidents) to death, such a directive would be contrary to the Prophetic directives and would amount to criticism on 'Ali's decision.[224] Moreover, Hashim Kamali references past jurists who held that the *fatwā* (religious edict) of a Companion did not constitute a binding proof in Islamic jurisprudence and also mentions Shāfiʿī (d. 820), who stated that scholars have sometimes abandoned the *fatwā* of a Companion.[225]

Another text noted by al-ʿĀmilī alludes to Abu Abdullah mentioning that while the active partner in *liwāṭ* is flogged if he is unmarried, the passive partner should be killed irrespective of his marital status.[226] According to Versi, this suggests that if the passive partner is to be executed then the act was construed as having taken place between two consensual partners. Such a view may be substantiated on the basis of the fact that a person, upon whom the act is forcibly perpetrated, is not subjected to punishment based on the Hadith that Allah has forgiven acts based on forgetfulness, mistakes, and compulsion.[227]

However, in Islamic jurisprudence, exploitation has been viewed distinctly from coercion. The consent of the passive partner cannot be assumed given that the *maʾbūn* was viewed as suffering from *ʾubna* and in fact if anything, the death verdict, as also noted in Ibn al-Qayyim's opinion, was perhaps to relieve the passive partner from an incurable disease that was associated with humiliation and one that could not be cured except by disobeying God, that is, through repeated homosexual anal intercourse. Indeed, contemporary scholars reproduce the past texts which indicate that the receptive partner person in his youth only grows to be in the worst condition in an older age.[228] Moreover, as noted in Section 5.5, the past jurists did not understand consent and duress as is understood in contemporary times and as such, for them, exploitation of the passive partner did not mitigate the associated punishment.

Confirming the content of the texts attributed to 'Ali, narratives traced back to Jaʿfar al-Ṣādiq reflect the opinion that the active partner is to be struck with a sword if he penetrates the male anus and is lashed if he does not.[229] Likewise, texts traced back to Abu Jaʿfar also known as Shaykh Ṭūsī (d. 1067) indicate that the punishment of the active and passive partners is that of fornication in that the *iḥṣān* status would matter for both partners.[230] Another text attributed to Jaʿfar al-Ṣādiq indicates that the active partner is to be punished like a fornicator—lashed if he were unmarried and stoned if he were *muḥṣan*. However, the same text indicates that the passive partner is punished with death irrespective of his *iḥṣān* status.[231] This difference of opinion indicates that as in Sunnī jurisprudence, there are divergent opinions in Shīʿī jurisprudence on the issue and that given contradictory opinions there is a possible weakness in the authenticity of these texts.

Unlike Sunnī jurisprudence, where *liwāṭ* does not include acts other than penetration, in Shī'ī jurisprudence, according to Muqaddas Ardabili (d. 1585) and Shahid Thani (d. 1558), in the technical context for punishment, as opposed to the lexical meaning, *liwāṭ* includes acts other than penetration.[232] Some texts indicate that Ja'far al-Ṣādiq opined that pressing the penis between thighs constituted sodomy, whose perpetrator commits disbelief, and that anal intercourse with males is a greater sin than fornication for a whole nation was destroyed for the former act but not a single person was destroyed for the latter sin.[233] The 'Ali narrative, noted earlier, where lashing is prescribed as a punishment for nonpenetrative acts is corroborated by the texts of al-Mufīd (d. 1022) who specified 100 lashes for both the *fā'il* and the *maf'ūl bih* for *tafkhīdh* (intercrural intercourse)[234] and of al-Hakim (d. 2002) who also supported 100 lashes for *tafkhīdh*,[235] a punishment that is replaced by death if the perpetrators are caught for a third time.[236]

The texts that define intercrural intercourse between thighs as sodomy contradict the Sunnī classical definition of *liwāṭ* as specifically homosexual anal intercourse. The texts that indicate that God did not destroy any one for fornication but destroyed a whole nation for sodomy were opposed by jurists like Ibn Ḥazm, as noted in earlier in this chapter. Moreover, it also seems that the opinion of Ja'far al-Ṣādiq on the issue was also based on the knowledge of his times, as he is also reported to have suggested a cure that a person suffering from *'ubna*—the disease of requiring receptive homosexual anal intercourse—sit on a chopped off hump of a camel.[237]

A text attributed to 'Ali Reza (d. 818) indicates his opinion that adultery and sodomy are the causes of 72 ills in this life and the Hereafter.[238] Likewise, an eschatological text attributed to Abu al-Aswad (d. 688) indicates that 'Ali opined that when men satisfy themselves with men and women with women, earthquakes will occur, faces will become transformed, and stones will rain down from the skies.[239] Other Hadith texts traced through Ibn 'Umar (d. 693), quoted by Sunnīs, indicate that the Prophet warned about plagues and diseases that would arise in societies where public lewdness and its promotion become widespread.[240] Whereas some quote the Hadith text using the word "lewdness," others replace it with "adultery and homosexuality" to associate AIDS with queers,[241] which indicates the use of interpretive license on the part of the translators. Furthermore, the authenticity of the Hadith traced back to Ibn 'Umar has been questioned as the next person in the transmission chain 'Aṭā was not known to have met Ibn 'Umar enough to narrate a Hadith from him. Likewise, other narrators in the transmission chain have been critiqued.[242] Regardless, the texts are underscoring the issue with *fāḥisha*—lewdness or illegal sexual acts as opposed to monogamous opposite or same-sex relationships.

It also seems, in contrast to Sunnī jurists like Ibn Ḥazm (d. 1064), Shī‘ī jurists draw injunctions from the punishment meted out to the people of Lūṭ in the Qur'an for same-sex conduct. Alluding to verse 11:83 in the context of the people of Lūṭ, which states that punishment for the unjust has been marked by God, Abu al-Ḥusayn Dastghaib Shīrāzī (d. 1981) indicated that since the Qur'an described three kinds of punishment for the people of Lūṭ—terrible scream, shower of stones, and turning the earth upside down—any of these may be inflicted on those who commit similar acts.[243] In the context of verses 7:80–81, which depict the people of Lūṭ as *qawmun musrifūn*—an extravagant people, he further opined that the indecency in the verse referred to men squandering sperms instead of directing them toward wombs for procreation.[244] However, this opinion seemingly contrasts with the widely held Shī‘ī opinion on the qualified permissibility of heterosexual anal intercourse, where procreation is not involved.

While the text attributed to Abu al-Ḥasan depicts both partners "voluntarily" having intercrural intercourse, it seems that the text may have been improperly translated. A reason behind this contention is that the act of *liwāṭ* was inflicted on someone, based at least on the text attributed to Ja‘far al-Ṣādiq that mentions "allowing oneself to be sexually molested," and as such the act was associated with humiliation. Another reason behind this contention is that several Shī‘ī texts specifically address *liwāṭ* in the context of youth or male slaves.

An eschatological narrative attributed to the Prophet indicates that a person who commits sodomy with a boy would be cursed by God and acquire an impurity that not even all the waters of the world would be able to remove. The text distinguishes this act from the one in which a person allows himself to be mounted by another male, a sin that earns him the lowest pits of Hell for eternity.[245] The content of this narrative indicates that *liwāṭ* is committed with a boy or a person who allows himself to be used, and in both instances, it reflects a sense of exploitation of the boy or the passive partner. However, the text reflects severity of the eternal punishment of the passive partner, which contradicts other texts that indicate that anyone who believed in God would eventually be saved.

A text from Ja‘far al-Ṣādiq indicates that ‘Ali stated that the Prophet prescribed three punishments for sodomy with a boy that include beheading, being burnt alive, or being thrown from a cliff.[246] However, this text not only contradicts other texts where the Prophet prohibited killing by fire, but also the fact that in the presence of such a text, the Companions would not have differed on the punishment for *liwāṭ*. Other texts from Ja‘far al-Ṣādiq attributed to ‘Ali indicate that a person who sodomized his wife's son from another husband and in another instance a man who came onto a slave boy were both punished by the sword.[247] In contrast, in another text, Abu al-Ḥasan opined that the curse of God is upon the one who plays with a boy in his thighs without mentioning any punishment, which, as noted earlier, he reserved for two men having intercourse in the thighs.[248] This contradiction in text raises concerns about the authenticity of these texts. Regardless, the ruling on *liwāṭ* comes in the context of exploitation, that is, the act is committed on a boy, which according to Dastghaib Shīrāzī makes the mother, sister, or daughter of the boy forbidden to the perpetrator of the act.[249] A similar text exists in Ṣaḥīḥ Bukhārī that indicates that if a man commits *liwāṭ* with a youth, then the youth's mother becomes forbidden to the man.[250] Such texts indicate at the very least the absence of capital punishment for *liwāṭ* as the issue of marriage could not arise for a dead person and as such these texts cast further doubt on those texts and opinions that call for capital punishment.

An eschatological text attributed to 'Ali indicates that the Prophet stated that the person who dies without repenting for committing the act of the people of Lūṭ would be sucked in toward the dead of the people of Lūṭ and will be counted from amongst them. It deserves to be noted that the context of this text revolves around the case of a slave who killed his master after he had forcibly committed sodomy with him.[251] Notwithstanding authenticity issues, this text confirms that the act of *liwāṭ* was construed as inflicting humiliation on the penetrated partner to the extent that the slave took recourse to killing his master.

Apart from the texts that indicate punishment for *liwāṭ* with slaves and boys, there exist other texts that caution against glancing at boys and which prescribe punishment on sensually kissing boys. A Hadith cautions against lustfully looking at beardless slaves and youth of rich people, indicating that greater mischief is possible by glancing at beardless youth than by glancing at veiled girls.[252] The greater mischief alluded to in the text seems to be echoed in Sunnī jurist al-Nawawī's (d. 1278) opinion that male youths are more worthy of prohibition as access to vice in their case is easier.[253] A text attributed to Najīb as-Sirrī indicates that the pious elders would dislike looking at handsome boys.[254] However, responding to such opinions, the scholar al-Nābulsī (d. 1731) vehemently stated, "I wash my hands of this matter since these cows cannot fathom my reasoning. . . . Does he not see that he can occasionally look at even his wife or slave-girl without lust? And, besides, how can he read other men's hidden thoughts?"[255]

In one eschatological Hadith the Prophet is reported to have stated that the man who sensually kisses a youth would be punished for a thousand years in Hell whereas in another eschatological Hadith, mentioned by Ja'far al-Ṣādiq, the Prophet is reported to have stated that God would tie a rein of fire on his mouth.[256] Likewise, 'Ali Reza opined that the angels of earth, sky, mercy, and wrath all curse the man who sensually kisses a youth and that God decrees a place for such a person in Hell.[257] The text from 'Ali Reza seems similar to a text quoted by some Sunnī Muslims, according to which the Prophet is reported to have stated that God, angels, and people curse a man who sensually touches a youth.[258] Based on such texts, Shī'ī jurists deduced that lustfully kissing *ghulāms* (male slaves, usually youth) is a *kabīra* (major sin).[259]

However, Ibn al-Qayyim's (d. 1349/1350) statement that the danger of pederasty was absent during the Prophet's time[260] weakens the authenticity of the Hadith narratives that report *liwāṭ* in the context of youth and slaves. Likewise, the Syrian belletrist Aḥmad al-Barbīr (d. 1817), based on the absence of love poetry for boys, and the Egyptian scholar Mar'ī ibn Yūsuf al-Karmī (d. 1624) both opined that Arabs in pre-Islamic and Islamic times were not inclined toward pederasty.[261]

Regardless, based on the available texts, apart from extra-scriptural considerations, Shī'ī jurists prescribed punishments for sensually kissing youth. A text attributed to Ja'far al-Ṣādiq indicates his opinion that the man should be struck with 100 lashes.[262] In contrast, Dastghaib Shīrāzī opined that the wrong doer could be punished from 30 to 90 lashes.[263] It seems that where Ja'far al-Ṣādiq's opinion rests on treating the matter as of requiring a *Ḥadd*—scripturally sanctioned punishment—Dastghaib Shīrāzī's opinion seems to suggest that the matter be treated as one requiring the *ta'zir* (discretionary punishment) that in common practice[264] consisted of no more than 80 lashes.

A similar difference of opinion can be noted from texts that prescribe the punishment for two men found sleeping under a single piece of clothing. A text attributed to Abu al-Ḥasan prescribes 100 lashes, whereas a text attributed to Ja'far al-Ṣādiq indicates that 'Ali prescribed smearing a man discovered in the bed of another male with excrement.[265] The contradiction in punishing the action of sleeping under a single piece of clothing through *Ḥadd* or *ta'zir* raises questions on the authenticity of these texts. It is also not clear whether *ta'zir* punishments, which usually comprised of beatings, detention, and fines, included smearing with excrement.

In the context of such same-sex conduct, Dastghaib Shīrāzī quoted a Hadith in which the Prophet is reported to have suggested separating the beds of children over 10 years of age, be they two brothers, two sisters, or a brother and sister.[266] However, interpretive license is used in juxtaposing this text in the context of same-sex conduct, just as some conservative Muslims attempt to elicit the prohibition of same-sex unions on the basis of Hadith, reported by Abu Dawūd and Tirmidhī, which prohibits men and women from gazing at the *'awra*—nakedness of other men and women—and also forbids them from sleeping under the same cover.[267] The texts seem to emphasize the teachings on modesty and it would be a stretch to derive a ruling on marriage or same-sex legal contract on the basis of these texts.

In the context of verse 11:82 that describes the raining of stones on the people of Lūṭ, a text attributed to Ja'far al-Ṣādiq indicates his opinion that a person who dies deeming *liwāṭ* to be permissible is hit with the stones that fell on the people of Lūṭ.[268] While a variant text adds committing *liwāṭ* to believing in the permissibility of the act, referencing both texts, Dastghaib Shīrāzī opined that anyone who deems sodomy to be legal is a *kāfir* (unbeliever)—because deeming the act illegal is a requirement of faith.[269] Dastghaib Shīrāzī's opinion seems to have precedence in the opinion of Ja'far al-Ṣādiq who stated that the prohibition of *liwāṭ* is one of the necessary factors of religion and in the opinion of al-Ḥillī who classified *liwāṭ* as one of the gravest sins.[270]

Ja'far al-Ṣādiq's opinion that the prohibition of *liwāṭ* is one of the necessary factors of religion opinion seems to be similar to that of conservative Sunnī Muslims when they state that the prohibition of same-sex conduct is based on the legal maxim *ma'lūm min al-dīn bi-l-ḍarūra*—religious doctrines known by necessity as part of religious teachings. However, the legal maxim does not mean that the ruling in the context of such a matter is certain but that one does not need specialized training to understand God's ruling on the matter.[271] Furthermore, jurists like Ibn 'Ābidīn (d. 1836) opined that claiming the permissibility of *liwāṭ* with male slaves did not necessitate *kufr* (unbelief).[272] Indeed, the Ḥanafī jurist al-Kawākibī (d. 1685) clearly stated that based on the phrase "what their right hand possesses" in verses 23:6 and 70:30, which generally alluded to female concubines, there were those who deemed *liwāṭ* with male slaves permissible.[273] Most Sunnī jurists did not deem falling in love with a youth to be a sin and, based on the principle that one should not prohibit what God has made licit, resisted the efforts of zealous jurists to prohibit "preliminaries" of *liwāṭ* and allowed the composition of pederastic love poetry.[274]

5.6.1 Female Same-Sex Conduct

As in Sunnī jurisprudence, the Shī'ī authorities distinguish between *liwāṭ* and nonpenetrative sexual acts and prescribe capital punishment for the former, especially for those classified as *muḥṣans*. However, in contrast to Sunnī authorities, Shī'ī authorities seem to have taken a more rigid stance on nonpenetrative sexual acts, which also reflects their harsher position on female same-sex conduct predominately defined as *siḥāq* (tribadism).

As in the case of *liwāṭ*, Shī'ī authorities differ on the punishment for *siḥāq*. Ja'far al-Ṣādiq opined that the punishment for *siḥāq* should be that for fornication, whereas Shaykh Ṭūsī mentioned the punishment of lashing.[275] A Hadith reported by al-Faḍl al-Ṭabrisī (d. 1153) equates *siḥāq* with *liwāṭ* and prescribes the death penalty for both.[276] Likewise, a text from al-'Āmilī (d. 1693) mentions that Abu Abdullah was approached by a group of women, who asked him about *siḥāq* and he responded that the punishment is the same as that for fornication and that God mentioned about it in the Qur'an through the people of Rass.[277] However, as noted in Section 5.3.2, while the people of Rass are discussed in verses 25:38–39 and 50:12–14, the Qur'an does not connect them with lesbianism and neither do Zamakhsharī (d. 1143),[278] Ibn Kathīr (d. 1373), or Ṭabarī (d. 923) in their exegetical commentaries and as such the connection between the people of Rass and *siḥāq* does not seem to be justified in Sunnī jurisprudence. Moreover, as noted earlier, in Sunnī jurisprudence, Ibn Ḥazm (d. 1064) refuted the report that equated *liwāṭ* and *siḥāq* with *zinā* as one of the narrators is deemed as a weak transmitter and unconnected with other narrators in the transmission chain.[279] He also refuted Shihāb Zuhrī's (d. 741/2) position, who prescribed hundred lashes for *siḥāq*, a penalty deduced from the equivalence of *liwāṭ* and *siḥāq* with the gravest and least severe forms of *zinā*, respectively.[280]

The difference of opinion on the punishment of *siḥāq* among Shī'ī authorities is also observed in their opinions on the punishment of two women found under a single quilt. Ja'far al-Ṣādiq reported a narrative about 'Ali (d. 661) where he ordered the burning of two women.[281] However, Ja'far al-Ṣādiq also opined that after lashing for two instances of being under a single quilt, the two women must be killed if found for a third time, though, elsewhere he prescribed the killing if they were found under the quilt for the fourth time.[282] Another narrative mentioned by Shī'ī authorities prescribes 100 lashes. It is interesting to note that where there exist reports of burning two women for being found under a single quilt, two men, as noted earlier, were either prescribed lashing or be smeared with excrement. Regardless, it seems that various opinions have been attributed to Ja'far al-Ṣādiq on the issue of female same-sex conduct, which necessitates an inquiry into the authenticity of these texts.

Shī'ī authorities also mentioned rulings on a case scenario where a woman, after having sex with her husband, proceeds to have *siḥāq* with a virgin girl, impregnating her through the act. A narrative attributed to Ḥasan (d. 670) indicates his opinion that the woman is stoned and the virgin girl is lashed.[283] A similar opinion is attributed to Ja'far al-Ṣādiq in various texts. However, in other texts, which address the issue of a woman seizing and deflowering a virgin girl by hand, Ḥasan prescribed the *Ḥadd* punishment and Ja'far al-Ṣādiq prescribed 80 lashes respectively for the woman.[284] The difference between the punishment for *siḥāq* and deflowering by hand for a woman suggests that some Shī'ī authorities viewed *siḥāq* separately from other female same-sex acts. Moreover, it seems that not all nonpenetrative sexual acts are viewed in a similar fashion, in that intercrural sex between males merits the death penalty, whereas deflowering by hand between females warrants 80 lashes. To the extent that Sunnī authorities do not view one nonpenetrative sexual act different from another nonpenetrative act and to the extent the same holds true for Shīʿī authorities, the authenticity of these texts has to be questioned.

It also deserves to be noted that just as the rulings for same-sex conduct between males were made in the context of acts between an adult and youth or male slaves, likewise, it seems that the rulings on same-sex acts between females were made in the context of an adult woman exploiting a young girl or slave by seizing and taking her virginity. Furthermore, given that one of the text indicates a married woman deflowering a girl after she had sex with her husband, same-sex conduct between females was viewed as a superfluous act outside the folds of a legal contract. This observation between females seems to be consistent with the assumption upheld in the context of same-sex conduct between males in that the active partner's attraction toward male youth was not viewed as a sole desire toward them but the same that was directed toward women and therefore could be sated with lawful female partners.[285]

In conclusion, like their Sunnī counterparts, the varying and contradictory opinions on same-sex conduct among Shīʿī authorities necessitate a critical inspection of the authenticity of the Shīʿī texts. The Shīʿī texts also confirm that religious rulings in the context of same-sex conduct for both males and females were usually made in the context of exploitation of male youth, slaves, and young girls. To the extent that rulings were made in the context of exploitation of youth and slaves, or in the context of males classified as suffering from *ʾubna*, a renewed approach to same-sex relationships between equal partners, which accounts for the contemporary understanding of exclusive same-sex constitutional orientations, is warranted.

NOTES

1. Lagrange, "The Obscenity of the Vizier," 184.
2. Ali, *Sexual Ethics and Islam,* 88.
3. El-Rouayheb, *Before Homosexuality,* 65.
4. Ibid, 114.
5. Ibid, 71.
6. Ali, *Sexual Ethics and Islam,* 84.
7. "Sex and Psychiatry," Magnus Hirschfeld Archive for Sexology, accessed October 2012, http://zeus4.cms.hu-berlin.de/sexology/ATLAS_EN/html/sex_and_psychiatry.html.
8. Rosenthal, "Ar-Razi on the Hidden Illness," 50.
9. Ze'evi, *Producing Desire,* 38.
10. Rosenthal, "Ar-Razi on the Hidden Illness," 56–57.
11. El-Rouayheb, *Before Homosexuality,* 19.
12. Ibid, 20.

13. Amer, "Medieval Arab lesbians and Lesbian-Like Women," 216–17.
14. Ze'evi, *Producing Desire,* 22.
15. Ibid, 32.
16. Ibid, 33.
17. El-Rouayheb, "Review of Ze'evi," 1.
18. Ibn Jumuʿa, ʿAbd ʿAli. *Tafsīr Nūr al-Thaqalayn* (Qom: Intisharat Ismailiyan, 1415 AH/1994), 2: 375–407.
19. Ibn Kathīr, *The History of Ibn Kathir—Bidaya and Nihaya*, Volume 9, 185.
20. Shalakany, "Comparative Law as Archeology," 26.
21. Ze'evi, *Producing Desire,* 88.
22. El-Rouayheb, *Before Homosexuality,* 17.
23. Ali, *Marriage and Slavery in Early Islam*, 11.
24. Ābādī, *ʿAwn al-Maʿbūd fī Sharḥ Sunan Abu Dawūd*, Volume 6, 141.
25. Ali, *Marriage and Slavery in Early Islam*, 182.
26. Ibid.
27. Sara Omar, "From Semantics to Normative Law: Perceptions of *Liwāṭ* (Sodomy) and *Siḥāq* (Tribadism) in Islamic Jurisprudence (8th–15th century CE)," *Islamic Law and Society* 19 (2012): 251.
28. Arno Schmitt, "LIWĀṬ im Fiqh Mannliche Homosexualitat," *Journal of Arabic and Islamic Studies* 4, no. 3 (2001–2002): 49–110.
29. Christopher Scott Rose, "Owned by the Right Hand: The Theory and Practice of Slavery in Islamic Society," (M.A. Thesis, University of Texas at Austin, 2000), accessed January 27, 2016, http://www.academia.edu/354364/Owned_by_the_Right_Hand_The_Theory_and_Practice_of_Slavery_in_Islamic_Societies.
30. El-Rouayheb, *Before Homosexuality*, 124.
31. Hallaq, *A History of Islamic Legal Theories*, 246–51.
32. Ibn ʿAbd al-Barr, *Istidhkār*, Volume 7, 493.
33. Ibid.
34. Al-San'ani, *Muṣannaf Abul Razzāq*, Volume 7, 429.
35. Kamali, *Principles of Islamic Jurisprudence*, 40.
36. Adang, "Ibn Ḥazm on Homosexuality," 26.
37. Ibid, 21.
38. Javed Ghamidi, "Islamic Punishments: Some Misconceptions," *Renaissance*, September 2002, accessed January 26, 2016, http://www.renaissance.com.pk/septref122y2.html.
39. Amjad, "Regarding the Death Penalty."
40. Ibn ʿAbd al-Barr, *Istidhkār*, Volume 7, 493.
41. Adang, "Ibn Ḥazm on Homosexuality," 19.
42. Ibid, 21.
43. Abdullah Hasan, "Unnatural Offences: The Controversy," 2008, accessed October 2012, http://maqasid.wordpress.com/2008/07/30/unnatural-offences-the-controversy/.
44. El-Rouayheb, *Before Homosexuality,* 120.
45. Al-San'ani, *Muṣannaf Abdul Razzāq*, Volume 11, 243.
46. Hasan, "Unnatural Offences: The Controversy."

47. Adang, "Ibn Ḥazm on Homosexuality," 20.
48. For a detailed critique by Ibn Ḥazm, see: *Al-Muḥallā bi-l-Āthār: kitāb mā lā ḥadd fīh*: The question of the doing of the people of Lut.
49. Ibn ʿAbd al-Barr, *Istidhkār*, Volume 7, 493.
50. Kamali, *Principles of Islamic Jurisprudence*, 319.
51. Ibid, 320.
52. Ibid, 194, 198.
53. Al-Bayhaqī, *Sunan al-Bayhaqī al-Kubrā*, Volume 8, 233.
54. Adang, "Ibn Ḥazm on Homosexuality," 21.
55. Ibid, 24.
56. Rowson, "Homosexuality in Islamic law."
57. Ibn ʿAbd al-Barr, *Istidhkār*, Volume 7, 493.
58. Ibn Ḥajar al-ʿAsqalānī, *Talkhīṣ al-Ḥabīr*, Volume 4, in الموسوعة الذهبية للحديث النبوي الشيف و علومه [*The Golden Encyclopedia of the Prophetic Golden Hadeeth and its Sciences*], 2nd edition, (London: Turath Publishing), CD-ROM, 55.
59. Adang, "Ibn Ḥazm on Homosexuality," 27.
60. Lange, *Justice, Punishment and the Medieval Muslim Imagination*, 206.
61. Hasan, "Unnatural Offences: The Controversy."
62. Kamali, *Principles of Islamic Jurisprudence*, 265.
63. Lange, *Justice, Punishment and the Medieval Muslim Imagination*, 181.
64. Shalakany, "Comparative Law as Archeology," 23.
65. Lange, *Justice, Punishment and the Medieval Muslim Imagination*, 183.
66. Ibid, 208.
67. Al-Rāzī, *Tafsīr al-Rāzī* of 24:2.
68. Lange, *Justice, Punishment and the Medieval Muslim Imagination*, 208.
69. Shalakany, "Comparative Law as Archeology," 23–24.
70. Ābādī, *ʿAwn al-Maʿbūd fī Sharḥ Sunan Abu Dawūd*, Volume 12, 99.
71. Lange, *Justice, Punishment and the Medieval Muslim Imagination*, 210.
72. Adang, "Ibn Ḥazm on Homosexuality," 27.
73. Al-Rāzī, *Tafsīr al-Rāzī* of 24:2.
74. Lange, *Justice, Punishment and the Medieval Muslim Imagination*, 210.
75. Ibid, 212.
76. Shalakany, "Comparative Law as Archeology," 25.
77. Ibn ʿAbd al-Barr, *Istidhkār*, Volume 7, 493.
78. Lange, *Justice, Punishment and the Medieval Muslim Imagination*, 202.
79. Ibid, 205.
80. El-Rouayheb, *Before Homosexuality*, 119.
81. Ibn Ḥazm, "Chapter 28: Of the Vileness of Sinning."
82. Adang, "Ibn Ḥazm on Homosexuality," 26.
83. Ibn Ḥazm, *Al-Muḥallā bi-l-Āthār: kitāb mā lā ḥadd fīh*: The question of the doing of the people of Lut, in الموسوعة الذهبية للحديث النبوي الشيف و علومه [*The Golden Encyclopedia of the Prophetic Golden Hadeeth and its Sciences*], 2nd edition, (London: Turath Publishing), CD-ROM. Translation by the authors.
84. Adang, "Ibn Ḥazm on Homosexuality," 28.
85. Ibn Ḥazm, *Al-Muḥallā bi-l-Āthār: kitāb mā lā ḥadd fīh*: The question of the doing of the people of Lut.

86. Al-Mizzī, *Tahdhīb al-Kamāl*, Volume 20, 278–82; Volume 31, 508–10.

87. Ibn Ḥazm, *Al-Muḥallā bi-l-Āthār: kitāb mā lā ḥadd fīh*: The question of the doing of the people of Lut.

88. Adang, "Ibn Ḥazm on Homosexuality," 14.

89. El-Rouayheb, *Before Homosexuality,* 124.

90. Ali, *Sexual Ethics and Islam*, 77.

91. George F. Hourani, *Islamic Rationalism: The Ethics of Abd Al Jabbar*, (Oxford: Clarendon Press, 1971), 29.

92. Ibid, 69–70.

93. Ibid, 104.

94. A. Kevin Reinhart, *Before Revelation: The Boundaries of Muslim Moral Thought*, (Albany: State University of New York Press, 1995), 41.

95. Ibid, 42.

96. Adang, "Ibn Ḥazm on Homosexuality," 28.

97. Ibn Ḥazm, *Ṭawq al-Ḥamāma fī al-ulfa wa-l-Allāf* (Damascus: Maktaba ʿArafa. 1349 A.H./1929-30 C.E.), 138–39.

98. Ibn Ḥazm, *Al-Muḥallā bi-l-Āthār: kitāb mā lā ḥadd fīh*: The question of the doing of the people of Lut, in الموسوعة الذهبية للحديث النبوي الشيف و علومه [*The Golden Encyclopedia of the Prophetic Golden Hadeeth and its Sciences*], 2nd edition, (London: Turath Publishing), CD-ROM. Translation by Anas Mahafzah.

99. Ali, *Sexual Ethics and Islam*, 78.

100. Abu Bakr Aḥmad ibn Ḥusayn ibn ʿAli ibn Mūsā al-Khusrawjirdī Al-Bayhaqī, *Knowledge of the Sunan and narrated stories,* Volume 6, in الموسوعة الذهبية للحديث النبوي الشيف و علومه [*The Golden Encyclopedia of the Prophetic Golden Hadeeth and its Sciences*], 2nd edition, (London: Turath Publishing), CD-ROM, 349. Translation by the authors.

101. Mohammad Omar Farooq, "The Doctrine of Ijma': Is there a consensus?" Upper Iowa University, 2006, accessed January 26, 2016, http://www.scribd.com/doc/45747285/The-Doctrine-of-Ijma-Is-there-a-consensus, 8.

102. Lange, *Justice, Punishment and the Medieval Muslim Imagination,* 209.

103. Ibid, 205.

104. Ibid, 207.

105. Ibid, 214.

106. Ibid, 102–103.

107. El-Rouayheb, *Before Homosexuality*, 119.

108. We are grateful to an anonymous critic for this point.

109. El-Rouayheb, (2005), *Before Homosexuality,* 119.

110. Elyse Semerdjian, *Off the Straight Path, Illicit Sex, Law and Community in Ottoman Aleppo*, (Syracuse: Syracuse University Press, 2008), 47.

111. Ibid, 41, 54.

112. Isik, "*Uqubat*—Penal Code."

113. Abdelwahab Bouhdiba, *Sexuality in Islam*, (London: Routledge and Kegan Paul, 1985), 31.

114. El-Rouayheb, *Before Homosexuality,* 137.

115. Ibid, 138.

116. Siddiq Bukhary, "Classifying Sins Into Minor and Major Category," March 2, 2003, Understanding Islam Q&A, accessed January 26, 2016, http://

www.understanding-islam.com/q-and-a/cleansing-and-purification/classifying-sins-into-minor-and-major-category-6166.

117. Muhammad Ibn Adam, "Nikaah, Zina, Fornication: it is overlooked by Allah?" Central-Mosque.com, accessed January 26, 2016, http://www.central-mosque.com/index.php/Relationships/fornication-adultery-masturbation-a-pornography.html.

118. El-Rouayheb, *Before Homosexuality*, 139.

119. Ibn Adam, "*Nikaah*, *Zina*, Fornication: it is overlooked by Allah?"

120. Bell, *Love Theory in later Hanbalite Islam*, 128.

121. El-Rouayheb, *Before Homosexuality*, 138.

122. Habib, *Arabo-Islamic Texts on Female Homosexuality*, 104.

123. Ibid, 88.

124. Email correspondence with Miqdaad Versi.

125. Al-Ṭabarānī. *Musnad al-Shāmiyyīn*, Hadith No. 3341, in الموسوعة الذهبية للحديث النبوي الشيف و علومه [*The Golden Encyclopedia of the Prophetic Golden Hadeeth and its Sciences*], 2nd edition, (London: Turath Publishing), CD-ROM.

126. Razi Allah, "What's the classical definition of Zina?" May 31, 2003, Understanding Islam Q&A, accessed January 27, 2016, http://www.understanding-islam.com/q-and-a/penal-law/what-s-the-classical-definition-of-zina-6254.

127. "Abnormal relationship between women," Islam QA, accessed May 12, 2016, https://islamqa.info/en/591.

128. Kamali, "The Sharia: Law as the Way of God," 164.

129. "Abnormal Relationship Between Women," Islam QA.

130. Habib, *Arabo-Islamic Texts on Female Homosexuality,* 83.

131. Mohammad Fadel, "The True, The Good and the Reasonable: The Theological and Ethical Roots of Public Reason in Islamic Law," University of Toronto Legal Studies Series, Research Paper No. 977206. 2007, 83.

132. Ibn al-Qayyim. *Al-Jawāb al-Kāfī li Man Saʾala ʿan al-Dawāʾ al-Shāfī.*

133. El-Rouayheb, *Before Homosexuality,* 14.

134. Hisham M. Ramadan, *Understanding Islamic Law: From Classical to Contemporary*, (Lanham, MD: AltaMira Press, 2006), 55.

135. Recep Senturk, "Sociology of Rights: Inviolability of the other in Islam between universalism and communalism," in *Contemporary Islam: Dynamic not Static*, eds. Abul Said, Mohammed Abu-Nimer, and Meena Sharify-funk, (London and New York: Routledge, 2006), 30, 38.

136. Muhammad Khalid Masud, *Shatibi's Philosophy of Islamic Law*, (Delhi: Adam Publishers and Distributors, 1997), 216.

137. Ibid, 216.

138. Ibid, 217.

139. Ibid, 222.

140. Ibid, 223.

141. Ali, *Sexual Ethics and Islam,* xxvi.

142. El-Rouayheb, *Before Homosexuality,* 127.

143. Ibid, 127.

144. Ibid, 127–128.

145. Ibid, 139.
146. Bell, *Love Theory in later Hanbalite Islam*, 196–197.
147. Ibid, 129.
148. El-Rouayheb, *Before Homosexuality in the Arab-Islamic World,* 129.
149. Imani et al., *An Enlightening Commentary*, Parts 7 & 8, 306.
150. Ibn Jumuʿa, ʿAbd ʿAli. *Tafsīr Nūr al-Thaqalayn* (Qom: Intisharat Ismailiyan, 1415 AH/1994), 2: 375–407.
151. Hassan El-Menyawi, "Same-sex marriage in Islamic law," *Wake Forest Journal of Law & Policy* 2, no. 2 (2012): 468.
152. Ibid, 483.
153. Ibid, 470.
154. Ramadan, *Radical Reform,* 169.
155. Ali, *Sexual Ethics and Islam,* xv.
156. Kecia Ali, "Progressive Muslims and Islamic Jurisprudence: The Necessity for Critical Engagement with Marriage and Divorce Laws," in *Progressive Muslims,* ed. Omid Safi, (Oxford: Oneworld Publications, 2003), 179.
157. Munawar Aḥmad Anees, *Islam and Biological Futures: Ethics, Gender, and Technology*, (London: Mansell, 1989), 102.
158. El-Menyawi, "Same-sex marriage in Islamic law," 484–85.
159. El-Rouayheb, *Before Homosexuality,* 131.
160. Ibid, 125. *Talkhīṣ al-Ḥabīr.*
161. Ibn Ḥajar al-ʿAsqalānī, *Talkhīṣ al-Ḥabīr*, Book of Nikāḥ, in الموسوعة الذهبية للحديث النبوي الشيف و علومه [*The Golden Encyclopedia of the Prophetic Golden Hadeeth and its Sciences*], 2nd edition, (London: Turath Publishing), CD-ROM.
162. Ibid, Chapter that addresses anal intercourse.
163. Moiz Amjad, "Narratives on the Prohibition of anal sex," Understanding Islam Q&A, accessed May 11, 2016, http://www.understanding-islam.com/narratives-on-the-prohibition-of-anal-sex/.
164. See *Talkhīṣ al-Ḥabīr* by Ibn Ḥajar.
165. Ṭabāṭabāʾī, *Tafsīr al-Mīzān*, commentary on verses 2:222–223.
166. "What is the Islamic law regarding anal intercourse? Is there any objection in it?" Islam Quest, Question Archive, accessed January 26, 2016, http://www.islam-quest.net/en/archive/question/fa1075.
167. Shalakany, "Comparative Law as Archeology," 20–21.
168. Qur'anic Path, "Does the Qur'an Prohibit Anal Sex between Husband & Wife?", accessed May 11, 2016, http://www.quranicpath.com/misconceptions/anal_sex.html.
169. Ṭabāṭabāʾī, *Tafsīr al-Mīzān*, commentary on verses 2:222–223.
170. El-Rouayheb, *Before Homosexuality,* 124.
171. Schmitt and Sofer, *Sexuality and Eroticism,* 14.
172. El-Rouayheb, *Before Homosexuality,* 124.
173. Ibid, 129.
174. Amjad, "Opinions Expressed by Muslims regarding masturbation," Understanding Islam Q&A, accessed May 11, 2016, http://www.understanding-islam.com/opinions-expressed-by-muslims-regarding-masturbation/.

175. Juferi, "The Consensus on Homosexuality."
176. Adang, "Ibn Ḥazm on Homosexuality," 24.
177. El-Rouayheb, *Before Homosexuality*, 128.
178. Ibid, 114.
179. Lange, *Justice, Punishment and the Medieval Muslim Imagination,* 211.
180. Norman Calder, *Islamic Jurisprudence in the Classical Era*, (New York: Cambridge University Press, 2010), 43.
181. Amjad, "Is Fornication a Universally Recognized Moral Sin?" Understanding Islam Q&A, accessed May 11, 2016, http://www.understanding-islam.com/is-fornication-a-universally-recognized-moral-sin/.
182. El-Rouayheb, *Before Homosexuality,* 132.
183. Reinhart, *Before Revelation,* 41.
184. Ibid, 42.
185. El-Rouayheb, *Before Homosexuality,* 133.
186. Ibid, 133.
187. Ibid, 132–33.
188. Ibid, 115.
189. Lange, *Justice, Punishment and the Medieval Muslim Imagination,* 211.
190. El-Rouayheb, *Before Homosexuality in the Arab-Islamic World,* 129.
191. Ibid, 115.
192. Muwaffaq al-Dīn Abdullah ibn Aḥmad ibn Qudāma Al-Maqdisī, *Al-Mughnī* The *ḥadd* of *liwāṭ*, In الموسوعة الذهبية للحديث النبوي الشيف و علومه [*The Golden Encyclopedia of the Prophetic Golden Hadeeth and its Sciences*], 2nd edition, (London: Turath Publishing), CD-ROM.
193. El-Rouayheb, *Before Homosexuality,* 126.
194. Ibid, 26.
195. Ibid, 14.
196. Ibid, 13.
197. Ibid, 14.
198. Rowson, "The Categorization of Gender," 68.
199. Ali, *Marriage and Slavery in Early Islam*, 183.
200. Rowson, "The Categorization of Gender," 68.
201. Ibid, 66.
202. "Ruling on one who has intercourse with his wife in her back passage during the day in Ramadaan," Islam QA, accessed May 11, 2016, https://islamqa.info/en/50452. Translation by anonymous and the authors.
203. Abd el-Wahab Ahmed El-Hassan, "The Doctrine of Duress *(Ikrāh)* in Sharia, Sudan and English Law," *Arab Law Quarterly* 1, no. 2 (February 1986): 236.
204. El-Rouayheb, *Before Homosexuality,* 136.
205. Ibid, 236.
206. Isik, "*Ikrāh*—Intimidation, Duress and Hijr-forbidding."
207. El-Rouayheb, *Before Homosexuality,* 20.
208. Ibid, 137.
209. Ibid, 123.

210. Abdullah ibn Abi Zayd Al-Qayrawani, *The Risala-A treatise on Maliki fiqh*, trans. Bello Mohammad Daura, London, Section 37:30, accessed January 25, 2016, http://www.archive.org/stream/TheRisala/TheRisala-ATreatiseOnMalikiFiqh_djvu.txt.

211. We are grateful to Peter Gray for this point.

212. Imber, "Why you should poison your husband," 208.

213. Ibid, 211.

214. El-Hassan, "The doctrine of duress," 231–36.

215. El-Rouayheb, *Before Homosexuality,* 28.

216. Shalakany, "Comparative Law as Archeology," 25.

217. Lange, *Justice, Punishment and the Medieval Muslim Imagination,* 193.

218. "Chapter Fourteen: Nasibi propaganda relating to sexual ethics." Shia Pen.

219. "Chapters on the Hadd of sodomy." Tashayyu, accessed January 27, 2016, http://www.tashayyu.org.

220. Shahid e Mehraab Ayatullah-ul-Uzma Sayed Abdul Husain Dastghaib Shīrāzī, "Eleventh Greater sin: Sodomy," in *Greater Sins*, Volume 1, trans. Sayyid Athar Husain S.H.Rizvi, accessed March 21, 2016, http://www.al-islam.org/greater-sins-volume-1-ayatullah-sayyid-abdul-husayn-dastghaib-shirazi.

221. "Chapter Fourteen: Nasibi propaganda relating to sexual ethics." Shia Pen.

222. Email correspondence with Miqdaad Versi.

223. El-Shinqiti, "Threats to behead homosexuals."

224. Amjad, "Why Did Ali Burn Some Apostates?" Understanding Islam Q&A, accessed May 11, 2016, http://www.understanding-islam.com/why-did-ali-burn-some-apostates/.

225. Kamali, *Principles of Islamic Jurisprudence*, 256, 318–19.

226. We are grateful to Miqdaad Versi for this point.

227. "The reason why the one to whom a homosexual act is done is to be executed." Islam QA.

228. Ibid.

229. "Chapters on the Hadd of sodomy." Tashayyu.

230. Ibid.

231. Ibid.

232. We are grateful to an anonymous critic for this point.

233. Shīrāzī, "Greater Sins."

234. We are grateful to an anonymous critic for this point.

235. Email correspondence with Miqdaad Versi.

236. We are grateful to an anonymous critic for this point.

237. Ibn Jumu'a, 'Abd 'Ali. *Tafsīr Nūr al-Thaqalayn* (Qom: Intisharat Ismailiyan, 1415 AH/1994), 2: 375–407.

238. Shīrāzī, "Greater Sins."

239. "Lesbian sex is strictly forbidden in Islam?" Islam QA, accessed May 11, 2016. http://islamqa.org/hanafi/darulifta-deoband/27772.

240. Al-Bazaar. *Musnad Ibn Abbas*, Hadith No. 1751, in الموسوعة الذهبية للحديث النبوي الشيف و علومه [*The Golden Encyclopedia of the Prophetic Golden Hadeeth and its Sciences*]. 2nd edition, (London: Turath Publishing), CD-ROM.

241. Wizdom, "*Sexuele anarchie bestraft met geslachtziekten!*"
242. Al-Mizzī, *Tahdhīb al-Kamāl*, Biography of Nafi'a bin Abdullah, in الموسوعة الذهبية للحديث النبوي الشيف و علومه [*The Golden Encyclopedia of the Prophetic Golden Hadeeth and its Sciences*]. 2nd edition, (London: Turath Publishing), CD-ROM.
243. Shīrāzī, "Greater Sins."
244. Ibid.
245. Ibid.
246. Ibid.
247. "Chapters on the Hadd of sodomy." Tashayyu.
248. Ibid.
249. Shīrāzī, "Greater Sins."
250. Bukhari, Authentic Traditions, BOOK LXII (Marriage), Chapter 25.
251. Shīrāzī, "Greater Sins."
252. Ibid.
253. El-Rouayheb, *Before Homosexuality,* 114.
254. Murtada Gusau, "The Dangers of Homosexuality and Lesbianism in Islam," *Premium Times*, December 18, 2015, accessed May 11, 2016, http://blogs.premiumtimesng.com/2015/12/18/the-dangers-of-homosexuality-and-lesbianism-in-islam-by-murtada-gusau/.
255. Semerdijan, *Off the Straight Path,* 45.
256. Shīrāzī, "Greater Sins."
257. Ibid.
258. Doi, *Sharia the Islamic Law*, 242.
259. We are grateful to an anonymous critic for this point.
260. Bell, (1979), *Love Theory in later Hanbalite Islam*, 129.
261. El-Rouayheb, *Before Homosexuality,* 77–78.
262. "Chapters on the Hadd of sodomy." Tashayyu.
263. Shīrāzī, "Greater Sins."
264. We are grateful to an anonymous critic for this point.
265. "Chapters on the Hadd of sodomy." Tashayyu.
266. Shīrāzī, "Greater Sins."
267. Yusuf Al-Qaradawi, *The Lawful and the Prohibited in Islam*, (Cairo: Al-Falah Foundation, 2005), 14–16.
268. Shīrāzī, "Greater Sins."
269. Ibid.
270. "Chapter Fourteen: Nasibi propaganda relating to sexual ethics." Shia Pen.
271. We are grateful to Mohammad Fadel for this point.
272. El-Rouayheb, *Before Homosexuality,* 124.
273. Ibid.
274. Ibid, 12.
275. "Chapters on the Hadd of Tribadism and Pimping." Tashayyu.
276. Ibid.
277. Email correspondence with Miqdaad Versi.
278. Ibid.
279. Adang, "Ibn Ḥazm on Homosexuality," 27.

280. Ibid, 26.
281. "Chapters on the Hadd of Tribadism and Pimping." Tashayyu.
282. Ibid.
283. Ibid.
284. Ibid.
285. Ali, *Sexual Ethics and Islam,* 88.

Chapter 6

Addressing the Opinions of Contemporary Scholars

Some contemporary Muslim leaders wield enough power among Muslim masses and as such are in a position to shape the discourse on the concerns of Muslim gays and lesbians. They fall back to the Qur'an, Hadith, and juristic literature, which were critically reviewed in the previous chapters, to formulate strong opinions on same-sex relationships. In what follows, the arguments brought by some conservative Muslim leaders will be critically addressed. These arguments include viewing orientation as a desire or urge and as a social construct based on French philosopher Michel Foucault's (d. 1984) opinions. The argument that same-sex orientation goes against the Islamic concept of *fiṭra*—inclination of the soul toward monotheism—will also be addressed indicating that like the argument that borrows from Foucault, the *fiṭra*-based argument is a modern invention. Having reviewed these three arguments that characterize same-sex orientation, the charges of apostasy will be addressed. The prescription of lifelong celibacy will be critiqued, along with arguments based on consensus, texts, obedience, and trials. Miscellaneous arguments used by contemporary scholars will be addressed next, thereby setting the stage for the arguments for same-sex unions in chapter 7.

Developments in psychology and a changed medical paradigm may necessitate a renewed approach for the issue of any possible right to same-sex legal relationships for gays and lesbians. Some contemporary scholars issue opinions based on classical juristic manuals and the statements of Ḥanbalī scholars like Ibn Taymiyya (d. 1328). However, others use arguments alluding to *fiṭra* (nature); for instance, Moiz Amjad (a Pakistani scholar) has opined that from an intellectual perspective, "homosexuality," in contrast to sexual relationships outside *nikāḥ* (marriage) between men and women, is a natural prohibition instead of a religious prohibition.[1] However, as will be demonstrated in the following, the arguments made by several contemporary scholars appear to be selective in that they do not take into account the full breadth of classical Muslim opinions.

6.1 DESIRE VERSUS ORIENTATION

Some conservative Muslim preachers reject the innateness of sexual orientation of gays and lesbians by referencing the Qur'anic verses and Hadith texts—sayings attributed to the Prophet—on the people of Lūṭ, to argue that God cannot make people gay and then punish them for their behavior for that would entail that God is unjust.[2] Several such thinkers, preachers, and other professionals sideline the viewpoints upheld by mainstream psychological and psychiatric professional bodies, and view the sexual orientation of gays and lesbians as constituting base desires or categorize it within a context that includes *khawāṭir al-shayṭān* (satanic whims).[3]

In contrast, the Qur'anic verse 3:47 indicates that Allah creates whatsoever He wills, and opposing the more zealous jurists, several past Muslim jurists defended their composition of love poetry in praise of the beauty of beardless youth arguing that one cannot prohibit what God made licit and that one ought not to think ill of fellow Muslims.[4] Putting aside the issue of pederasty for a while, and in contrast to several contemporary Muslim thinkers, many past jurists, including the more conservative scholars like Ibn Taymiyya,[5] (d. 1328), whom many current conservative Muslims seem to follow, while upholding the conventional view on the prohibition of same-sex acts, did not view the tilt toward the same sex as an aberration, deviance, or an inspiration from Satan. Scholars like 'Alam al-dīn Sanjar al-Jāwulī (d. 1343) who admired Ibn Taymiyya not only wrote love poems on both sexes but also interspersed them with quotations from the Qur'an.[6] Jurists like Ibn Ḥazm (d. 1064) went so far as to state that "love is neither disapproved by Religion, nor prohibited by the Law; for every heart is in God's hands."[7]

Past jurists viewed the desire for beardless boys and even male slaves as consistent with the desire to penetrate the vagina of a female or the anus of a beardless boy or whomever. Therefore, they felt that the vagina may suffice as more than an adequate alternate therapy for such desire, even though they acknowledged that this may not work for all. Such scholars did not have a problem acknowledging that some people have genuinely natural desires toward things that are prohibited. They certainly emphasized that the prohibition is against the action rather than the desire, and they did feel that there were legitimate alternatives that are available for such people through marriage, as the desire to penetrate would have been fulfilled. Thus, while they were prescribing patience, they were asking for patience as a temporary solution to a genuine desire that would have been eventually fulfilled through marriage. To past scholars, whether a desire is innate or acquired is irrelevant for they acknowledged it as real. However, contemporary Muslim scholars seem to have problems with any desire toward something that is deemed prohibited and therefore may use arguments that such desires go against or corrupt *fiṭra* (nature). Indeed, such arguments were rarely used by traditional scholars of the past.

6.2 FOUCAULT'S SOCIAL CONSTRUCTION OF SEXUALITY

In a similar vein of rejecting the sexual orientation of gays and lesbians, a researcher at the *International Institute of Advanced Islamic Studies* in Malaysia has argued in a 2012 paper that "there is no such thing as a homosexual" and that "dignity and rights can be accorded only to human beings."[8] He opines that the medical view of "sodomy" emerged in the nineteenth century, and borrowing from Foucault, he rejects the essentialist view of sexual orientation as depicted by Foucault's choice of words "interior androgyny" or the "hermaphrodism of the soul," in favor of viewing it as an artificial construct or a "biological aberration."

However, Mark Brustman,[9] a writer and an avid reader of the classical texts on same-sex relationships, takes the novel, contrarian view that Foucault himself implies the existence of constitutional gays and lesbians when he refers to "the sensuality of those who did not like the opposite sex" as having been subjected to the scrutiny of nineteenth-century medical science. He asserts that Foucault's phrase ("those who did not like the opposite sex") is a clear allusion to an existing group that would form the core of the homosexual "species" that Foucault claimed was invented by medical discourse. Brustman further argues that what Foucault views as a social and historical construct is specifically the assignment of same-sex feelings exclusively to a small minority of anomalous people defined as "homosexuals," whereas other historical periods have seen same-sex desire as unremarkable and widespread. Examples of such same-sex conduct indeed abound within gender-segregated societies, a point noted in chapter 1, and in specific contexts as prisons.

The point that Foucault argued for same-sex sexuality as a social construct can also be understood based on the fact that he viewed identity as a form of subjugation or as a way of exercising power over people[10] through medical encroachment. Kugle indicates that the term "homosexuality" was used in medical clinics to identify a deviant sexuality in order to classify people as deviants and to control, cure, or confine them.[11] Foucault's opposition to a gay identity can also be understood on the basis that given his risqué same-sex encounters including sado-masochism and his involvement in drugs,[12] he would potentially be opposed to a life that involved the strictures of lifelong same-sex monogamous couple-hood. As such, Foucault needs to be read based on the context of his disposition and context, instead of being misappropriated to reject a reasonable understanding of the issues of constitutional gays and lesbians and deny them any recognition.

The emphasis on Foucault's point that the essentialist view of sexual orientation is a nineteenth-century invention can also be critiqued on the basis of John Thorpe's reading of Aristophanes' speech in the *Symposium*, which depicts the existence of males who, while marrying for societal conventions, wish to live with other males beyond copulation as their souls long for something which they cannot name.[13] The fact that constitutional gays existed without having a label or identity indicates that while adopting a specific identity might be a social construct, it does not negate the underlying existence of the constitutional gay individual. This point may be understood on the basis of a quotation from Muhammad Asad's book *Road to Mecca*, which suggests that the absence of an adoptive identity, in this case that of a Muslim, does not negate the fact that the person with the characteristics marked by that identity actually exists.

> I laughed, and replied: "No, I am not a Muslim, but I have come to see so much beauty in Islam that it makes me sometimes angry to watch you people waste it."
>
> But my host shook his head. "No, it is as I have said: you are a Muslim, only you don't know it yourself."[14]

Indeed, according to John Corvino, just because something is culturally constructed does not mean that it is of insignificance for religion is a profound element of human identity despite being a cultural construct.[15] Furthermore, according to Frederic Lagrange, based on the tenth-century libel of Abu Ḥayyān al-Tawḥīdī (d. 1010), it is possible to construe that effeminacy in manners could sometimes be associated with *liwāṭ* (active sodomy) and as such while the "homosexual" identity did not exist, libel accidentally constructs what is denounced.[16]

The view of sexual orientation as a nineteenth-century invention can also be critiqued by noting that medieval physicians like al-Samaw'al ibn Yaḥyā (d. 1180) wrote of the physiological causes of lesbianism and that medieval Arabic erotic treatises had terms like *ẓarīfāt* (courtly ladies lovers) and *ḥabā'ib* (beloveds) to refer to lesbians.[17] The essentialist view of sexual orientation can also be supported from medieval Arabic medical opinions, such as those of al-Rāzī (d. 925) and Qusṭā ibn Lūqā (d. 912), as noted in chapter 1. Furthermore, notwithstanding the medical views on same-sex desire manifestations, the truth of an identity or disposition in Islamic jurisprudence is not necessarily based on medical viewpoints in that it can be substantiated on the basis of an oath. As an example, *'unna* (asynodia), understood by Dr. Ahmad

Kanan as a man's inability to penetrate a woman for psychological reasons that may include revulsion, is established by a confession or oath.[18] Likewise, some jurists permitted the marriage of the *khunthā mushkil* (intersex individuals) on the basis of a personal statement on gender and orientation.

> The Ḥanbalīs differed in his marriage. Al-Khiraqī mentioned that the *khunthā* decides according to what he says. If he said that he is a man and that he desires women, then he can do it. If he said that he is a woman and he desires men, then he can do it. This is because only he can decide and no one other than him can decide this. So, his word is accepted as the word of the woman is accepted when she says that she has menstruation or the period. He, the *khunthā*, may know himself according to the desires as he sees which of the two sexes he desires.[19]

Indeed, if Islamic jurisprudence accepts the state of a person's disposition based on an oath, the rejection of sexual orientation by contemporary conservative Muslim scholars seems to be based more on polemics that are usually involved in the context of the same-sex marriage debate in the West, than on Islamic scholarship. In the absence of developments in psychology, past jurists like al-Āmidī (d. 1233) based their opinions on the apparent, as hidden things were left to God,[20] which may include inner attributes like sexual orientation. This helps to shed light on why oaths were accepted on the state of a person's inner constitution and helps frame the question that how can contemporary conservative leaders state with conviction that the sexual orientation of gays and lesbians is not innate. Moreover, it is not clear why would such leaders not withhold opinion, as would be appropriate, rather than indulge in speculation based on their personal convictions.

Nonetheless, conservative Muslim leaders depict the issue of sexual orientation of gays and lesbians through the lens of "abnormal urges" and as an aberration or deviance,[21] which has a psychological appeal of making the issue not worthy of being properly considered. However, as noted above, while contemporary conservative Muslim thinkers seek to reject the existence of gays and lesbians on the basis of their personal convictions, a careful reading of the opinions of past jurists and that of thinkers like Foucault fails to lend support to their viewpoints that same-sex desires are not a profound and constitutive part of gay and lesbian individuals or that they are unnatural, abnormal, or deviant.

6.3 THE *FIṬRA* ARGUMENT

Contemporary conservative scholars also go beyond rejecting the existence of gays and lesbians or making arguments that depict gays and lesbians as having abnormal or unnatural urges. As such, an argument is made that the artificial concept of a "homosexual" distorts the Qur'anic concept of *fiṭra*—human nature that relates to body, mind, and spirit instead of just the psychobiological constitution.[22] In essence, it is argued that compassion and mercy cannot be realized through demanding "special rights" on the basis of artificial constructs. While allusion to the common humanity of people based on *fiṭra* is made, irrespective of any sins or misdeeds that are committed by them, the core existence of gay and lesbian individuals is rejected based on the understanding that verse 30:30, a part of which reads "the nature made by Allah in which He has made men; there is no altering of Allah's creation," suggests that *fiṭra* does not change.

In a similar vein, it is stated that people corrupt their *fiṭra,* in whose definition is included the term "opposites attract," through external means or by themselves. An argument is made that the "primary reason" behind the "rise in unnatural inclinations" is "the proliferation of sexual images and public sexuality."[23] Likewise, it is asserted that one way a person can become gay "very easily" is by watching too much pornography.[24] Ignoring the consensus amongst mainstream psychological and psychiatric organizations that same-sex orientation is a profoundly constitutive part of gays and lesbians, conservative scholars go beyond the biological concept of nature to the spiritual concept of *fiṭra* to argue that gays and lesbians have a *fiṭra* that has been distorted or corrupted.

It is not clear how contemporary conservative scholars can state with full conviction that the Islamic concept of *fiṭra* includes the idea that all people are born straight, for such a claim does not seem to have been made by past jurists. Since *fiṭra* has usually been understood as the inclination of the soul to worship the one true God, by conflating it with sexuality, it seems that contemporary conservative scholars are mimicking the opinions prevalent within Catholic circles wherein same-sex orientation itself, in the absence of any same-sex acts, is viewed as unnatural. The Hadith texts wherein *fiṭra* is viewed in the context of body grooming and hygiene practices also do not mention the inclusion of sexuality within the definition. Moreover, even past conservative scholars like Ibn Taymiyya (d. 1328), while acknowledging that some people are afflicted with the love of beardless youth, did not state that such people are going against *fiṭra*.

Since the concept of *fiṭra* is distinguished from that of *tabi'a*—which refers to mankind's passions, desires, and impulse toward survival, conflating *fiṭra* with sexuality or same-sex desires seems more like a polemical move than one warranted by the definition of *fiṭra*. However, when conservative scholars try to claim that "homosexuality" goes against *fiṭra*, it seems that they are essentially trying to reconcile their prescription of the prohibition of same-sex relationships to constitutional gays and lesbians with the claim, as highlighted by Andrew March, that Islamic law is compatible with *fiṭra* in that the law is "perfectly suited to the needs, desires, and inclinations of human beings."[25] Since they would uphold that Islamic law is suited to people's legitimate human needs, they reject the innateness of same-sex orientation and conclude that such an orientation comes about as the corruption of *fiṭra*. In this regard, as in the case of Foucault, they can summon the many cases of same-sex conduct, which are perpetrated in gender-segregated societies and in prisons, allude to public obscenity and pornography, and eventually conflate all this with the context of constitutional gays and lesbians. Moreover, in a polemical move, contemporary conservative scholars can reference Ibn Taymiyya's (d. 1328) opinion that notwithstanding the Qur'anic claim in verse 30:30 that *fiṭra* does not change, God has granted people the ability to change through willful disobedience.[26] However, Ibn Taymiyya's context is that of unbelief rather than same-sex acts, which necessitates the polemical move on part of contemporary conservative scholars to argue that through their actions of watching pornography, masturbation, and same-sex conduct, that is, by committing bad deeds, people willfully disobey God and hence end up distorting or corrupting their *fiṭra*.

However, such an opinion of deliberate change in *fiṭra* in the case of constitutional gays and lesbians is difficult to hold. In contrast to the argument that *fiṭra* does not change, conservative scholar Syed Qutb (d. 1966) indicated that God is capable of altering human nature or creating him with a different nature,[27] which in a general sense lends support to the view that not all human beings can be assumed to have the same disposition or orientation. Another argument against people being responsible for the change in their *fiṭra* through willful disobedience can be made as follows. Based on a Hadith text in which it is recommended to teach children to pray at the age of seven and admonish them for not praying at the age of 10, it is construed that at the age of seven, children begin to discern between good and bad and that at the age of 10, mental faculties are able to properly digest information.[28] While, based on various Hadith texts, rights and responsibilities are listed for youth at the age of 15, according to the jurist Abu Ḥanīfa (d. 767) the age of majority is considered to be 18 for males and 17 for females.[29] These ages are important to note for even Joseph Nicolosi, a founding member of *NARTH,* suggests about preventing the development of "homosexuality" in children as young as 4 years old.[30] It has also been indicated that Nicolosi takes clients as young as 3 years old for ex-gay therapy.[31] Thus, based on the juxtaposition of Islamic texts and Nicolosi's comments, how can gay and lesbian youth be held responsible for deliberately changing their *fiṭra* when responsibility in Islam does not get attributed before the age of 18 or 15 and when the ability to discern between right and wrong does not develop before the ages of 10 or seven and when one of the arch proponents of reparative therapy focuses on children as young as three or four?

It is clear from the above analysis that contemporary conservative Muslim leaders misappropriate the Muslim tradition to frame the discussion on sexual orientation of gays and lesbians as one about people who willfully corrupt their *fiṭra* through disobedience by following their abnormal urges. By framing the issue as such, they are actually not being consistent with the Islamic tradition that at least did not classify such desires as unnatural. As noted earlier, by borrowing ideas on social construction of sexuality from Foucault and reparative therapy from *NARTH*, contemporary conservative Muslim leaders end up making arguments that are far removed from the Islamic tradition and share more with the strict Catholic Christian position that views same-sex desires themselves, in the absence of any acts, as unnatural. This is reminiscent of the observation noted by Kecia Ali, in the context of issues related to women, that while conservative Muslim leaders may believe that they are adhering to the classical legal doctrines, their justification is Victorian and far removed from the classical Muslim discourse.[32]

Finally, it deserves to be underscored that searching the Hadith corpus for the term *fiṭra* indicates that the term appears mainly in matters of belief, preferring milk to wine, matters of personal hygiene, as in shaving the moustache and letting the beard grow, shaving the pubic area, plucking the underarm hair, and cleaning the nose and mouth. However, not a single Hadith declares *fiṭra* as being related to sexuality. Therefore, some contemporary scholars extrapolate the term *fiṭra* to matters that were not related to Muslims by the Prophet whether through a strong or even a weak Hadith.

6.4 SHUNNING DIALOGUE: THE *IJMĀʿ* (CONSENSUS) ARGUMENT

Kecia Ali states how any meaningful dialogue on the issue of Muslim gays and lesbians is thwarted based on a “don’t ask don’t tell model” that is perpetuated by conservative Muslim scholars, who argue that sinful behavior should not be disclosed and that it is a greater offense to deny rules than to break them.[33] Some conservative Muslim scholars continue to view the orientation of gays and lesbians as an “inclination” and state that acting on “desire” is a sin as known by *ijmāʿ* (consensus), which if denied would constitute *fisq*—deviation from the Islamic path.[34] It is asserted that Muslims “should not be intimidated or bullied into failing to state this ruling.”[35]

In the context of issues related to women’s rights, Kecia Ali has noted that too often warnings are given to desist from challenging widely held views by charges of heresy, blasphemy, and apostasy.[36] Dr. Omar Farooq has noted how *ijmāʿ* has been abused to silence opponents and underscores the fact that there is no *ijmāʿ* on the definition of *ijmāʿ* itself for a great majority of scholars do not even restrict the definition to the *ijmāʿ* of the Companions of the Prophet, which is usually given precedence.[37] Farooq references the jurist Shāfiʿī (d. 820) as highlighting how rare it was to find an opinion from a Companion, which was not contradicted by another, and also references the scholar al-Ghāzālī (d. 1111) who asserted that perhaps the validity of *ijmāʿ* was simply based on customary norms rather than the foundational texts of Islam.[38]

The problem with asserting the claim that there exists *ijmāʿ* on a particular issue is the existence of competing definitions in that whether *ijmāʿ* refers to the consensus of all Muslims, just the *Salaf*—pious elders that constitute the first three generations of Muslims, all Muslim scholars, or only those of a particular sect. Some Muslim groups, such as the *Naẓẓām* faction of the *Mutazilah* and some *Kharijites,* also rejected the acceptance of *ijmāʿ* as a proof of binding opinions.[39] The jurist Shāfiʿī (d. 820) defined *ijmāʿ* as the consensus of all Muslims, thereby making it nearly impossible to have consensus. Indeed, given Shāfiʿī's position, the most one can assert on an issue is that one is unaware of a dissenting opinion, instead of asserting that an *ijmāʿ* exists, since a dissenting opinion may have existed earlier but not documented.

Farooq not only references the jurist al-Bazdawī (d. 1100) to assert that if a past *ijmāʿ* is later found unsuitable, it can be replaced through reasoning with a new *ijmāʿ*, but also mentions Muslim reformer Sayyid Aḥmad Khan (d. 1898) who sometimes invalidated the *ijmāʿ* of the Companions to contend for a fresh *ijmāʿ* in light of changed circumstances, as well as the Muslim thinker Iqbal (d. 1938) who like some past jurists believed that *fiqh* (Islamic jurisprudence) ought to be changed in view of changed circumstances.[40]

Like what Farooq has done, Muslim scholar Dr. Hashim Kamali has referenced the jurist Abu Ḥanīfa (d. 767) who stated that while he did not altogether abandon the views of the Companions, he did abandon their ruling, which did not appeal to him.[41] Kamali also references past jurists who held that the *fatwā* (edict) of a Companion did not constitute a binding proof in Islamic jurisprudence, and also referenced both Shāfiʿī (d. 820) who stated that scholars have sometimes abandoned the fatwā of a Companion, as well as Iqbal (d. 1938), who opined that later generations were not bound by the decisions of the Companions.[42]

The fact that *ijmāʿ* can be challenged can be noted from how Wahabi scholar Ibn al-Uthaymeen (d. 2001) went against the *ijmāʿ* on the validity of forced marriages of minor girls that was based on the Hadith pertaining to ʿĀ'isha mentioned in Ṣaḥīḥ Bukhārī.[43] It may also be noted that two analogies can coexist as two *ijtihādī* opinions without one abrogating the other and a subsequent *ijmāʿ* can abrogate an existing *ijmāʿ* based on *maṣlaḥa mursala* (public interest) and *ʿurf* (custom).[44] According to Shaltūt (d. 1963), the objective of *ijmāʿ* is to realize *maṣlaḥa,* which varies with time and place and *ijmā*ʿ has to be reviewed if it is the only way to realize *maṣlaḥa*.[45] This indicates that if a past *ijmā*ʿ fails to uphold public interest with changing social mores, then the past consensus has to be revisited as *maṣlaḥa* trumps *ijmā*ʿ. In the context of same-sex unions, since the issue of a legal contract for same-sex couples was not addressed and the framework of *liwāṭ* is grossly distinct from intimacy between same-sex couples, any supposed *ijmā*ʿ upheld by conservative scholars has to be reviewed for the welfare of Muslim gays and lesbians.

However, notwithstanding the issues associated with the definition of *ijmā*ʿ, including the difference of opinion on the definition as being the consensus of the Companions, contemporary conservative scholars continue to use it as a tool to silence dissenting opinions in contemporary Islamic thought. This intransigence may be explained through Muslim academic Dr. Kugle's observation that such scholars in the West are scared to lose their status and following in the Muslim minority communities that remain closed minded on this issue since they feel under threat.[46] Some conservative Muslim scholars have tried to project a consensus against same-sex relationships by alluding to the majority views within major world religions and spiritual traditions, including Hinduism, Buddhism, Judaism, and Christianity, that condemn and forbid "homosexuality," and opine that the call to Muslims to accept "homosexuality" is bound to fail even within reformist Islam.[47]

However, the supposed prohibition of same-sex unions cannot be extrapolated from Judeo-Christian laws as laws revealed before the advent of Islam are not applicable to Muslims.[48] Maimonides (d. 1208) specifically and repeatedly equated homosexual acts with matters like the hybridization of cattle, rules which have no bearing on Muslim law.[49] Furthermore, the word *toevah* (abomination) used in Leviticus 18:22, which admonishes a man lying with another man like a woman, does not refer to something intrinsically evil but something ritually unclean like eating shellfish, trimming beards, mixing fibers in clothing, etc.[50]

A consensus does not exist within world religions given that various Church denominations like the United Church and Unitarian Church as well as both Conservative and Reform Judaism along with Muslims for Progressive Values and the el-Tawhid Juma Circle mosques affirm same-sex relationships. Moreover, the opinion on various world religions having a consensus against "homosexuality" is not supported by some Muslims, who, in the context of the support for same-sex relationships by Jews and Christians, are quick to point out the eschatological Hadith that depicts Muslims following the Jews and Christians into a lizard hole. As an aside, it is interesting to note that the context of the Hadith is about infighting amongst the Jews and Christians, but conservative Muslims conflate the text with the issue of same-sex unions.

Despite this difference of opinion, some Muslim thinkers distinguish between an individual's public and private life to assert that while "homosexuality" is morally reprehensible under Islam and that it should not be "promoted," a practicing homosexual who is Muslim cannot be excommunicated.[51] However, they perpetuate the same "don't ask don't tell" model that seeks to stifle any discussion on the legitimate concerns of practicing gay and lesbian Muslims. It seems that Muslim gays and lesbians can be respected enough as human beings to let them live their lives in private but not human enough to allow them the right to fulfill their genuine human need for intimacy and companionship as visible couples who are part of a religiously vibrant Muslim community. This raises concerns of justice in the public sphere, for if a Muslim gay couple lives as a couple in the private sphere, then accessing public benefits in the public sphere becomes incredibly impossible. For instance, according to Muslim academic Dr. Mohamed Fadel, it does not seem fair that accessing health care causes great problems if decisions on behalf of someone hospitalized are usually given to a spouse.[52]

In conclusion, notwithstanding the difficulties with the definition of *ijmāʿ*, the consensus among past scholars will have to be defined. In this sense, it may be argued that Muslim scholars of the past ruled on the prohibition of same-sex relationships but in the context of absence of marriage or legal arrangement. This consensus does not hold for the question that was never addressed, that is, about the legitimacy of same-sex unions. Thus, it cannot be assumed that the previous consensus applies to the issue of same-sex unions.

6.5 THE SLIPPERY SLOPE ARGUMENT

Conservative Muslim leaders, instead of viewing the totality of the lives of Muslim gays and lesbians of which the need for intimacy and companionship is a legitimate part, focus exclusively on the sexual aspect of same-sex relationships. A *fatwā* (religious edict) was issued in 2006 stating that sincere love does not legitimize a prohibited practice.[53] The argument that that sincere love does not legitimize a sexual practice does not do justice to the position of Muslim gay and lesbians. It is an argument that conservative Muslim scholars usually like to make when they view the orientation of gays and lesbians as an impulse or desire and rely upon the horror of the audience to make the slippery slope argument that if actions were legitimized by feelings then that opens avenues for the justification of all sorts of crimes based on feelings and desires. Moreover, despite the fact that some like to distinguish between people and acts, that is, constitutional gays and lesbians on the one hand and acts of bestiality and incest on the other, the argument for same-sex relationships does not necessarily stem from the fact that since the orientation is constitutional same-sex relationships should be justified, for conservative Muslim leaders are quick to point out the existence of zoophiles and pedophiles.

The argument for same-sex relationships could be based on the fact that the case of constitutional gays and lesbians is different from those who indulge in adultery, incest, or bestiality as the latter acts involve issues of consent and the fact that those who indulge in adultery or incest already have options to satisfy their needs through marital union with opposite gender spouses. Moreover, since constitutional gays and lesbians are denied a legitimate avenue to forge same-sex unions and since marriage with an opposite gender spouse[54] does not seem to be an ethical alternative, for it involves toying with the life and aspirations of a heterosexual spouse, the analogy between gays and lesbians and those who engage in adultery and incest is not an appropriate one to make. However, according to Dr. John Corvino, even the argument that gays and lesbians are asking for equal options instead of extra options as in the case of polygamy and incest can be countered by conservative thinkers by conceding that the prohibition of same-sex relationships places greater burden on gays and lesbians than the prohibition of incest places on those who indulge in those acts.[55] Indeed, Muslim leader Dr. Maher Hathout (d. 2015) made this argument in his podcast talk in which he states that the parallel between the "homosexual" and the straight person is not accurate in that the latter has an option for release, and that the former must face the extra *jihad*—struggle within to remain celibate or that whatever happens must remain in the private sphere.[56] As such, conservative Muslim leaders remain unmoved by the injustice in relegating the constitutional gay and lesbian Muslim to a lifetime of celibacy and seek to deploy the "don't ask don't tell" tactic by relegating the issue to the private sphere.

The above indicates that the argument that sincere love does not legitimize same-sex relationships will have to be addressed in a better manner than the usual arguments that distinguish between constitutional gays who are denied their basic need for intimacy and companionship and those who commit acts of incest and adultery for whom the option of a marital union remains available. As such, instead of a weak analogy between incest, bestiality, and adultery with same-sex relationships, a better analogy, according to Corvino, would be to compare the latter with nonprocreative heterosexual relationships[57] to argue that if the benefits of marriage, as mentioned in the Qur'anic verse 30:21—tranquility, mercy and *mawadda* (affection)—can be realized in same-sex relationships, just as they are in nonprocreative heterosexual relationships. The burden of proof is then on conservative Muslim leaders to clarify on what basis are they denying gays and lesbians the *ḥaqq* (right) to a life of intimacy and companionship with a same-sex partner.

6.6 THE TEXT-BASED ARGUMENTS

It is argued that the prohibition of "homosexuality" is a *ḥukm qaṭʿī* (absolute injunction) based on *qaṭʿī al-thubūt* (indisputable evidence) and that the prohibition is *qaṭʿī al-dilāla* (unquestionable in purport). Likewise, it is argued that the prohibition of same-sex relationships is based on the principle of *maʿlūm min al-dīn bi-l-ḍarūra*—religious doctrines known by necessity to be part of religious teachings, that is, no inference is required to understand them.[58]

Such arguments, which merit careful consideration, are based on the Hadith texts and the Qur'anic verses on the people of Lūṭ, chiefly verses 7:80–81, 26:165–166, 27:55, and 29:28–29 that depict the condemnation of the actions of the people of Lūṭ. It is important to highlight that conservative Muslims usually like to project that the plain reading of the verses explicitly condemns same-sex relationships. However, they substantiate their argument by quoting one of the three verses—7:81, 26:165–166, or 27: 55—noted in chapter 2, without referring to the context formed by other verses: 7:80 and 29:28–29.

Conservative Muslims apparently feel that by quoting such verses plainly, they can halt any dialogue on the issue of same-sex relationships. However, if such verses are construed as condemning same-sex relationships and if the sexual orientation of gays and lesbians is considered to be innate, then this leads to the issue of the injustice of God for that would mean that God creates gay people and expects them to forgo the legal fulfillment of their legitimate human need, which would go against the notion that the objective of Islamic law is to attain the *maṣlaḥa* (welfare) of man and also the notion that Islamic directives are easy to follow, in that the law is harmonious with the needs of man. To address the issue of the injustice of God, conservative Muslim thinkers either argue that the sexual orientation of gays and lesbians is not innate or that while the "inclination" might be natural, one must not act on those "urges" as part of the trial decreed by God for which the person undergoing the trial will be rewarded in the Hereafter.

The argument that the sexual orientation of gays and lesbians is not innate or that it is a consciously elected choice goes against the consensus within the medical and psychological professional communities. Since conservative Muslims and their leaders derive their convictions on the same-sex unions issues from the Qur'anic verses and Hadith texts, they end up viewing the consensus within the medical and psychological professional bodies with great suspicion. They also end up making arguments based on conspiracy theories that the removal of "homosexuality" from the list of disorders was forced under pressure from gay rights groups, thereby discounting the progress on the issue made within the psychological and psychiatry professional bodies over several decades. Such a rigid attitude of conservative Muslims and their leaders contradicts their general claims, made in contrast to other religions, on how Islam prizes scientific enterprise and how Islam views sex as a legitimate human need for which it provides a legitimate avenue for fulfillment.

In contrast to the reality of gays and lesbians, the Qur'anic verses 7:81, 26:165–166, or 27:55 do seem to indicate that the conduct of the people of Lūṭ was a deliberately elected choice to approach men lustfully instead of women. While there is no explicit limitation mentioned in the verses—*laysa ʿalā ẓāhirihā*—that excepts gays and by analogy lesbians from the general category of men who, despite not having a sexual orientation toward the same-sex, pursue other men,[59] there are cases where the *ẓāhir* (manifest) meaning of the Qur'anic text has been subject to limitation by *takhṣīṣ* (specification). As an example, the Jews and Christians, referred to in verse 5:51 that forbids Muslims from taking them as friends, are specified as those of a particular context in seventh-century Arabia instead of those from other times. As such, whether through the method of *takhṣīṣ* or the observation that the general rulings of the Qur'an are open to exceptions, applying these verses to the case of constitutional gays and lesbians would be a gross conflation. Indeed, no interpretational or hermeneutic jugglery is needed to note that since *dhakar* (males) are linguistically and generally viewed as nonreceptive entities and that *unthā* (females) are viewed as receptive entities, the above quoted verses are reproving the people of Lūṭ on approaching men, who are not generally partial to the advances of other men, instead of women, who are likelier to be partial to the advances of men.

In short, a plain reading of the relevant Qur'anic verses suggests that the people of Lūṭ elected to pursue men instead of women, and that it makes sense to not conflate the import of these verses with the case of gays and lesbians. By avoiding such a conflation, conservative Muslim leaders will not only avoid the issue of divine injustice but also avoid having to resort to conspiracy theory-based arguments that are unnecessarily evoked by those who pit their religious convictions with science. Indeed, far from shunning the dialogue, by plainly reading the Qur'anic verses 7:81, 26:165–166, or 27:55, conservative Muslims and their leaders end up raising more questions than resolving them.

Conflating these verses to exclusively refer to gays and lesbians also goes against the principle as elucidated by the Muslim scholar Maududi (d. 1979) that the Qur'an merely seeks to chart a broad code of law and only deals with fundamental questions.[60] What this suggests is that instead of viewing these Qur'anic verses as exclusively applicable to a minority of people, which would go against the Qur'anic style of avoiding secondary details, it seems more appropriate to view these verses as applicable to all people. The relevant verses do not directly address the reality of gays and lesbians but "men who pursue other men instead of women." However, conservative Muslim leaders conflate the category of "men who pursue other men instead of women" with gay men. This conflation seems to be based on *qiyās* (analogical deduction) instead of a plain reading of the verses as "men who pursue other men instead of women" are not necessarily gay men looking for a loving same-sex relationship, a point which can be substantiated by a holistic analysis of verses 7:80, 11:77–79, 15:67–72, and 29:28–29, that form the context of the acts of the people of Lūṭ. Indeed, as noted earlier, based on the observation highlighted by the jurist al-Āmidī (d. 1233) that hidden attributes are left to God,[61] the Muslim tradition does not account for hidden attributes like orientation and deals only with apparent actions.

Deducing a prohibition based on *qiyās*, as in the case of equating "men who pursue other men instead of women" with gays and by deduction with lesbians, is prone to bias and error given human limitations in the formulation of analogy. Given the speculation involved in the determination of the *'illa* (causes) and *maqāṣid* (objectives) of divine injunctions, several past scholars affiliated with the *Mu'tazila*, *Ẓāhirī*, *Shī'ī*, and *Ḥanbalī* schools of jurisprudence questioned the validity of *qiyās*,[62] which as an inferential method was deemed to yield only *ẓannī* (probabilistic) instead of *qaṭ'ī* (certain) knowledge.[63] Moreover, a ruling based on *qiyās* is open to challenge and is rarely considered final, which is perhaps why a whole school of jurisprudence, the *Ẓāhirī* school, was built on the rejection of *qiyās* as a method to determine legal injunctions.

Since in determining legal injunctions, *qiyās* is viewed as yielding only *ẓannī* knowledge, just as al-Amidi (d. 1233) noted that *ijmā'* yielded probabilistic knowledge of legal injunctions, and that even Hadith that are not *mutawātir*—successively transmitted by an overwhelming majority of narrators—yield only probabilistic knowledge,[64] indicates that the argument that the prohibition of "homosexuality" is a *ḥukm qaṭ'ī* (absolute injunction) based on *qaṭ'ī* al-thubūt (indisputable evidence) and *qaṭ'ī* al-dilāla (unquestionable in purport), warrants further consideration. First, it has already been noted that a plain reading of the Qur'anic verses leads to more questions than answers. Second, it is not clear if conservative Muslim leaders can deduce *qaṭ'ī* injunctions based on methods—non-*mutawātir Hadith*, *ijmā'* and *qiyās*—that yield *ẓannī* knowledge. It may be asserted that after an *ijmā'* coalesces around a *ḥukm ẓannī*—legal injunction based on methods that yield probabilistic knowledge—may attain the status of *ma'lūm min al-dīn b-il-ḍarūra*—religious doctrine known by necessity to be part of religious teachings. However, such an assertion does not do justice to the concept of *ma'lūm min al-dīn b-il-ḍarūra,* which simply means that one does not require specialized training to decipher the *ḥukm* (legal injunction) as opposed to implying that the injunction was *qaṭ'ī* (certain).[65] As such, when conservative Muslim leaders try to deduce the prohibition of same-sex relationships within a legal contract by arguing that the prohibition is an essential part of faith, they end up making claims far stronger than their *ẓannī* (probabilistic) methods would allow. Indeed, making strong claims based on probabilistic knowledge could be construed as mere conjecture and speculation.

6.7 ARGUMENTS BASED ON APOSTASY, WHIMS, AND "WHAT YOUR RIGHT HAND POSSESSES"

Conservative Muslim leaders adopt a bullying tactic to intimidate any points of view that oppose their viewpoint on the prohibition of same-sex relationships. Some state that while acting upon same-sex urges constitutes a major sin, any justification through articles or any arguments to deem same-sex conduct as Islamic would constitute *kufr* (disbelief).[66] It is argued that the prohibition of "homosexuality" is part of the *ḍarūriyyāt al-dīn* (essentials of the Islamic faith), therefore any person denying the prohibition would be an apostate, and that any dissenting opinion that associates the prohibition with lust rather than love would be inadmissible. In a similar vein, it is argued that the prohibition of same-sex relationships is *ma'lūm min al-dīn b-il-ḍarūra* (religious doctrines known by necessity to be part of religious teachings).[67] Thus, some may argue that since a person who commits *inkār al-ḍarūrī* (rejects the necessary aspect of Islam) is a *kāfir* (disbeliever), therefore to deny the prohibition of same-sex unions is to invite charges of *fisq* (disobedience) or *kufr*.

However, the issue of a legal contract for same-sex couples is not *ma'lūm min al-dīn b-il-ḍarūra* and according to Ibn Ḥazm, not only can a Muslim not be charged with *kufr* or *fisq* regarding *i'tiqād aw fatwā* (dogmatic or juridical issues) but also *ijtihādī* (independently reasoned) opinion merits a reward[68] even if it were to be wrong based on the Prophetic Hadith on twice as much reward on being correct and once on being wrong as it is the exertion of intellectual effort that mattered. Furthermore, charges of *kufr* were laid for reasons that might be deemed repugnant based on contemporary sensibilities. For instance, when the seventeenth-century Ḥanafī jurist Ḥaṣkafī opined that if a man, who had four wives and a thousand concubines, was reproached for taking another concubine, it was as if the critic had committed disbelief by reproaching a permissible conduct.[69]

Conservative Muslim leaders use the apostasy argument as a polemical move in the same manner as they link same-sex relationships with the violation of *fiṭra*. In essence, by making arguments that connect the reality of gays and lesbians and their genuine concern on the right to a life with intimacy and companionship with the metaphysical realm of *fiṭra* and putting the issue on par with the essentials of the faith, conservative Muslim thinkers end up usurping and inflecting the tradition to silence dissenting opinions, which are also rooted in the Islamic tradition. Indeed, it can been argued that the Qur'anic verses 3:47 and 42:49 indicate that Allah creates whatsoever He wills and that the requirement of being a heterosexual Muslim is not included within the six articles of faith as espoused by Sunnī Muslims, which include belief in God, angels, the divine books, the prophets, the Day of Judgment, and destiny. Moreover, the six articles of faith also do not include the criterion that one has to believe that same-sex relationships are Islamically incompatible and that claiming otherwise would take one outside the folds of Islam. Indeed, al-Ghāzālī (d. 1111) opined that the three roots of belief are belief in God, the Apostle, and the Last day, and anything else is a branch of belief on which the charge of unbelief cannot be imputed.[70]

There exist opinions from past scholars that indicate that arguing for the permissibility of *liwāṭ* would be tantamount to committing apostasy. Ibn al-Qayyim (d. 1350) mentioned that construing the phrase *aw mā malakat aymānukum* (what your right hand possesses) to refer to male slaves in order to argue for the permissibility of *liwāṭ* with them would be distorting the meaning of the Qur'an as it would be in contradiction to the severe Qur'anic condemnation of *liwāṭ* and referred to such distortions as *fitna al-shubuhāt* (trial of doubt).[71] He opined that the origin of all *fitna* (trials) could be explained by giving priority to *ra'y* (personal opinion) and *hawā* (caprice) over *shar*ʿ (the legal) and ʿ*aql* (reason) respectively and that a person who embraces the view of the permissibility of *liwāṭ* would be a *kāfir* (infidel) by consensus of the entire *umma* (Muslim community).[72]

In contrast to Ibn al-Qayyim, who believed that a person commits apostasy by opining the permissibility of *liwāṭ*, there were other scholars who actually sanctioned such sexual relationships and rejected the apostasy charge. Male slaves were sexually used by their masters[73] and at times this was sanctioned by some Mālikī jurists[74] and some Shīʿī scholars[75] on the basis of the *mulk yamīn* (ownership of the right hand) rationale that allowed sexual relationship with female concubines.[76] The Ḥanafī jurist al-Kawākibī (d. 1685) confirmed that based on the phrase "what their right hand possesses" verses 23:6 and 70:30, which generally alluded to female concubines, there were those who deemed *liwāṭ* with male slaves permissible.[77] Moreover, the jurist Ibn ʿĀbidīn (d. 1836) stated that claiming the permissibility of *liwāṭ* with male slaves did not necessitate *kufr* (unbelief).[78]

In terms of Ibn al-Qayyim invoking *ijmā*ʿ for bolstering his position of excommunicating those who held an opinion contrary to his views on *liwāṭ*, it may be noted from Section 6.4 how Dr. Omar Farooq asserted that *ijmā*ʿ has been abused to silence opponents. There are various issues revolving around defining *ijmā*ʿ, which is relative in the sense that one can only claim that one is unaware of a dissenting voice on a particular issue as a dissenting voice may have existed but then later disappeared or not documented. Thus, invoking *ijmāʿ* on the position of same-sex relationships does not seem reasonable as alternate opinions presented above clearly indicate the absence of *ijmāʿ* on the issue and even if one were to give precedence to Ibn al-Qayyim's opinions over the others, one cannot conflate "*ijmāʿ*" on *liwāṭ* to same-sex relationships given the stark difference between the two.

Ibn al-Qayyim views personal opinions and caprice as a source of trials, which have to be eschewed in formulating Islamic legal opinions. However, one cannot conflate that to refer to carefully thought out opinions based on the spirit of addressing human need in a starkly different human and social context of contemporary gays and lesbians. Dr. Hashim Kamali provides us with principles that allow for adopting reasonable positions in Islamic law, even if such opinions were to go against the grain of traditionally held dogma and even in the face of hostility from the masses, who may be uninformed and in need of guidance, as long as the values of *tawḥīd* (monotheism) and the clear guidance of the Qur'an were not denied.[79] He asserts that there is no objection to publishing books, which challenge prevailing views and doctrines[80] and that the findings of a qualified scholar cannot be classified a *bid'a* (innovation) even if they were to go against the majority opinion or seemed innovative.[81]

Kamali references the Prophet who advised that people should make up their own minds and not follow others in injustice[82] and warned them to avoid suspecting the worst in the speech of others while they can still attribute a favorable interpretation.[83] Kamali asserts that one should reserve judgment on someone's statement even if it were construed to be evil as there might be an extenuating explanation behind the statement.[84] He references Abu Ḥanīfa (d. 767) who stated that a statement comprising of 99 percent of disbelief but only 1 percent of belief would still not amount to *kufr* (apostasy) and Ibn ʿĀbidīn (d. 1836) who stated that those who passed charges of *kufr* were essentially writers of lesser caliber whose works did not merit high credibility.[85]

This suggests that instead of judging, caricaturing, and condemning gay Muslims as those bent on destroying Islamic values by spreading *fāḥisha* (obscenity), people might do better to understand that they might be formulating alternative less popular opinions based on the premise of alleviating human suffering by addressing the basic legitimate human need for companionship and a life based on *mawadda*—love and affection.

Conservative Muslims occasionally warn those who seem to adopt different viewpoints than those present in the classical jurisprudence tradition. Like Ibn al-Qayyim, they warn about indulging in *ra'y* (personal opinion) and *hawā* (caprice). According to Kamali, *hawā* is characterized by selfishness and pursuit of one's desire, and *bid'a* (innovation) is characterized by an attempt to distort or interpret the principles of Islam as one wishes.[86] However, the issue of same-sex unions is not based on whims and on a deliberate attempt to distort Islamic principles. If anything, the argument for same-sex unions is made with the intention to hold the Islamic principle of justice in providing for the basic need for *mawadda* (affection) and intimacy for constitutional gays and lesbians, whose concerns have not been addressed outside the scope of *liwāṭ*.

Moreover, the notions of *hawā* and *bid'a* can be counterbalanced by the concepts of *baghy* and *istibdād bi-l-ra'y* that refer to indulging in self-righteousness, imposing one's opinion on others and denouncing those who oppose it.[87] Kamali also refers to *khusumah*—argumentation without malice to establish a right denied by the opponent[88] and also indicates that even *ra'y* (personal opinion) that does not lead to certain knowledge but conjecture, may be used in cases of emergency when no better alternative exists and in order to avoid an indefinite delay in the quest for certainty.[89] All of this suggests that instead of being bogged down by the nature versus nurture debate and waiting for scientific certainty on issues such as the gay gene, progress on the concerns of constitutional gays and lesbians can be made based on the principles of alleviating hardships, on granting them rights to fulfill their legitimate need for companionship. Furthermore, those who seek to thwart the resolution of same-sex unions by charging others with *bid'a* and *hawā* may well reflect whether in the garb of defending the tradition, they themselves end up indulging in *baghy* and *istibdād bi-l-ra'y*.

The term *mā malakat aymānukum* that appears in verses 23:5–7 and 70:29–30 can be revisited to determine if it could potentially refer to a relationship between two free members of the same sex instead of a master-slave relationship on the basis of exegetical and linguistic analysis. The relevant portion from both these sets of verses reads as follows.

> And who guard their private parts, except before their mates or those whom their right hands possess . . . (23:5–7 and variant in 70–29–30).[90]

While the term *mā malakat aymānukum* is usually translated to refer to ownership of slaves, it is also used to refer to legal authority over an entity or person, marriage or a legal contract that keeps a relationship firm and intact. According to Ibn Taymiyya,[91] the word *mulk* means ownership or legal authority, which the legislator may allow a human over others and which is different than the case of inheritance. Viewed through this lens, the case for a legal contract between two free persons could potentially be made and that would be different from the patriarchal authority exercised by a slave owner over his male slaves.

Even in the case of ownership of male slaves, some past jurists permitted sexual relationships, which can be determined form the refutation of these opinions by other jurists. Some Shī'ī authorities allowed for anal intercourse with wives, and both female and male slaves,[92] in contrast to other opinions that indicate that there is no legal authority to have sex with male slaves.[93] Whereas one Ibaḍī exegetical work suggests that the phrase *mā malakat aymānukum* refers to having sex with ownership or legal authority as a person's desires,[94] another Ibaḍī exegetical work indicates that the relevant verse refers to male ownership of female slaves even if "some people in the East" misconstrue it to support the permissibility of sex with male slaves.[95] Likewise, al-Kawākibī, the Ḥanafī Mufti of Aleppo, stated that no *Ḥadd* punishment could be implemented on a man who had sex with his male slaves due to the potential reasoning of those who held such a sexual relationship as permissible.[96]

Jurists generally refuted opinions that allowed for sexual relationship between male owners and their male slaves. This seems to be based on how they construed gender as the male was viewed as the one who initiates, the one who owns and penetrates, whereas the female was viewed as the one who receives, the one who gets owned and penetrated. The Tafsīr of Ibn 'Ādil indicates that the phrase *mā malakat aymānukum,* which starts with the term *ma* that is not used for human beings, can be explained by either the possibility that there are different types of what the right hand possesses or the possibility that the phrase referred to slave women.[97] The later possibility would suggest that since females were generally construed as owned based on the notion of gender of the times of the jurists, the phrase would not encapsulate the category of male slaves. This notion of gender can also be discerned from texts that allude to the issues of female taking male concubines. Such texts include the narrative on ʿUmar (d. 644) indicating that the interpretation that a woman gave to the Qur'anic verses 23:5–7 on taking male concubines was incorrect,[98] and a similar narrative involving two women, which indicates the friends of ʿUmar (d. 644) stating, "they disputed you on the book of God," thereby suggesting that they did not deem the understanding of the women as completely wrong.[99] Thus, the way gender was construed influenced the understanding of the phrase *mā malakat aymānukum.*

To the extent contemporary understanding of gender does not depend on the owner-owned paradigm and to the extent legal authority can be exercised between two free individuals, the phrase *mā malakat aymānukum* could potentially allow for the unions between members of the same sex through some type of legal authority.

6.8 ARGUMENT BY OBEDIENCE

Based on Ibn Kathīr's (d. 1373) words, conservative Muslims argue that Allah does not enjoin what is not in the best interests of the people and does not forbid except to protect people from harm and thus believers have to submit to the rulings of Allah even if they do not know the reason behind the ruling. They quote verses 4:64,[100] 33:36, and 24:51 in support of this opinion as follows.[101,102]

> But no, by your Lord, they will not [truly] believe until they make you, [O Muhammad], judge concerning that over which they dispute among themselves and then find within themselves no discomfort from what you have judged and submit in [full, willing] submission. (4:64)
>
> It is not for a believing man or a believing woman, when Allah and His Messenger have decided a matter, that they should [thereafter] have any choice about their affair. And whoever disobeys Allah and His Messenger has certainly strayed into clear error. (33:36)
>
> The only statement of the [true] believers when they are called to Allah and His Messenger to judge between them is that they say, "We hear and we obey." And those are the successful. (24:51)

They also reference a text from Abu Hurayra (d. 681) that states that the Companions complained to the Prophet that verse 2:284, a part of which reads, "Whether you show what is within yourselves or conceal it, Allah will bring you to account for it," asks of them what they are not capable of bearing. The text from Abu Hurayra indicates that the Prophet responded that instead of saying "we hear and rebel," they should be responding as "we hear and obey." It is in this context that the subsequent abrogating verse 2:286 was revealed, a portion of which reads, "Allah does not charge a soul except [with that within] its capacity."[103]

Conservative Muslims may use verse 2:284 to argue that believers submit to the ruling of God for their response should be the one of "we hear and obey." However, it is to be noted that verse 2:284 was abrogated by verse 2:286, which clearly states that God does not burden a soul beyond its capacity. Viewed in this light the argument on submitting without questioning needs to be qualified in light of the verse that God does not impose more than what a human being can bear. While some conservative Muslim leaders may claim that gay and lesbian Muslims can live a life of celibacy, this ignores their legitimate need to fulfill their right to a life with intimacy and companionship.

Conservative Muslims apply the argument of submitting without questioning to reject same-sex unions, arguing that since a plain reading of the verses on the people of Lūṭ and the Hadith texts on *liwāṭ* is clear, any viewpoint going against the classical grain cannot be tolerated, as it would mean that one is not submitting to Allah. For conservative Muslims, *ʿaql* (reason)-based arguments are irrelevant as Muslim norms are determined by the text instead of pure reason. They also indicate that any attempt to justify same-sex unions would be tantamount to making the *ḥarām* (forbidden) *ḥalāl* (permissible).

However, while the general point on submitting to the ruling of Allah without questioning is acknowledged, the argument for same-sex unions is not based on questioning the reason behind the ruling but rather based on determining whether a ruling exists in the first place and if so whether it is applicable to same-sex unions. It is to this effect that both the relevant verses and the Hadith texts were explored in previous chapters. Moreover, it is also clear based on the principles of jurisprudence that in matters of worship, things are deemed forbidden unless expressly allowed, whereas in matters of social transactions that include marriage, things are deemed permissible unless expressly prohibited. To the extent an express prohibition of same-sex unions is not to be found in the primary sources of Muslim knowledge—the Qur'an and the Sunnah—but rather contemporary conservative scholars derive the prohibition from the classical prohibition of *liwāṭ*, which itself is based on *qiyās* (analogical deduction) that leads to probable instead of certain knowledge, the argument of making the *ḥarām ḥalāl* is not warranted.

Conservative Muslims reference a Hadith text found in the collections of Bukhārī (d. 870) and Muslim (d. 875) and amongst the 40 that have been collected by al-Nawawī (d. 1277). The essence of this Hadith is on leaving doubtful matters. A portion of this text is presented below[104]:

> That which is lawful is plain and that which is unlawful is plain and between the two of them are doubtful matters about which not many people know. Thus he who avoids doubtful matters clears himself in regard to his religion and his honor, but he who falls into doubtful matters falls into that which is unlawful.

Based on this Hadith, conservative Muslims may argue that even if it is conceded that the story of the people of Lūṭ in the Qur'an does not apply to constitutional gays and lesbians, to the extent that express approval for same-sex unions is absent in the primary sources—Qur'an and Sunnah—then the dictates of *taqwā* (God consciousness) would imply that as human beings prone to error, we stay away from approving such unions just as we stay away from doubtful matters.

However, according to scholarly authorities, this Hadith is not prescriptive but rather suggestive on the issue of *mustabāḥāt*—matters which many people go through in their lives. Moreover, the Hadith text is neither on an expressly forbidden matter nor does it declare permissibility or prohibition on an issue, but rather suggests avoiding a matter would be better than pursuing it. An application of this text may include avoiding walking on a street with prostitutes if one is prone to having sex with them. Therefore, it seems like a stretch to argue against same-sex unions based on this Hadith. It may also be noted that in matters of *ijtihād* (independent reasoning), if one scholar holds something permissible, whereas another deems it prohibited, then if one is capable of doing so, one can study the evidences of the respective scholars and derive conclusions on one's own. However, this Hadith text would be applicable for someone who is unable to navigate through the lines of evidence provided by the scholars and who has no business with the matter at hand. Thus, this Hadith does not prove to be a bar against an argument for same-sex unions.

Conservative Muslims may allude to the story of Khidr and Moses in the Qur'an, which indicates that human beings are not always aware of how divine justice works, in order to substantiate the point that we should follow the ruling of God even if we are unable to grasp the reasoning behind them. However, the same story also carries another equally plausible implication. According to Kamali, the fact that Moses criticized Khidr for his actions suggests that when a person has investigated an issue to the best of his abilities, then that would provide normally sufficient evidence to base one's criticism on the issue.[105] The Moses-Khidr story also indicates that the Qur'an provides reasonable justifications for Khidr's actions, which implies that the audience of the Qur'an possesses the necessary capacity to understand Khidr's actions. Moreover, Khidr's actions—sinking a boat, killing a youth, and collapsing a wall—are only rationalized when the logic is provided, in the absence of which, all of these actions would be deemed unjust.[106] Thus, it does not seem reasonable to argue against same-sex unions or to counter those who argue for such unions on the basis of arguments that do not carry any reason or rationale.

6.9 THE TRIAL ARGUMENT

Some conservative Muslim leaders concede that sexual orientation could very well be innate but argue that gays and lesbians should check their desires and remain celibate as part of the trials of life, passing which would earn them a place in heaven. Essentially, gays and lesbians are viewed as those burdened with a different set of trials than those faced by the straight population. However, nothing unreasonable can be deemed Islamic and as such the usual tests as that of handicap, infertility, cancer, etc. do not evoke scriptural condemnation. This would mean that the analogy, as is sometimes made, between handicap and infertility as a test on the one hand and "homosexuality" on the other might be a weak one to make.

Conservative Muslims may allude to the works of Ibn Taymiyya (d. 1328) in building their case for "homosexuality" being a test from God. In his commentary of chapter 3 in the Qur'an, he comments on the phrase "the people of desire wish that you tilt" that while generally people tilt toward women, some of them would also be tested in their tilt toward beardless boys. He alludes to the "martyr of love Hadith" that states "whoever loved and kept it hidden and did not follow through but remained patient, then he died a martyr." However, Ibn Taymiyya also acknowledges the weakness of this text and it is important to take a holistic view of his opinions on the subject. The question arises why Ibn Taymiyya and his disciple Ibn al-Qayyim (d. 1350) did not allow for the legitimate need for a male inclined toward other males. In this regard, it is important to understand that they viewed same-sex sexual expression through the lens of *'ubna* (disease) and on the basis of the understanding that the legal contract for marriage in their time was not between two equals but between a master and the subordinate. Indeed, al-Ghāzālī (d. 1111) attributed a saying to the Prophet that marriage is *riqq* (slavery).[107]

It is clear from Ibn Taymiyya's words that those who are tested in a tilt toward beardless youth do not have an exclusive tilt toward them, but rather have this superfluous tilt despite having a general orientation toward women. Indeed, as Kecia Ali writes, most medieval writers did not consider the desire for youth as an exclusive desire, but the same that was directed toward women and as such could be satisfied with opposite gender spouses.[108] Likewise, Afsaneh Najmabadi writes in the context of nineteenth-century Iran that men were assumed to be sexually inclined to both women and *murdān* (young male adolescents) and Dror Ze'evi indicates that the classical single-sex model of human body, in which a woman is considered an imperfect version of man, suggests that sexual desire did not differentiate according to the gender of the object of desire.[109] As such, the notion of men and women complementing one another is a modern development in Islamic thought as a woman was classically viewed as an imperfect man based on the single-sex model.[110]

Moreover, by referring to beardless youth, the issue addressed is one of pederasty instead of a relationship between two equal partners. Indeed, as noted earlier, Ibn Taymiyya, in his commentary of chapter 24, asserts that it is the active partner who has the desire for sex, whereas the passive partner has no sexual desire except for disease/affliction, financial reasons, or other aims. This confirms that Ibn Taymiyya is viewing sex-same relationships in the context of exploitation as according to him the active partner pursues the passive partner, who has no sexual desire for the specific act of homosexual anal intercourse. It may also be noted that past authorities assumed nonconsent on the part of males and assumed consent on the part of females for penetrative sexual intercourse. The argument made earlier in chapter 2 in the context of the words *dhukran* (nonreceptive) and *unthā* (receptive) can be evoked to support this line of thought. This argument also gets bolstered from Ibn Qudāma's (d. 1223) words in his treatise "*Al Mughnī*" in the section

"The *Ḥadd* on *Liwāṭ*" that "the male is not a place of intercourse for another male."

Ibn Taymiyya is concerned with a specific sexual act rather than affection and mercy that are part of an intimate relationship. As such, it is not clear if Ibn Taymiyya's argument on same-sex desire being a test is applicable to constitutional gays and lesbians, given that he views same-sex desire in the context of exploitation of beardless youth or of those passive males who were viewed through the lens of *'ubna*, which, as noted earlier, referred to the disease of the anus that the sufferer was expected to resist.[111]

In his commentary of chapter 24, Ibn Taymiyyah states that if the repentance of the passive partner were not accepted, then Lūṭ would not have ordered his people to repent. Commenting on the appropriate cure for *'ubna*, Ibn Taymiyya's disciple Ibn al-Qayyim (d. 1350) opined that it would be better for the passive partner in homosexual anal intercourse to be killed instead of getting penetrated as by getting penetrated he is dealt a death after which no life can be wished, although he qualified his opinion by stating that killing such a person would confer martyrdom on that person as it be tantamount to a transgression against him.[112]

In contrast, Al-Ruḥaybānī states that the passive partner is better off being killed as he is damaged beyond repair, that the semen of the active partner would poison his body to the extent that he would not remain deserving of any good, and that he cannot be helped by helpful knowledge, helpful deeds, or repentance.[113] He felt that the passive partner in homosexual anal intercourse has no hope for reform, neither does he repent sincerely nor does he deserve to be guided to anything good and that vain would be such a person's efforts toward good.[114] He seemed to be reflecting the opinion, as upheld by physicians like al-Rāzī (d. 925), that *'ubna* was incurable, a viewpoint also captured by al-Tha'ālibī (d. 1038) as "the disease which cannot be treated except by disobeying God."[115] Ibn Kathīr (d. 1373) has opinions parallel to those of Al-Ruḥaybānī on repentance as he is noted to have stated in the *al-Bidāya wa-l-Nihāya*, "Homosexuality is the worst abomination. . . . Whoever has this likeness, there is nothing within them that is beneficial for creation if they remain. So if Allah saves us from them, our faith and lives will be more righteous."[116]

The opinions of Ibn Taymiyya, Ibn al-Qayyim, and Ibn Qudāma indicate how their opinions on receptive homosexual anal intercourse were shaped by their cultural norms and medical knowledge of their times, as such opinions are not textually substantiated. In other words, extra-textual reasoning informed their reasoning. Such extra-scriptural arguments are extremely limited to the knowledge base of the time of the past jurists. Therefore, having access to greater extra-scriptural knowledge on human sexuality and given our social mores, it would be reasonable to argue that the discourse on "homosexuality" be moved away from treating it as a test or illness, and toward facilitating a healthy life for gays and lesbians.

However, Ibn Taymiyya is also reported as stating that the Companions had agreed that the participants in sodomy should be killed and disagreed on the method of killing,[117] and as such he is presented as having claimed *ijmāʿ* on the death penalty for sodomy. He is also presented as having claimed the capital punishment for both the *fāʿil* and *mafʿūl bih*—active and receptive partner—which contrasts with the Ibn Zubayr text in Section 3.3.5 that the punishment was that of *zinā,* that is, unmarried perpetrators of *liwāṭ* were lashed and that weakens the claim of *ijmāʿ* on capital punishment. Ibn Taymiyya is also reported as excommunicating the person who denied the prohibition of sodomy even by *ta'wil*—esoteric interpretation of the Qur'an.[118] This opinion on there being an *ijmāʿ* on the death penalty was earlier rejected by Ibn Ḥazm, although like Ibn Taymiyya, he was of the opinion that *ʿamal qawm Lūṭ* was one of the *kabāʾir* (major sins)—akin to the consumption of pork or wine, and like *zinā* (fornication) and that anyone who declared these sins as licit was a *kāfir* (disbeliever) whose life could be taken.[119]

However, the claim of excommunication does not hold in light of Prophetic narratives that forbid declaring another Muslim as a disbeliever as being a Muslim is solely based on the recitation of the testimonial of faith. Such a claim also does not hold as the six articles of faith, which include belief in God, the angels, books, prophets, the Day of Judgment, and fate, do not include the belief in *ʿamal qawm Lūṭ* as being one of the *kabāʾir*. Moreover, comparing *ʿamal qawm Lūṭ*, which did not have a concrete definition until the jurists specified its meaning, with the consumption of wine or pork or with *zinā* is based on *qiyās* (analogical deduction) which can be disproved as noted in an earlier section. Indeed, many Ḥanafī jurists rejected the analogy between *zinā* and *ʿamal qawm Lūṭ*. Thus the claims of *ijmāʿ* on the death penalty, equating sodomy with other acts, or excommunicating those who uphold the legitimacy of sodomy are all problematic.

The notion of *ʿamal qawm Lūṭ* as being one of the *kabāʾir* is also problematic especially in the context of Ibn Taymiyya's opinion on the "tilt toward beardless boys" being a test. The problem arises as *ʿamal qawm Lūṭ* is viewed as an abomination perpetrated by a vile people, whereas a test is usually considered in the context of people who are deemed as virtuous enough to be accorded a trial from God.

Contemporary scholar Mushfiqur Rahman references Hadith texts attributed to the Prophet that indicate that tests are a sign of love from Allah, who sends trials if he intends good for His servants and does not hasten to take a person to task if He intends evil.[120] Rahman references verses 2:286, 23:62, 6:152, and 7:42 to indicate that Allah does not test beyond a person's capacity to bear that burden for Allah is not unjust. He references Hadith that suggests that trials are harder and rewards are greater for those with strong faiths but they are lighter for those with weaker faith. Amongst the common types of trials, he lists sickness and quotes Hadith texts that suggest that affliction leads to expiation of sins and that patience through affliction leads to heaven. Amongst other trials, he lists facing injustice to one's honor and dignity and that a believer can take comfort in justice on Judgment Day.

Rahman's exposition of trials makes it clear that if trials are not meant to be beyond a person's capacity, if they are a sign of Allah's love, and if they are harder for those with stronger faith, then viewing the lives of gays and lesbians as a trial from Allah is problematic on at least three counts. First, the trial exposition would suggest that in contrast to the straight population. gays and lesbians have perhaps a greater threshold to bear a life of celibacy. Moreover, since even a contemporary conservative scholar such as Abdul Hakim Murad acknowledges that given that long-term abstinence fails for most individuals, as they are not super moral figures, and that most Muslims with a same-sex orientation would commit transgressions,[121] such an acknowledgment stands in stark contrast to the view that tests are not meant to be beyond a person's capacity. Second, the view of trials as a sign of Allah's love contrasts with the conservative Muslim view of holding the lives of gays and lesbians in contempt. Third, the views of conservative Muslims that gays and lesbians are to be scorned stand in contrast to the view that harder tests are meant for those with stronger faith. In short, viewing the lives of gays and lesbians as a trial from Allah that is meant for those with stronger faith contrasts with the popular conflation of gay and lesbian expression of love with *'amal qawm Lūṭ*, which is viewed as an abomination. Viewing gay and lesbian lives through the lens of tests for the righteous starkly contrasts with viewing their lives through the lens of abomination. The above suggests that applying the trial argument to the lives of gays and lesbians is fraught with several inconsistencies and seems to be as unreasonable to address a social reality as conflating *'amal qawm Lūṭ* with the lives of gays and lesbians.

Rahman's opinion that patiently bearing affliction leads to expiation of sins and heaven and that one can find comfort in delayed justice on Judgment Day for violation to one's dignity have to be balanced with other opinions on trials delineated by him. Based on verse 4:97, he indicates that remaining passive and continuing to suffer is also a form of injustice that one inflicts upon the self and that since life is a trust from Allah, it has to be fully utilized. Moreover, he also indicates that no matter how pious one might be, one must not give into pride and ask for trials from Allah. In the context of gays and lesbians, this means that the oft-churned argument on patiently bearing a celibate life, that even if the situation seems bleak there is hope and comfort to be found on Judgment Day, can be replaced by alternate opinions that indicate that it would be unreasonable and inappropriate to invoke tests of celibacy based on the inability to fathom that the classical jurists addressed *'amal qawm Lūṭ* and not the case of same-sex unions between two equal partners who are constitutionally and exclusively attracted to members of the same gender. Moreover, needlessly suffering celibacy would be tantamount to inflicting injustice upon oneself and that life being a trust from Allah ought to be fully lived, which would include sexual expression based on love, affection, and mercy between partners joined in a legal contract.

Like Rahman, contemporary writer Ruqaiyah Abdullah indicates that people are tested to distinguish between those who worship Allah from those who ascribe partners to Him, to distinguish between those who believe in the Hereafter from those who do not, to encourage good deeds, to allow for making up for sins, and to earn Paradise through patience and faith.[122] She further mentions that Allah tests his creations through depriving of good health, death of loved ones or children, removing material wealth, sexual temptations, poverty, social relationships, and natural disasters. She also states that when Allah's punishment falls indiscriminately on a nation as it is perhaps a mercy for the innocent who are saved pain and suffering in this world, and that one can cope with tests through worship, placing trust in Allah, patience, looking at people who are worse-off, and detaching oneself from this world.

Abdullah's description of the objectives and types of tests and how to cope with them do not seem to make sense in the context of Muslim same-sex relationships. Many Muslim gays and lesbians believe in Allah, are involved in responsible societal conduct, exhibit qualities of patience, and like other Muslims also strive to eschew unethical behavior. Sexual orientation toward the same gender does not seem to fit in the general category of tests including that of sexual temptations, as that would suggest that God instilled an exclusive same-sex desire only to expect people to remain celibate for the rest of their lives, which provides a picture of an unjust God and paints Islam as a religion that does not account for the needs of human beings. Finally, the various techniques of coping with tests are not helpful in the context of changing one's sexual orientation. Thus, transposing the test framework onto sexual orientation seems unreasonable as the objective, type, and method of coping with tests do not seem to possess any applicability to sexual orientation.

In expounding on the aims of the Islamic law, Wael Hallaq states that none of the attributes that man is born with may be subjected to legal rulings that would adversely affect it.[123] In the context of long prayers, the Prophet is reported to have admonished Mu'ādh (d. 639) on invoking trials for people and cautioned people against driving people away from Islam, and in the context of fasting, the Prophet asserted, "It is not piety to fast during a journey."[124] The above indicates that if the Prophet has cautioned against invoking trials from Allah, if excessive hardship is not piety, and if people's disposition cannot be subjected to legal rulings that would harm them, then the prohibition against gays and lesbians on forming same-sex unions on the basis of compassion and mercy would go against the spirit of Islamic teachings.

The argument for celibacy as a test from God can also be challenged on the basis of the work of past jurists who rejected the justification of unreasonable suffering as a test. According to Shāṭibī (d. 1388), hardship is accepted unless it is continuous or perpetual[125] and that patience is encouraged unless the hardship interferes with reason or religion.[126] Shāṭibī's work indicates that hardship differs in intensity according to the circumstances based on the rule, time, and nature of the act,[127] and that *rukhaṣ* (licenses) can be provided in cases without there being a basis for those in the Sharīʿa.[128] According to ʿAbd al-Jabbar (d. 1025), useless suffering is evil, that is, if there is no benefit beyond the suffering and no repulsion of harm greater than it.[129] His work also indicates that if God inflicts pain without reason but which is concomitant with a reward in the Hereafter, such an act would still be evil as it would be useless.[130] In the context of ʿAbd al-Jabbar's (d. 1025) work, Hourani indicates that it is reasonable for every rational being to repel harm from oneself.[131] In light of such opinions, the test-based prescription of celibacy cannot be reasonably justified.

In general, the test argument is limited mainly to individual cases as opposed to societal issues, where its application would require further evidence. The commands and prohibitions in the Qur'an are mainly for the welfare of humanity and individuals. As such, alcohol is forbidden because of its harmful effects and therefore it is a test for the person addicted to alcohol to avoid it even though his or her body desires its consumption. Allowing the consumption of alcohol would harm rather than help the addict. Thus, it may be opined that an alcoholic is tested with addiction and that he must be helped against his addiction by keeping prohibited the consumption of alcohol. However, in order for gay Muslims to accept the test argument, the harm from same-sex intimacy should be clear, which it is not. Certainly, unregulated sexual acts in a society have clear harms to individuals and society, but this is not limited to homosexuality, and since regulation helps solve the majority of those issues for heterosexuals, regulation through a legal contract may also help gays and lesbians. Viewed in this light, the case for a legal contract between members of the same gender can be supported.

6.10 OTHER ARGUMENTS BY CONTEMPORARY SCHOLARS

Apart from the above focal arguments, there are several other arguments that conservative Muslim scholars use to prevent Muslim gays and lesbians from living a life with the joy of marital union with their partners. Alluding to the Qur'anic teaching that Allah does not inflict a burden greater than the capacity of the individual, it is argued that having same-sex feelings does not mean that one should act upon them.[132] However, this argument rests on the premise that the demand for same-sex unions is flimsily based on feelings, which does not make sense, as lifelong partnerships are not based on mere whims or fanciful emotions. Indeed, the case of gays and lesbians with the constitutional orientation toward members of the same gender stands in stark contrast to the issue of superfluous desire and feelings toward male youth that was addressed by the classical jurists. Moreover, the issue of same-sex unions is one of a legal contract to bind two parties in marital union and not one of acting upon whims and desires. Thus, it is unreasonable to conflate the issue of unbridled desires with that of a meaningful life with sexual expression based on love and affection within the bounds set by a legal contract.

In the context of major sins indulged in so regularly so as to constitute a lifestyle, some opine that while it would be praiseworthy to minimize sin, it might be futile and even antireligious to completely eliminate it.[133] It is argued that willful sin and religiosity are not mutually exclusive and by referring to a case of the Companion who habitually drank wine but loved Allah and His Messenger, the point is made for the context of gays and lesbians that instead of seeking an interpretation of permissibility, the Companion accepted his moral frailty with the associated guilt.

However, traditionalists, who might argue that the case of the Companion who drank was only applicable for those times when the Prophet was in the process of teaching the law, might reject the above opinion. Some might argue on the basis of the Qur'anic verse 53:32 that Allah's forgiveness and hence heaven is awarded to those who avoid major sins. Dr. Khalid Zaheer refers to verses 53:31–32 and indicates that for those who believe in Allah, it is not possible to continue to remain disobedient and especially for the pious, moral failings are not a rule but an exception.[134] As such, the argument on the futility of stamping out sin may be appropriate for those who are addicted to alcohol, drugs, or sex; however, such an argument does not have a bearing on the issue of a legal contract for same-sex couples as sexual orientation is not viewed as an addiction but is simply a facet of an individual's existence. To the extent that such an argument helps put a human face to gays and lesbians who are viewed by conservative Muslims as vile sinners, it might be useful to inhibit the strong condemnation of gays and lesbians although ultimately such arguments perpetuate viewing gays and lesbians as sinners instead of as human beings with the God-given legitimate need for affection and intimacy.

Arguing against same-sex relationships, some reference a Hadith to opine that we must judge based on apparent matters and that commanding the good and forbidding evil is both an individual as well as a community obligation.[135]

Verses 5:44–47 are referenced to indicate that whoever does not judge by Allah's revelation is from the ingrates, wrongdoers, and transgressors, and also references verse 33:36 to indicate that one cannot have an opinion on a matter on which Allah and His Prophet have already decreed.

However, the referenced Hadith also indicates that while apparent matters are judged, the hidden matters are left to God. Past jurists left issues such as gender identity of intersex individuals for them to decide and as noted earlier, scholars like al-Khiraqī even opined that only the intersex individual could decide about her gender and the associated orientation. Conservative Muslim scholars seem to conflate commanding the good and forbidding evil with judging other people. As noted earlier in chapter 5, this directive is not clear and scholars usually warn that great wisdom is required in this regard. Indeed, there is a Hadith text narrated through Abu Hurayra (d. 681) and recorded by Abu Dawūd (d. 889) that cautions very strongly through the punishment of Hell against judging others.[136] Referencing verses 5:44–47 is problematic as by ignoring the message of tolerance in verse 5:48, such selective quoting unnecessarily instigates intolerance as verses 5:44–47 were used by the extremist group *Khawārij* to declare ʻAli (d. 661) and Muʻāwiya (d. 680) as non-Muslims. Finally, verse 33:36 and other similar verses were addressed in the section on the arguments based on obedience, where a distinction was made between following Allah's decree and ascertaining the existence of a decree on a matter in the first place. By bypassing the matter of ascertaining the existence of the decree in the first place, conservative Muslim scholars go against the methodology of traditional scholars, who discussed an issue based on evidence and accepted opposing arguments as a matter of legitimate difference in opinion when they could not prove the opposing arguments completely wrong. In short, judgmental approaches seem to go against the grain of previous Islamic directives on matters of presenting a new argument and especially when the Qur'anic verse 2:44 clearly cautions against judging other people by stating, "Do you order righteousness of people and forget yourselves."

Some Muslim scholars like to reference Western anti-LGBTQ arguments to make the claim that same-sex relationships are not justifiable even within a secular context.[137] These arguments are borrowed from religious groups in the United States that are politically involved against the LGBTQ rights movement and whose views of history, such as the Greeks did not condone same-sex relationships,[138] are shaped by anti-LGBTQ values. However, for Muslim scholars to quote non-Islamic arguments is problematic to the extent they critique Muslim LGBTQ groups on their recourse to secular scholarship and affirming interfaith groups that support same-sex relationships. Furthermore, many of the secular arguments alluded to by such Muslim scholars occasionally clash with viewpoints in Islamic jurisprudence. For instance, arguments against same-sex relationships on the basis of infertility are not countenanced in Islamic jurisprudence, which holds no bar for elderly and divorced women to get married.

The asymmetrical nature of sexual relationships in ancient Greece and not between coequal adult males or females only substantiates the point that the issue of same-sex relationships was not countenanced in history due to different medical assessments of same-sex orientation and different social and cultural mores and as such it would also have been anachronistic for Muslim jurists to address the issue of same-sex unions.

Muslim scholars have to be careful when referencing explanations like "dominant mother, absent father" that treat same-sex orientation as pathology or a form of arrested development, from groups like NARTH. John Thorpe argues that such psychoanalytic theories have failed to establish causality between such factors and sexual orientation for such factors can produce contrary results.[139] Such scholars also have to be careful in drawing from the tradition to substantiate their arguments against gays and lesbians. As an example, some reference an opinion by al-ʿAsqalānī (d. 1448) that males whose speaking and walking is similar to women owing to innate disposition must burden themselves to unlearn such behavior.[140]

However, by invoking this opinion, conservative Muslim scholars conflate sexual orientation with gender expression, which is a separate issue. One theological model indicates that the inner soul takes precedence over the outer body and it is on this basis that Ṭanṭāwī (d. 2010) argued in his fatwā on gender reassignment surgery that it would be self-deception to behave in a manner inconsistent with one's inner essence.[141] Just as jurists acknowledge nationality or cultural background, both of which are not genetic but part of a person's identity, they can view sexual orientation that cannot be changed or only so at an excessive cost as part of a person's identity for sexual orientation can be viewed as a *shakila* (inner disposition),[142] which takes precedence over the outer body. Finally, al-ʿAsqalānī's opinion is a viewpoint that is not necessarily binding in the absence of clear and authentic textual evidence and in the absence of any such restrictions on the *mukhannathūn* of Medina during the time of the Prophet.

Sometimes it is argued that in the Islamic worldview people are not labeled by their sexual orientation or practices and that human beings are more than sexual orientation and behavior.[143] It is correct that people are more than their sexual orientation, which substantiates the point that by obsessively focusing on the singular issue of homosexual anal sex, conservative Muslim authorities fail to reasonably address the issue of same-sex relationships that do not necessarily include that particular activity and go beyond it to encompass love, compassion, and affection between the spouses. Moreover, it is not entirely true that in the Islamic worldview people are not labeled according to their disposition, for then, classical Islamic discourse would not have contained terms like *khunthā mushkil* and *mukhannathūn*.

6.11 ONLINE ARGUMENTS OF MUSLIMS LEADERS

Influential Muslim leaders who provide online guidance to Muslim masses have a captive audience that places their trust on them. Ignoring a careful reading of the texts, such scholars superimpose the paradigm of *liwāṭ* in addressing the concerns of Muslim gays and lesbians. Their general arguments, which may reflect some of the arguments critiqued above, are critically delineated as follows.

At the onislam site, a response was presented to a query on LGBTQ organizations.[144] It was asserted that the word *fāḥisha* in the context of the verses on the people of Lūṭ refers to sodomy and lesbianism. The response indicated that there does not have to be a connection between legal punishment and sin by illustrating that *shirk* (attributing partners to Allah) has no punishment but still remains a grave sin. It was mentioned that great sins are often punished in the Hereafter, as the punishment is more harmful than worldly punishment. Furthermore, the assertion was made that the *umma* has reached a consensus on the prohibition of same-sex sexual conduct as it destroys the family and clashes with the divine aim of establishing sexual instincts between males and females leading toward marriage. Moreover, it was opined that the main aim of marriage is not sexual desire but to realize tranquility through love and mercy between spouses. The Qur'anic verses 4:15–16 were referenced to allude to gays and lesbians, and it was argued that Hadith texts define same-sex sexual conduct between two men and between two women as adultery and also indicate that the Prophet thrice mentioned Allah's curse on the one who commits the acts of the people of Lūṭ. Moreover, the narrative of Abu Bakr implementing punishment was referenced to mention the punishment of stoning and burning, and to advise that Muslims should keep their children away from gays and lesbians, who are neither fit to attend mosques nor lead prayers.

Given the critical review of the Islamic texts in previous chapters, it becomes clear that the above response takes a very selective view of the tradition, one that supports a more hardline viewpoint. Even by classical scholarship, the word *fāḥisha* has to be equated with *liwāṭ* through *qiyās*, an argument that becomes even weaker for *siḥāq* as no penetration is involved. It seems that *siḥāq* and anal sex between males, a conduct that cannot be defined by *liwāṭ* that involves exploitation or coercion, are superimposed on the verses on Lūṭ's people. The response mentions that greater sins are punished more gravely in the Hereafter, but then paradoxically presents the worldly punishments of stoning and burning, neither of which can be substantiated by authentic Hadith texts. The opinion of verses 4:15–16 flies against classical scholarship. The opinion on there being a consensus on the issue of gays and lesbians does not hold as the question was not addressed by classical scholars, who dealt with the issue of *liwāṭ* in the context of *'ubna*, exploitation, or coercion. The argument that the aim of marriage is to foster love and mercy between spouses and not just sexual desire does not seem to acknowledge the human dignity of gays and lesbians in establishing relationships beyond sexual gratification. In light of these criticisms, it becomes apparent that the onislam response does not properly reflect the nuanced scholarship of classical Islam.

In another onislam response, one of the questioners was advised on giving up "homosexuality."[145] Ignoring the position of mainstream medical and psychology organizations, those who indulge in "homosexual behavior" were equated with those who have been conditioned to fornicate, commit theft, murder, or those who have become addicted to pornography. Instead of making an analogy between sterile couples and same-sex couples, gays and lesbians were equated with murderers, thieves, addicts, and those who have sex despite having recourse to marriage. Such arguments are not unique for many online Muslim authorities connect same-sex orientation with addiction and same-sex relationships with imbibing alcohol. Such conflations by demonizing and dehumanizing gays and lesbians prevent a reasonable understanding of their issues. As an example, in Arab societies, often lesbians are portrayed as drug addicts and promiscuous, which has led to the coining of the word *sharmuta*—whore for a lesbian[146]—and thus has prevented a reasonable understanding of the importance of the right to live a life with compassion and affection with a same-gender spouse.

The tips offered in the struggle to overcome "homosexuality" include elements of aversion therapy, associating the suffering of Hell with same-sex behavior, reading Qur'anic verses depicting Hell fire, praying for Allah's help, desiring to be in the company of the righteous instead of the wicked, cutting off relations with those involved in a gay lifestyle, or relocating to a different city and getting married after repentance. The diagnosis of same-sex orientation as an addiction and prescription based on aversion therapy fly against the consensus amongst mainstream medical and psychology organizations. Given that aversion therapy prescriptions may cause harm in gays and lesbians, and since such remedies are the opinions of an Islamic Studies researcher and not a physician or psychologist, they cannot be taken seriously as per the Prophet's directive to "do no harm and to accept no harm."

The response to the query on sexual perversions[147] indicates that "homosexuality" in Western countries puts men in positions worse than animals, and that the acceptance of such perversions is against women's rights and is tantamount to involvement in filth. In this query, several Muslim scholars are referred to, including one, who indicates that "homosexuality" results from repression that stems from the misunderstanding that any contact between opposite genders is sinful, bad friends who exchange spiritual emptiness, lack of proper sex education, carelessness in buying anything young people desire, excessive freedom, lack of monitoring, lack of understanding of the harms of sexual perversion in this world and the Hereafter.

This list of explaining "homosexuality" defies a reasonable understanding of sexual orientation. It seems to be based on quack theories and does not account for the consensus among medical and psychology professionals. While the explanation that "homosexuality" is on the rise in the West because of early sexual experimentation only confirms the pseudo nature of arguments, it also reflects that such an understanding is shaped by situational homosexuality that sometimes manifests in prisons and gender-segregated societies, both of which are mostly about exploitation and control through using a weaker person as a surrogate for women.

The response also alludes to verses 7:80–84 to make the point that the people of Lūṭ got involved in abnormality, a claim that is neither supported by the text of these verses nor supported by classical scholarship that viewed desire for male youth as natural but superfluous. It is also asserted that "homosexuality" is a reversal of natural order. Crime against women's rights makes those who practice "homosexuality" slaves to their lusts, deprives them of a decent manner of living and that notwithstanding the cruelty of Islamic punishments, they are essential to maintain the purity of Islamic society.

This argument based on the natural order goes against the grain of classical scholarship that did not view same-sex desire as unnatural. While other arguments defy a sense of reasonability, the point on cruel punishments does not fully account for the Islamic tradition, specifically the Ḥanafī school that rejected *Ḥadd* punishment for *liwāṭ,* as it did not acknowledge *qiyās* for the case of punishments.

It is also stated that the homosexual "act" is against pure human nature, spreads diseases, affects birth rate, harms innocent children through rape, and it should be uprooted as it spreads *fisād fī al-arḍ* (corruption on earth). It is further stated that homosexual acts cannot be practiced without taking drugs and that they destroy the lives of women whose husbands leave them to practice homosexual acts. Moreover, it is argued that such reasoning explains the prohibition of "homosexuality" and the Hadith on killing the active and passive partners is referenced along with the opinion of Mālik, Shāfiʿī and Ibn Ḥanbal on the stoning of such people regardless of their marital status. Finally, it is indicated that the testimony of the lesbian cannot be accepted because of her perversion.

Such arguments conflate *fisād fī al-arḍ*, usually in the context of armed groups that spread terror and anarchy, and child abuse with loving same-sex unions. The other arguments seem bereft of reasonability and the Hadith that is quoted has already been demonstrated to be extremely weak in chapter 3. Moreover, the classical tradition is selectively parsed by narrating only one strand of opinion within the three juristic schools and by completely ignoring the Ḥanafī school of jurisprudence. The response conflates lesbians with *siḥāq* done outside the folds of a legal contract between two women. Moreover, the response reflects the opinions of scholars who reject the testimony of sinners at the expense of other scholars who accepted testimony of sinners under certain situations. Kamali writes that while a mufti bases his *fatwā* on religious considerations, a judge must only look at objective evidence and as such a pious individual in a court case is not treated differently from an impious person or one without a religion.[148]

It has also been noted in medieval Arabic literature that *sāḥiqāt* (lesbians) were known to form exclusive, reciprocal relationships based on love and devotion and that according to the physician Al-Samaw'al ibn Yaḥyā (d. 1180), who wrote of the physiological causes of lesbianism, specifically grinding, through rationales of coldness, shortness, deficiencies, or illnesses of wombs,[149] many Arab lesbians were writers, poets, scholars, and even Qur'an reciters.[150] However, it seems such representations have not been accounted for in both classical and contemporary juristic writings where they are viewed quite negatively due to rulings like the unacceptability of the testimony of lesbians on account of them being evildoers.

In the query on why Islam forbids homosexuality,[151] it is opined that "homosexuality" goes against *fiṭra* of not only human beings but also animals, causes diseases, causes the breakup of the family, and leads people to give up work and study in pursuit of perversions. Whereas the *fiṭra*-based arguments were addressed in an earlier section, the other arguments seem quite unreasonable in light of contemporary information on human sexuality and sexually transmitted diseases through unsafe sex practices.

In another response to a query,[152] it is indicated that the people of Lūṭ were destroyed because they made "homosexuality" commonplace and acceptable. Verse 11:83 is referenced to depict homosexuals as polytheists and Ibn Ḥajar (d. 852) is referenced to indicate that lesbianism is a major sin. However, as argued in chapter 2, if "homosexuality" is construed as a major sin, then it is the rare one that did not get explicitly addressed in the Qur'an as did *kufr*, murder, highway robbery, and slander. Moreover, equating the polytheistic people of Lūṭ with Muslim gays and lesbians fails due to many reasons including the fact that the people of Lūṭ rejected God's Messenger, exploited guests through demanding them, forbidding hospitality, engaging in evil deeds in public assemblies, and committing highway robbery. As such, instead of the simplistic explanation of making "homosexuality" commonplace, it is making such practices of inhospitality commonplace that provides a reasonable understanding behind the destruction of a society that was bent upon exploitation and coercion.

Based on a skewed view of the tradition, it is argued that the correct punishment of "homosexuality" is execution by the sword and that the punishment is severe as intercourse not permissible under any circumstances is worse than intercourse permissible in some circumstances. Moreover, selectively referencing Ibn Taymiyya (d. 1328), it is asserted that a "homosexual" can repent and not confess sins to anyone, and it is further opined that marriage might be obligatory as a safeguard after repentance. Based on this and previous chapters, it becomes clear that the response to the query clearly lacks nuance and fails to look at diverse sources in the corpus of Muslim tradition. As noted earlier, Ibn Taymiyya has differing opinions on repentance, and the issue of severely punishing intercourse impermissible in any circumstance is countered by the fact that the Ḥanafī jurists rejected *qiyās* in *Ḥadd* punishments. Moreover, as noted in chapter 5, the reprehensibility of same-sex conduct has to be understood in light of the extra-textual assumptions made by the classical jurists, who were informed by the medical knowledge and social mores of their times.

In yet another response to a query,[153] the Companions are projected as having a consensus that the sin of "homosexuality" is greater than that of murder and second only to *kufr*. While the issue concerning *ijmāʿ* was addressed earlier in this chapter, the issue of "homosexuality" as a major sin was addressed in chapter 5 through a critique of Ibn Ḥazm's opinion on the issue. Since the issue of same-sex unions was never classically addressed, the point on consensus becomes moot, and the point on same-sex relationships in a legal contract being a major sin is inappropriate as conflating such unions with *liwāṭ,* a conduct based on exploitation and coercion outside the folds of a legal contract, is unreasonable.

Qur'anic verses are employed to yield unreasonable conclusions. Based on 7:80, it is argued that no one among human beings or *jinns* (fiery creatures) was tested with the major sin of "homosexuality" prior to the people of Lūṭ. It is also argued that since the people of Lūṭ twisted the natural order, Allah turned their houses upside down. However, as noted in chapter 2, archaeological evidence indicates the existence of homosexual practices prior to the time of the people of Lūṭ and bringing the *jinns* into the context does not make sense as their conduct, like that of animals, is irrelevant to that of human beings. Such explanations are reflective of reading too much into the verses. Furthermore, connecting the people of Lūṭ, described as rebellious to God in verse 21:74 and as polytheist wrongdoers in verse 29:31, to Muslim gays and lesbians, amounts to lazy analysis and speculation. The solutions prescribed as cures, such as not looking at women or movies, always being preoccupied with worship and emphasizing guilt, also belie a reasonable understanding of human sexuality.

6.12 CRITICAL SUMMARY OF ONLINE ARGUMENTS AGAINST MUSLIM GAYS AND LESBIANS

Usually a heated debate erupts in various online forums on Islam and same-sex unions. The followers of conservative Muslim scholars and religious authorities vehemently oppose any recognition of the right of Muslim gays and lesbians to live a life with affection and mercy with their partners. While major arguments proffered by online conservative Muslim leaders and scholars were deconstructed above, the following provides a critical summary of several salient points that are usually raised in online discussions.

One argument raised is that gay Muslims are themselves responsible for the alienation they bring upon themselves by hurting the feelings of fellow Muslims through their brazen activism. Such a line of thought seeks to silence the voices of gay Muslims through shaming them by putting down their sexual orientation as deviant desires or by equating the constitutionality of same-sex orientation with the genetic component for the urge to murder, consume alcohol, or engage in sociopathic behavior. Furthermore, instead of supporting the already vulnerable gay Muslims, the absurd burden to prove the constitutionality of their same-sex orientation is placed upon them.

However, tactics to shame and silence Muslim voices that reflect social changes are not new as Hashim Kamali points out that past Muslim jurists in the age of *taqlīd* (imitation) denounced social changes by deeming them as aberrations.[154] Moreover, deeming something *shādhdh* (aberration) is one way to make it not worthy of being mentioned or considered and instead of furthering dialogue, such a strategy has the psychological appeal to intimidate people who disagree with popular opinions.

In line with such scare tactics, instead of equating the case of gay and lesbian Muslims with that of nonchild-bearing couples, online discussants equate the sexual orientation of gay and lesbian Muslims with the proclivities of alcoholics, sociopaths, and murderers. Apparently, the analogy is made to fit based solely on the basis of any genetic component behind the actions of alcoholics, sociopaths, and murderers. Ignoring the harms associated with alcoholism that include impairing of judgment and motor functions and increased violence, reputable Muslim scholars and their followers often make the analogy between alcoholism and same-sex relationships as they view both as addictions.

However, equating the case of couples who wish to live in love and affection with those who seek to inflict harm on themselves and others simply indicates that gay Muslims are denied their human dignity and that their human need for affection is viewed through the lens of addiction, aberration, and disease. It is here that online Muslim discussants choose to ignore developments in psychology and instead prefer to view advances in human understanding of sexuality through the lens of conspiracy theories. Paradoxically, while they accept understanding of transexuality, as advanced by professional psychologists, they reject the same on homosexuality, which simply indicates the deep rootedness of their bias on the subject as shaped by the framework of *liwāṭ*.

Instead of affording space to gay Muslims, online discussants expect them to bear the burden of proving the innateness of their sexual orientation, all the while rejecting the consensus amongst professional psychologists. In other words, an unfair task is laid before gay Muslims, which is nothing but a strategy to avoid reasonably addressing the issue of Muslim same-sex unions through accommodation and facilitation. However, it deserves to be noted that the burden of proof falls on the side that wishes to argue for a case. To the extent that rejection of the fulfillment of human need for intimacy through a legal contract violates the human dignity of Muslim gays and lesbians, the onus falls on contemporary Muslim scholars and their followers to establish on what basis they wish to inflict harm on their fellow coreligionists with a minority sexual orientation by denying them the right to live in affection, mercy, and compassion with a same-sex spouse.

This unreasonable position on Muslim gays and lesbians is often justified through the argument that human reason cannot be deemed superior to God's judgment on a particular issue. However, this is just another device to silence a reasonable discussion of the subject. According to Hassan el-Menyawi, the idea that God's law is immediately understandable and does not require interpretation suggests that human beings can directly access the will of God without biases and subjectivities.[155] Such an idea was not supported by 'Ali (d. 661) who is reported to have asserted that the Qur'an does not speak by itself and thus requires human interpreters.[156]

According to Abu Ḥanīfa (d. 767), the texts of the Sharīʿa, unless they relate to *ʿibāda* (worship), are rational in that their causes can be ascertained.[157] Similarly, according to al-Rāzī (1209), we can use reason to assert Sharīʿa norms.[158] Both al-Juwaynī (d. 1085) and al-Samʿānī (1096) justified *istdilāl* (legal reasoning) by arguing that the Companions used reason without turning to the foundational sources of legal authority.[159] In a similar vein, according to al-Qarāfī (d. 1285), *maṣlaḥa* (public interest) and *istiḥsān* (juristic preference) indicate that the authority of reason is recognized in Islamic jurisprudence.[160] Likewise, according to Allal al-Fasi (d. 1974), the rationale behind God's law falls within the bounds of human comprehension.[161] Al-Ṭūfī (d. 1316) even held that for *fī ḥaqq al-makhlūqīn* (matters that affect the created world) without a rational basis, God's acts would be *'abath* (futile).[162]

With such significance on the authority of reason in the reading of the texts and in jurisprudence, it would be inappropriate to adopt an unthinking attitude based on a reading of the Muslim texts that lacks both depth and nuance. It would be equally inappropriate to shun a reasonable view on the right of Muslim gays and lesbians to live their lives with the same affection with their spouses as is enjoyed by heterosexual spouses. Some conservative Muslims, however, may argue that since differential treatment based on gender is not considered wrong in jurisprudence, the argument on not discriminating on the basis of sexual orientation may not be applicable in jurisprudence.[163] Furthermore, the test-based argument is made that since God does not task beyond capacity, the prescription of struggling with same-sex desires at the very least would not be deemed unjust.[164]

There are several issues in deeming that the prescription to ask gay Muslims to remain celibate is neither discrimination nor unjust according to classical jurisprudence. First, while differential treatment on the basis of gender does exist in classical jurisprudence, it does not exist on the basis of ethnicity, which indicates that differential treatment based on one characteristic does not necessarily translate to another characteristic of human beings. Second, even in the case of differential treatment of women, many such rulings have been subject to change given the changing socioeconomic conditions. As an example, the Tunisian legal reforms indicate that if the wife assumed financial responsibility for the family, her duty of obedience became moot and that she too had the right of unilateral divorce and guardianship over children.[165] Third, differential treatment in classical jurisprudence is based on socioeconomic conditions as opposed to the genuine needs of human beings. For instance, while the testimony of two women is deemed equivalent to one man and the conditions of *'awra* are different for women, the right of women to fulfill their human need for intimacy through a legal contract is not impinged. This indicates that justifying discrimination against gay Muslims by denying them the right to intimacy is rather based on one's prejudices and capacity for disgust rather than the Islamic ethos that upholds compassion, mercy, and justice.

Justice is a cardinal value in Islam just as its converse—oppression—is antithetical to the Islamic ethos. The argument that God does not task beyond capacity so asking gay Muslims to live a life of permanent celibacy would not be unjust is problematic on at least two counts. First, the point that God does not task beyond capacity implies that He does not ask a lot from human beings in terms of His laws. His laws are not meant to cause undue or intolerable *'usr* (hardship) and as such the Sharīʿa forbids *ṣawm al-wiṣāl* (continuous fasting) or staying up all night for worship[166] and by extension asking people to deny their legitimate need for intimacy and affection permanently for a lifetime. Many jurists have shown that God detests an exaggerated ideal of strictness.[167] Ibn Qutayba (d. 884) mentioned that God has neither set overly burdensome commandments in religion nor prohibited things solely for the purpose of *bi-l-isti'bād* (subjugation).[168] Ayatollah Fadlallah (d. 2010) indicated that like eating and drinking, sexual practice is a natural need[169] and Wael Hallaq noted that none of the attributes that a man is born with is subject to adverse legal rulings,[170] which allow one to question the prescription of permanent celibacy for gay Muslims.

Second, according to Ibn Ḥazm (d. 1064), Allah has not forbidden anything without providing better lawful substitutes.[171] Ibn Qutayba (d. 884) indicated that while God prohibited fornication, usury, wine, gambling, and swine, He respectively allowed marriage, trade, many beverages, competitive sport, and the flesh of nonpredatory beasts and birds.[172] This suggests that if marriage has been allowed in lieu of fornication, then the prescription of permanent celibacy not only imposes undue hardship but also binds gay Muslims without a reasonable alternative, both of which violate the Islamic ethos of justice. However, some may argue that the prohibited item does not necessarily have an identical ḥalāl counterpart in that marital sex does not contain the elements of taboo or thrill associated with fornication or that permissible beverages do not contain the intoxication feature of wine and thus marriage to an opposite gender spouse could be the alternative that the Sharī'a offers gay Muslims. This argument, however, is based on the silly notion that there has to be a ḥalāl equivalent intoxication and taboo or thrill. It downplays the basic idea that the Sharī'a provides for the basic need for intimacy and quenching thirst, which is not met for gay Muslims through either the prescription of permanent celibacy or the equally unjust prescription of marriage to an opposite gender spouse, whose concern in such a sham marriage is completely sidelined.

Some might admit that the prescription for permanent celibacy is made on the basis of the fear that if same-sex relationships were allowed then that would lead to a slippery slope of allowing for the permissibility of other conduct like the consumption of wine. Others deny same-sex unions to gay Muslims as they feel that in doing so they are being merciful by protecting them from committing a crime against God and thus from the torments of Hell fire. Still others question the necessity for a same-sex union in the first place or claim that "because God said so" is a sufficient reason for believers to abide by His rules including those on the prohibition of "homosexuality."

However, it is not clear how allowing for same-sex unions based on human dignity and justice for a people to meet their basic need for intimacy would lead to a lifting of prohibition on wine or for that matter conduct like pedophilia, bestiality, incest, or prostitution. Consumption of wine is not a basic human need; pedophilia and bestiality are respectively a violation of children and species of a different genus; incest destroys families and relations tied through blood, semen, or milk; and prostitution even if consensual simply allows for sexual gratification without a legal contract and the associated responsibilities.

Likewise, the idea that human beings must be protected, as an act of mercy, from a God who burns in eternal Hell those who engage in same-sex intimacy, is based on the idea that like fornication, *liwāṭ* was a transgression against *ḥaqq Allah* (right of God) as opposed to *ḥaqq ādamī* (rights of other humans).[173] Notwithstanding the conflation of *liwāṭ* with same-sex intimacy confined by a legal contract, the idea generally propounded is that the greatest sin is *shirk* (associating partners with Allah), which is viewed as worse than murder or rape despite the fact that worshiping idols does not entail harming other human beings. However, such a line of reasoning conflates the rejection of *Tawḥīd* (oneness of God) with a superficial worship of idols. According to Kugle, *Tawḥīd* in general means urging harmonious unity by rejecting alienation, violence, egotism, and hypocrisy that keep people fragmented and societies unjust.[174] As such, murder and rape are manifestations of *ẓulm* (oppression) that arise as a consequence of rejecting this unity of all human beings. Viewed in this light, *shirk* is not mere idol worship but the source of *ẓulm* of which murder and rape are a few manifestations. Thus, denying same-sex unions, far from being a merciful position, actually violates the core kernel of Islam of not inflicting *ẓulm* as a consequence of belief in *Tawḥīd*.

Finally, the argument that "God says so" is a sufficient explanation for believers violates the premium that the Qur'an places on faith guided by reason. In fact, the Qur'an warns against placing blind faith in scholars and preachers by admonishing against making lords out of scholars and monks in verse 9:31. Moreover, people in general interpret the divine command based on what they reasonably understand to be good, just, and ethical.[175]

The above critical summary underscores the limitations of the arguments propounded by online conservative Muslim scholars and their followers. The critical analysis presented in previous chapters indicates that the question of Muslim same-sex unions, that is, the possibility of a legal contract between members of the same gender, was not entertained by the classical jurists, who were informed by the social norms and medical knowledge of their times. Given changed social mores and advanced medical knowledge of human sexuality and given the silence of the Muslim texts on the issue, a case for same-sex unions can be advanced in chapter 7.

NOTES

1. Amjad, "What is the standpoint of Islam on gays and lesbians?" Understanding Islam Q&A, accessed May 11, 2016, http://www.understanding-islam.com/gays-and-lesbians/.

2. Bilal Philips, "Islam's Position on Homosexuality," Islamweb, accessed January 27, 2016. http://www.islamweb.net/en/article/135433/.

3. Mohamed Ghilan, "LGBTQIA Islam?" February 1, 2013, accessed January 26, 2016, http://mohamedghilan.com/2013/02/01/lgbtqia-islam-2/.

4. El-Rouayheb, *Before Homosexuality*, 12.

5. Aḥmad ibn ʿAbd al-Ḥalīm Ibn Taymiyya, *Al-Istiqāma*; MF 11:543; 28:335, in الذهبية للحديث النبوي الشيف و علومه الموسوعة [*The Golden Encyclopedia of the Prophetic Golden Hadeeth and its Sciences*], 2nd edition, (London: Turath Publishing), CD-ROM.

6. Everett K. Rowson, "Homoerotic Liaisons among the Mamluk elite in late medieval Egypt and Syria," in Islamicate Sexualities, eds. K. Babayan and A. Najmabadi, (Cambridge: Harvard University Press, 2008), 226.

7. Ibn Ḥazm, *Ṭawq al-Ḥamāma fī al-ulfa wa-l-Allāf* (Damascus: Maktaba ʿArafa. 1349 A.H./1929-30 C.E.), 4.

8. Tengku Aḥmad Hazri, "Whither 'Homosexual Rights'?" *Islam and Civilizational Renewal* 3, no. 3 (April 2012): 543.

9. Personal correspondence with Mark Brustman.

10. Clare O'Farrell, "Identity," *Michel Foucault*, (London: SAGE Publications, 2005), 140.

11. Kugle, "Sexuality, Diversity, and Ethics," 195.

12. James Miller, *The Passion of Michel Foucault*, (New York: Simon and Schuster, 1993), 245, 252–54.

13. John Thorp, "Review article / Discussion: The social construction of homosexuality." *Phoenix* 46, no. 1 (1992), accessed January 27, 2016. http://www.fordham.edu/halsall/med/thorp.asp, 54–65.

14. Muhammad Asad, *Road to Mecca,* (New Delhi: Islamic Book Service, 2004), accessed January 25, 2016, http://muhammad-asad.com/Road-to-Mecca.pdf, 298.

15. Corvino, "Homosexuality and the PIB Argument," 507.

16. Lagrange, "The Obscenity of the Vizier," 189.

17. Sahar Amer, "Naming to Empower: Lesbianism in the Arab Islamicate World Today," *Journal of Lesbian Studies* 16, no. 4 (2012): 381–97.

18. Vardit Rispler-Chaim, *Disability in Islamic law*, Dordrecht, (The Netherlands: Springer, 2006), 117–18.

19. Entry on the marriage of the khuntha, *Kuwaiti Encyclopedia of Fiqh*. Translation by the authors.

20. Lange, *Justice, Punishment and the Medieval Muslim Imagination*, 193.

21. Yasir Qadhi, "Dealing With Homosexual Urges: Yasir Qadhi to Muslim Student, Sex and the Ummah," *Muslim Matters*, April 13, 2009, accessed January 27, 2016, http://muslimmatters.org/2009/04/13/dealing-with-homosexual-urges/.

22. Hazri, "Whither 'Homosexual Rights'?" 544.

23. Qadhi, "Dealing with homosexual urges."

24. Rollo Romig, "Where Islam meets America," *The New Yorker*, May 22, 2013, accessed January 27, 2016, http://www.newyorker.com/online/blogs/books/2013/05/where-islam-meet-america.html.

25. Andrew F. March, "The Uses of Fitra (Human Nature) in the Legal and Political Theory of 'Allal Al-Fasi: Natural Law or 'Taking People as They Are'?" Yale Law School, Public Law Working Paper No. 190. 2009. New title: "Naturalizing

Sharīʿa: Foundationalist Ambiguities in Modern Islamic Apologetics, Islamic Law and Society" 22 (2015) 1–37, accessed January 26, 2016, http://papers.ssrn.com/sol3/papers.cfm?abstract_id=1500009, 2.

26. Livnat Holtzman, "Human Choice, Divine Guidance and the *Fitra* Tradition-The Use of Hadith in Theological Treatises by Ibn Taymiyya and Ibn Qayyim al-Jawziyya." in *Ibn Taymiyya and His Times,* eds. Y. Rapoport and S. Ahmed, (Karachi: Oxford University Press, 2010), 176–77.

27. Andrew F. March, "Taking People as They Are: Islam as a 'Realistic Utopia' in the Political Theory of Sayyid Qutb," *American Political Science Review*, 104, no. 1 (February 2010): 197.

28. Anisah Che Ngah, "The Position of Informed Consent under Islamic Law," *The International Medical Journal of Malaysia* 4, no.1 (June 2005), http://www.eimjm.com/Vol4-No1/Vol4-No1-H1.htm.

29. Ibid.

30. Joseph Nicolosi and Linda Ames Nicolosi, *A Parent's Guide to Preventing Homosexuality,* (Downers Grove, *IL:* InterVarsity Press, 2002), 182–85.

31. "Truth wins out," NARTH, accessed January 27, 2016, http://www.truthwinsout.org/narth/.

32. Ali, "Progressive Muslims and Islamic Jurisprudence," 173.

33. Ali, *Sexual Ethics and Islam,* 73, 78.

34. Abdal Hakim Murad, "Bayan—a clarification," May 5, 2013, accessed January 26, 2016, http://www.masud.co.uk/ISLAM/ahm/bayan.htm.

35. Ibid.

36. Ali, *Sexual Ethics and Islam,* xiii.

37. Farooq, "The Doctrine of Ijma."

38. Ibid.

39. Kamali, *Principles of Islamic Jurisprudence*, 14.

40. Farooq, "The Doctrine of Ijma."

41. Kamali, *Principles of Islamic Jurisprudence*, 320.

42. Ibid, 256, 318–19.

43. We are grateful to Anas Mahafzah for this point.

44. Kamali, *Principles of Islamic Jurisprudence*, 205.

45. Ibid, 258.

46. Omar Shahid, "Muslim and gay: Islam begins to confront the issue," *The Times*, November 29, 2012, accessed January 27, 2016, http://omarshahid.co.uk/2012/11/29/muslim-and-gay-islam-begins-to-confront-the-issue-the-times/.

47. Tariq Ramadan, "Islam and Homosexuality," May 29, 2009, accessed January 27, 2016, http://tariqramadan.com/english/2009/05/29/islam-and-homosexuality/.

48. Kamali, *Principles of Islamic Jurisprudence*, 307.

49. John Boswell, *Christianity, Social Tolerance and Homosexuality* (Chicago: University of Chicago Press, 2015), 101.

50. "Serious Study Of Leviticus: Has Nothing to do with today's homosexuality," Liberated Christians, accessed January 26, 2016, http://www.libchrist.com/other/homosexual/leviticus.html.

51. Ramadan, "Islam and Homosexuality."

52. Sarah Moawad, “On Same-sex marriage, What Islamic Law says about the issues,” Islawmix, accessed February, 2014, http://islawmix.org/election2012/samesex.html.

53. Mufti Muhammad Zubair Butt, “What is the status of one who considers homosexuality to be permissible?” Last modified May 7, 2006, http://attalib.blogspot.ca/2009/05/what-is-status-of-one-who-considers.html.

54. Qadhi, “Dealing with homosexual urges.”

55. Corvino, “Homosexuality and the PIB Argument.”

56. “When homosexuality hits home” Straight Talk.

57. Corvino, “Homosexuality and the PIB Argument.”

58. Hamza Yusuf, “Islam and Homosexuality,” YouTube video, accessed January 27, 2016. http://www.youtube.com/watch?v=5idZNhc-iqc.

59. We are grateful to Mohamed Fadel for this point.

60. Maududi, *Towards Understanding the Qur’an,* Verses 4:15–16.

61. Lange, *Justice, Punishment and the Medieval Muslim Imagination,* 193.

62. Kamali, *Principles of Islamic Jurisprudence*, 265.

63. Hallaq, *A History of Islamic Legal Theories*, 77.

64. Farooq, “The Doctrine of Ijma.”

65. We are grateful to Mohamed Fadel for this point.

66. Qadhi, “Dealing with homosexual urges.”

67. Yusuf, “Islam and Homosexuality.”

68. Kamali, *Freedom of Expression in Islam*, 219.

69. Ali, *Sexual Ethics and Islam,* 39.

70. Kamali, *Freedom of Expression in Islam*, 220.

71. Ibid, 202–203.

72. Ibid, 202–204.

73. Ali, *Marriage and Slavery in Early Islam*, 11.

74. Husni and Newman, *Muslim Women in Law and Society*, 76.

75. Ābādī, *ʿAwn al-Maʿbūd fī Sharḥ Sunan Abu Dawūd*, Volume 6, 141.

76. Ali, *Marriage and Slavery in Early Islam*, 182.

77. El-Rouayheb, *Before Homosexuality,* 124.

78. Ibid.

79. Kamali, *Freedom of Expression in Islam*, 65.

80. Ibid, 209.

81. Ibid, 138.

82. Ibid, 52.

83. Ibid, 58.

84. Ibid, 60.

85. Ibid, 186, 221.

86. Ibid, 186, 131.

87. Ibid, 131, 146.

88. Ibid, 153.

89. Ibid, 72.

90. Shakir’s translation of the verse as noted in Note in chapter 2.

91. Ibn Taymiyya, *Majmūʿ Fatāwā*. Tadmuri letter: statement of Imam Aḥmad; The Chapter of Waqf: the chapter of changing the *hady* and *uḍḥiya*.

92. Ābādī, *ʿAwn al-Maʿbūd fī Sharḥ Sunan Abu Dawūd* 6, 141.

93. Muhammad ibn Abdullah al-Kharshi Al-Mālikī, *Sharḥ Mukhataṣar Khalīl*, *Ḥadd* of *zinā* and its rule, in الموسوعة الذهبية للحديث النبوي الشيف و علومه [*The Golden Encyclopedia of the Prophetic Golden Hadeeth and its Sciences*], 2nd edition (London: Turath Publishing), CD-ROM.

94. Hūd ibn al-Muḥakkam Al-Hawwārī, *Tafsīr al-Hawwārī*, Commentary on verse 23:6, in الموسوعة الذهبية للحديث النبوي الشيف و علومه [*The Golden Encyclopedia of the Prophetic Golden Hadeeth and its Sciences*], 2nd edition, (London: Turath Publishing), CD-ROM.

95. Muhammad ibn Yūsuf ibn ʿĪsā Ibn Ṣāliḥ Iṭmayyish, *Hamayān al-Zād ilā Dār al-Mīʿād*. Commentary on verse 23:6, in الموسوعة الذهبية للحديث النبوي الشيف و علومه [*The Golden Encyclopedia of the Prophetic Golden Hadeeth and its Sciences*], 2nd edition, (London: Turath Publishing), CD-ROM.

96. El-Rouayheb, *Before Homosexuality,* 124.

97. ʻUmar ibn ʻAli ibn ʻĀdil Al-Dimashqī, *Tafsīr Ibn ʿĀdil*. Commentary on verse 23:6. In الموسوعة الذهبية للحديث النبوي الشيف و علومه [*The Golden Encyclopedia of the Prophetic Golden Hadeeth and its Sciences*], 2nd edition, (London: Turath Publishing), CD-ROM.

98. Ibn Kathīr, *Tafsīr Ibn Kathīr,* for 23:6.

99. Ibn ʿUthmān, *Muṣannaf Ibn Abi Shayba* 5, 537.

100. Al-Nawawī. *Riyad as-Salihin (The Meadows of the Righteous)*, trans. Ibrahim Ma'rouf (El-Mansoura: Dar Al-Manarah, 2003), 245–46.

101. "Why is fasting haraam for menstruating women?" Islam QA.

102. The translation of these verses is from the sources cited in End Note 101 and 102.

103. Al-Nawawī. *Riyad as-Salihin (The Meadows of the Righteous)*, 245–46.

104. Ibid.

105. Mohammad Hashim Kamali, (1997) *Freedom of Expression in Islam*, The Islamic Texts Society, 54.

106. We are grateful to Peter Gray for this point.

107. G. J. H. Van Gelder, *Close Relationships: Incest and Inbreeding in Classical Arabic Literature*, (New York: I.B. Tauris and Co. Ltd., 2005), 115.

108. Ali, *Sexual Ethics and Islam,* 88.

109. Najmabadi, "Types, Acts or What?" 276, 285.

110. Ibid, 292.

111. *Kuwaiti Encyclopedia of Fiqh*, Entry: *khunthā mushkil*, in الموسوعة الذهبية للحديث النبوي الشيف و علومه [The Golden Encyclopedia of the Prophetic Golden Hadeeth and its Sciences], 2nd edition, (London: Turath Publishing), CD-ROM.

112. Ibn al-Qayyim. *Al-Jawāb al-Kāfī li Man Saʾala ʿan al-Dawāʾ al-Shāfī*, in الموسوعة الذهبية للحديث النبوي الشيف و علومه [*The Golden Encyclopedia of the Prophetic Golden Hadeeth and its Sciences*], 2nd edition, (London: Turath Publishing), CD-ROM.

113. Muṣṭafā ibn Saʿd ibn ʿAbduh Al-Ruḥaybānī, *Maṭālib Ūlī al-Nuhā fī Sharḥ Ghāya al-Muntahā; kitāb al-ḥudūd; bāb al-zinā*, in الموسوعة الذهبية للحديث النبوي الشيف و علومه [*The Golden Encyclopedia of the Prophetic Golden Hadeeth and its Sciences*], 2nd edition, (London: Turath Publishing), CD-ROM.

114. "The reason why the one to whom a homosexual act is done is to be executed," Islam QA, accessed May 12, 2016, https://islamqa.info/en/84140.

115. Husni and Newman, *Muslim Women in Law and Society*, 77–78.

116. Ibn Kathīr. *The History of Ibn Kathir—Bidaya and Nihaya*. Translated by Abul Fida Imad uddin Ibn Kathir Damishqi (Karachi: Nafees Academy Urdu Bazaar, 1988), Volume 9, 186.

117. Juferi, "The Consensus on Homosexuality."

118. Ibn Taymiyya, *Al-Istiqāma*; MF 11:543; 28:335.

119. Adang, "Ibn Ḥazm on Homosexuality," 14.

120. Mushfiqur Rahman, "Islamic Perspectives on Trials and Tribulations." 2004, accessed January 27, 2016, https://groups.yahoo.com/neo/groups/InterfaithDialogueCenter/conversations/topics/20471.

121. Ali, *Sexual Ethics and Islam*, 88.

122. Ruqaiyah Abdullah, *Overcoming Trials & Tribulations according to the Qur'an and Sunnah*, Last modified August 8, 2010, Serving Islam Team, http://www.servingislamteam.com/lectures_files/1359314686overcoming%20trials%20%26%20tribulations%20.pdf.

123. Hallaq, *A History of Islamic Legal Theories*, 182.

124. Ibrāhīm ibn Mūsā Abu Isḥāq Al-Shāṭibī, *The Reconciliation of the Fundamentals of Islamic Law*, trans. Imran Ahsan Khan Nyazee, reading: Garnet Pub. Ltd., 2012, 245.

125. Ibid, 234.

126. Ibid, 239.

127. Ibid, 224.

128. Ibid, 250.

129. Hourani, *Islamic Rationalism*, 32.

130. Ibid, 75.

131. Ibid, 134.

132. Qadhi, "Dealing with homosexual urges."

133. Sherman Jackson, "Islam: Between Old Fundamentalism, New Fundamentalism and Modern Sincerity," *American Learning Institute for Muslims*, April 18, 2013, accessed January 26, 2016, http://www.alimprogram.org/articles/islam-between-old-fundamentalism-new-fundamentalism-and-modern-sincerity/.

134. Khalid Zaheer, "Some Popular Misconceptions of the Muslims," accessed January 27, 2016, http://www.khalidzaheer.com/essays/kzaheer/criticism/some_popoular_misconceptions_of_the_muslims.html.

135. Dawud Walid, "How 'don't judge' has taken a wrong turn among American Muslims," January 28, 2014, accessed January 27, 2016, https://dawudwalid.wordpress.com/2014/01/28/how-dont-judge-has-taken-a-wrong-turn-among-american-muslims/.

136. "The Insolent," Hadith Explanation, accessed December 2014, http://dailyhadith.adaptivesolutionsinc.com/hadith/The-Insolent.htm.

137. Adam Kolasinski, "The Secular case against gay marriage," *The Tech: Online Edition* 124, no. 5 (2004) accessed January 26, 2016, http://tech.mit.edu/V124/N5/kolasinski.5c.html.

138. Robert R. Reilly, "What Would the Greeks Have Thought of Gay Marriage?" *Catholic Exchange*, March 11, 2013, accessed January 27, 2016, http://catholicexchange.com/what-would-the-greeks-have-thought-of-gay-marriage.
139. Thorp, "The Social Construction of Homosexuality."
140. Ali, "The Homosexual Challenge to Muslim Ethics."
141. El-Menyawi, "Same-sex marriage in Islamic law," 448, 521.
142. Ibid, 462.
143. Ghilan, "Islam, Homosexuality & Same-sex marriage."
144. Al-`Alawani, "Islam's Stance on Homosexual Organizations."
145. Kutty, "How to give up homosexuality."
146. Amer, "Naming to Empower."
147. Yusuf Al-Qaradawi and Muhammad Saalih al-Munajjid, "Homosexuality and Lesbianism: Sexual Perversions," accessed January 28, 2016, http://www.prophetmuhammadforall.org/webfiles/fatwa/HomosexualityNLesbianis.pdf.
148. Kamali, "The Sharia: Law as the Way of God," 164.
149. Habib, *Arabo-Islamic Texts on Female Homosexuality,* 84–85.
150. Amer, "Naming to Empower."
151. "Why does Islam forbid lesbianism and homosexuality?" Islam QA.
152. "Can those who have committed homosexual acts be forgiven, and is it permissible for such a person to get married?" Islam QA, accessed May 12, 2016, https://islamqa.info/en/5177.
153. "He wants to repent from homosexuality and needs help." Islam QA.
154. Kamali, *Principles of Islamic Jurisprudence*, 519.
155. El-Menyawi, "Same-sex marriage in Islamic law," 396.
156. Ibid.
157. Kamali, *Principles of Islamic Jurisprudence*, 271.
158. Emon, *Islamic Natural Law Theories*, 154.
159. Ibid, 128.
160. Ibid, 125.
161. Hallaq, *A History of Islamic Legal Theories*, 225.
162. Emon, *Islamic Natural law theories*, 163.
163. Email correspondence with Miqdaad Versi.
164. Ibid.
165. El-Menyawi, "Same-sex Marriage in Islamic Law," 480.
166. Kamali, *Principles of Islamic Jurisprudence*, 447.
167. El-Menyawi, "Same-sex Marriage in Islamic Law," 530.
168. Ibn Qutayba, *Kitāb al-ashriba wa dhikr ikhtilāf al-nās fīhā*, 26.
169. Fadlallah, "Jurisprudence of Sex."
170. Hallaq, *A History of Islamic Legal Theories,* 182.
171. Ibn Ḥazm, "Chapter 28: Of the Vileness of Sinning."
172. Ibn Qutayba, *Kitāb al-Ashriba wa Dhikr Ikhtilāf al-Nās fīhā*, 26.
173. El-Rouayheb, *Before Homosexuality,* 118.
174. Kugle, "Sexuality, Diversity, and Ethics," 234.
175. We are grateful to Mohammad Fadel for this point.

Chapter 7

Conclusion

Toward a Queer-Positive Muslim Jurisprudence

Despite the authenticity issues of the various Hadith attributed to the Prophet, the weakness of the narratives on the conduct of the Companions and the lack of consensus amongst the followers, traditionally at least three schools of Muslim jurisprudence prescribe the capital penalty for *liwāṭ*. However, Ibn Ḥazm effectively refutes the capital penalty and prescribes a *ta'zīr* (discretionary) penalty, which cannot exceed 10 lashes.[1,2] This suggests that just as Ibn Ḥazm's critiqued three schools of jurisprudence, the use of the *liwāṭ* and *siḥāq* framework by conservative Muslims can be critiqued, given its irrelevance to Muslim gays and lesbians.

Ibn al-Qayyim (d. 1350) summarized the three traditional opinions of Muslim scholars related to anal intercourse between men. These opinions were critically addressed in chapter 5. The first opinion is that the punishment is worse than that of *zinā*, the second is that the punishment is the same as that for *zinā*, while the third suggests no punishment at all.[3] The third strand of Muslim opinions lends support to the case for decriminalization of same-sex acts as made in chapter 5.

Gamal al-Banna (d. 2013), the youngest brother of the founder of the Muslim brotherhood Hassan al-Banna, stated that while he learned from Imam Shāfi'ī, he also had the added benefit of centuries worth of knowledge after him.[4] Alluding to Gamal al-Banna, and while respecting the Muslim tradition, one could potentially argue for a queer-positive Muslim jurisprudence especially in light of our understanding of human sexuality and the drastically different socioeconomic environment of our time.

7.1 FROM *LIWĀṬ* TO SEXUAL ORIENTATION

It is important to underscore that several past jurists employed juristic tools like *istiṣlāḥ* (juristic preference) or *maṣlaḥa mursala* (public interest) even in the presence of clear verses. Given their milieu, it is reasonable to understand that, while their decisions seem inconsistent with our socioeconomic realities, the past jurists sought to protect women and vulnerable segments of the Muslim society from exploitation. The medieval jurists understood *liwāṭ* to exclusively refer to anal intercourse in the context of men involved with youth or those suffering from *ʾubna*. However, as noted in chapter 2, Muhammad Salih al-Munajjid, a contemporary scholar, conflates this understanding to same-sex relationships by stating that "in Sharīʿa terminology it (homosexuality) refers to inserting the tip of the penis into the anus of a male."[5] Past Muslim jurists viewed the desire to penetrate separately from the action of penetration in that while the desire was viewed as a superfluous one directed at youth or the *ma'buns*, only the act was subject to the scrutiny of law. As such, the question of "unnaturality" would be foreign to Muslim jurisprudence, wherein, while the *maʾbūn* was viewed as suffering from an incurable disease, the desire to penetrate youth was viewed as the same desire that was directed toward women. In fact, as noted in previous chapters, past Muslim physicians sought to provide a biological underpinning for both *ʾubna* and *siḥāq*.[6,7]

The past jurists provided reasoned positions on the prohibition and subsequent punishments for *liwāṭ*. In contrast to the blanket condemnation of "homosexuality" by contemporary conservative Muslims, the past jurists, as noted in chapter 2, were concerned about the exploitation of male slaves, men suffering from *ʾubna*, and beardless youth. Furthermore, they viewed same-sex acts as taking place outside a legal contract.[8] As such, while jurists like Abu Ṭālib Makkī (d. 996) and Ibn Ḥajar al-Haytamī (d. 1567) included *liwāṭ* in the list of major sins, and the latter even included *siḥāq* in that list,[9] those instances were defined by sex outside the folds of a legal contract.

Thus, while the past authorities addressed same-sex acts outside a legal contract and were concerned about the exploitation of males and beardless youth, they never addressed the question whether it would be possible to have a legal contract between two members of the same gender. Obviously, this anachronistic question could only be reasonably brought up in our contemporary socioeconomic environment defined by our current knowledge of human sexuality. However, there is some evidence that in some subcultures marriage contracts were written. Ibn Ḥazm (d. 1064) noted that in the eleventh century while some Muslim tribes punished homosexuality, others permitted homosexual relations.[10] Likewise, several tribes in Sudan had a bride price for boys and in Siwa, marriage contracts were written between men and boys, where the money paid amounted to 15 pounds, in contrast to one pound for women.[11] It may, however, be noted that such marriages were between men and youth in age and status asymmetrical relationships, in contrast to contemporary marriage between two equal consenting adults bound by the responsibilities defined by a legal contract.

It is also important to note that while Sunnī jurisprudence is clear on its taboo on heterosexual anal intercourse, Shī'ī jurisprudence, while considering the act reprehensible, generally allows for it given the consent of the wife. However, even the Shī'ī authorities are concerned about the welfare of the woman and take a stand to deem the act as forbidden on a precautionary basis to avoid harm to the wife,[12] who under classical jurisprudence is required to submit to the husband. As noted in chapter 4, there exist three strands of texts on *ityān fī al-dubur* (anal intercourse). While one strand of texts prohibits the act, the other strand allows for it. The third strand of texts on anal intercourse, therefore, maintains a neutral stance. In this regard, Shāfi'ī (d. 820) is reported to have mentioned through one of his opinions that there does not exist strong evidence for or against the act of heterosexual anal intercourse.[13]

The analysis in chapter 4 indicated that the Hadiths related to anal intercourse with one's wife are not strong enough and also seem to go in opposite directions—acceptance and prohibition. This inconclusiveness on the issue is also substantiated by the clear lack of *ijmā'* (consensus) amongst the early Muslim society on the issue of anal intercourse with the wife. Therefore, one cannot use the argument that anal intercourse is Ḥarām in an absolute manner. As such, the argument of prohibiting anal intercourse between males in a same-sex relationship also becomes weak as there is not even a consensus on the act within a heterosexual context. Regardless, it is important to underscore that many gays and lesbians do not indulge in homosexual anal intercourse. In his book "Gay and Single Forever," Steven Bereznai notes that even within the casual encounters of sexually active gay men, anal intercourse would only be the fourth preferred activity.[14] Thus, the issue of one particular sexual act should not be conflated with that of a legal contract for Muslim gays and lesbians to fulfill the human need for affection and intimacy, like their straight coreligionists.

Kecia Ali notes the distinction between acts that are prohibited because of their being intrinsically evil like bestiality and necrophilia and acts prohibited because of lack of a legal contract like "homosexuality." However, Kecia Ali also notes that past authorities like Ibn Ḥajar Haytamī have not made such distinctions.[15] It may be noted that one reason past authorities did not make the distinction was probably because they believed that bestiality, necrophilia, and anal penetration (to male or female) were viewed as one-sided sexual acts aimed solely for the pleasure of the active penetrating partner irrespective of the status of the one on the receiving end. To the extent that conservative

Muslims are unwilling to make such distinctions, the move toward instituting Muslim same-sex unions might remain controversial. Nonetheless, four arguments for establishing same-sex Muslim contracts may be advanced.

These arguments become feasible because of the absence of a narrative in the Qur'an or Hadith that marriage or *mulk yamīn* relationships are between two people of opposite genders. Some may refer to verse 16:72 that indicates that Allah has made sons and grandsons from *azwājikum* (one's spouses), verses 53:45 and 75:39 that refer to the two mates—male and female, and that linguistically the word *zawj* (mate) refers to the opposite part of a pair to substantiate their case that marriage is between opposite gender spouses for the purpose of having offspring. However, it is also clear that the scope of such verses allow for exceptions as in the case of the marriage of sterile couples, elderly women, and the intersex persons. Moreover, while the word *zawj* is gender neutral and as such includes pairs irrespective of gender, the phrase *ʿalā azwājihim* used in verse 23:6 indicates that the word *ʿalā* connotes the meaning of above or on top and therefore suggests that addressees are the male partner over or above the female partners. The observation that the exegetes understood marriage through the lens of the partner on the top and the one on the receiving end also substantiates the argument that same-sex legal contracts were not feasible in a context based on a hierarchy of power and as such the question of same-sex unions was not addressed by the past jurists.

Some past jurists did have a list of entities that Muslim men could not marry. For instance, according to Ibn ʿĀbidīn (d. 1836), jurists defined marriage as a legal contract that allows for lawful sex between spouses in the absence of lawful prohibitions that include other men, intersexed people, polytheist women, closely related women, and female jinn.[16] However, such lists were not uniformly accepted, which is perhaps why some jurists, as noted in chapter 5, allowed masters to have sex with their male slaves and others even allowed marriage to Hindu women in India, who were considered as polytheists by some but referred to as people of the Book by other jurists. Several jurists allowed marriage with the *khunthā muskhil* (intersex persons), which included Sunnī jurists, as noted in chapter 6, and even Shī'ī jurists like al-Yazdi (d. 1919), whose work indicates that a *khunthā* can engage in relations with a woman as a man; and with a man as a woman.[17]

Moreover, in contrast to other jurists, Shāfiʿī (d. 820) opined that marriage to a daughter born out of wedlock was not forbidden as based on the rule that "the child belongs to the marriage bed" irrespective of biological paternity and that from the perspective of the law such a girl is not deemed to be the man's daughter.[18] While Islam is stricter than Judaism in prohibiting marriage to nieces, Christianity is stricter than Islam in not favoring marriage with first cousins[19] and treating as incest what would be allowed in Islam. Furthermore, it is also true that Ibn Ḥazm alluded to the case of Abraham marrying his half-sister and to the case of the Khawārij allowing marriage between grandparents and grandchildren or between uncles and nieces.[20]

Likewise, the marriage to *jinns* (fiery creations) was contested. The prohibition of marriage to *jinns* includes the rationales that the spouse has to be of the same kind based on verse 30:21, the issue of the jinn incarnating in a different gender, the ability of the man to impose restrictions on the female *jinn*, the issue of progeny with jinn characteristics, and the potential lack of tranquility, peace, and compassion with the *jinn* spouse.[21] Notwithstanding these reservations, some jurists considered such a marriage permissible and even Mālik could not find textual prohibition against men marrying female *jinns*.[22]

Thus, given the absence of a conclusive definition that marriage is between two people of opposite genders, the following four arguments are advanced.

7.2 THE ABSENCE OF A REASONABLE ALTERNATIVE

The first argument may be based on revisiting the traditional understanding of verses 23:5–7 wherein the Qur'an declares that anyone going beyond their spouses or concubines would be deemed as transgressing limits. However, the pertinent question to raise here would be whether a gay individual could really be deemed as a transgressor if the option of marriage with a female was not feasible in the first place. According to Ibn Ḥazm,[23] and many other scholars of Islam, nothing in Islam is forbidden without there being a legitimate substitute for the prohibited act. Classic examples in this line of thought include marriage in lieu of fornication and trade in lieu of *ribā* (usury). Given the point that there exists no such alternative for Muslim gays and lesbians, it would be reasonable to move the discourse on "homosexuality" from absolute prohibition to facilitation or legal accommodation within clear limits. While some conservative Muslims might claim that not every prohibition is supposed to have a lawful alternative, it is also true that every hardship has a facility in that Allah has given a way out as a choice in a burdensome matter.[24] The Qur'anic verses and the Prophet's sayings on facilitation of hardships should provide Muslim jurists sufficient scriptural backing on accommodating Muslim gays and lesbians in Islam. The argument for alleviation of hardships will be further elaborated in Section 7.6.

The second argument may be to distinguish between "homosexuality" on the one hand and bestiality and necrophilia on the other. While traditional scholars do not differentiate between the two, it deserves to be noted that the element of consent in the former and the absence of that consent in the latter should at least differentiate between the gravity of the two types of conduct. Many conservative Muslims advance the argument that accommodation of "homosexuality" would lead to a slippery slope of accepting all forms of sexual conduct. However, sexual conducts like bestiality, incest, necrophilia, and pedophilia allude to actions as opposed to persons, whereas "homosexuality" alludes to individuals.[25] Conservative Muslims believe that "homosexuality" is an action like the other forms of conduct and as such the prescription, as for the other forms of conduct, would be heterosexual marriage. However, this erroneous juxtaposition of "homosexuality" with other sexual conduct would lead to an unsatisfactory solution for Muslim gays and lesbians. The crux of the argument is simply that for other sexual conduct, to the extent that the perpetrator is heterosexual, the alternative of a heterosexual marriage exists, whereas for gays and lesbians that option is infeasible or not offered.

It was reflected through Ibn al-Qayyim that the desire for the same-sex among males was viewed as bereft of love and compassion. Such an understanding is also common amongst contemporary conservative Muslims who reduce the issue of gays and lesbians to that of the permissibility of intercourse. It is therefore understandable that same-sex relationships cannot be countenanced within a framework that views same-sex desire in the absence of compassion and through the lens of disease. However, this view of same-sex desire as superfluous, bereft of love, or based on disease as evident in the writings of the classical jurists was not based on Islamic texts but instead shaped by the medical knowledge and social mores of their times. A more informed understanding of sexual orientation based on the consensus among medical and psychology professionals challenges the position of conservative Muslim scholars and allows for a case for Muslim same-sex unions.

7.3 THE *ḌARŪRA* (NECESSITY) FRAMEWORK

Contemporary scholars like Tariq Ramadan have critiqued relying too much on the *ḍarūra* (extreme necessity) framework to address difficult issues in contemporary times.[26] Regardless, many contemporary authorities have used the *ḍarūra* framework to address controversial issues. As an example, the European Council for Fatwa and Research has used the *ḍarūra* principle to address mortgage acquisition despite the fact that the issue is not one that invokes a life or death situation.[27] While recognizing usury as a major sin and as one whose perpetration is depicted as waging war with Allah and the Prophet, the Council allows for home mortgages on the principle of *ḍarūra* and restricts this facility to those Muslims in real need for a house. The Council treats *ḥāja* (need) on a par with *ḍarūra* (extreme necessity) by asserting, "Jurists have established that *ḥāja* or the necessity or need, whether for an individual or a group, can be treated in equal terms with *ḍarūra* or extreme necessity."[28] It also quotes the Prophet that a spacious house is an element that constitutes happiness and also concedes that rental houses would not fulfill all the Muslim needs, especially in old age given the possibility of eviction.[29]

It is sometimes argued, based on linguistics, that the relevant Qur'anic verse allows for paying interest but not taking interest. However, some scholars have even accommodated old pensioners for taking interest based on a *ḍarūra* (necessity) framework. Contemporary scholar Khalid Zaheer states that his mentor Ghamidi holds the opinion "that poor pensioners were very likely not to be considered sinning if they received interest-based earnings, given that they had no alternative arrangements to survive."[30] The parallel case for Muslim gays and lesbians would be no different.

According to a jurisprudential rule in the absence of express prohibition, permissibility holds, and according to another rule necessity trumps prohibition. Traditional jurists, by referring to verse 2:185, which indicates that God does not wish to inflict hardship, and verse 22:78, which indicates that God has not laid hardship in religion, reason that Islamic law is mindful of genuine public or private needs and that it allows overstepping even the clear scriptural text under exceptional situations. The Ottoman Civil Code Majallah incorporated this notion in articles 17 and 21, and jurists like al-Māwardī (d. 1058) even considered the maxim "necessity trumps prohibitions" as one of the pillars of Islamic jurisprudence.[31] The traditional jurists did not define "need" except by indicating that it occurs in the absence of things that are essential for a healthy, respectable, and dignified life. In fact, the traditional jurists left it for the future Muslim generations to define need according to circumstances and changing times.[32] Perhaps, this is why, following Ghamidi, contemporary scholar, Tariq Mahmood Hashmi, holds the permissibility of interest-based loans for lodging in the absence of alternatives,[33] and in the context of left-handedness asserts, "The Sunnah has been established keeping in view the fact that it is natural for right-handed people to eat with their right hand for the Sharī'a does not ignore the natural human built. Similarly when it is not natural and therefore not easy for a natural lefty to eat with right hand he is not bound to eat with his right hand."[34]

The fourteenth-century Mālikī jurist Ibn Farḥūn (d. 1396) proposed a classification of Islamic law that advanced the pursuit of human needs for well-being.[35] Based on Bouhdiba's work, a pious son has to help his widower father marry again to guard his chastity for this duty is no less important than that of *kafāla* (food pension),[36] which suggests the significance of the facilitation of human needs including intimacy. At the popular "onislam" website, Umm Zakiyyah asks that by merely providing "food, clothing and shelter to widows and divorced women" would all their needs would be met? She questions how human beings can suggest a lifestyle bereft of intimate interaction with the opposite gender when they would not accept such a lifestyle for themselves.[37] Indeed, if that is the case with heterosexuals then what rationale prevents the posing of such a question for gays and lesbians? Thus, invoking the silence of the scriptures, and given genuine human need for physical and emotional intimacy for a healthy life, any contemporary position that views same-sex unions with contempt can be overruled to facilitate the hardships faced by gays and lesbians and by allowing them to form same-sex unions.

However, Ibn Taymiyya (d. 1328) referenced verse 7:33 to opine that *shirk* (attributing partners to Allah), injustice, and acts of lewdness are not permissible whether for need or otherwise for any situation. He believed that since verse 7:33 was revealed in Mecca, the prohibition is absolute as opposed to the latter prohibitions of blood, carrion, and pork, where the prohibition is lifted based on dire necessity.[38] Thus, the *ḍarūra* framework would perhaps not be applicable to the case of sexuality. Indeed, there is a reference made to Ibn Ḥajar, who states that even if fornication were the only way to provide for her food, a woman could not engage in that activity due to the social repercussions of the action.[39]

However, it could be argued that to a limited extent the *ḍarūra* framework was applied even to sexuality. Despite indicating that desires cannot be equated to needs and that man can survive without sexual intercourse but not without food, Ibn al-Qayyim (d. 1350) opined in the context of a person prone to bursting of testicles due to abstinence during daytime fasting in Ramadan, that he could resort to masturbation, failing which, he could make use of the hand of an *ajnabiyya* (impermissible female) for emission without looking at her for such a procedure would be analogous to a female physician touching to treat him.[40] Likewise, based on Khaled el-Rouayheb's work, the jurist Shihāb al-dīn Aḥmad al-Ramlī (d. 1550 CE) is recorded to have stated that kissing the object of one's affection, usually a woman or a beardless boy, was a duty if in line with the then medical theory that such frustration would contribute to the lover's death. This observation may lead one to conclude that while the past jurists predominately addressed *liwāṭ*, they never seriously entertained the issue of intimacy between adult members of the same gender. This conclusion, however, may be tempered by noting the principle of *sadd dharī'a* (closing the door) according to which if an act leads to a prohibited act then it is prohibited and as such if intimacy leads to anal intercourse, assuming the strand of opinion on the prohibition of anal intercourse, then that intimacy is prohibited.

In conclusion, the *ḍarūra* framework might be problematic as it is usually applicable in life or death situations as in the case of the lifting of the ban on the consumption of pork when no other food is available under dire and extenuating circumstances. In this framework, the act of pork consumption is still deemed prohibited but it is tolerated under the extreme need to preserve life. Given that man can live without sexual expression, the *ḍarūra* framework cannot be applied for sexual expression unless there was an extenuating situation involving the choice between sexual expression and death as considered by Ramlī (d. 1550 CE), Ibn al-Qayyim (d. 1350), and others, and even then, the framework would not be likely helpful in supporting same-sex unions.

7.4 THE *MAṢLAḤA MURSALA* (PUBLIC INTEREST) FRAMEWORK

Shāṭibī (d. 1388) defines *ḍarūra* as what is necessary for the fulfillment of worldly and religious interests such that if the *ḍarūra* were not fulfilled, a person's welfare would be drastically affected and he would be kept from success and comfort and end up in clear loss.[41] On the other hand, *ḥāja* is defined as a need, which if not fulfilled, puts a person in difficulty even if that person can live without it.[42] Thus, while intimacy may not be a *ḍarūra* (necessity) in that a life or death scenario does not arise in the absence of its provision, it is a *ḥāja* (need) which if not facilitated causes extreme *'usr* (undue hardship). Indeed, it was noted through Hakim Murad that most people are not super moral figures in that long-term abstinence will fail for most individuals. Thus, it is important to underscore that would it be better for conservative Muslims to deny Muslim gays and lesbians the right to intimacy, which would still exist in an unregulated fashion, or would it be better if they facilitated Muslim gays and lesbians through the provision of a same-sex legal contract, which would regulate intimacy just as it is regulated in the case of straight couples.

To the extent that no satisfactory alternative exists for Muslim gays and lesbians and given the immense duress that they experience in their lives, it would be reasonable to employ tools of jurisprudence to address their plight. The available tools of *maṣlaḥa mursala* (public interest) and *istiṣlāḥ* (juristic preference) are subject to debate among Muslim scholars. The debate arises from the differences in the philosophical outlook of people, in that those who oppose juristic tools like *istiḥsān* (juristic preference) view such efforts as means of circumventing the law on the basis of *hawā* (whims), whereas others may use such juristic tools to root the Sharī'a *aḥkām* (commands) on the basis of equity, *maṣlaḥa*, and necessity,[43] and henceforth support same-sex unions.

The case for same-sex unions may be critiqued by noting that *maṣlaḥa* is supposed to be *kulliya* (general), in that it secures benefit for the largest possible number or people as opposed to a subsection of the community.[44] In other words, the criticism is based on the argument that restricted *ḥāja* (needs) for a part of the community are not like universal *ḥāja*, which are treated like *ḍarūra* and as such the principle of *rukhṣa* (license) may not apply for gays and lesbians. However, as noted in Section 7.3, such a criticism did not prevent the European Council for Fatwa and Research from treating the need of housing, a *ḥāja*, on par with *ḍarūra* and facilitating a subsection of Muslims in obtaining housing based on interest-based mortgage in cases where that was the only option available. Furthermore, such criticisms are predicated on the assumption that there exists a prior prohibition on a legal contract for same-sex couples, an issue that has not been addressed by classical jurisprudence. Moreover, such arguments ignore the fact that human dignity and welfare is a central concern of Islamic law.[45]

The argument of not facilitating the *ḥāja* for a subsection of the community may arise out of the fear that facilitating a subsection might come at the expense of the decrease in welfare of the general population. Such fears are expressed in the case of same-sex unions when it is incorrectly argued that facilitating gays and lesbians would come at the expense of the societal order. It could be argued that the social repercussions of fornication are absent in the case of "homosexuality." In fact, if anything, and purely from a social perspective, by sanctioning such unions, society would witness a reduction in such social repercussions through a reduction in extramarital affairs. This line of argument may, however, invite charges of using a very "utilitarian" perspective on Muslim mores, although such charges could be addressed by recourse to the *maṣlaḥa mursala* framework that kept paramount the benefit of the Muslim society over the strict application of Muslim law.

Thus, given that accommodating gays and lesbians does not tear the fabric of the society, the argument of not facilitating restricted *ḥāja* in this context cannot be justified. Moreover, ʿIzz al-dīn b. ʿAbd al-Salām (d. 1263) indicated that if benefits exceeded harms, then the benefit is accepted and the harm is tolerated.[46] To the extent that the harms of same-sex unions are negligible, if any, the case for facilitating gays and lesbians can be supported.

7.5 FACILITATION OF INTERSEX AND TRANSPERSONS

The third argument toward Muslim same-sex unions may be to pinpoint how past jurists accommodated intersex persons. Conservative Muslims might argue that all sexual relationships would be prohibited unless expressly allowed. However, past jurists have established legal contracts for those other than a strict male and female(s). Paula Sanders states that past jurists did not consider the marriage of an intersex person to a cissexual person as prohibited and in fact casually considered the error of marrying an intersex person to a woman if the former turned out to be a woman.[47]

While the Shafiis and Mālikīs prohibit the marriage of the *khunthā mushkil* (intersex person) and the Hanafis allow their marriage to the opposite gender in the case their gender becomes certain,[48] the Ḥanbalī scholar al-Khiraqī stated that the *khunthā mushkil* could marry either a male or female based on her or his inner disposition. He reasoned that only the *khunthā mushkil* was able to make this decision and that her or his word was to be accepted as the word of the woman on menstruation is accepted. In the marriage section for *khunthā*, the Kuwaiti Encyclopedia of Fiqh states:

> The Ḥanbalīs differed in his marriage. Al-Khiraqī mentioned that the khunthā decides according to what he says. If he said that he is a man and that he desires women, then he can do it. If he said that he is a woman and he desires men, then he can do it. This is because only he can decide and no one other than him can decide this. So, his word is accepted as the word of the woman is accepted when she says that she has menstruation or the period. He, the Khunthā, may know himself according to the desires, that is, based on, which of the two sexes he desires.[49]

Thus, to the extent that al-Khiraqī accepts inner gender orientation despite external ambiguity and allows for a legal marriage contract, based on our contemporary knowledge of human sexuality, Muslim jurists could put forth a case for Muslim same-sex unions in much the same way. Some may argue that while the past jurists accommodated the *khunthā mushkil* by allowing them to marry, they assigned them a ritual gender and as such upheld straight marriage apart from reinforcing the idea that desires are secondary to anatomy. However, the past jurists were interested in gender to the extent it allowed them to decide on issues such as inheritance and otherwise, for the *khunthā mushkil* and the *mukhannathūn* socially adopted the role between men and women. Moreover, the jurists who allowed the *khunthā mushkil* to marry according to their inner disposition allowed them to do so, based on the gender they were attracted to as opposed to the anatomy they found desirable. Thus, the framework that allowed the *khunthā mushkil* to marry on the basis of their constitution could possibly be applied to Muslim gays and lesbians in that they could be viewed as *khunthā* in orientation, parallel to the term *khunthā nafsiyya* (psychological intersexuality)[50] as used by Ṭanṭāwī.

Notwithstanding the Islamic teachings on not tampering with the creation of Allah, the late Egyptian Grand Mufti Sayed Ṭanṭāwī (d. 2010) endorsed gender reassignment surgery in the case of *al-khunutha al-nafsiya* (psychological intersexuality) through the logic of giving precedence to the hidden disposition of a human being as his or her true nature.[51] In allowing for such a procedure, Ṭanṭāwī actually ruled on the basis of a hidden attribute, which is in contrast to the opinion of al-Āmidī, who had stated that jurists only rule on the external and leave hidden aspects to Allah. It is quite possible that such a framework of *khunthā nafsiya* can be extended to accommodate the sexual orientation of gays and lesbians.

The constitutionality of the orientation of gays and lesbians can also be supported on the basis that al-Ghāzālī (d. 1111) is noted to have stated that

Allah's creations are not subject to the arrows of accident.[52] The Qur'an can also be read to note that Allah creates whatsoever He wills and that includes, according to verses 17:84 and 30:22,[53] those with alternate inner dispositions, as captured by the words *shākila* (manner) and *lawn* (color). Likewise, in verse 24:31, the phrase *ghayr ulī al-irba* (male attendants who lack vigor) was elaborated in Tafsīr Ṭabarī as describing various categories of men, which include a man who follows his fellow man and does not have desire in women, a man who is mentally retarded, or a man who cannot have an erection in response to women.[54] Based on texts attributed to Ibn ʿAbbās (d. 687), the *ghayr ulī al-irba* mentioned in verse 24:31 refers to effeminate men who cannot have arousal or men from whom women do not feel shy. Likewise, Mujāhid (d. 722) and Qatada (d. 735) mentioned that such a man has no desire for women.[55] In a similar vein, al-Rāzī (d. 1209) indicated that scholars differed on the categories of men the phrase referred to and the list included the poor, the mentally disabled, children, the old, and anyone without desire for women. Al-Rāzī concludes that the construction of the phrase does not exclude any of the categories of such men.[56] He also alludes to the Hadith in which a *mukhannath* was banned from the Prophet's household and referred to the *mukhannath* as the *ghayr ulī al-irba,* which substantiates the use of this phrase for noncissexual males, which may potentially include gay men.

Muslim authorities, both Shīʿī and Sunnī, have been extremely mindful of the plight of intersex and transpersons in that they have been allowed to undergo gender reassignment surgeries. Shīʿī scholars base their opinion on the juristic principle that what is not expressly prohibited is in principle permissible.[57] Vardit Rispler-Chaim states that in permitting gender reassignment, Shīʿī authorities like Ayatollah al-Khaminai have a broader definition of individuals that include males who emotionally and sexually incline toward female behavior or appearance.

However, Sunnī scholars base their ruling on gender reassignment surgery on medical grounds.[58] Rispler-Chaim states that in the determination of gender, psychological and emotional inclinations also need to be examined apart from external organs, chromosomes, and hormonal levels.[59] This leads to the question that if contemporary Muslim scholars accept medical and psychological opinion on the issue of intersex and transpersons, then on what basis they deny the same in the case of gays and lesbians.

7.6 THE JURISTIC TREATMENT OF MARRIAGE

The fourth argument can be based on noting how the past jurists understood marriage as a legal contract and then discerning whether such a framework could be extrapolated to Muslim gays and lesbians. Contrary to the claims of conservative scholars, past jurists did not relegate the main purpose of marriage to reproduction. Many jurists defined the purpose of marriage, distinctly from reproduction, in terms of sexual enjoyment.[60] In general, classical jurists viewed marriage as a legal contract to regulate sexual intercourse for that was the reason that elderly women were allowed to get married despite bearing no potential for children.

Among the five main purposes of marriage, al-Ghāzālī (d. 1111) included the satisfaction of sexual desire. In one of the Shī'ī Lexicons, the main purpose of marriage is considered to be included in the meaning of the word *nikāḥ* deemed equivalent to the word *waṭ'*, which means sexual intercourse between a man and a woman sanctioned by marital contract.[61] Generally, the word *nakaḥa* means both marriage and sexual intercourse, and where the Shafii and Mālikī jurists upheld the former meaning, the Ḥanafī and Ḥanbalī jurists upheld the latter meaning.[62] Vardit Rispler-Chaim writes, "More pivotal for the preservation of marital relations than bearing children a child seems to be that the couple are both healthy enough to engage in physical and emotional intimacy and in sexual intercourse."[63]

In Islam, sex is viewed as having the attributes of kindness, reciprocity, and generosity[64] as is clear from verse 30:21 that reads, "And of His signs is that He created for you from yourselves mates that you may find tranquility in them; and He placed between you affection and mercy." Sex is viewed as a natural need and while its social utility lies in procreation, it is considered as the primary reason for marriage.[65] Sex is viewed as both pleasure and duty, and the spouse is deemed as harmed if the duty is not fulfilled.[66]

Several Hadith invoking the sayings of the Prophet have been used to underscore the importance of marriage in Islam. One Hadith, circulated in online Muslim sites, has the Prophet stating, "Marriage is my tradition who so ever keeps away there from is not from amongst me."[67] The reason perhaps has to do with the regulation of human sexual need. Where, a contemporary scholar, Moiz Amjad confirms that wanting to avoid fornication "is indeed one of the most commendable and pious reasons for marriage,"[68] another scholar, Shehzad Saleem, indicates in the context of the Hadith that angels curse the wife till dawn who refuses sex to her husband, that refusal of spouses to engage in marital sex, "which puts chastity in jeopardy is disliked by the Almighty."[69] Thus, anyone who refuses to marry has been counseled to not fight against human nature.[70]

So strong is the recognition of the human sexual need that, in one of his queries, Shehzad Saleem responds to a questioner, "If you think that in spite of all the good mannerisms found in your fiancé, it is difficult for you to stand your fiance's physical appearance, it is better to take this seemingly harsh step of terminating your engagement than to psychologically suffer all your life."[71] Khalid Zaheer, another contemporary scholar, even asserts, "Even if we were to imagine that a husband isn't quite as careful in his conduct . . . and as a consequence he gets interested in another lady to the extent that he wants to marry her, why should the first wife not be given the option to either live with her husband, adjusting to the new reality, or leaving him?"[72]

According to classical jurists, while the wife may not dissolve the marriage contract even if the husband suffers from leprosy, she is allowed divorce in the case the husband can no longer serve the primary purpose of marriage—sexual intercourse, specifically in cases of *jabb* (being amputated of penis), *unna*, and *khiṣā* (castrated).[73] Dr. Aḥmad Kanan understands *unna* (asynodia), which, according to classical jurists, is established by a confession or oath, as a man's inability to penetrate a woman for psychological reasons that may include revulsion.[74] This indicates the importance given by classical jurists to the provision of a legitimate avenue for sexual intercourse and also provides a justification for same-sex unions for Muslim gays and lesbians, whose human need for intimacy is viewed with contempt by conservative scholars.

7.7 BUILDING A CASE FOR MUSLIM SAME-SEX UNIONS

While some might argue that if some matter such as same-sex unions is of legal significance, then the Prophet would have mentioned it because of his obligation to convey the meaning of revelation as the Qur'an being the word of God is for all times to come. However, it is also true that being bound by the socioeconomic and political confines of his time, there were many issues on which the Prophet could not directly comment and as such the general principles of Islam have to be evoked and a decision has to be made based on *ijtihād*. This is specifically true given that while the Prophet encountered the case of the *mukhannathūn*, the case of same-sex couples was not presented to him or for that matter the Companions and the following generations of the followers and the jurists.

On the basis of the scholarship by Khaled el-Rouayheb and Kecia Ali and as pointed out in previous chapters, while classical Islam addressed the issues of *liwāṭ* and *ma'buns,* it did not address the concerns of gays and lesbians and the issue of a legal contract for same-sex partners. This can be substantiated by the general observation of Mustafa Zayd that many circumstances of the modern world have no precedent in the authoritative Muslim texts.[75] Thus, in the absence of texts that would unambiguously allow for the possibility of same-sex unions, the overarching principles, essence, and spirit of Islam have to be invoked to establish the case for Muslim same-sex unions.

According to Hassan el-Menyawi, past jurists were able to go against the grain of their societies based on the principle of '*adl* (justice) as opposed to explicit Qur'anic backing and jurists like al-Ṭūfī (d. 1316), 'Abduh (d. 1905), and Riḍā (1935) advocated deriving rules even if they were not directly confirmed by the texts.[76] Likewise, Kamali asserts that it is the responsibility of the *mujtahid* (independent thinker) to exert himself for the fulfillment of the legitimate needs of the society and benefit of people even if no specific authority is found for the purpose of justification[77] and that efforts for justice, even in the absence of rulings in the Sharīʿa, will always be in harmony with the Sharīʿa.[78]

Part of the final sermon of the Prophet reads, "All those who listen to me shall pass on my words to others and those to others again; and may the last ones understand my words better than those who listen to me directly," which suggests the responsibility of future generations to contribute to the Islamic tradition. Such texts reject the tendency of conservative scholars to freeze the Islamic tradition to the times of the classical jurists and actually bolster the efforts of Muslim reformers toward change.

The sayings of various Muslim jurists also substantiate this point on change given new socioeconomic and political realities. In this regard, eleventh-century scholar al-Samʿānī stated, "*Fiqh* (jurisprudence) is an ongoing science continuing with the passage of centuries and changing with the change of circumstances and conditions of men, without end or interruption."[79] Likewise, Ibn Ḥazm (d. 1064) is reported to have stressed that *taqlīd* (imitation) is prohibited according to jurists like Abu Ḥanīfa (d. 767), Mālik (d. 795), and Shāfiʿī (d. 820), a point that was supported by al-Shawkānī (d. 1839).[80]

Al-Qarāfī (d. 1285) is quoted as having declared,

> Persons handing down legal judgments while adhering blindly to the texts in their books without regard for the cultural realities of their people are in gross error. They act in contradiction to established legal consensus and are guilty of iniquity and disobedience before God, having no excuse despite their ignorance; for they have taken upon themselves the art of issuing legal rulings without being worthy of that practice. . . . Their blind adherence to what is written down in the legal compendia is misguidance in the religion of Islam and utter ignorance of the ultimate objectives behind the rulings of the earlier scholars and great personages of the past whom they claim to be imitating.[81]

Likewise, Ibn al-Qayyim (d. 1350) is quoted as having harrowingly asserted,

> Whoever issues legal rulings to the people merely on the basis of what is transmitted in the compendia (law books) despite differences in their customs, usages, times, places, conditions, and the special circumstances of their situations has gone astray and leads others astray. His crime against the religion is

> greater than the crime of a physician who gives people medical prescriptions without regard to the differences of their climes, norms, the times they live in, and their physical natures but merely in accordance with what he finds written down in some medical book about people with similar anatomies. He is an ignorant physician, but the other is an ignorant jurisconsult but much more detrimental.[82]

Shāṭibī (d. 1388) is also quoted as having stated,

> Because incidents in our lives are unlimited therefore it is not correct to enlist them under restricted indications and thus it was necessary to keep the door open for ijtihād (assiduity), comparison and so on. It is certain that some incident will occur while no texts related to their ruling exist and the predecessor did not practice any assiduity on them.[83]

Shāṭibī's words are quite relevant given the argument that the past jurists did not countenance the issue of a legal contract for same-sex couples.

In recent times, Muhammad Asad (d. 1992) echoed the point on change based on changing circumstances by stating,

> Every age requires a new approach to the Qur'an for the simple reason that the Qur'an is made for all ages. It is our duty to look for deeper meanings in the Qur'an in order to increase our knowledge and experience. The Qur'an wants your intellect to be always active and trying to approach the message of God. God himself dedicated this book to people who think.[84]

The above quotations are only a snapshot of a whole array of scholars from various time periods, who have consistently upheld the theme of eschewing *taqlīd* and exerting *ijtihād* based on changing socioeconomic and political circumstances. Given the developments in psychology and increased understanding of human sexuality, it seems reasonable to address the concerns of Muslim gays and lesbians through the framework of sexual orientation as opposed to through *liwāṭ* and *'ubna*. Viewing Muslim gays and lesbians as human beings with genuine need for intimacy and affection, instead of as diseased individuals suffering from the disease of the anus or vulva, would allow supporting the case of same-sex unions.

However, instead of basing the case for Muslim same-sex unions on the *ḍarūra* framework, which is technically limited to life or death situations, the case can be built on the principle of not inflicting harm and on the principle to facilitate the legitimate human need for affection and intimacy. In this regard, the prescription of permanent celibacy can be rejected as it inflicts harm and undue suffering upon gays and lesbians. In this regard, it may be noted that the Sharīʿa represents *al-ṭarīq al-wasaṭ* (the middle path) between *ʿusr* (undue difficulty) and *yusr* (extreme ease).[85] As such, the issue is not considered through the lens of tolerating the prohibited but based on verse 65:2 that Allah would make an opening for whoever acts consciously of Him.

Al-Ṭūfī built a jurisprudential methodology based on a single Prophetic text, "Do not inflict harm or repay one harm with another"[86] and this provides a scope to argue for the case for Muslim same-sex unions from the point of view of not inflicting harm by prescribing permanent celibacy to Muslim gays and lesbians. In al-Ṭūfī's methodology, any conflict between the *naṣṣ* (text) and *maṣlaḥa* (public welfare) is actually the conflict between one text and another, which reads *lā ḍarar wa lā ḍirār fī al-Islām* (there is no harm or reciprocating harm in Islam).[87]

The idea of avoiding undue hardship denotes a cardinal value in Islam, one that is substantiated by various scholars through various texts and juristic maxims. According to Sarakhsī (d. 1097), *rafʿ al-ḥaraj* (avoidance of hardship) is the cardinal principle of Islam substantiated by the Qur'an and Hadith that reads, "The best of religion is what brings ease to the people."[88] The Qur'anic verses on facilitation of hardship include verse 22:78 that reads, "Allah has not placed any difficulty in religion" and verse 5:6 that reads, "Allah does not intend to impose any difficulty."[89] The principle of *rafʿ al-ḥaraj* has its variant in the maxim *dafʿ al-ḍarar* (prevention of harm) and verses 22:78 and 5:6 have variants in verse 4:28 that reads, "Allah intends to put you at ease,"[90] and verse 2:185 that reads, "Allah intends ease and does not intend hardship."[91] Other maxims, similar in wording on preventing harm, include *al-mashaqqa tajlub al-taysīr* (hardship begets facility), *al-ḍārru yuzāl* (harm must be eliminated), *idhā ḍāq al-amru ittasaʿ* (an opening must be found where matters become exceedingly difficult),[92] and Shāfiʿī's saying *mā ḍāqa al-shay'u illā ittasaʿ* (there is an exception for something extremely restrictive).[93]

It may also be noted that except ritual worship, all other areas of law are changeable to achieve *maṣlaḥa* (public welfare) based on the social context and that one avenue of obtaining *maṣlaḥa* is through the protection of *ird* (human dignity).[94] The promotion of human dignity is an overriding objective of the Sharīʿa along with justice, equality, realization of lawful benefits for people, prevention of harm, and removal of hardship.[95] In this regard, the case for a legal contract for same-sex couples can be supported on the basis of the fact that prescriptions to ignore legitimate human needs lead to *taklīf mā lā yuṭāq* (creation of obligations that cannot be met) and which is why Shāṭibī (d. 1388) recognized that some human dispositions are so inherent that to deny them would be to harm human beings irreparably.[96] Potentially, a case for Muslim same-sex unions could be built as follows.

7.8 THE CASE FOR MUSLIM SAME-SEX UNIONS

Following the approach developed in this book, the starting point would be to state that the verses on the people of Lūṭ are not applicable to contemporary gays and lesbians and that the Hadith related to the Prophet are suspect and weak. Having established the silence of the principal sources of Muslim knowledge, the narratives alluding to the conduct of the Companions and the understanding of the followers can be revisited to indicate that the *Salaf* (pious ancestors) did not have a consensus on the understanding of later juristic terms of *liwāṭ* and *Lūṭī*. Rather, notwithstanding the weak traditions, the Companions addressed *'amal qawm Lūṭ*, which were a composite of apostasy and murder and perhaps coercive sexual conduct.

It is important to note that every Companion, *tabi'i* (follower), and jurist who equated the punishment of *liwāṭ* with that of *zinā*, essentially reflected the understanding that the analogy of *zinā* better explained *liwāṭ* rather than the story of Lūṭ. Furthermore, every *tabi'i* and jurist who prescribed the *taʿzīr* punishment reflected the understanding that it was problematic to explain *liwāṭ* through the story of Lūṭ or through the analogy of *zinā*. Acknowledging the absence of a clear directive from the *Salaf*, the next step would be to argue that the jurists while predominately prohibiting *liwāṭ,* defined in the context of *ʾubna* and beardless youth, did not actually address the anachronistic issue of a same-sex legal contract. In general, jurists do not have to mention exceptions in their rulings that are theoretically present in any general ruling once valid reasons for the exception are delineated. Thus, the issue of homosexuality is predominately one of the absence of a legal contract, which was not feasible in the time of the jurists, who defined the marriage contract through the framework of ownership.

Sidelining minority opinions that allowed for sexual access to male slaves, generally men were not allowed to have sex with their male slaves as men were viewed as nonreceptive entities and to get penetrated was indicative of suffering from *ʾubna*, a model that originated from Galen, as opposed to Islamic, texts. However, with increased knowledge of psychology, the framework of sexual orientation can replace the outdated *ʾubna* framework. Moreover, same-sex sexual acts are not viewed as intrinsically evil as acts that include necrophilia and bestiality, where the concern is that of the exploitation of the perceiving party, but rather illegal due to a lack of legal contract, which substantiates the reframing of the issue as one of a legal contract for same-sex couples.

While some contemporary scholars may try to dismiss the case for Muslim same-sex unions as *shādhdh* (absurd), it is a valid dissenting opinion based on human dignity and justice. Moreover, the textual evidence against same-sex unions is not strong for even if one were to uphold the prohibition of heterosexual anal sex, it has no bearing on the issue of a legal contract for same-sex couples and also because prohibiting anal intercourse with a woman does not automatically render the extrapolation of that prohibition to the context of men owing to differences in physiology.

Conservative Muslims may argue against making permissible the forbidden; however, the converse also holds true as is reflected in verse 5:87 that indicates to not prohibit the good things that Allah has made lawful. This would hold true in the case of same-sex unions on which the primary texts are silent. While some may argue that the Qur'an emphasizes opposite gender pairings, verses that refer to the coupling of Adam and Eve do not universally prescribe opposite gender coupling for all, as the scope of the verse is *mu'ayyan* (specific) and not intended to be *'āmm* (generalized to all individuals).[97]

Since the Qur'an refers to marriage as *mīthāq ghalīẓ* (firm covenant) in verse 4:21,[98] matrimonial laws fall in the category of *mu'āmalāt* (social transactions),[99] which are subject to changes based on changing social conditions, as opposed to *'ibāda* (worship), which is not subject to such changes. According to Shāṭibī (d. 1388), matters that can be rationally understood, in that they are not merely *ta'abbudi* (based on obedience) like worship rituals, and whose goodness and badness can be known include marriage and punishments, for which the term *bid'a* (innovation) is not applicable.[100] With social changes, marriage is no longer viewed as *riqq* (slavery) in that the husband does not own the wife, which is perhaps why contemporary Muslims do not support the Ḥanafī position to allow forcible sex with a wife when she does not have a legitimate excuse.[101] Indeed, in popular Egyptian culture marriage is not referred to as *'aqd nikāḥ* (legal contract for marriage or sexual intercourse) but as *'aqd qiran* (legal contract for marriage or union) and the spouse is referred to as *sharīkat/sharīk hayati* (my life partner).[102] In contemporary times, social changes include women being better off economically than their husbands, and also the reframing of marriage as a contract between two equals as opposed to between a head and a subordinate. Therefore, given that the marriage contract is modified to include two equal partners, the case of same-sex unions is justified on the basis of the ethos to alleviate human suffering and to uphold human dignity.

According to the Ḥanbalī jurists, in the absence of a clear text that prohibits contracts, the normative position on contracts including marriage is *ibāḥa* (permissibility) and as such, on the basis of Qur'anic verse 4:19 that teaches that contracts be based on mutual consent, and given that consent alone creates binding rights and responsibilities,[103] the case for same-sex unions can be justified. Likewise, according to the Ḥanafī jurists, a valid contract requires freedom of *ikhtiyār* (choice) and *riḍā* (consent) which is defined as real willingness,[104] which substantiates the point that a legal contract for same-sex couples based on mutual consent can be justified. In this regard, the Tunisian family law reforms that view marriage as a contract and that stipulate the feasibility of marriage only through consent provide a model for same-sex unions.[105]

Same-sex unions can be justified on the basis of the values espoused by the Qur'an on marriage. In verses 30:21 and 2:187, the Qur'an views marriage as forming the basis of *mawadda* (affection), *raḥma* (compassion), and as an institution through which spouses find tranquility and companionship as they become a *libās* (protective garment) to each other, guarding their dignity and honor.[106] Same-sex unions can also be supported on the basis of verse 9:71 that depicts mutual protectorship of men and women and verse 2:187 that depicts cooperation and harmony between them instead of verse 4:34 that focuses on male providership.[107] Thus, given that the Quran allows marriage for the purpose of contentment, *mawadda*, and compassion, and given that sterile couples and elderly women are allowed to get married, there seem no reasonable grounds to prohibit the realization of these benefits for same-sex couples.

7.9 LIMITATIONS TO MUSLIM SAME-SEX UNIONS

Some may argue that Muslim same-sex unions cannot be justified on the basis of the classical understanding of marriage. They feel that such unions could not be covered by the rules and restrictions that are usually associated with marriage. They would question the application of '*idda*—a woman's period of waiting after divorce or death of the husband—to same-sex relationships and the associated issue of who gets to offer support money during the '*idda*. Other questions include which of the spouses would pay *mahr* (mandatory payment paid to the bride), would gays and lesbians be also allowed for a maximum of four spouses and could a bisexual take spouses of both genders, who would be the protector and held responsible for providing for the family, who gets the right to divorce, which of the spouses would have a *walī* (custodian), who would be the *maḥram* (unmarriageable kin) and before whom would the gaze have to be lowered, would someone else be allowed in the home when the spouse is away, and finally do explicit scriptural texts exist that ban same-sex incest with fathers and brothers just as they exist for mothers and sisters.

However, all such questions emerge from an understanding of marriage rooted in patriarchal norms that prevailed during the times of the classical jurists. As noted earlier, marriage falls under the rubric of *muʿāmalāt* and not *ʿibāda* and as such all these regulations are subject to change based on time, location, and circumstances. Furthermore, applying rules without regard to the spirit behind those rules can at times lead to unreasonable situations.

This indicates that the purpose behind the rules can guide their applicability in cases that do not fit regular situations and circumstances. In the context of rules pertaining to marriage, the purpose behind *'idda* is to reveal any hidden pregnancy; a rule that may be relaxed in the case of elderly women and sterile couples irrespective of their sexual orientation. The contemporary understanding of *mahr* can be radically distinguished from that of the classical jurists, who viewed it as the price offered to have exclusive access to the vulva. Also, in pre-Islamic Arabia *mahr*, a practice selectively sanctioned by Islam was the compensation that was paid to the bride's family to deem her offspring as part of the husband's tribe as opposed to that of her father and brother.[108] Given that marriage is no longer viewed as an ownership-based contract and that offspring are not a necessary part of marriage, the understanding of *mahr* can be recast through its symbolic value and in cases of economic inequality between the spouses, the one who is better off socially and economically can offer it to the other spouse.[109]

Nikāḥ is a legal contract, which means stipulations can be made in an egalitarian setting that is radically different from times where the female was entirely dependent on the male for sustenance. This indicates, as has been observed in the Tunisian family law reforms, that stipulations can be placed in marriage against polygamy, for the right to divorce for both partners, the optionality of a *walī*, and for the economically better off spouse to uphold family responsibility as opposed to the husband, who was traditionally required to provide for the family. Such family reforms allow for the facilitation of the procedural concerns regarding same-sex unions. The issue of lowering the gaze concerns modesty and is irrelevant to the sanctioning of same-sex unions. Finally, just as prohibition of marriage to paternal and maternal aunts of one's wife was extended from the prohibition of marrying to two sisters at the same time,[110] the prohibition of same-sex incest can be deduced from the prohibition to one's mother and sister in verse 4:23. Moreover, according to the body fluids theory of incest,[111] ties between people established due to blood, milk, and semen prohibit sexual relationship between them. Likewise, Afsaneh Najmabadi confirms that the transfer of bodily fluids as milk or semen is indicative of close kinship and hence prohibitive of marriage.[112]

In conclusion, such limitations can all be reasonably addressed and as such they do not pose a hindrance to establishing Muslim same-sex unions.

7.10 RECENT DEVELOPMENTS IN MUSLIM COMMUNITIES ON SAME-SEX UNIONS

While conservative Muslims have largely sustained the viewpoint of not accommodating same-sex unions, some amongst them have come out strongly against homophobia. Differentiating between a sin and crime and alluding to the absence of a Qur'anic punishment, prominent Sunnī and Shia scholars in India like Asghar Ali Engineer (d. 2013), Maulana Nadvi, and Maulana Rizvi have favored the decriminalization of "homosexuality."[113] Their views have a precedent in the Tanzimat Ottoman reforms, which decriminalized homosexuality in 1858.[114] In Pakistan, while upholding the traditional position on same-sex unions, Shehzad Saleem has movingly expressed that gay Muslims "might be nearer to God than many of the righteous we see around us." He has eloquently stated, "What right have we to malign and abuse them and regard them among the untouchables. Is this not vanity and overinflated self-esteem on our part?"[115]

In Europe, France-based Imam Tarek Oubrou[116] and Netherlands-based Imam El-Ouazzani[117] have clearly condemned attacking, insulting, or despising gay people. The late Imam Zaki Badawi[118] in the United Kingdom went so far as to state that provided they remained chaste, gay Muslims could benefit from civil unions. Sudan-based Sheikh Hashim Al-Hakim has indicated that while he used to be "hard against homosexuals," he has "learned to respect their humanity." Likewise, Bangladesh-based mosque leader Sheikh Abul Kalam Azad has sympathized with the suffering of gay Muslims.[119]

In the United States, Imam Johari Malik expressed, "It's time to get past our homophobia to help human beings,"[120] and Imam Suhaib Webb expressed regret on his referral to a reparative therapy group and argued against the discrimination of gay Muslim congregants.[121] Dr. Maher Hathout (d. 2015), a retired physician and founder of the Muslim Public Affairs Council, discussed how gays are not given an outlet for sexual expression in Islam and how Muslim families, struggling to reconcile their child's sexual and religious identity, can be compassionate toward their children.[122] Ayman Fadel wrote a moving piece on how he abandoned acquired homophobic behavior and attitudes. He asks if straight Muslims can at least recognize that the "party line does not make a lot of sense in today's world," that there are no amulet-based cures for sexual orientation, and that gay Muslims should not be pressured into fraudulent marriages.[123]

Muslim academics like Omid Safi and Mohammad Fadel have even expressed support for same-sex marriage in a secular North American context. Omid Safi wrote an article on why he supports same-sex marriage by indicating, "I have seen these families show the same love, affection, and attention on their children that my own heterosexual family does. Love is love. Family is family, though they come in different shapes. My children have gay and lesbian friends. They belong [*sic*] a social club at school that is an alliance of straight, gay, lesbian, and bi-sexual students."[124]

Likewise, in the context of the 2012 elections in the United States, Mohammad Fadel expressed, "We can support the idea of same-sex marriage because what we want is to make sure that all citizens have access to the same kinds of public benefits that other people do. . . . Islamic law can at least qualify the endorsement of the idea, at least in the context of democratic, non-religious states."[125]

Muslim law has always contained majority and minority opinions, especially on controversial issues. As such, in contrast to conservative Muslims, progressive Muslims fully support same-sex unions. In the United States, Imam Khaleel Mohammad has stated that there is cause to reinterpret the relevant Qur'anic verses on the issue.[126] Whereas, Dr. Arash Naraghi has gone further to explore theological accommodation for gay Muslims.[127] Spain-based Abdennur Prado has stated that the scriptural texts do not refer to loving relationships but rather inhospitality and rape of foreigners.[128] In Indonesia, Dr. Siti Musdah Mulia and other Muslim scholars were reported to have concluded that same-sex orientation was from God and that same-sex relationships were permissible in Islam.[129] Likewise, the Grand Mufti of Zambia, Sheikh Assadullah Mwale, has asserted on LGBT Muslims that, "you were created the way you are" and therefore "everyone is allowed in Islam and very much welcomed."[130]

Muslims for Progressive Values (*MPV*) in the United States and Universalist Muslims in Canada have come out in full support of same-sex unions. Pamela Taylor of MPV stated that condemning gay Muslims to celibacy would go against the "fundamental Islamic ideals of fairness, equality of all human beings, compassion and mercy."[131] Progressive Muslims of varying theological backgrounds have created spaces that are inclusive of LGBTQ Muslims, such as the el-Tawhid Juma Circle Unity Mosques, MPV Unity mosques and Inclusive Mosque Initiatives.[132]

7.11 TOWARD DERIVING REASONABLE CONCLUSIONS FROM THE SCRIPTURES

While in North America and Europe, some Muslims have adopted more lenient positions on same-sex unions, in many Muslim countries, cultural taboos preclude a rational assessment of the concerns of Muslim gays and lesbians. To this end, one could state that on other controversial issues like Muslim testimonial laws, several contemporary scholars genuinely grapple with the texts without being precluded by any cultural taboo. In fact, it might be instructive to view the following excerpt from Dr. Khalid Zaheer, a contemporary Islamic scholar in Pakistan, on the issue of testimonial laws.

> Is the need to have two women instead of one man still relevant today when there are many women who have become professionals in the field of finance

> and they are much less likely to forget financial issues than many of the men who are non-professionals in this field? I think it is a tough question, far beyond my domain of competence. I don't want to see the Qur'anic formula changing, but then I do understand that there was a definite reason why it was needed. Perhaps the fact that ladies are getting professional expertise in these fields is not in line with the ideals of Islam. I do not know. I invite you to think about it and give your opinion on the subject. Forgive me for being unclear here.[133]

It is instructive to note that given social changes, and in the absence of taboos, conservative scholars genuinely grapple with issues that necessitate changes in Islamic rules that at times go against even clear-cut Qur'anic verses. Such issues, to mention a few, include testimonial laws, the wife-beating clause in verse 4:34, and taking or paying *ribā* (interest). Moreover, it is not unreasonable to expect that conservative Muslim academics and intellectuals may end up making similar statements on "homosexuality" if the cultural taboos were sidelined. If the issue of "homosexuality" was genuinely grappled with as done by Christian authorities like Desmond Tutu and Jewish authorities like Rabbi Harold Schulweis, Muslim academics and intellectuals might also end up safeguarding the right of Muslim gays and lesbians to a healthy Muslim life. Rabbi Harold Schulweis has mentioned that the curse we have put on our gay children is not the will of God but solely our doing.[134] Likewise, Bishop Desmond Tutu has categorically stated that we do not have any earthly reason to state that a committed homosexual relationship does not lead to compassion.[135] He further adds that he would not worship a homophobic God.[136] Bishop Tutu's words might reflect the equivalent "conscientious pause" of Khaled Abou Fadl,[137] which in this context would ask of conservative Muslims to pause to think about the import of the verses on the people of Lūṭ before applying them without regard to the distinction between the people of Lūṭ and Muslim gays and lesbians.

7.12 CONCLUDING REMARKS

We have argued that the principal sources of Muslim knowledge—the Qur'an and the Hadith—do not address the issue of same-sex unions. The texts address *'amal qawm Lūṭ* in the context of the people of Lūṭ, whose actions depict coercion, inhospitality, and exploitation. Any ruling on same-sex unions based on such texts is made through *qiyās* (analogy), which is contestable, as believing Muslim gays and lesbians with an exclusive orientation toward the same gender and whose concern is of the basic human need for affection, intimacy, and companionship cannot be reasonably compared to a people who engaged in highway robbery and evil deeds in public assemblies by approaching unwilling men traveling through their land.

We also argued that past jurists addressed *liwāṭ* in the context of male slaves, beardless youth, and men suffering from the *'ubna* disease. Moreover, they addressed *liwāṭ* outside the folds of a legal contract. For them, while the penetrated partner was diseased, the penetrator was acting on superfluous desire, that is, the same desire that was channeled toward women. Thus, past jurists did not address the question of a legal contract between members of the same gender, outside the context of disease. It is important to note that contemporary Muslim scholars and the masses look at "homosexuality" very differently from the traditional scholars, that is, with contempt, especially for the receptive male partner. Contemporary scholars prescribe permanent celibacy to Muslim gays and lesbians as a test or trial from God. Such a vision is alien to the classical scholars of Islam.

In terms of the issue of heterosexual anal intercourse, we argued that there is no *ijmā'* (consensus) on the prohibition of the act, which was addressed in the context of unwilling receptive partners, who were deemed to be harmed by the act. However, even the assumed prohibition of anal intercourse between husbands and wives is not readily transferable to between two men bound by a legal contract, given the physiological difference between men and women due to pleasure derived from the massage of the prostate gland. Furthermore, even the blanket prohibition on anal intercourse should not affect the issue of Muslim same-sex unions, as they are not defined by a single sexual act. In terms of nonpenetrative sexual acts within a legal contract, we argued that such acts cannot be construed as *qubḥ* (evil) as they do not possess the features of *ẓulm* (oppression).

We deconstructed the arguments used by contemporary scholars that include, among others, viewing the human need for intimacy through the lens of urges and whims, depicting Muslim gays and lesbians as going against *fiṭra* (nature), making analogies with unethical sexual conduct that include bestiality and necrophilia and invoking *ijmā'* (consensus). We argued that permanent celibacy is an unreasonable prescription that violates the Islamic emphasis on *ird* (human dignity) and *'adl* (justice). Furthermore, in light of our better understanding of human sexuality, we argued to shift the discourse from that of *'ubna* to that of sexual orientation. Based on the jurisprudential principles of *raf' al-harj* (repelling harm) and *maṣlaḥa* (public interest) that eventually rest on promoting *ird* (human dignity) and *'adl* (justice), we argued for facilitating Muslim same-sex unions. We also argued that the limitations to same-sex unions in terms of rules related to marriage, modesty, and sexual misconduct can all be reasonably addressed and that they do not pose a hindrance to establishing Muslim same-sex unions.

We acknowledged some positive changes that have taken place in Muslim subcultures, specifically in North America. However, much more remains to be done in terms of creating spaces for queer Muslims. We strongly exhort contemporary Muslims to abandon outdated constructs of *ʾubna* and reasonably facilitate the human need for intimacy, affection, and companionship for Muslim gays and lesbians who, after all, are our own sons and daughters, brothers and sisters, and part of the Muslim faith-based family. We invite them to reject invoking needless trials and support Muslim same-sex unions on the basis of the cardinal Islamic values of *ʻirḍ* (human dignity) and *ʻadl* (justice). Indeed, given that Islam allows marriages for elderly women and sterile couples to realize the benefits of intimacy, affection, and companionship, there seems no reasonable argument against allowing same-sex couples to realize the same benefits within a legal contract.

We invite Muslim academics and jurists to help alleviate human suffering, based on the teachings of the Prophet, who is reported to have said, "Facilitate and do not cause difficulties and do not cause people to detest (the Islamic law), but treat people like brothers."[138] We invite them to protect the self-worth and humanity of gays and lesbians from the sermons of fiery "Imams" and to safeguard both their virtue and *imaan* (faith) from the vacuous alternatives they face in cloistered or sinful lives lived under immense duress. We leave our readers with a reminder from Ibn Taymiyya. "When the scholars find out that their decisions are causing lots of suffering, or that people are looking for worse loopholes than the actual prohibition, or that people end up living in the Ḥarām, then it is time for the scholars to think again about their conclusions."[139]

NOTES

1. Adang, "Ibn Ḥazm on Homosexuality."
2. Habib, *Arabo-Islamic Texts on Female Homosexuality,* 80–84
3. Ibn al-Qayyim. *Al-Jawāb al-Kāfī li Man Saʾala ʿan al-Dawāʾ al-Shāfī*, 161.
4. We are grateful to Emran El-Badawi for this point.
5. "Why does Islam forbid lesbianism and homosexuality?" Islam QA, accessed May 12, 2016, https://islamqa.info/en/10050.
6. Ze'evi, *Producing Desire*, and Amer, "Medieval Arab lesbians and Lesbian-Like Women."
7. Habib, *Arabo-Islamic Texts on Female Homosexuality,* 84–88; Samar Habib, *Female Homosexuality in the Middle East: Histories and Representations*, (New York and London: Routledge, 2009), 47–62.
8. Kecia Ali, "Muslim Sexual Ethics: Same-Sex Sexual Activity and Lesbian and Bisexual Women," *The Feminist Sexual Ethics Project*. Brandeis University, 2002, accessed January 25, 2016, http://www.brandeis.edu/projects/fse/muslim/same-sex.html.

9. Elizabeth M. Bucar and Fagheh Shirazi, "The 'Invention' of Lesbian Acts In Iran: Interpretative Moves, Hidden Assumptions, and Emerging Categories of Sexuality," *Journal of Lesbian Studies* 16, no. 4 (2012): 416–34.

10. Habib, *Arabo-Islamic Texts on Female Homosexuality,* 17.

11. Will Roscoe and Stephen O. Murray. *Islamic Homosexualities*, (New York: New York University Press, 1997), 40.

12. Rizvi, "Chapter 3: The Islamic Sexual Morality."

13. Ibn Ḥajar al-ʿAsqalānī, *Talkhīṣ al-Ḥabīr.*

14. Steven Bereznai, *Gay and Single Forever*, (New York: Marlowe & Company, 2006).

15. Ali, "Muslim Sexual Ethics."

16. "May a Human Marry a Jinni?" Islam Awareness, accessed January 26, 2016, http://www.islamawareness.net/Jinn/fatwa_marry.html.

17. Email correspondence with Miqdaad Versi.

18. Van Gelder, *Close Relationships,* 91.

19. Ibid, 93.

20. Bouhdiba, *Sexuality in Islam*, 198.

21. "May a Human Marry a Jinni?" Islam Awareness.

22. Muallimah Sauda, "Can Humans Marry Jinn?" Madrasah Ummul Hasanaat, August 10, 2012, accessed January 27, 2016, http://www.ummulhasanaat.co.za/can-humans-marry-jinn.

23. Ibn Ḥazm, "Chapter 28," *Ṭawq al-Ḥamāma fī al-ulfa wa-l-Allāf*, (Damascus: Maktaba ʿArafa. 1349 A.H./1929-30 C.E).

24. Al-Shāṭibī, *The Reconciliation of the Fundamentals of Islamic Law*, 246.

25. Dan Savage, "Incestathon," August 1, 2002, accessed January 27, 2016, http://www.thestranger.com/seattle/SavageLove?oid=11500.

26. Ramadan, *Radical Reform.*

27. European Council for Fatwa and Research, "Ruling on Buying Houses with mortgages," Islamic Mortgages, accessed January 26, 2016, http://www.islamicmortgages.co.uk/index.php?id=259.

28. Ibid.

29. Ibid.

30. Khalid Zaheer, "Ghamidi Sb's Opinion on Government Investment Schemes," accessed January 27, 2016, http://www.khalidzaheer.com/qa/946.

31. Mohammad Muslehuddin, *Islamic Jurisprudence and the Rule of Necessity and Need*, (New Delhi: Kitab Bhavan, 1982), 31, 58–63.

32. Khaled Abou El-Fadl, *The Great Theft: Wrestling Islam from the Extremists*, (San Francisco: Harper San Francisco, 2005), 187–89.

33. Tariq Mahmood Hashmi, "Paying interest on buying apartments," Query response, Studying Islam., An Affiliate of The Al Mawrid Institute of Islamic Sciences, March 9, 2005, accessed January 26, 2016, http://www.studying-islam.org/querytext.aspx?id=283.

34. Tariq Mahmood Hashmi, "The dilemma of natural left handers," Query response, Studying Islam, An Affiliate of The Al Mawrid Institute of Islamic Sciences,

October 31, 2005, accessed January 26, 2016, http://www.studying-islam.org/showcounterqa.aspx?id=133.

35. Fadel, "The True, The Good and the Reasonable."

36. Bouhdiba, *Sexuality in Islam*, 90.

37. Umm Zakiyyah, "Muslim Girls Don't Want Sex?" OnIslam, January 19, 2014, accessed January 28, 2016, http://onislam.orkiservers.com/english/family/your-society/468227-muslim-girls-dont-want-sex-.html.

38. Ibn Taymiyya, *Tafsīr Sūra Āl ʿImrān*: *Tafsir* of do not make what is permitted prohibited, in الموسوعة الذهبية للحديث النبوي الشيف و علومه [*The Golden Encyclopedia of the Prophetic Golden Hadeeth and its Sciences*], 2nd edition, (London: Turath Publishing), CD-ROM.

39. Karamali, "Is fornication allowed to alleviate extreme poverty?" accessed May 12, 2016, http://islamqa.org/shafii/qibla-shafii/33827.

40. Bell, *Love Theory in Later Hanbalite Islam*, 132–33.

41. "Ikrah (Coercion)" Ummah, accessed May 12, 2016, http://www.ummah.com/forum/showthread.php?177400-Ikrah-And-Taqiyyah.

42. European Council for Fatwa and Research. "Ruling on Buying Houses with mortgages."

43. Mohammad Hashim Kamali, "Istihsan and the Renewal of Islamic law," International Institute of Advanced Islamic Studies, accessed January 26, 2016, http://www.iais.org.my/e/index.php/publications-sp-1447159098/articles/item/16-istihsan-and-the-renewal-of-islamic-law.html, 8.

44. Kamali, *Principles of Islamic Jurisprudence*, 359.

45. Kamali, "The Sharia, Law as the Way of God," 170.

46. Fadel, "The True, The Good and the Reasonable."

47. Paula Sanders, "Gendering the Ungendered Body: Hermaphrodites in Medieval Islamic Law," in *Women in Middle Eastern History*, eds. Nikki Keddie and Beth Baron, (New Haven and London: Yale University Press, 1991), 87.

48. *Kuwaiti Encyclopedia of Fiqh*, Entry: *khunthā mushkil*, in الموسوعة الذهبية للحديث النبوي الشيف و علومه [*The Golden Encyclopedia of the Prophetic Golden Hadeeth and its Sciences*], 2nd edition, (London: Turath Publishing), CD-ROM.

49. Translation by authors.

50. Bucar and Shirazi, "The "Invention" of Lesbian Acts In Iran."

51. Ibid.

52. Kugle, "Sexuality, Diversity, and Ethics," 198.

53. Ibid, 196.

54. Al-Ṭabarī, *Tafsīr al-Ṭabarī*, verse 24:31.

55. Ibid.

56. Al-Rāzī, *Tafsīr al-Rāzī*, verse 24:31.

57. Sayyed Muhammed Hussein Fadlallah, "Jurisprudence of Sex," *Bayynat*, accessed January 26, 2016, http://english.bayynat.org/Jurisprudence/sex.htm.

58. Jakob Skovgaard Peterson, "Sex change in Cairo: Gender and Islamic law," *The Journal of the International Institute* 2, no. 3 (Spring, 1995), accessed January 27, 2016, http://quod.lib.umich.edu/cgi/t/text/text-idx?c=jii;view=text;rgn=main;idno=4750978.0002.302.

59. Rispler-Chaim, *Disability in Islamic Law*, 73–74.
60. Ali, *Sexual Ethics and Islam,* 179.
61. Rispler-Chaim, *Disability in Islamic Law*, 47.
62. Kamali, *Principles of Islamic Jurisprudence*, 163.
63. Rispler-Chaim, *Disability in Islamic Law*, 47.
64. Bucar and Shirazi, "The "Invention" of Lesbian Acts In Iran."
65. Husni and Newman, *Muslim Women in Law and Society*, 60.
66. Ibid.
67. Dr. Sherif Mohammed, "On Marriage in Islam," *Jannah Organization,* accessed January 26, 2016, http://www.jannah.org/sisters/marr.html.
68. Amjad, "Is Wanting to Avoid Fornication a Good Reason for Marriage?" accessed May 12, 2016, http://www.understanding-islam.com/is-wanting-to-avoid-fornication-a-good-reason-for-marriage/.
69. Shehzad Saleem, "'Refusing sex to the husband,' Islam and Women: Misconceptions and Misperceptions." *Renaissance*, February 2005, accessed January 27, 2016, http://www.monthly-renaissance.com/issue/content.aspx?id=154.
70. Amjad, "Celibacy," accessed May 12, 2016, http://www.understanding-islam.com/celibacy/.
71. Shehzad Saleem, "Separating from an unattractive fiancé," Query Response, *Renaissance*, September 2001, accessed January 27, 2016, http://www.monthly-renaissance.com/issue/query.aspx?id=491.
72. Khalid Zaheer, "Rationale behind polygamy and the consent of wife," accessed January 27, 2016, http://www.khalidzaheer.com/qa/154.
73. Rispler-Chaim, *Disability in Islamic Law*, 56.
74. Ibid, 117–18.
75. Emon, *Islamic Natural Law Theories*, 35.
76. El-Menyawi, "Same-sex marriage in Islamic law," 419, 421.
77. Kamali, *Principles of Islamic Jurisprudence*, 48.
78. Kamali, "The Sharia, Law as the Way of God," 174.
79. We are grateful to Peter Gray for this point.
80. Moulay al-Hussain ibn Al-Hayyan, "Imitation and its effect on the efficiency of Assiduity in Islamic jurisprudence Part 1 / 2," The Message of Islam, accessed January 25, 2016, http://islamicstudies.islammessage.com/ResearchPaper.aspx?aid=708.
81. Umar Faruq Abd-Allah, *Islam and the Cultural Imperative*, (Nawawi Foundation, 2004), accessed January 25, 2016, http://www.nawawi.org/wp-content/uploads/2013/01/Article3.pdf, 6–7.
82. Ibid, 7.
83. Al-Hayyan, "Imitation and its effect."
84. The American Muslim, "A Road to Mecca," December 20, 2012, accessed January 27, 2016, http://theamericanmuslim.org/tam.php/features/articles/film-announcement-a-road-to-mecca-muhammad-asad.
85. Hallaq, *A History of Islamic Legal Theories,* 174.
86. El-Menyawi, "Same-sex Marriage in Islamic Law," 421.
87. Kamali, *Principles of Islamic Jurisprudence*, 360.
88. Ibid, 325.

89. Ibid, 353.
90. Kamali, "The Sharia, Law as the Way of God," 176.
91. Mohammad Hashim Kamali, "Legal maxims and other genres of literature in Islamic jurisprudence," *Arab Law Quarterly* 20, no. 1 (2006): 77–101.
92. Ibid.
93. We are grateful to Mohammad Fadel for this point.
94. El-Menyawi, "Same-sex Marriage in Islamic Law," 421, 426.
95. Kamali, "The Sharia, Law as the Way of God," 166.
96. Emon, *Islamic Natural Law Theories*, 175.
97. El-Menyawi, "Same-sex Marriage in Islamic Law," 468.
98. Ibid, 474.
99. Kamali, "The Sharia, Law as the Way of God," 151.
100. Masud, *Shatibi's Philosophy of Islamic Law*, 222.
101. Ali, *Sexual Ethics and Islam,* 12.
102. We are grateful to Mohammad Fadel for this point.
103. Kamali, "The Sharia, Law as the Way of God," 162.
104. El-Hassan, "The Doctrine of Duress."
105. El-Menyawi, "Same-sex Marriage in Islamic Law," 477.
106. Mohammad Hashim Kamali, "Human Dignity in Islam," International Institute of Advanced Islamic Studies, accessed January 26, 2016, http://www.iais.org.my/e/index.php/publications-sp-1447159098/articles/item/36-human-dignity-in-islam.html.
107. Ali, *Sexual Ethics and Islam,* 183.
108. Ibid, 3.
109. Kugle, *Homosexuality in Islam,* 208.
110. "It is not permissible to be married to a woman and her paternal or maternal aunt at the same time," Islam QA, accessed May 12, 2016, http://islamqa.info/en/147367.
111. Van Gelder, *Close Relationships,* 96.
112. Najmabadi, "Types, Acts or What?" 281.
113. "Homosexuality immoral, but not criminal: Religious leaders," The Times of India, July 4, 2009, accessed January 27, 2016, http://timesofindia.indiatimes.com/india/Homosexuality-immoral-but-not-criminal-Religious-leaders/articleshow/4736152.cms?referral=PM.
114. Ishtiaq Hussain, "The Tanzimat: Secular Reforms in the Ottoman Empire," Faith Matters, accessed January 26, 2016, http://faith-matters.org/images/stories/fm-publications/the-tanzimat-final-web.pdf.
115. Shehzad Saleem, "Response to "Trivializing Homosexuality,'" June 2006, accessed January 27, 2016, http://www.monthly-renaissance.com/issue/content.aspx?id=74.
116. Ben Hanan Rhouma, "Islam, homosexualité et homophobie, vus par Tareq Oubrou," May 29, 2010, accessed January 27, 2016, http://www.saphirnews.com/Islam-homosexualite-et-homophobie-vus-par-Tareq-Oubrou_a11544.html.
117. "Eindhoven: Imam to fight homophobia," Islam in Europe, June 24, 2009, accessed January 26, 2016, http://islamineurope.blogspot.ca/2009/06/eindhoven-imam-to-fight-homophobia.html.

118. "Tribute to Sheikh Zaki Badawi, News and Views 2006," Safra Project, January 24, 2006, accessed August, 2015, http://www.safraproject.org/newsviews06.htm.

119. "Middle East: Doors of tolerance begin to open for gay Muslims," IRIN, December 4, 2007, accessed January 26, 2016, http://www.irinnews.org/report/75673/middle-east-doors-of-tolerance-begin-to-open-for-gay-muslims.

120. Ify Okoye, "Islam & Homosexuality: Muslim Perspectives," November 26, 2008, accessed January 26, 2016, http://ifyokoye.com/2008/11/26/islam-homosexuality-muslim-perspectives/.

121. Omar Sacirbey, "With a New Imam, a New Outlook," *Boston Globe*, December 3, 2011, accessed January 27, 2016, https://www.bostonglobe.com/metro/2011/12/03/islamic-society-boston-cultural-center-introduces-william-suhaib-webb-new-imam/GcyTn4n4g9ADqIsgV089xH/story.html.

122. "When homosexuality hits home," Straight Talk.

123. Ayman Fadel, "My Journey from Homophobe to Less Bad of a Human!" Aym Playing, 2013, accessed January 26, 2016, https://aymplaying.wordpress.com/2013/02/15/my-journey-from-homophobe-to-less-bad-of-a-human/.

124. Omid Safi, "Why I support same-sex marriage: a religious argument in solidarity. What would Muhammad do?" *Religion News Service*, March 27, 2013, accessed January 27, 2016, http://omidsafi.religionnews.com/2013/03/27/why-i-support-same-sex-marriage-a-religious-argument-in-solidarity/.

125. Junaid Jahangir, "Can Pamela Geller Work With Straight and Queer Muslims?" *Huffington Post*, March 28, 2013, accessed January 26, 2016, http://www.huffingtonpost.ca/junaid-jahangir/can-pamela-geller-work-wi_b_2958190.html.

126. Pamela White, "Ending the Silence," *Boulder Weekly*, accessed August 2015, http://archive.boulderweekly.com/092905/coverstory.html.

127. Arash Naraghi, "Islam and Moral Status of Homosexuality," *Arash Naraghi, personal website,* 2005, accessed January 26, 2016, http://www.scribd.com/doc/245696236/Arash-Naraghi-Islam-and-Moral-Status-of-Homosexuality-2005#scribd.

128. El Pais Miguel Angel Medina, "For the Gay Muslim, the Closet Has Seven Keys," February 27, 2012, accessed January 26, 2016, https://en-pi.facebook.com/note.php?note_id=263343820409588.

129. Abdul Khalik, "Islam 'recognizes homosexuality.'" *The Jakarta Post*, March 28, 2008, accessed January 26, 2016, http://www.thejakartapost.com/news/2008/03/27/islam-039recognizes-homosexuality039.html.

130. "An interview about homosexuality with Sheikh Assadullah Mwale," E-Motive, July 2, 2015, Last accessed November 2015, http://emotiveprogram.org/2015/07/02/an-interview-about-homosexuality-with-sheikh-assadullah-mwale/.

131. Junaid Jahangir, "Queer Muslims Get Straight Respect," *Huffington Post*, September 15, 2012, accessed January 26, 2016, http://www.huffingtonpost.ca/junaid-jahangir/muslim-homophobia_b_1882244.html.

132. Junaid Jahangir, "Why All Muslims Are Talking About Queer Sexuality," *Huffington Post*, March 13, 2013, accessed January 26, 2016, http://www.huffington-post.ca/junaid-jahangir/queer-muslims_b_2855300.html.

133. Khalid Zaheer, "Why is woman's testimony half that of a man in the court of law?" accessed January 27, 2016, http://www.khalidzaheer.com/qa/165.

134. Rabbi Harold Schulweis, "A second look at homosexuality," Valley Beth Shalom, accessed January 27, 2016, https://www.vbs.org/worship/meet-our-clergy/rabbi-harold-schulweis/sermons/second-look-homosexuality.

135. Desmond Tutu, "Homophobia is as unjust as that crime against humanity, apartheid," *The Times*, July 1, 2004, accessed January 27, 2016, http://www.thetimes.co.uk/tto/law/columnists/article2047533.ece.

136. "Tutu chides Church for gay stance," BBC, November 18, 2007, accessed January 25, 2016, http://news.bbc.co.uk/2/hi/africa/7100295.stm.

137. Khaled Abou El-Fadl, "The Ugly Modern and the Modern Ugly," in *Progressive Muslims: On Justice, Gender, and Pluralism*, ed. Omid Safi, 33–77 (Oxford: Oneworld Publications, 2003).

138. Ṣaḥīḥ al-Bukhārī. Book of Knowledge, Number 68.

139. Ibn Taymiyya, *Majmūʿ Fatāwā,* Book of selling. Translation by authors.

Bibliography

Ābādī, Muhammad Shams al-Ḥaqq al-ʿAẓīm. *ʿAwn al-Maʿbūd fī Sharḥ Sunan Abu Dawūd*. Volume 6, 12. In الموسوعة الذهبية للحديث النبوي الشيف و علومه [*The Golden Encyclopedia of the Prophetic Golden Hadeeth and its Sciences*]. 2nd edition. London: Turath Publishing. CD-ROM.

Abd-Allah, Umar Faruq. *Islam and the Cultural Imperative*. Nawawi Foundation, 2004. Accessed January 25, 2016. http://www.nawawi.org/wp-content/uploads/2013/01/Article3.pdf.

Abdullah, Ruqaiyah. *Overcoming Trials & Tribulations according to the Qur'an and Sunnah*. Last modified August 8, 2010. Serving Islam Team. http://www.servingislamteam.com/lectures_files/1359314686overcoming%20trials%20%26%20tribulations%20.pdf.

Adang, Camilla. "Ibn Ḥazm on Homosexuality. A Case-Study of Zahiri Legal Methodology." *Al-Qantara* 24, no. 1 (2003): 5–31.

"An-Nawawi's 40 Hadith, Hadith No. 1." ahadith.co.uk. Accessed January 25, 2016. http://ahadith.co.uk/hadithwithcommentary.php?id=441&cid=11.

Aḥmad, Mirza Bashīruddin Maḥmūd. *The Holy Qur'an with English Translation and Commentary*. Volume 3. Published under the auspices of Mirza Tahir Aḥmad. U.K.: Islam International Publications Limited, 1988. Accessed January 25, 2016. http://www.alislam.org/quran/tafseer/guide.htm?region=E1.

Al-ʿAlawani, Taha Jabir. "Islam's Stance on Homosexual Organizations." *Prophetmuhammadforall.org*. Accessed January 28, 2016. http://www.prophetmuhammadforall.org/webfiles/fatwa/islamstance.pdf.

Al-Ajuree, Al-Hafith Abu Bakr Muhammad bin al-Hussain. *The Forbiddance of Homosexuality*. Translated by Mustafa George Deberry. Wilkes-Barre: Masjid At-Tawheed, 2010.

Al-Bājī, Sulaymān ibn Khalaf. *Al-Taʿdīl wa-l-Tajrīḥ li Man Kharraja ʿanhu al-Bukhārī fī al-Jāmiʿ al-Ṣaḥīḥ*. Volume 2. In الموسوعة الذهبية للحديث النبوي الشيف و علومه [*The Golden Encyclopedia of the Prophetic Golden Hadeeth and its Sciences*]. 2nd edition. London: Turath Publishing. CD-ROM.

Al-Bayḍāwī. *Anwār al-Tanzīl wa Asrār al-Ta'wīl*. Commentary on verses 7:80–82. In الموسوعة الذهبية للحديث النبوي الشيف و علومه [*The Golden Encyclopedia of the Prophetic Golden Hadeeth and its Sciences*]. 2nd edition. London: Turath Publishing. CD-ROM.

Al-Bayhaqī, Abu Bakr Aḥmad ibn Ḥusayn ibn 'Ali ibn Mūsā al-Khusrawjirdī. *Sunan al-Bayhaqī al-Kubrā*. Volume 4, 8. In الموسوعة الذهبية للحديث النبوي الشيف و علومه [*The Golden Encyclopedia of the Prophetic Golden Hadeeth and its Sciences*]. 2nd edition. London: Turath Publishing. CD-ROM.

Al-Bayhaqī, Abu Bakr Aḥmad ibn Ḥusayn ibn 'Ali ibn Mūsā al-Khusrawjirdī. *Knowledge of the Sunan and narrated stories*. Volume 6. In الموسوعة الذهبية للحديث النبوي الشيف و علومه [*The Golden Encyclopedia of the Prophetic Golden Hadeeth and its Sciences*]. 2nd edition. London: Turath Publishing. CD-ROM.

Al-Bazaar. *Musnad Ibn Abbas*. In الموسوعة الذهبية للحديث النبوي الشيف و علومه [*The Golden Encyclopedia of the Prophetic Golden Hadeeth and its Sciences*]. 2nd edition. London: Turath Publishing. CD-ROM.

Al-Dimashqī, 'Umar ibn 'Ali ibn 'Ādil. *Tafsīr Ibn 'Ādil*. Commentary on verse 23:6. In الموسوعة الذهبية للحديث النبوي الشيف و علومه [*The Golden Encyclopedia of the Prophetic Golden Hadeeth and its Sciences*]. 2nd edition. London: Turath Publishing. CD-ROM.

Al-Hawwārī, Hūd ibn al-Muḥakkam. *Tafsīr al-Hawwārī*. Commentary on verse 23:6. In الموسوعة الذهبية للحديث النبوي الشيف و علومه [*The Golden Encyclopedia of the Prophetic Golden Hadeeth and its Sciences*]. 2nd edition. London: Turath Publishing. CD-ROM.

Al-Hayyan, Moulay al-Hussain ibn. "Imitation and its effect on the efficiency of Assiduity in Islamic jurisprudence Part 1 / 2." The Message of Islam. Accessed January 25, 2016. http://islamicstudies.islammessage.com/ResearchPaper.aspx?aid=708

Al-Kashani, Abd al-Razzaq. *Tafsir Kashani*. Amman: Royal Aal al-Bayt Institute for Islamic Thought. Accessed May 10, 2016. http://altafsir.com/.

Al-Maghribī, Shams al-Dīn Abu Abdullah Muhammad ibn Muhammad ibn 'Abd al-Raḥmān al-Ṭarābulsī. *Mawāhib al-Jalīl fī Sharḥ Mukhtaṣar Khalīl*. In الموسوعة الذهبية للحديث النبوي الشيف و علومه [*The Golden Encyclopedia of the Prophetic Golden Hadeeth and its Sciences*]. 2nd edition. London: Turath Publishing. CD-ROM.

Al-Mālikī, Muhammad ibn Abdullah al-Kharshi. *Sharḥ Mukhataṣar Khalīl*. *Ḥadd* of *zinā* and its rule. In الموسوعة الذهبية للحديث النبوي الشيف و علومه [*The Golden Encyclopedia of the Prophetic Golden Hadeeth and its Sciences*]. London: Turath Publishing, 2nd edition. CD-ROM.

Al-Maqdisī, Muwaffaq al-Dīn Abdullah ibn Aḥmad ibn Qudāma. *Al-Mughnī*. The *ḥadd* of *liwāṭ*. In الموسوعة الذهبية للحديث النبوي الشيف و علومه [*The Golden Encyclopedia of the Prophetic Golden Hadeeth and its Sciences*]. 2nd edition. London: Turath Publishing. CD-ROM.

Al-Maqrīzī, Aḥmad ibn 'Ali. *Mukhtaṣar al-Kāmil fī al-Ḍu'afā'*. Volume 4. In الموسوعة الذهبية للحديث النبوي الشيف و علومه [*The Golden Encyclopedia of the Prophetic Golden Hadeeth and its Sciences*]. 2nd edition. London: Turath Publishing. CD-ROM.

Al-Mizzī, Yūsuf ibn 'Abd al-Raḥmān. *Tahdhīb al-Kamāl*, Volume 2, 4, 8, 11, 13, 14, 16, 20, 22, 27, 30, 31. In الموسوعة الذهبية للحديث النبوي الشيف و علومه [*The Golden*

Encyclopedia of the Prophetic Golden Hadeeth and its Sciences]. 2nd edition. London: Turath Publishing. CD-ROM.

Al-Muḥārib, Ruqayyah bint Muḥammad. "The Islamic Ruling on Female Secretion [Part Three]." The Message of Islam. Accessed January 25, 2016. http://islamic-studies.islammessage.com/ResearchPaper.aspx?aid=303.

Al-Nawawī. *Riyad as-Salihin (The Meadows of the Righteous)*. Translated by Ibrahim Ma'rouf. El-Mansoura: Dar Al-Manarah, 2003.

Al-Naysabūrī, al-Ḥākim. *Mustadrak*. Volume 4. In الموسوعة الذهبية للحديث النبوي الشيف و علومه [*The Golden Encyclopedia of the Prophetic Golden Hadeeth and its Sciences*]. 2nd edition. London: Turath Publishing. CD-ROM.

Al-Oadah, Sheikh Salman. "Masturbation, Sexuality." IslamToday. Accessed January 25, 2016. http://en.islamtoday.net/node/1513.

Al-Qaradawi, Yusuf. *The lawful and the prohibited in Islam*. Cairo: Al-Falah Foundation, 2005.

Al-Qaradawi, Yusuf and Muhammad Saalih al-Munajjid. "Homosexuality and Lesbianism: Sexual Perversions." Accessed January 28, 2016. http://www.prophetmuhammadforall.org/webfiles/fatwa/HomosexualityNLesbianis.pdf.

Al-Qayrawani, Abdullah ibn Abi Zayd. *The Risala-A treatise on Maliki fiqh*. Translated by Bello Mohammad Daura. London. Accessed January 25, 2016. http://www.archive.org/stream/TheRisala/TheRisala-ATreatiseOnMalikiFiqh_djvu.txt

Al-Qazwīnī, Abū Abdullah Muḥammad ibn Yazīd ibn Mājah al-Rab'ī. *Sunan Ibn Mājah*. Volume 2. In الموسوعة الذهبية للحديث النبوي الشيف و علومه [*The Golden Encyclopedia of the Prophetic Golden Hadeeth and its Sciences*]. 2nd edition. London: Turath Publishing. CD-ROM.

Al-Qurṭubī, Abu Abdullah Muhammad ibn Aḥmad ibn Abu Bakr al-Anṣārī. *Tafsīr al-Qurṭubī*. Amman: Royal Aal al-Bayt Institute for Islamic Thought. Accessed May 10, 2016. http://altafsir.com/.

Al-Rāzī, Fakhr al-Dīn Abu Abdullah Muhammad ibn Umar ibn al-Ḥusayn at-Taymī al-Bakrī at-Ṭabaristānī. *Tafsīr al-Rāzī*. Commentary on verses 2:223, 7:80–81, 24:2, 24:31. In الموسوعة الذهبية للحديث النبوي الشيف و علومه [*The Golden Encyclopedia of the Prophetic Golden Hadeeth and its Sciences*]. 2nd edition. London: Turath Publishing. CD-ROM.

Al-Rāzī, Muhammad ibn Idris ibn al-Mundhir al-Hanẓali. *Al-Jarḥ wa-l-Ta'dīl*. Volume 2–4, 9. In الموسوعة الذهبية للحديث النبوي الشيف و علومه [*The Golden Encyclopedia of the Prophetic Golden Hadeeth and its Sciences*]. 2nd edition. London: Turath Publishing. CD-ROM.

Al-Ruḥaybānī, Muṣṭafā ibn Sa'd ibn 'Abduh. *Maṭālib Ūlī al-Nuhā fī Sharḥ Ghāya al-Muntahā*; *kitāb al-ḥudūd*; *bāb al-zinā*. In الموسوعة الذهبية للحديث النبوي الشيف و علومه [*The Golden Encyclopedia of the Prophetic Golden Hadeeth and its Sciences*]. 2nd edition. London: Turath Publishing. CD-ROM.

Al-Ṣan'ānī, 'Abd ar-Razzāq. *Muṣannaf 'Abd al-Razzāq*. Volume 7, 11. In الموسوعة الذهبية للحديث النبوي الشيف و علومه [*The Golden Encyclopedia of the Prophetic Golden Hadeeth and its Sciences*]. 2nd edition. London: Turath Publishing. CD-ROM.

Al-Shāmī, Sulaymān ibn Aḥmad ibn Ayyūb al-Lakhmī. *Musnad al-Shāmiyyīn*. Volume 1, 2. In الموسوعة الذهبية للحديث النبوي الشيف و علومه [*The Golden Encyclopedia of the*

Prophetic Golden Hadeeth and its Sciences]. 2nd edition. London: Turath Publishing. CD-ROM.

Al-Shāṭibī, Ibrāhīm ibn Mūsā Abu Isḥāq. *The Reconciliation of the Fundamentals of Islamic Law*. Translated by Imran Ahsan Khan Nyazee. Reading: Garnet Pub. Ltd., 2012.

Al-Sijistānī, Abu Dāwūd Sulaymān ibn al-Ash'ath al-Azdī. *Sunan Abu Dawūd*. Chapter: rule of the *mukhannathūn*. In الموسوعة الذهبية للحديث النبوي الشيف و علومه [*The Golden Encyclopedia of the Prophetic Golden Hadeeth and its Sciences*]. 2nd edition. London: Turath Publishing. CD-ROM.

Al-Suyūṭī, Jalāl al-Dīn. *Al-Durr al-Manthūr fī al-Tafsīr bi-l-Ma'thūr*. In الموسوعة الذهبية للحديث النبوي الشيف و علومه [*The Golden Encyclopedia of the Prophetic Golden Hadeeth and its Sciences*]. 2nd edition. London: Turath Publishing. CD-ROM.

Al-Ṭabarānī. *Mu'jam Awsaṭ*. Volume 5. In الموسوعة الذهبية للحديث النبوي الشيف و علومه [*The Golden Encyclopedia of the Prophetic Golden Hadeeth and its Sciences*]. 2nd edition. London: Turath Publishing. CD-ROM.

Al-Ṭabarānī. *Musnad al-Shāmiyyīn*. In الموسوعة الذهبية للحديث النبوي الشيف و علومه [*The Golden Encyclopedia of the Prophetic Golden Hadeeth and its Sciences*]. 2nd edition. London: Turath Publishing. CD-ROM.

Al-Ṭabarī, Abu Ja'far Muhammad ibn Jarīr. *The History of al-Ṭabarī: Prophets and Patriarchs*. Translated by William Brinner. Albany: State University of New York, 1986.

Al-Ṭabarī, Abu Ja'far Muhammad ibn Jarīr. *Tafsīr Ṭabarī*. Commentary on verses 11:78, 24:31, 29:28–30. In الموسوعة الذهبية للحديث النبوي الشيف و علومه [*The Golden Encyclopedia of the Prophetic Golden Hadeeth and its Sciences*]. 2nd edition. London: Turath Publishing. CD-ROM.

Al-Ṭabrasī, *Majma' al-Bayān fī Tafsīr al-Qur'an*. Commentary on verses 7:80–82. In الموسوعة الذهبية للحديث النبوي الشيف و علومه [*The Golden Encyclopedia of the Prophetic Golden Hadeeth and its Sciences*]. 2nd edition. London: Turath Publishing. CD-ROM.

Al-Ṭabrasī, Abu Ali Fadhl ibn Ḥasan. *Tafsīr Ṭabrasī*. Commentary on verse 15:70. In الموسوعة الذهبية للحديث النبوي الشيف و علومه [*The Golden Encyclopedia of the Prophetic Golden Hadeeth and its Sciences*]. 2nd edition. London: Turath Publishing. CD-ROM.

Al-Tamīmī, Abu Muhammad al-Ḥārith ibn Muhammad ibn Dāhir. *Musnad al-Ḥārith*. Volume 2. In الموسوعة الذهبية للحديث النبوي الشيف و علومه [*The Golden Encyclopedia of the Prophetic Golden Hadeeth and its Sciences*]. 2nd edition. London: Turath Publishing. CD-ROM.

Al-Turayri, Sheikh Abd al-Wahhab. "Oral sex, Sexuality." Islam Today. Accessed January 25, 2016. http://en.islamtoday.net/node/1514.

Al-Zamakhshari. Commentary of 7:80. Amman: Royal Aal al-Bayt Institute for Islamic Thought. Accessed May 10, 2016. http://altafsir.com/.

Ali, Abdullah bin Hamid. "The Homosexual Challenge to Muslim Ethics." Lamppost Education Initiative. Accessed January 25, 2016. http://www.lamppostproductions.com/the-homosexual-challenge-to-muslim-ethics/.

Ali, Kecia. "Muslim Sexual Ethics: Same-Sex Sexual Activity and Lesbian and Bisexual Women." The Feminist Sexual Ethics Project. Brandeis University,

2002. Accessed January 25, 2016. http://www.brandeis.edu/projects/fse/muslim/same-sex.html

Ali, Kecia. "Progressive Muslims and Islamic Jurisprudence: The Necessity for Critical Engagement with Marriage and Divorce Laws." In *Progressive Muslims*, edited by Omid Safi. Oxford: Oneworld Publications, 2003.

Ali, Kecia. *Sexual Ethics and Islam: Feminist Reflections on Quran Hadith*. Oxford: Oneworld Publications, 2006.

Ali, Kecia. *Marriage and Slavery in Early Islam*. Cambridge: Harvard University Press, 2010.

Alice! Health Promotion. "Not all gay men have anal sex." Last modified June 13, 2008. http://goaskalice.columbia.edu/not-all-gay-men-have-anal-sex.

Alli, Habeeb. *Intimacy and the Sacred in Muslim Communities*. Edited by Elizabeth Rahman. Bloomington: iUinverse Inc., 2011.

Alul Bayt Foundation. "Rulings of Grand Ayatollah Sistani. Marriage." Accessed January 25, 2016. http://www.alulbayt.com/rulings/11.htm.

Amer, Sahar. "Cross Dressing and Female Same-Sex Marriage in Medieval French and Arabic Literatures." In *Islamicate Sexualities*, edited by Kathryn Babayan and Afsaneh Najmabadi, 72–113. Cambridge: Harvard University Center for Middle Eastern Studies, 2008.

Amer, Sahar. "Medieval Arab lesbians and lesbian-like women." *Journal of the History of Sexuality* 18 (2009): 215–36.

Amer, Sahar. "Naming to Empower: Lesbianism in the Arab Islamicate World Today." *Journal of Lesbian Studies* 16, no. 4 (2012): 381–397.

Amjad, Moiz. "What is the Punishment for Adultery?" Renaissance Monthly Journal. Last modified May 1, 2002. http://www.javedahmadghamidi.com/renaissance/view/what-is-the-punishment-for-adultery.

Amjad, Moiz. Understanding Islam Q&A. Accessed May 11, 2016. http://www.understanding-islam.com

Anees, Munawar Aḥmad. *Islam and Biological Futures: Ethics, Gender, and Technology*. London: Mansell, 1989.

Asad, Muhammad. *Road to Mecca*. New Delhi: Islamic Book Service, 2004. Accessed January 25, 2016. http://muhammad-asad.com/Road-to-Mecca.pdf.

Avert. "HIV, AIDS and men who have sex with men." Accessed January 25, 2016. http://www.avert.org/men-sex-men.htm.

Babayan, Kathryn. "'In spirit we ate each other's sorrow': Female Companionship in seventeenth century Safavi Iran." In *Islamicate Sexualities*, edited by Kathryn Babayan and Afsaneh Najmabadi, 239–274. Cambridge: Harvard University Center for Middle Eastern Studies, 2008.

BBC. "Tutu chides Church for gay stance." November 18, 2007. Accessed January 25, 2016. http://news.bbc.co.uk/2/hi/africa/7100295.stm.

Bell, Joseph Norment. *Love Theory in later Hanbalite Islam*. Albany: State University of New York Press, 1979.

Bereznai, Steven. *Gay and Single Forever*. New York: Marlowe & Company, 2006.

Boswell, John. *Christianity, Social Tolerance and Homosexuality*. Chicago: University of Chicago Press, 2015.

Boswell, John. "Revolutions, universals, and sexual categories." In *Hidden from history: reclaiming the gay and lesbian past,* edited by Duberman M., Vicinus M., Chauncey Jr, G. New York: Meridian, 1989. Accessed January 26, 2016. http://history.msu.edu/hst420/files/2013/03/Boswell__Revolutions__Universals__and_Se.pdf.

Bouhdiba, Abdelwahab. *Sexuality in Islam.* London: Routledge and Kegan Paul, 1985.

Bucar, Elizabeth M. and Fagheh Shirazi. "The 'Invention' of Lesbian Acts In Iran: Interpretative Moves, Hidden Assumptions, and Emerging Categories of Sexuality." *Journal of Lesbian Studies* 16, no. 4 (2012): 416–434.

Butt, Mufti Muhammad Zubair. "What is the status of one who considers homosexuality to be permissible?" Last modified May 7, 2006. http://attalib.blogspot.ca/2009/05/what-is-status-of-one-who-considers.html.

Calder, Norman. *Islamic Jurisprudence in the Classical Era*. New York: Cambridge University Press, 2010.

Corvino, John. "Homosexuality and the PIB Argument." *Ethics* 115 (April 2005): 501–534. Accessed January 26, 2016. http://johncorvino.com/academic/Corvino-PIB.pdf.

Daniel, Marc. "Arab Civilization and Male Love." Translated by Winston Leyland. In *Reclaiming Sodom*, edited by Jonathan Goldberg, 59–65. New York: Routledge, 1994.

Daryabadi, Abdul Majid. *Tafsīr-Ul-Qur'an Translation and Commentary of the Holy Qur'an*, Volume I. Pakistan: Darul-Isha'at Urdu Bazar, 1991.

Desai, Mufti Ebrahim. "Fatwa on Oral Sex." Zawaj.com. Accessed January 28, 2016. http://www.zawaj.com/articles/fatwa_oral_desai.html.

El-Fadl, Khaled Abou. "The Ugly Modern and the Modern Ugly." In *Progressive Muslims: On Justice, Gender, and Pluralism*, edited by Omid Safi, 33–77. Oxford: Oneworld Publications, 2003.

El-Fadl, Khaled Abou. *The Great Theft: Wrestling Islam from the Extremists*. San Fransisco: Harper San Fransisco, 2005.

El-Hassan, Abd el-Wahab Ahmed. "The Doctrine of Duress *(Ikrāh)* in Sharia, Sudan and English Law." *Arab Law Quarterly* 1, no. 2 (February 1986): 231–236.

El-Menyawi, Hassan. "Same-sex marriage in Islamic law." *Wake Forest Journal of Law & Policy* 2, no. 2 (2012): 375–531.

El-Rouayheb, Khaled. *Before Homosexuality in the Arab-Islamic World, 1500–1800*. Chicago: University of Chicago Press, 2005.

El-Rouayheb, Khaled. Review of Ze'evi, Dror. *Producing Desire: Changing Sexual Discourse in the Ottoman Middle East, 1500–1900 (Studies on the History of Society and Culture)*. H-Levant, H-Net Reviews. Accessed January 26, 2016. http://www.h-net.org/reviews/showrev.php?id=13235.

El-Shinqiti, Mohamed El-Moctar. "Threats to Behead Homosexuals: Shari`ah or Politics?" Islamic Research Foundation International. Accessed January 28, 2016. http://www.irfi.org/articles2/articles_2951_3000/Threats%20to%20Behead%20Homosexuals.HTM.

El-Shinqiti, Mohamed El-Moctar. "Should beheading be the penalty for homosexuals." *The Brunei Times*, June 13, 2008. Accessed January 26, 2016. http://www.bt.com.bn/friday_special/2008/06/13/should_beheading_be_the_penalty_for_homosexuals.

Emon, Anver. *Islamic Natural Law Theories*. Oxford: Oxford University Press, 2010.

E-Motive. "An interview about homosexuality with Sheikh Assadullah Mwale." July 2, 2015. Last accessed November 2015. http://emotiveprogram.org/2015/07/02/an-interview-about-homosexuality-with-sheikh-assadullah-mwale/.

European Council for Fatwa and Research. "Ruling on Buying Houses with mortgages." Islamic Mortgages. Accessed January 26, 2016. http://www.islamicmortgages.co.uk/index.php?id=259

European Council for Fatwa and Research's Resolution on "Permissibility of conventional mortgage under necessity," 1999. Accessed January 26, 2016, http://www.globalwebpost.com/farooqm/study_res/i_econ_fin/ecfr-fatwa_mortgage.htm.

Fadel, Ayman. "My Journey from Homophobe to Less Bad of a Human!" Aym Playing, 2013. Accessed January 26, 2016. https://aymplaying.wordpress.com/2013/02/15/my-journey-from-homophobe-to-less-bad-of-a-human/.

Fadel, Mohammad. "Is Historicism a Viable Strategy for Islamic Law Reform? The Case of 'Never Shall a Folk Prosper Who Have Appointed a Woman to Rule Them." *Islamic Law & Society*, 2011. Accessed January 26, 2016. http://papers.ssrn.com/sol3/papers.cfm?abstract_id=1712968.

Fadel, Mohammad. "The True, The Good and the Reasonable: The Theological and Ethical Roots of Public Reason in Islamic Law." University of Toronto Legal Studies Series. Research Paper No. 977206. 2007.

Fadlallah, Sayyed Muhammed Hussein. "Jurisprudence of Sex." *Bayynat*. Accessed January 26, 2016. http://english.bayynat.org/Jurisprudence/sex.htm.

Farooq, Mohammad Omar. "The Doctrine of Ijma': Is there a consensus?" Upper Iowa University, 2006. Accessed January 26, 2016. http://www.scribd.com/doc/45747285/The-Doctrine-of-Ijma-Is-there-a-consensus.

Frontline. *The Dancing Boys of Afghanistan*. PBS Documentary, 2010. Accessed January 26, 2016, http://www.pbs.org/wgbh/pages/frontline/dancingboys/.

Furber, Musa. "Is Oral sex permitted?" The Modern Religion. Accessed January 26, 2016. http://www.themodernreligion.com/misc/sex/sex-oral.html.

Ghamidi, Javed. "Hifz al-Furuj (Guarding the Private Parts). Translated by Shehzad Saleem." *Renaissance*. Accessed January 26, 2016. http://www.monthly-renaissance.com/issue/content.aspx?id=1242

Ghamidi, Javed. "Islamic Punishments: Some Misconceptions." *Renaissance*. September 2002. Accessed January 26, 2016. http://www.renaissance.com.pk/septrefl22y2.html.

Ghilan, Mohamed. "LGBTQIA Islam?" February 1, 2013. Accessed January 26, 2016, http://mohamedghilan.com/2013/02/01/lgbtqia-islam-2/.

Ghilan, Mohamed. "Islam, Homosexuality & Same-sex marriage." Last modified May 6, 2013. Accessed January 26, 2016. http://mohamedghilan.com/2013/05/06/religion-homosexuality-same-sex-marriage/.

Gilani, Aziz. "Homosexuality in Islam." Texas Islam, October 10, 2012. Accessed January 26, 2016. http://www.texasislam.com/2012/10/homosexuality-in-islam.html.

Global Health Council. "HIV/AIDS At risk groups – other groups." [n.d]. Accessed January 26, 2016, http://web.archive.org/web/20110728031548/http://www.globalhealth.org/hiv_aids/risk_groups2/.

Gusau, Murtada. "The Dangers of Homosexuality and Lesbianism in Islam." *Premium Times*, December 18, 2015. Accessed May 11, 2016. http://blogs.premiumtimesng.com/2015/12/18/the-dangers-of-homosexuality-and-lesbianism-in-islam-by-murtada-gusau/.

Habib, Samar. *Arabo-Islamic Texts on Female Homosexuality, 850 - 1780 A.D.* New York: Teneo Press, 2009.

Habib, Samar. *Female Homosexuality in the Middle East: Histories and Representations*. New York and London: Routledge, 2009.

Haddad, Gibril F. "Oral Sex, Questions on Sexuality." Living Islam. Accessed January 26, 2016. http://www.abc.se/~m9783/fiqhi/fiqha_e92.html.

Hadith Explanation. "The Insolent." Accessed December 2014. http://dailyhadith.adaptivesolutionsinc.com/hadith/The-Insolent.htm.

Hallaq, Wael. *A History of Islamic Legal Theories: An Introduction to Sunni Usul Al Fiqh*. Cambridge: Cambridge University Press, 1999.

Haq Cha Yar. Accessed January 25, 2016, http://islamic-forum.net/index.php?showtopic=1496.

Hartford, Hedaya. *Initiating and Upholding an Islamic Marriage*. Damascus and Beirut: Dar al-Fikr, 2000.

Hasan, Abdullah. "Unnatural Offences: The Controversy." 2008. Accessed October 2012. http://maqasid.wordpress.com/2008/07/30/unnatural-offences-the-controversy/.

Hashmi, Tariq Mahmood. "Paying interest on buying apartments," Query response. Studying Islam. An Affiliate of The Al Mawrid Institute of Islamic Sciences. March 9, 2005. Accessed January 26, 2016. http://www.studying-islam.org/querytext.aspx?id=283.

Hashmi, Tariq Mahmood. "The dilemma of natural left handers," Query response. Studying Islam. An Affiliate of The Al Mawrid Institute of Islamic Sciences. October 31, 2005. Accessed January 26, 2016. http://www.studying-islam.org/showcounterqa.aspx?id=133.

Hazri, Tengku Aḥmad. "Whither 'Homosexual Rights'?" *Islam and Civilizational Renewal* 3, no. 3 (April 2012): 543–546.

Holtzman, Livnat. "Human Choice, Divine Guidance and the *Fitra* Tradition- The Use of Hadith in Theological Treatises by Ibn Taymiyya and Ibn Qayyim al-Jawziyya." In: *Ibn Taymiyya and His Times,* edited by Y. Rapoport and S. Ahmed, 163–188. Karachi: Oxford University Press, 2010.

Hourani, George F. *Islamic Rationalism: The Ethics of Abd Al Jabbar*. Oxford: Clarendon Press, 1971.

Hussain, Ishtiaq. "The Tanzimat: Secular Reforms in the Ottoman Empire." Faith Matters. Accessed January 26, 2016. http://faith-matters.org/images/stories/fm-publications/the-tanzimat-final-web.pdf.

Husni, Ronak and Daniel L. Newman. *Muslim Women in Law and Society*. London and New York: Routledge, 2007.

Ibn Abbas. Commentary of 4:15-16. Amman: Royal Aal al-Bayt Institute for Islamic Thought. Accessed May 10, 2016. http://altafsir.com/.

Ibn ʿAbd al-Barr. *Al-Istidhkār fī Sharḥ Madhāhib ʿUlamāʾ al-Amṣār*. Volume 7. In الموسوعة الذهبية للحديث النبوي الشيف و علومه [*The Golden Encyclopedia of the Prophetic*

Golden Hadeeth and its Sciences]. 2nd edition. London: Turath Publishing. CD-ROM.

Ibn ʿAbd al-Barr. *Al-Tamhīd li Mā fī al-Muwaṭṭaʾ min al-Maʿānī wa-l-Asānīd*. Volume 5, 22. In الموسوعة الذهبية للحديث النبوي الشيف و علومه [*The Golden Encyclopedia of the Prophetic Golden Hadeeth and its Sciences*]. 2nd edition. London: Turath Publishing. CD-ROM.

Ibn Adam, Muhammad. "Nikaah, Zina, Fornication: it is overlooked by Allah?" Central-Mosque.com. Accessed January 26, 2016. http://www.central-mosque.com/index.php/Relationships/fornication-adultery-masturbation-a-pornography.html.

Ibn Ameen, Shaykh Muhammad. "The Islamic Ruling on masturbation." Accessed January 26, 2016. http://www.ibnamin.com/masturbation_en.htm.

Ibn Ḥajar al-ʿAsqalānī. *Fatḥ al-Bārī*. Volume 12. In الموسوعة الذهبية للحديث النبوي الشيف و علومه [*The Golden Encyclopedia of the Prophetic Golden Hadeeth and its Sciences*]. 2nd edition. London: Turath Publishing. CD-ROM.

Ibn Ḥajar al-ʿAsqalānī. *Tahdhīb al-Tahdhīb*. Volume 8. In الموسوعة الذهبية للحديث النبوي الشيف و علومه [*The Golden Encyclopedia of the Prophetic Golden Hadeeth and its Sciences*]. 2nd edition. London: Turath Publishing. CD-ROM.

Ibn Ḥajar al-ʿAsqalānī. *Talkhīṣ al-Ḥabīr*. Volume 3, 4, Book of Nikāḥ, Chapter that addresses anal intercourse. In الموسوعة الذهبية للحديث النبوي الشيف و علومه [*The Golden Encyclopedia of the Prophetic Golden Hadeeth and its Sciences*]. 2nd edition. London: Turath Publishing. CD-ROM.

Ibn Ḥanbal. *Musnad Aḥmad*. Musnad Abu Hurayra, Musnad Abdullah Ibn ʿUmar. In الموسوعة الذهبية للحديث النبوي الشيف و علومه [*The Golden Encyclopedia of the Prophetic Golden Hadeeth and its Sciences*]. 2nd edition. London: Turath Publishing. CD-ROM.

Ibn Ḥazm. *Al-Muḥallā bi-l-Āthār: kitāb mā lā ḥadd fīh*: The question of the doing of the people of Lūṭ. In الموسوعة الذهبية للحديث النبوي الشيف و علومه [*The Golden Encyclopedia of the Prophetic Golden Hadeeth and its Sciences*]. 2nd edition. London: Turath Publishing. CD-ROM.

Ibn Ḥazm, ʿAli al-Andulusī. *Ṭawq al-Ḥamāma fī al-ulfa wa-l-Allāf*. Damascus: Maktaba ʿArafa. 1349 A.H./1929-30 C.E.

Ibn Ḥibbān, Muhammad. *Al-Majrūḥīn*. Volume 2. In الموسوعة الذهبية للحديث النبوي الشيف و علومه [*The Golden Encyclopedia of the Prophetic Golden Hadeeth and its Sciences*]. 2nd edition. London: Turath Publishing. CD-ROM.

Ibn Jumuʿa, ʿAbd ʿAli. *Tafsīr Nūr al-Thaqalayn*. Qom: Intisharat Ismailiyan, 1415 AH/1994.

Ibn Kathīr. *The History of Ibn Kathir – Bidaya and Nihaya*. Translated by Abul Fida Imad uddin Ibn Kathir Damishqi. Karachi: Nafees Academy Urdu Bazaar, 1988.

Ibn Kathīr, Abū l-Fidāʾ Ismāʿīl ibn ʿUmar. *Tafsīr Ibn Kathīr*. Commentary on verses 23:6, 29:33. In الموسوعة الذهبية للحديث النبوي الشيف و علومه [*The Golden Encyclopedia of the Prophetic Golden Hadeeth and its Sciences*]. 2nd edition. London: Turath Publishing. CD-ROM.

Ibn Manẓūr. *Lisān al-ʿArab*. Volume 7. In الموسوعة الذهبية للحديث النبوي الشيف و علومه [*The Golden Encyclopedia of the Prophetic Golden Hadeeth and its Sciences*]. 2nd edition. London: Turath Publishing. CD-ROM.

Ibn Mūsā al-ʿAqīlī, Abu Jaʿfar Muhammad ibn ʿAmr. *Kitāb al-Ḍuʿafāʾ al-Kabīr.* Volume 3. In الموسوعة الذهبية للحديث النبوي الشيف و علومه [*The Golden Encyclopedia of the Prophetic Golden Hadeeth and its Sciences*]. 2nd edition. London: Turath Publishing. CD-ROM.

Ibn al-Qayyim. *Al-Jawāb al-Kāfī li Man Saʾala ʿan al-Dawāʾ al-Shāfī.* In الموسوعة الذهبية للحديث النبوي الشيف و علومه [*The Golden Encyclopedia of the Prophetic Golden Hadeeth and its Sciences*]. 2nd edition. London: Turath Publishing. CD-ROM.

Ibn Qutayba, Abū Muḥammad ʿAbd-Allāh b. Muslim. *Kitāb al-Ashriba wa Dhikr Ikhtilāf al-Nās fīhā*, edited by Yāsīn Muḥammad al-Sawwās. Beirut, Damascus: Dār al-Fikr, 1999.

Ibn Ṣāliḥ Iṭmayyish, Muhammad ibn Yūsuf ibn ʿĪsā. *Hamayān al-Zād ilā Dār al-Mīʿād.* Commentary on verse 23:6. In الموسوعة الذهبية للحديث النبوي الشيف و علومه [*The Golden Encyclopedia of the Prophetic Golden Hadeeth and its Sciences*]. 2nd edition. London: Turath Publishing. CD-ROM.

Ibn Taymiyya, Aḥmad ibn ʿAbd al-Ḥalīm. *Majmūʿ Fatāwā.* Tadmuri letter: statement of Imam Aḥmad; The Chapter of Waqf: The Chapter of Changing the *hady* and *uḍḥiya;* Book of selling. In الموسوعة الذهبية للحديث النبوي الشيف و علومه [*The Golden Encyclopedia of the Prophetic Golden Hadeeth and its Sciences*]. 2nd edition. London: Turath Publishing. CD-ROM.

Ibn Taymiyya, Aḥmad ibn ʿAbd al-Ḥalīm. *Tafsīr Sūra Āl ʿImrān*, Tafsīr of do not make what is permitted prohibited; *Tafsīr Sūra Āl ʿImrān,* Tafsīr on the people of desire wish that you tilt. In الموسوعة الذهبية للحديث النبوي الشيف و علومه [*The Golden Encyclopedia of the Prophetic Golden Hadeeth and its Sciences*]. 2nd edition. London: Turath Publishing. CD-ROM.

Ibn Taymiyya, Aḥmad ibn ʿAbd al-Ḥalīm. *Al-Istiqāma*; MF 11:543; 28:335. In الموسوعة الذهبية للحديث النبوي الشيف و علومه [*The Golden Encyclopedia of the Prophetic Golden Hadeeth and its Sciences*]. 2nd edition. London: Turath Publishing. CD-ROM.

Ibn ʿUthmān, Abu Bakr ibn Abi Shayba Abdullah ibn Muhammad ibn Ibrāhīm. *Muṣannaf Ibn Abi Shayba.* Vol. 5. In الموسوعة الذهبية للحديث النبوي الشيف و علومه [*The Golden Encyclopedia of the Prophetic Golden Hadeeth and its Sciences*]. 2nd edition. London: Turath Publishing. CD-ROM.

Imani, Ayatollah Sayyid Kamal Faghih et al. *An Enlightening Commentary into the Light of the Holy Qur'an, Parts 7 & 8.* Translated by Sayyid ʿAbbās Sadr Ameli. Isfahan, Iran: Amir ul Mumineen Ali Library, 2005.

Imber, Colin. "Why you should poison your husband: A note on liability in Hanafi law in the Ottoman period." *Islamic Law and Society* 1, no. 2 (1994): 206–216.

IRIN. "Middle East: Doors of tolerance begin to open for gay Muslims." December 4, 2007. Accessed January 26, 2016. http://www.irinnews.org/report/75673/middle-east-doors-of-tolerance-begin-to-open-for-gay-muslims.

Isik, Huseyn Hilmi. "Ikrah—Intimidation, Duress and Hijr-forbidding." In *Seadet i Ebediyye - Endless Bliss*, 1st edition, Hakikat Kitabevi Publications No: 6. Accessed January 26, 2016, http://imanveislam.com/kitaplar/english/read/endless6/017.htm.

Isik, Huseyn Hilmi. "Uqubat—Penal Code." In *Seadet i Ebediyye - Endless Bliss*, 1st edition. Hakikat Kitabevi Publications No: 6. Accessed January 26, 2016, http://imanveislam.com/kitaplar/english/read/endless6/013.htm.

Islam Awareness. "May a Human Marry a Jinni?" Accessed January 26, 2016. http://www.islamawareness.net/Jinn/fatwa_marry.html.

Islam Awareness. "'What is the fatwa on masturbation in Islam?' Islamic Ruling on Masturbation." 2002. Accessed January 26, 2016. http://www.islamawareness.net/Sex/fatwa_sex_003.html.

Islamic Awakening. Accessed August, 2015, http://forums.islamicawakening.com.

Islam in Europe. "Eindhoven: Imam to fight homophobia." June 24, 2009. Accessed January 26, 2016. http://islamineurope.blogspot.ca/2009/06/eindhoven-imam-to-fight-homophobia.html.

IslamOnline Fatwa Committee. "Islamic Ruling on Anal Sex. Reprinted from IslamOnline's Fatwa Bank." Accessed January 26, 2016. http://www.zawaj.com/articles/ruling_anl_sx.html.

Islam QA. Accessed January 25, 2016. http://islamqa.info.

Islam QA. Accessed May 11, 2016. http://islamqa.org/hanafi/darulifta-deoband/27772.

Islam Quest. What is the Islamic law regarding anal intercourse? Is there any objece tion in it? Question Archive. Accessed January 26, 2016, http://www.islamquest.net/en/archive/question/fa1075.

Islamweb. "Fatwa #: 86457, Anal sex strictly forbidden." Accessed January 26, 2016. http://www.islamweb.net/emainpage/index.php?page=showfatwa&Option=FatwaId&Id=86457.

Jackson, Sherman. "Islam: Between Old Fundamentalism, New Fundamentalism and Modern Sincerity." American Learning Institute for Muslims. April 18, 2013. Accessed January 26, 2016. http://www.alimprogram.org/articles/islam-between-old-fundamentalism-new-fundamentalism-and-modern-sincerity/.

Jahangir, Junaid. "Queer Muslims Get Straight Respect." *Huffington Post*. September 15, 2012. Accessed January 26, 2016. http://www.huffingtonpost.ca/junaid-jahangir/muslim-homophobia_b_1882244.html.

Jahangir, Junaid. "Why All Muslims Are Talking About Queer Sexuality." *Huffington Post*. March 13, 2013. Accessed January 26, 2016. http://www.huffingtonpost.ca/junaid-jahangir/queer-muslims_b_2855300.html.

Jahangir, Junaid. "Can Pamela Geller Work With Straight and Queer Muslims?" *Huffington Post*. March 28, 2013. Accessed January 26, 2016. http://www.huffingtonpost.ca/junaid-jahangir/can-pamela-geller-work-wi_b_2958190.html.

Juferi, Mohd Elfie Nieshaem. "The Consensus on Homosexuality and The Illiteracy of Christian Polemicists." *Bismika Allahuma*. September 18, 2007. Accessed January 26, 2016. http://www.bismikaallahuma.org/archives/2007/the-consensus-on-homosexuality-and-the-illiteracy-of-christian-polemicists/.

Kamali, Mohammad Hashim. *Freedom of Expression in Islam*. Cambridge: The Islamic Texts Society, 1997.

Kamali, Mohammad Hashim. *Principles of Islamic Jurisprudence*, 3rd edition. Cambridge: The Islamic Texts Society, 2005.

Kamali, Mohammad Hashim. "Legal maxims and other genres of literature in Islamic jurisprudence." *Arab Law Quarterly* 20, no. 1 (2006): 77–101.

Kamali, Mohammad Hashim. "The Sharia, Law as the Way of God." In *Voices of Islam (5 vols.), Vol I: Voices of Tradition*, edited Vincent J. Cornell, 149–183. Wesport, CT: Praeger Publishers, 2007.

Kamali, Mohammad Hashim. "Transgenders and justice in Islam." *New Straits Times*. November 24, 2011. Accessed January 26, 2016. http://www.hashimkamali.com/index.php/publications/item/23-transgenders-and-justice-in-islam.

Kamali, Mohammad Hashim. "Human Dignity in Islam." International Institute of Advanced Islamic Studies. Accessed January 26, 2016. http://www.iais.org.my/e/index.php/publications-sp-1447159098/articles/item/36-human-dignity-in-islam.html.

Kamali, Mohammad Hashim. "Istihsan and the Renewal of Islamic law." International Institute of Advanced Islamic Studies. Accessed January 26, 2016, http://www.iais.org.my/e/index.php/publications-sp-1447159098/articles/item/16-istihsan-and-the-renewal-of-islamic-law.html.

Karamali, Hamza. Islam QA. Accessed May 12, 2016, http://islamqa.org/shafii/qibla-shafii/33827.

Kasem, Abul. *Sex and Sexuality in Islam, Part 6,* November 2005. Accessed January 26, 2016, http://www.islam-watch.org/abulkasem/SexInIslam/sex_and_sexuality_in_islam6.htm.

Khalik, Abdul. "Islam 'recognizes homosexuality.'" *The Jakarta Post*. March 28, 2008. Accessed January 26, 2016. http://www.thejakartapost.com/news/2008/03/27/islam-039recognizes-homosexuality039.html.

Kidwai, Saleem and Ruth Vanita. *Same Sex love in India*. New York: Palgrave McMillan, 2001.

Knappert, Jan. *Islamic Legends: Histories of the Heroes, Saints, and Prophets of Islam*. Leiden: E.J. Brill., 1985.

Knight, Michael Muhammad. "Queering the Qur'an." *Vice*. November 13, 2012. Accessed January 26, 2016. http://www.vice.com/en_ca/read/queering-the-quran.

Kolasinski, Adam. "The Secular case against gay marriage," *The Tech: Online Edition* 124, no. 5 (2004) Accessed January 26, 2016. http://tech.mit.edu/V124/N5/kolasinski.5c.html.

Kugle, Scott Siraj al-Haqq. "Sexuality, Diversity and Ethics in the Agenda of Progressive Muslims." In *Progressive Muslims*, edited by Omid Safi, 190–234. Oxford: Oneworld Publications, 2003.

Kugle, Scott Siraj al-Haqq. *Homosexuality in Islam: Islamic Reflection on Gay, Lesbian, and Transgender Muslims*. Oxford: Oneworld Publications, 2010.

Kutty, Shaikh Aḥmad. Ask the Scholar. Accessed January 26, 2016. http://www.askthescholar.com/question-details.aspx?qstID=1700.

Kutty, Sheikh Aḥmad. "Fatwa on Oral Sex." September 29, 2003. Accessed January 28, 2016. https://8lan.wordpress.com/2011/01/24/fatwa-on-oral-sex/.

Kutty, Aḥmad. "How to give up homosexuality." January 24, 2015. Accessed January 28, 2016. http://www.prophetmuhammadforall.org/webfiles/fatwa/homosexuality1.pdf.

Kuwaiti Encyclopedia of Fiqh, Entry: *khunthā mushkil*. In الموسوعة الذهبية للحديث النبوي الشيف و علومه [*The Golden Encyclopedia of the Prophetic Golden Hadeeth and its Sciences*]. 2nd edition. London: Turath Publishing. CD-ROM.

Labi, Nadya. "The Kingdom in the closet." *The Atlantic Magazine*. May 2007. Accessed January 26, 2016. http://www.theatlantic.com/magazine/archive/2007/05/the-kingdom-in-the-closet/5774/.

Lagrange, Frederic. "The Obscenity of the Vizier." In *Islamicate Sexualities*, edited by Kathryn Babayan and Afsaneh Najmabadi, 161–203. Cambridge: Harvard University Center for Middle Eastern Studies, 2008.

Lakdawala, M. Hanif. "Muslim Intellectual Inertia and Ijtehad." *Islamic Voice* 13, no. 2 (February 1999): 146. Accessed January 28, 2016. http://www.irfi.org/articles3/articles_4601_4700/muslim%20intellectual%20inertia%20and%20ijtehadhtml.htm.

Lane, Edward William. *Arabic-English Lexicon*. Beirut: Librairie Du Liban, 1968.

Lange, Christian. *Justice, Punishment and the Medieval Muslim Imagination*. Cambridge: Cambridge University Press, 2008.

Liberated Christians. "Serious Study Of Leviticus: Has Nothing to do with today's homosexuality." Accessed January 26, 2016. http://www.libchrist.com/other/homosexual/leviticus.html.

Maghen, Ze'ev. *Virtues of the flesh – passion and purity in early Islamic jurisprudence*. Leiden: Brill, 2005.

Maqsood, Ruqayyah Waris. *The Muslim Marriage Guide*. New Delhi: Goodword Books, 2005.

March, Andrew F. "Taking People as They Are: Islam as a 'Realistic Utopia' in the Political Theory of Sayyid Qutb." *American Political Science Review* 104, no. 1 (February 2010): 189–207.

March, Andrew F. "The Uses of Fitra (Human Nature) in the Legal and Political Theory of 'Allal Al-Fasi: Natural Law or 'Taking People as They Are'?" Yale Law School, Public Law Working Paper No. 190. 2009. New title: "Naturalizing *Sharī'a*: Foundationalist Ambiguities in Modern Islamic Apologetics, Islamic Law and Society" 22 (2015) 1–37. Accessed January 26, 2016, http://papers.ssrn.com/sol3/papers.cfm?abstract_id=1500009.

Mussi, Margherita. *Earliest Italy: An Overview of the Italian Paleolithic and Mesolithic*. NewYork: Kluwer Academic/ Plenum Publisher, 2001.

Maroc. NL Community. Accessed January 27, 2016. http://www.maroc.nl/forums.html

Masud, Muhammad Khalid. *Shatibi's Philosophy of Islamic Law*. Delhi: Adam Publishers and Distributors, 1997.

Maududi, Syed Abul A'ala. *Towards Understanding the Qur'an*. Translated by Zafar Ishaq Ansari. Leicester: The Islamic Foundation, 2006. Accessed January 26, 2016. http://www.tafheem.net/main800.html.

Miguel Angel Medina, El Pais. "For the Gay Muslim, the Closet Has Seven Keys." February 27, 2012. Accessed January 26, 2016. https://en-pi.facebook.com/note.php?note_id=263343820409588.

Miller, James. *The passion of Michel Foucault*. New York: Simon and Schuster, 1993.

Mission Islam. "Islam and Homosexuality." Accessed January 26, 2016. http://www.missionislam.com/knowledge/homosexuality.htm.

Moawad, Sarah. "On Same-sex marriage, What Islamic Law says about the issues." Islawmix. Accessed February, 2014. http://islawmix.org/election2012/samesex.html.

Mohammed, Dr. Sherif. "On Marriage in Islam." Jannah Organization. Accessed January 26, 2016. http://www.jannah.org/sisters/marr.html.

Murad, Abdal Hakim. "Bayan – a clarification." May 5, 2013. Accessed January 26, 2016. http://www.masud.co.uk/ISLAM/ahm/bayan.htm.

Muslehuddin, Mohammad. *Islamic Jurisprudence and the Rule of Necessity and Need*. New Delhi: Kitab Bhavan, 1982.

Nagamia, Husain F. and Nasir Puyan. "Abū Zayd Ḥunayn ibn Isḥāq al-'Ibādī: a physician translator par excellence." *Journal of Islamic Medical Association of North America* 40 (2008): 9–14. Accessed January 26, 2016, http://dx.doi.org/10.5915/40–1-5279. _

Najmabadi, Afsaneh. "Types, Acts or What? Regulation of sexuality in nineteenth century Iran." In *Islamicate Sexualities*, edited by Kathryn Babayan and Afsaneh Najmabadi, 275–296. Cambridge: Harvard University Center for Middle Eastern Studies, 2008.

Naraghi, Arash. "Islam and Moral Status of Homosexuality." *Arash Naraghi, personal website*. 2005. Accessed January 26, 2016. http://www.scribd.com/doc/245696236/Arash-Naraghi-Islam-and-Moral-Status-of-Homosexuality-2005#scribd.

NARTH. "Truth wins out." Accessed January 27, 2016. http://www.truthwinsout.org/narth/.

Nathan, Bassem. "Medieval Arabic medical views on male homosexuality." *Journal of Homosexuality* 26 (1994): 37–39.

Neill, James. *The Origins and Role of Same-Sex Relations in Human Societies*. Jefferson, NC: McFarland, 2011.

Ngah, Anisah Che. "The Position of Informed Consent under Islamic Law." *The International Medical Journal of Malaysia* 4, no. 1 (June 2005). http://www.eimjm.com/Vol4-No1/Vol4-No1-H1.htm.

Nicolosi, Joseph and Linda Ames Nicolosi. *A Parent's Guide to Preventing Homosexuality*. Downers Grove, IL: InterVarsity Press.

O'Farrell, Clare. "Identity." *Michel Foucault*. London: SAGE Publications, 2005.

Okoye, Ify. "Islam & Homosexuality: Muslim Perspectives." November 26, 2008. Accessed January 26, 2016. http://ifyokoye.com/2008/11/26/islam-homosexuality-muslim-perspectives/.

Omar, Sara. "From Semantics to Normative Law: Perceptions of *Liwāṭ* (Sodomy) and *Siḥāq* (Tribadism) in Islamic Jurisprudence (8th – 15th century CE)." *Islamic Law and Society* 19 (2012): 222–256.

Pellat, Charles. "*Liwāṭ*". *The Encyclopedia of Islam*, Vol. 5. Edited by C. E. Bosworth, E. Van Donzel, B. Lewis and Ch. Pellat, 776–779. Leiden: E.J. Brill, 1983.

Peterson, Jakob Skovgaard. "Sex change in Cairo: Gender and Islamic law." *The Journal of the International Institute* 2, no. 3 (Spring 1995). Accessed January 27, 2016. http://quod.lib.umich.edu/cgi/t/text/text-idx?c=jii;view=text;rgn=main;idno=4750978.0002.302.

Philips, Bilal. "Islam's Position on Homosexuality." *Islamweb*. Accessed January 27, 2016. http://www.islamweb.net/en/article/135433/.

Qadhi, Yasir. "Dealing With Homosexual Urges: Yasir Qadhi to Muslim Student, Sex and the Ummah." *Muslim Matters*. April 13, 2009. Accessed January 27, 2016. http://muslimmatters.org/2009/04/13/dealing-with-homosexual-urges/.

Qarashi, Muhammad Bāqir. "Combating Sexual Deviation." *Imam Reza Network*. Accessed January 27, 2016. http://www.imamreza.net/eng/imamreza.php?id=3145.

Questions on Islam. "Is it permissible for a person who is biologically and physiologically a man or a woman to have an operation and be equipped with some of the features and organs of the opposite sex just because he/she feels as a member of the opposite sex?" December 7, 2010. Accessed January 27, 2016. http://www.questionsonislam.com/question/it-permissible-person-who-biologically-and-physiologically-man-or-woman-have-operation-and-

Quran Tafsir Ibn Kathir. Accessed January 26, 2016. http://www.qtafsir.com.

Qur'anic Path. Accessed May 11, 2016. http://www.quranicpath.com/misconceptions/anal_sex.html.

Rahman, Mushfiqur. "Islamic Perspectives on Trials and Tribulations." 2004. Accessed January 27, 2016, https://groups.yahoo.com/neo/groups/InterfaithDialogueCenter/conversations/topics/20471.

Ramadan, Hisham M. *Understanding Islamic Law: From Classical to Contemporary*. Lanham, MD: AltaMira Press, 2006.

Ramadan, Tariq. "Islam and Homosexuality." May 29, 2009. Accessed January 27, 2016. http://tariqramadan.com/english/2009/05/29/islam-and-homosexuality/.

Ramadan, Tariq. *Radical Reform: Islamic Ethics and Liberation*. New York: Oxford University Press, 2008.

Reilly, Robert R. "What Would the Greeks Have Thought of Gay Marriage?" *Catholic Exchange*. March 11, 2013. Accessed January 27, 2016. http://catholicexchange.com/what-would-the-greeks-have-thought-of-gay-marriage.

Reinhart, A. Kevin. *Before Revelation: The Boundaries of Muslim Moral Thought*. Albany: State University of New York Press, 1995.

Reznick, Rabbi Leibel. "Does archeological data support the Biblical story? Biblical Archeology: Sodom and Gomorrah, Science and Medicine." Aish.com. April 5, 2008. Accessed January 27, 2016. http://www.aish.com/ci/sam/48931527.html.

Rhouma, Ben Hanan. "Islam, homosexualité et homophobie, vus par Tareq Oubrou." May 29, 2010. Accessed January 27, 2016. http://www.saphirnews.com/Islam-homosexualite-et-homophobie-vus-par-Tareq-Oubrou_a11544.html.

Rispler-Chaim, Vardit. *Disability in Islamic Law*. Dordrecht, The Netherlands: Springer, 2006.

Rizvi, Sayyid Muhammad. *Marriage and Morals in Islam*. Ahlul Bayt Digital Islamic Library Project, Ontario, Canada. Accessed January 27, 2016. http://www.al-islam.org/marriage-and-morals-islam-sayyid-muhammad-rizvi/chapter-three-islamic-sexual-morality-2-its#c-marriage.

Romig, Rollo. "Where Islam meets America." *The New Yorker*. May 22, 2013. Accessed January 27, 2016. http://www.newyorker.com/online/blogs/books/2013/05/where-islam-meet-america.html.

Roscoe, Will and Stephen O. Murray. *Islamic Homosexualities*. New York: New York University Press, 1997.

Rose, Christopher Scott. "Owned by the Right Hand: The Theory and Practice of Slavery in Islamic Society." M.A. Thesis, University of Texas at Austin, 2000. Accessed January 27, 2016. http://www.academia.edu/354364/

Owned_by_the_Right_Hand_The_Theory_and_Practice_of_Slavery_in_Islamic_Societies.

Rosenthal, Franz. "Ar-Râzî on the hidden illness." *Bulletin of the History of Medicine* 52 (1978): 45–60. Accessed January 27, 2016, http://williamapercy.com/wiki/images/Ar-Razi_on_the_Hidden_Illness.pdf.

Rowson, Everett K. "Homoerotic Liaisons among the Mamluk elite in late medieval Egypt and Syria." In *Islamicate Sexualities*, edited by K. Babayan and A. Najmabadi, 204–238. Cambridge: Harvard University Press, 2008.

Rowson, Everett K. "Homosexuality In Islamic law." *Encyclopaedia Iranica*. Last modified March 23, 2012. Accessed January 27, 2016. http://www.iranicaonline.org/articles/homosexuality-ii.

Rowson, Everett K. "The categorization of gender and sexual irregularity in medieval Arabic vice lists." In *Body Guards: The Cultural Politics of Gender Ambiguity*, edited by Julia Epstein and Kristina Straub, 50–79. New York: Routledge, 1991.

Rowson, Everett K. "The Effeminates of Early Medina." *Journal of the American Oriental Society* 111, no. 4 (1991): 671–693.

Sacirbey, Omar. "With a New Imam, a New Outlook." *Boston Globe*. December 3, 2011. Accessed January 27, 2016. https://www.bostonglobe.com/metro/2011/12/03/islamic-society-boston-cultural-center-introduces-william-suhaib-webb-new-imam/GcyTn4n4g9ADqIsgV089xH/story.html.

Saeed, Muhammed. "Fatwa on Oral Sex." Dec 13, 2003. Accessed January 28, 2016. https://8lan.wordpress.com/2011/01/24/fatwa-on-oral-sex/.

Safi, Omid. "Why I support same-sex marriage: a religious argument in solidarity. What would Muhammad do?" *Religion News Service*. March 27, 2013. Accessed January 27, 2016. http://omidsafi.religionnews.com/2013/03/27/why-i-support-same-sex-marriage-a-religious-argument-in-solidarity/.

Safra Project. "Tribute to Sheikh Zaki Badawi, News and Views 2006." January 24, 2006. Accessed August, 2015. http://www.safraproject.org/newsviews06.htm.

Ṣaḥīḥ al-Bukhārī. In الموسوعة الذهبية للحديث النبوي الشيف و علومه [*The Golden Encyclopedia of the Prophetic Golden Hadeeth and its Sciences*]. 2nd edition. London: Turath Publishing. CD-ROM.

Ṣaḥīḥ Muslim. Vol. 4. In الموسوعة الذهبية للحديث النبوي الشيف و علومه [*The Golden Encyclopedia of the Prophetic Golden Hadeeth and its Sciences*]. 2nd edition. London: Turath Publishing. CD-ROM.

Saleem, Shehzad. "Separating from an unattractive fiancé." Query Response. *Renaissance.*, September, 2001. Accessed January 27, 2016. http://www.monthly-renaissance.com/issue/query.aspx?id=491.

Saleem, Shehzad. "'Refusing sex to the husband,' Islam and Women: Misconceptions and Misperceptions." *Renaissance*. February 2005. Accessed January 27, 2016. http://www.monthly-renaissance.com/issue/content.aspx?id=154.

Saleem, Shehzad. "Response to ''Trivializing Homosexuality.'" June 2006. Accessed January 27, 2016. http://www.monthly-renaissance.com/issue/content.aspx?id=74.

Sanders, Paula. "Gendering the Ungendered Body: Hermaphrodites in Medieval Islamic Law." In *Women in Middle Eastern History*, edited by Nikki Keddie and Beth Baron. New Haven and London: Yale University Press, 1991.

Saqr, Sheikh `Atiyyah. "A Guide to Controlling One's Sexual Desire." Onislam. December 21, 2014. Accessed January 28, 2016. http://onislam.orkiservers.com/english/ask-the-scholar/morals-and-manners/morals-and-values/174577-a-guide-to-controlling-ones-sexual-desire.html.

Sauda, Muallimah. "Can Humans Marry Jinn?" Madrasah Ummul Hasanaat. August 10, 2012. Accessed January 27, 2016. http://www.ummulhasanaat.co.za/can-humans-marry-jinn.

Savage, Dan. "Incestathon." August 1, 2002. Accessed January 27, 2016. http://www.thestranger.com/seattle/SavageLove?oid=11500.

Schmitt, Arno and Jehoeda Sofer. *Sexuality and Eroticism among Males in Moslem Societies*. New York: The Haworth Press, 1992.

Schmitt, Arno. "LIWĀṬ im Fiqh Mannliche Homosexualitat." *Journal of Arabic and Islamic Studies* 4, no. 3 (2001–2002): 49–110.

Schulweis, Rabbi Harold. "A second look at homosexuality." Valley Beth Shalom. Accessed January 27, 2016. https://www.vbs.org/worship/meet-our-clergy/rabbi-harold-schulweis/sermons/second-look-homosexuality.

Semerdjian, Elyse. *Off the Straight Path, Illicit Sex, Law and Community in Ottoman Aleppo*. Syracuse: Syracuse University Press, 2008.

Senturk, Recep. "Sociology of Rights: Inviolability of the other in Islam between universalism and communalism. In *Contemporary Islam: Dynamic not Static*, edited by Abul Said, Mohammed Abu-Nimer, and Meena Sharify-funk, 24–49. London and New York: Routledge, 2006.

"Sex and Psychiatry." Magnus Hirschfeld Archive for Sexology. Accessed October 2012. http://zeus4.cms.hu-berlin.de/sexology/ATLAS_EN/html/sex_and_psychiatry.html.

Shafaat, Aḥmad. "'*Death Penalty For Homosexuality, Incest, And Bestiality.*' Punishment for adultery in Islam: A detailed examination." March 6, 2005. Accessed January 27, 2016. http://www.islamicperspectives.com/Stoning5.htm#Chapter5.

Shahid, Omar. "Muslim and gay: Islam begins to confront the issue," *The Times*. November 29, 2012. Accessed January 27, 2016. http://omarshahid.co.uk/2012/11/29/muslim-and-gay-islam-begins-to-confront-the-issue-the-times/.

Shalakany, Amr. "Comparative Law as Archeology: On Sodomy, Islamic Law and the Human Rights Activist." Draft: October 9, 2006. Accessed January 27, 2016, http://www.utexas.edu/law/centers/humanrights/events/speaker-series-papers/Shalakany.pdf.

Shia Pen. Accessed January 27, 2016. http://www.shiapen.com.

Shīrāzī, Shahid e Mehraab Ayatullah-ul-Uzma Sayed Abdul Husain Dastghaib. "Eleventh Greater sin: Sodomy." In *Greater Sins*, Vol 1. Translated by Sayyid Athar Husain S.H.Rizvi. Accessed March 21, 2016, http://www.al-islam.org/greater-sins-volume-1-ayatullah-sayyid-abdul-husayn-dastghaib-shirazi.

ShiaChat. Accessed January 27, 2016. http://www.shiachat.com/forum/topic/234978790-i-need-hadith-about-homosexuality-by-imams-as/.

Siraj, Asifa. "The Construction of the homosexual 'other' by British Muslim heterosexuals." *Contemporary Islam* 3 (2009): 41–57.

Straight Talk. "When homosexuality hits home." Accessed January 27, 2016. http://www.stitcher.com/podcast/straight-talk-podcast-with-dr-maher-hathout/e/when-homosexuality-hits-home-22033123.

Ṭabāṭabā'ī, Allama Muhammad Hussein. *Tafsīr al-Mīzān.* ed. Husayn al-A'lamī, Beirut: Manshurat Mu'assasat al-A'lamī li'l-Maṭbū'āt, 1394/1974.

Tashayyu. Accessed January 27, 2016. http://www.tashayyu.org.

The American Muslim. "A Road to Mecca." Dec 20, 2012. Accessed January 27, 2016. http://theamericanmuslim.org/tam.php/features/articles/film-announcement-a-road-to-mecca-muhammad-asad.

The Official website of Grand Ayatollah Muhammad Fazel Lankarani. "Anal Intercourse." Accessed January 27, 2016. http://www.lankarani.com/eng/faq/a.php.

The Times of India. "Homosexuality immoral, but not criminal: Religious leaders." July 4, 2009. Accessed January 27, 2016. http://timesofindia.indiatimes.com/india/Homosexuality-immoral-but-not-criminal-Religious-leaders/articleshow/4736152.cms?referral=PM.

Thorp, John. "Review article / Discussion: The social construction of homosexuality." *Phoenix* 46, no. 1 (1992): 54–65. Accessed January 27, 2016. http://www.fordham.edu/halsall/med/thorp.asp.

Tutu, Desmond. "Homophobia is as unjust as that crime against humanity, apartheid." *The Times*. July 1, 2004. Accessed January 27, 2016. http://www.thetimes.co.uk/tto/law/columnists/article2047533.ece.

Umm Zakiyyah. "Muslim Girls Don't Want Sex?" OnIslam. January 19, 2014. Accessed January 28, 2016. http://onislam.orkiservers.com/english/family/your-society/468227-muslim-girls-dont-want-sex-.html.

Ummah: The Online Muslim community. Accessed January 25, 2016, http://www.ummah.com.

Understanding Islam Q&A. Accessed January 28, 2016. http://www.understanding-islam.com.

Van Gelder, G. J. H. *Close Relationships: Incest and Inbreeding in Classical Arabic Literature*. New York: I.B. Tauris and Co. Ltd., 2005.

Walid, Dawud. "How 'don't judge' has taken a wrong turn among American Muslims." January 28, 2014. Accessed January 27, 2016. https://dawudwalid.wordpress.com/2014/01/28/how-dont-judge-has-taken-a-wrong-turn-among-american-muslims/.

Wenham, Gordon. "The Old Testament attitude to Homosexuality." *Expository Times* 102 (1991): 259–363. Accessed January 27, 2016. http://www.biblicalstudies.org.uk/article_attitude_wenham.html.

White, Pamela. "Ending the Silence." *Boulder Weekly*. Accessed August 2015. http://archive.boulderweekly.com/092905/coverstory.html.

Wilson, Glenn and Qazi Rahman. *Born Gay: The Psychobiology of Sex Orientation*. London: Peter Owen, 2005.

Yusuf, Hamza. "Islam and Homosexuality." YouTube video. Accessed January 27, 2016. http://www.youtube.com/watch?v=5idZNhc-iqc.

Yusuf, Hamza. "Tempest in a teapot: Islamophobia meets homophobia." *Sandala*. May 8, 2013. Accessed January 27, 2016. https://www.sandala.org/blog/tempest-in-a-teapot-islamophobia-meets-homophobia.

Zaheer, Khalid. "Ghamidi Sb's Opinion on Government Investment Schemes." Accessed January 27, 2016. http://www.khalidzaheer.com/qa/946.

Zaheer, Khalid. "Rationale behind polygamy and the consent of wife." Accessed January 27, 2016. http://www.khalidzaheer.com/qa/154.

Zaheer, Khalid. "Some Popular Misconceptions of the Muslims." Accessed January 27, 2016. http://www.khalidzaheer.com/essays/kzaheer/criticism/some_popoular_misconceptions_of_the_muslims.html.

Zaheer, Khalid. "Why is woman's testimony half that of a man in the court of law?" Accessed January 27, 2016. http://www.khalidzaheer.com/qa/165.

Zanghellini, Aleardo. "Neither homophobic nor (hetero) sexually pure: contextualizing Islam's objections to same-sex sexuality." In *Islam and Homosexuality*, edited by Samar Habib, 269–296. Santa Barbara: Praeger, 2009.

Zawaj. "Masturbation, Answer from Islam Online's Fatwa Bank at Islam-Online.net." December 14, 1999. Accessed January 27, 2016. http://www.zawaj.com/articles/masturbation_islamonline.html.

Ze'evi, Dror. *Producing Desire: Changing Sexual Discourse in the Ottoman Middle East, 1500–1900*. Berkeley: University of California Press, 2006.

Zollner, Barbara. "Mithliyyun or Lutiyun? Neo-Orthodoxy and the debate on the unlawfulness of same-sex relations in Islam." In *Islam and Homosexuality*, edited by Samar Habib, 193–222. Santa Barbara: Praeger, 2010.

Index

About the Authors

Dr. Junaid Jahangir is an assistant professor of economics at MacEwan University. For the last decade he has worked with Dr. Hussein Abdullatif on developing a renewed perspective on Muslim same-sex unions. He frequently presents community workshops and contributes to the *Edmonton Journal* and the *Huffington Post*. His publications include a chapter in the two-volume book *Islam and Homosexuality*. With Dr. Abdullatif, he has coauthored an article in the *Journal of Homosexuality*.

Dr. Hussein Abdullatif is a pediatric endocrinologist in Birmingham, Alabama, and is affiliated with multiple hospitals in the area, including The Children's Hospital of Alabama and University of Alabama Hospital. He received his medical degree from University of Jordan Faculty of Medicine and has been in practice for 30 years. He has a keen interest in Islamic literature and has a strong grasp of classical Arabic. With Dr. Jahangir, he has coauthored an article in the *Journal of Homosexuality*.

www.ingramcontent.com/pod-product-compliance
Ingram Content Group UK Ltd.
Pitfield, Milton Keynes, MK11 3LW, UK
UKHW041633031026
15587UKWH00001B/250

9 780739 189375